Death and the
Quest for Meaning

Death and the Quest for Meaning

Essays in Honor of Herman Feifel

Edited by

Stephen Strack, Ph.D.

JASON ARONSON INC.
Northvale, New Jersey
London

Production Editor: Elaine Lindenblatt

This book was set in 10 pt. Cheltenham by Alpha Graphics of Pittsfield, New Hampshire and printed and bound by Book-mart Press of North Bergen, New Jersey.

Library of Congress Cataloging-in-Publication Data

Death and the quest for meaning : essays in honor of Herman Feifel /
    edited by Stephen Strack.
        p.   cm.
    Includes bibliographical references and index.
    ISBN 0-7657-0014-X (hardcover : alk. paper)
    l. Death—Psychological aspects.   2. Feifel, Herman.
3. Bereavement—Psychological aspects.   4. Grief.   5. Care of the
sick.   6. Children and death.   7. Teenagers and death.
8. Thanatology.   I. Strack, Stephen.   II. Feifel, Herman.
BF789.D4D346   1997
306.9—dc20   96-16028

Manufactured in the United States of America. Jason Aronson Inc. offers books and cassettes. For information and catalog write to Jason Aronson Inc., 230 Livingston Street, Northvale, New Jersey 07647.

For
Herman Feifel
father of the modern death movement
with admiration, affection, and gratitude
from his students, colleagues, and friends

Contents

Preface

Poised on the brink of the millennium, looking back at the awesome accomplishments of mankind during this century in science, technology, and medicine, it is humbling to note that just forty years ago there was no organized scrutiny of the everyday matters of death, dying, and bereavement. There were, of course, classical treatments, religious doctrine, folklore, and even "a few sporadic forays" (Feifel 1990, p. 537) by social scientists, but there was no death movement and no field of thanatology to speak of. A brief glimpse of the intellectual climate concerning death in the late 1950s comes from Robert Kastenbaum, one of Herman Feifel's first students and a contributor to this volume. When Kastenbaum was a graduate student in psychology, one of his professors was a consultant to the Veterans Administration Mental Hygiene Clinic in Los Angeles. Following a visit to the clinic the professor told her class about an unpleasant incident she had witnessed there. She had observed a psychologist addressing an elderly veteran in a rather loud and vigorous manner. If this lapse in gentility wasn't bad enough, the psychologist had compounded his error by asking him, "And what do you think about death?" The look of disdain on the professor's face communicated to everyone her feelings about the psychologist and the subject matter of death.

Some time after this, Kastenbaum began working at the mental hygiene clinic as part of his training, and had the opportunity to meet the psychologist to whom his professor had alluded, as well as the patient who had been the subject of his inquiry. The psychologist was none other than Herman Feifel, and the patient turned out to be a rather vital, if somewhat deaf, World War I veteran who had liked his meetings with Dr. Feifel, and who thought it was about time someone had asked him about death.

Today, of course, thanatology is a thriving, international field of study and practice encompassing anthropology, education, medicine, nursing, philosophy, psychiatry, psychology, religion, social work, sociology, the arts, and the humanities. There are professors of this subject at the finest universities, graduate programs for doctoral students, and courses for undergraduates—even high school students—taught throughout the United States and abroad. Dozens of books for professionals and lay persons are published each year on death, dying, and bereavement. There are scientific journals devoted to death studies, and there are societies and work groups to disseminate information, spawn ideas, and plot the future of death.

The 40-year history of the modern death movement can be traced to the first scientific symposium on "Death and Behavior," which was organized and chaired by Herman Feifel, and held at the 1956 annual meeting of the American Psychological Association in Chicago. Three years later, Feifel (1959) put together a provocative group of papers under the title *The Meaning of Death*, which was published by McGraw-Hill and later translated into Dutch and Japanese. The book galvanized the nascent energies of scholars and practitioners and directed them into what would later become the field of thanatology—the study of death, dying, and bereavement.

Rightfully considered the father of the modern death movement, Herman Feifel's literary contributions span six decades, and include over 100 articles and chapters, and two edited books. His writings have fundamentally influenced how we think about death, treat the dying and bereaved, and how we view our own lives. A number of his empirical reports are considered classics in the field, and his studies on death attitudes and coping behavior paved the way for two generations of researchers.

For many, Herman Feifel's personal contributions to thanatology are at least as great as his literary contributions. Only a unique individual would have had the qualities—the "right stuff"—needed to break the entrenched taboo against death that existed in the 1950s, and to inspire people all over the world to pick up the gambit along with him to make death, dying, and bereavement important areas of inquiry. Publicly and privately Herman Feifel is brilliant, fiery, and intense, a real fighter for what he believes in, and stubborn in determination. He is alive with enthusiasm and always has a sparkle in his blue eyes. He is full of humor and laughs from the gut. He is kind and compassionate. He's a lover of opera, good food, and especially good coffee ice cream. He can recite baseball trivia back to Honus Wagner. He loves boxing and was a competitive handball player until recently. He's a scholar and a showman, someone who can spout Latin, German, French, and Hebrew phrases at the drop of a hat, and finish up with an impish smile and an "alagarooooo!" Perhaps it was these qualities, together with the scholarly pen, that made Herman Feifel the shaping force that he was to an evolving death movement.

This volume of original essays was conceived as a *Festschrift* to honor the man who started it all. Participants include Feifel's students, colleagues, and friends from many areas of study: psychology, psychiatry, medicine, nursing, sociology, religion, education, and humanities. All of them have made important contributions to the death literature, and most have achieved wide recognition for their work. The variety of participants and chapter topics reflects the nature of the field of thanatology as well as the interests of the man being honored. A psychologist by education, Herman Feifel reached beyond his profession early in his career to embrace all of the social sciences, medicine, and the humanities.

In writing their chapters, contributors were allowed to select their topics and they were encouraged to reach beyond their previous accomplishments to write on state-of-the-art issues. Herman Feifel was their inspiration; their audience was to include professionals, students, and educated lay persons. The result is a cornucopia of cutting-edge ideas for all people who have an interest in death, dying, and bereavement. They speak of Feifel's lifelong quest for meaning in the face of the inevitability of death, and give new directions for society and the field of thanatology.

Editing this volume was made easier by the assistance of David Gosse, himself a budding thanatologist, who read most of the manuscripts; by Robert Kastenbaum's support and good humor; and by the forbearance of my wife, Lèni Ferrero, and children, Francesca and Eric. I am especially grateful for the cooperation and enthusiasm of the contributors who unanimously agreed to donate all royalties for the book in Herman Feifel's name to the International Work Group on Death, Dying, and Bereavement. Finally, all of us are indebted to Jason Aronson for sharing our vision and graciously extending himself to our cause.

Stephen Strack
Los Angeles
October 1996

References

Feifel, H., ed. (1959). *The Meaning of Death*. New York: McGraw-Hill.
Feifel, H. (1990). Death and psychology: meaningful rediscovery. *American Psychologist* 45:537–543.

Contributors

Charles Ansell received an Ed.D. from Columbia University and a J.D. from the John Marshall Law School in Chicago. He was Senior Analyst at the National Psychological Association for Psychoanalysis in New York City, and, since 1960, has practiced clinical psychology in Encino, California. He is a past president of the California Psychological Association and editor of its state publication for several years.

Jeanne Quint Benoliel is Professor Emeritus at the University of Washington School of Nursing. She holds a D.NSc. from the University of California at San Francisco, is a fellow of the American Academy of Nursing, and a charter member of the International Work Group on Death, Dying, and Bereavement. Her research and writing have centered on the impact of life-threatening situations on human identity, adaptive behaviors, and social relationships.

Sandra L. Bertman, Ph.D., is Professor of Humanities in Medicine and founding Director of the Medical Humanities Program at the University of Massachusetts Medical Center. A pioneer in the use of arts and humanities in the psychology of loss, she was recipient of the 1989 American Journal of Hospice Care Award and was named the 1992 "Outstanding Death Educator" by the Association for Death Education and Counseling. She is the author of *Facing Death Images, Insights, and Interventions* (1991).

S. Robin Cohen received her Ph.D. in psychology from McGill University in 1986, where she studied the neuroscience of pain. She is currently Research Fellow at the National Cancer Institute of Canada and Coordinator of Research for Palliative Care McGill, where her primary research focus has been on the development of a quality of life measure that can be used with persons who have life-threatening illnesses.

Charles A. Corr is Professor of Philosophy at Southern Illinois University in Edwardsville, and a volunteer at the Hospice of Madison County, Illinois. He received his doctorate from St. Louis University. Dr. Corr has published fifteen books related to dying, death, bereavement, and gerontological nursing. He was Chairperson of the International Work Group on Death, Dying, and Bereavement from 1989 to 1993.

Kenneth J. Doka, Ph.D., is Professor of Gerontology at the College of New Rochelle, and an ordained Lutheran clergyman serving a small parish in Stony Point, New York. His published works include forty articles and chapters as well as the books *Disenfranchised Grief, Living With Life-Threatening Illness, Death and Spirituality*, and *Mourning Children, Children Mourning*. Currently editor of the newsletter *Journeys* and associate editor of the journal *Omega*, in 1993 he was elected President of the Association for Death Education and Counseling.

Elliot N. Dorff is Rector and Professor of Philosophy at the University of Judaism in Los Angeles, California. Ordained a conservative rabbi by the Jewish Theological Seminary of America in 1970, he earned his Ph.D. in philosophy from Columbia University in 1971. He is the author of six books and over 100 articles and chapters on Jewish law, ethics, and theology, and in 1993 he served on the Ethics Committee of Hillary Rodham Clinton's Health Care Task Force.

Barry Fortner received his M.S. degree in clinical psychology at Murray State University in 1993, and attends the University of Memphis in pursuit of a doctorate in the same area. Author of a recent article on death anxiety in the second edition of the *Encyclopedia of Aging*, his current research includes the role of death anxiety and attitudes toward suicide in therapists' responses to suicidal verbalizations of their clients.

Alan W. Friedman received his Ph.D. from the University of Rochester and is Professor of English at the University of Texas at Austin, where he has taught for 30 years. Among the courses he regularly teaches is one entitled "Death as a Cultural Phenomenon." He has edited four books and written four others, the most recent of which is *Fictional Death and the Modernist Enterprise*.

Robert Fulton, Ph.D., is Professor of Sociology and Director of the Center for Death Education and Research at the University of Minnesota. In 1963 he conducted the first seminar on death offered at an American university. Dr. Fulton's numerous publications include *Death and Identity* (now in its third edition), and *Death and Dying: Challenge and Change* (with a readership of more than 12 million). He is the recipient of the National Forum for Death Education and Counseling's "Outstanding Achievement Award."

Robert Kastenbaum is Professor of Communication at Arizona State University in Tempe. He received his Ph.D. in psychology from the University of Southern California in 1959. Herman Feifel was one of his psychotherapy mentors during a predoctoral internship at the Veterans Administration. Editor of *Omega, Journal of Death and Dying* and *The International Journal of Aging and Human Development*, Kastenbaum's books include *The Psychology of Death*, *Death, Society, and Human Experience,* and *Dorian Graying: Is Youth the Only Thing Worth Having?*

Daniel Leviton, Ph.D., is Professor of Health Education at the University of Maryland, College Park. One of the founders and first President of the Association for Death Education and Counseling, he also founded and directs the Adult Health and Development Program, an intergenerational health promotion and rehabilitation program established at ten colleges and universities in the United States and Israel. Dr. Leviton is the author of two edited books, many chapters, and several articles on *Horrendous Death* and other aspects of thanatology.

John D. Morgan, Ph.D., Professor of Philosophy and Coordinator of the King's College Center for Education about Death and Bereavement in London, Ontario, Canada, offered the first undergraduate course on death in 1968 at (then) Loyola College in Montreal. He is Secretary/Treasurer of the International Work Group on Death, Dying, and Bereavement, and Consulting Editor for the 20-volume book series "Death, Values, and Meaning." Dr. Morgan has published thirty articles and chapters, and is the editor of ten books on grief issues.

Balfour M. Mount, CM, OQ, MD, FRCS (C), is founding Director of the Royal Victoria Hospital Palliative Care Service in Montreal, Quebec, Canada. He holds the Eric M. Flanders Chair in Palliative Medicine, and is Director of the Division of Palliative Care in the Department of Oncology at McGill University. He has written widely on topics related to care of the terminally ill.

Robert A. Neimeyer, Ph.D., is Professor of Psychology at the University of Memphis, where he also maintains a clinical practice. He has published over 160 articles and chapters, and fourteen books, including a *Death Anxiety Handbook: Research, Instrumentation and Application*; *Personal Meanings of Death* (with Franz Epting); and *Dying: Facing the Facts* (with Hannelore Wass). Dr. Neimeyer is editor of the international journal *Death Studies*, President of the Association for Death Education and Counseling, and a member of the International Work Group on Death, Dying, and Bereavement.

Therese A. Rando, Ph.D., is a clinical psychologist in private practice in Warwick, Rhode Island. She trained at the University of Rhode Island and at Case Western Reserve University Medical School and University Hospitals of Cleveland, Ohio. Author of over forty-five articles and chapters and five books, including *Treatment of Complicated Mourning* and *How to Go On Living When Someone You Love Dies*, she was the recipient of the Association for Death Education and Counseling's "Outstanding Contribution to the Study of Death, Dying, and Bereavement" award in 1987, and a 1990 grantee of its lifetime certificate as Certified Death Educator.

Florence S. Wald, M.N., M.S, is a graduate (1941) and former Dean (1957–1968) of the Yale University School of Nursing. A social activist and proponent of National Health Service from student days, she was inspired by Dame Cicely Saunder's work with the terminally ill to develop the first hospice in the United States. Since then she has helped draft the Assumptions and Principles of Care for the Terminally Ill, advocated for the future of hospice, and worked to broaden the concept of spiritual care.

Hannelore Wass received her Ph.D. from the University of Michigan, and is Professor Emeritus of Educational Psychology at the University of Florida. She is founding Editor of the journal *Death Studies*, and a Consulting Editor for the book series "Death Education, Aging, and Health Care." She has published numerous articles, chapters, and ten books including *Childhood and Death*, *Helping Children Cope With Death*, *Death Education* (two volumes), and *Dying: Facing the Facts*. Her body of work has been recognized by two awards for outstanding contributions to thanatological studies.

Avery D. Weisman, M.D., is Professor Emeritus of Psychiatry at Harvard Medical School, Senior Psychiatrist at Massachusetts General Hospital, and emeritus Training/Supervising Analyst at the Boston Psychoanalytic Institute. Now retired, he has shifted from professional writing to fiction and personal essays. His contribution to this volume, "Ambiguity in Aging," is an example.

Laurens P. White, M.D., is a clinician in private practice in San Francisco specializing in Medical Oncology and Internal Medicine. He holds faculty appointments at the University of California, San Francisco, as Clinical Professor of Medicine and Lecturer in Thanatology in the Department of Psychiatry. He has published forty-seven papers and edited two books, the most recent of which is *Care of Patients With Fatal Illness*. He is a former president of the California Medical Association and San Francisco Medical Society, and like Herman Feifel, an expert on coffee ice cream.

Introduction: A Personal Memoir of Herman Feifel

CHARLES ANSELL

The stature of the scholar is rightfully measured by the animating ideas that impelled him from early life. Perhaps the nub of man's earliest philosophy was stated by Socrates in his legendary remark, "The unexamined life is not worth living." At the height of Herman Feifel's early work in psychology, or perhaps at the depth of his studies, awash as he was in a rigorous study and application of tests and measurements, Herman never cut himself adrift from the question that haunted him throughout his studies: "Will this lead me to a conceptual system that can encompass not man, but the human being?"

When in 1988 the American Psychological Association honored him with its Award for Distinguished Professional Contributions to Knowledge, it noted:

> His burgeoning conviction that a vital psychology must be rooted in people, not in a mathematical physics model, convinced him to [focus on] clinical psychology. . . . He has been described as a person who blends the rigorous logic and systematic reasoning of the hard sciences with the warmth and sense of values that characterize the humanities. [American Psychological Association 1989, p. 645]

The essential humanist Herman Feifel, in his work on *The Meaning of Death* (1959), has advanced (or shall I say *returned*) psychology to its rightful place as the study of human life and its search after meaning. One remembers Alexander Pope's warning, in *An Essay on Man*, against turning away from the study of human life: "Presume not God to scan; The proper study of mankind is man."

My friendship with Herman Feifel began many years ago after a brief stint at occasional poker sessions with colleagues, but most enduring is our membership in a small discussion group that has been meeting for years in a continuing interest in dredging up the implicit values and directions contained in the wide spectrum of human concerns. It is here, with several close friends, that Herman is free to give voice to a scatter of reflections on the frontiers of psychological thought, on the emerging directions of social and political opinion, and on the errant course in postmodern literature and the arts.

From earliest adolescence Feifel throbbed with an awareness that there is much to know. He speaks of a recollection at perhaps 13 or 14. He is in the main room of a large public library and stands momentarily stunned at the sight of shelf upon shelf of books that rise from floor to ceiling. He is overcome with a great hunger to swallow each book. He flings his arms out in a wide embrace before the massive shelves in an impassioned wish that by some magic he can fill his mind instantly with each page of the thousands of books that rise above him.

Some years later he is an undergraduate at City College of New York. He has an early morning class. He rises at dawn to travel from faraway Brooklyn to 137th Street in Manhattan. The subway car is filled with workingmen. He senses that he is the youngest passenger in the crowded car. Some men, he notes, are easily twice his age, perhaps more. And soon his mind impels him to reflect on the meaning of his observation, his youth, their age. "They will be long gone when I am their age," he muses. But it will be time that will also bring him to their age. And slowly the image of time floods his thought. I am left to surmise that he was early aware of the meaning of time in life. Some years ago at a dinner party with colleagues, I turned to Herman and asked what led to his interest in death and dying. He answered simply, "Death organizes life." Now, years later, I think of the young Herman Feifel at the public library and the young Herman on the early morning subway ride to his class at CCNY and I begin to understand his reply. Indeed, time in Herman Feifel's life has been his taskmaster. His wide-ranging interests in knowledge, his search after knowing more of the thousand experiences he had seen and heard have left him not only familiar with the great philosophies, but have also made him a master of the rigorous demands of science. He is likewise at home with arts, letters, and sports. He is an opera buff and a devotee of classical music.

Writing this memoir is a personal delight for its major thread is not woven in the fabric of this scholarly tribute to Herman Feifel. It is at heart an impressionistic account of the man who founded a wholly new dimension of psychological inquiry. While I will be making references to his impressive curriculum vitae (see the bibliography and biographical highlights presented in this volume), these details are cited mainly to track his long struggle to reach the precious insight that finally led to his excursions into the unexplored realm in his search for the meaning of death and dying.

Developmental scientists speak of phases of growth from infancy to adulthood. One assumes that in our passage from one growth phase to another we retain the best of the past even as we take on the challenge of the next phase. We are an adaptive species, and for the most part we somehow manage to find a secure place in each stage of our ongoing development. Failing that, we are said to be left mired in an earlier developmental state.

But there are those few who are blessed with the gift of carrying the better part of an earlier phase to a later phase, much to their psychological (and physical) profit. A city boy at play in the streets of Brooklyn, Herman played handball. A sidewalk, a brick wall, a neighborhood park were his arena; at first a sturdy sponge-centered ball was his equipment, but later when he played in competitive tournaments it would be a hard black rubber ball. It is altogether a game for the swift, for the sharp-eyed who can anticipate the angle of the ball as it ricochets off the wall. Adult men who continue to play handball after 40 remain lean and agile. It is not a game for soft stomachs and fleshy arms. Herman played it competitively until just recently; in fact, he once vied for championship status, reaching the quarterfinals in national tournament play at the age of 72!

In this way Herman carried an adolescent passion for sports well past the age when his contemporaries complained of shortness of breath after crossing a busy street. Yet by far the most remarkable trait he carried even into his late seventies is a vibrant adolescent enthusiasm, an excitement, even a delight at coming upon a new facet in an ongoing interest. Herman, as the scholar before an audience of colleagues, is the well-tempered clavichord. His tone is firm, his speech steady. In the colorful language of the 1950s, he is a "cool cat." His scholarship impeccable and precise, he stands there a fount of wisdom carefully unraveling folds of knowledge until his thought is made clear.

But in his after-hours discussions with friends, his youthful excitement returns in an eruption of energy. It is in these moments that I, along with several others who meet with him regularly, have come to treasure a wisdom that seems to throb in a constant state of readiness. There is a charming paradox in his rapid verbal volleys reminiscent of a thousand spontaneous bull sessions at college, yet though delivered at breakneck speed, he dependably transmits a seasoned wisdom with the ease of reporting a news event. His presence among us makes the exercise of intelligence a joyous voyage into fresh waters.

Psychoanalysts speak of destinies as often "overdetermined" by early influences, but if it were so we would do well to examine the nature and the intensity of these overdetermined factors if we are to understand the eventual choices we make in life. There seems something quite simplistic in assuming that we are led reflexively onto paths that were prescripted for us. Herman Feifel's ultimate choice of studies into the meaning of death came to him far removed from the immediacy of early environmental influences.

A young man's career choices are too often cast in stone before he permits himself an essential *Wanderjahr* of free exploration. Herman entered college in an exploratory mood. He turned first to history, in which subject he had garnered medals in high school. He continued to do well in history at college until he learned that a New York City teacher's credential required candidates to pass a speech test. It apparently was the view of educators at the time to protect New York City children from listening to teachers whose speech was little different from their students' speech at home or on the street. It is a matter of interest that my Midwesterner's ear for dialects found no trace of Brooklynese in Herman's speech. I suspect he turned away from a potential career as a history teacher more as a protest against the pretensions of the school administrators of the time. He then turned to sociology, which held his fancy for a brief period. But he found the professor soporific and fatally flawed by his immersion in tables and graphs. The subject matter, he felt then, could not reach the soul of the human. Even in his first months at college, he found himself assessing subject after subject for their potential to illuminate the nature of man.

When I reflect on the origins of Herman's interest in death and dying I find it not in a cluster of overdetermined factors but in great part in his adventitious experiences in the United States military during World War II. In 1942 he enlisted in the Army Air Corps where he functioned as an aviation psychologist for two years, working in the selection and classification of flying crew members (e.g., navigators, pilots, and bombardiers). It was "human engineering," he said. He was then directly commissioned as an officer in the adjutant general's office where he spent his last two years in the service. It was during this latter period that he ended up overseas, stationed on the small island of Tinian in the Marianas. There he worked with flying crews engaged in bombing the Japanese mainland, and dealt with combat and operational fatigue cases incurred during the Iwo Jima and Okinawa campaigns. Tinian possessed the largest concentration of B-29s in the service, which contributed a major portion of the planes attempting to bomb the Japanese Empire into submission. In August 1945, in the final weeks of the war in the Pacific, the famed Enola Gay flew out of the small island of Tinian on its fateful mission to bomb Hiroshima, an event that ushered in a new world subject to instant megadeath. Several days later another B-29 flew out of Tinian to deliver a similar fate to the city of Nagasaki. Ironically, the Feifel family album contains a photograph of young Herman standing beside the historic Enola Gay, barely two days after its mission over Hiroshima.

Many years later he recalls Robert Oppenheimer's vivid outcry at witnessing the A-bomb test at Alamogordo, "I am become Death—the shatterer of worlds." Herman was dizzied by the death of thousands at one stroke. He remained restive with the memories of Hiroshima and Nagasaki. His reflections of the vast destruction over the ill-fated Japanese cities remained pivotal in his germinating thoughts about death. In the obscene count of thousands who perished savagely under the blast of an unearthly fury, all slaughtered in horrendous number, each of the fallen had been denied the dignity of dying. Death had become an ugly statistic. They had become victims of a sudden fate unleashed by one of the planes he stood beside barely two days after its dread mission. Days later he sensed that he would one day count the shattering events of an August day in 1945 in his reckoning with the meaning of death.

A far earlier experience strangely entered Herman's dawning awareness of death, not in its morbid aspects of grief and loss, but something quite romantic. He was in his eighteenth year when he saw the 1934 movie *Death Takes a Holiday,* starring the then-dashing romantic figure of Frederic March and the beauteous Evelyn Venable. In the film, Frederic March, playing Death, visits Earth from his haunts in the netherworld on a mission to understand those he would one day claim. He comes to Earth disguised as a nobleman without hint or knowledge of the psychological lives of his future charges. In time he comes upon the daughter of his host, Evelyn Venable, and he is soon caught up with the ways of mortals on earth: he falls in love. Suddenly life becomes precious to Death, for in his enchantment with his young lady he would order a halt to all dying on earth. At a visit to the annual auto races at Indianapolis, Death and his beloved sit in the stands and witness a shattering accident, a seven-car smash-up. When the drivers are rescued from their burning cars they walk away from the crash almost as fit as at the moment they took the wheel. Onlookers are astounded at the miracle. A man sitting behind Death remarks to a friend, "The old man must be asleep up there," at which handsome Frederic March adjusted his monocle and growls, "The old man?" There were no casualties that day or on any other day during his stay on earth. His beloved Evelyn Venable soon learns that her nobleman is Death himself. Nevertheless, her love for him overpowers her fear of death and she joins him in his dramatic departure from Earth. Leaving the movie, young Herman was delighted at the victory of love over death. There were powers within us all, he mused, which could de-demonize death, if not defeat death. It had been a warming thought and one that somehow removed the black veil that covered the face of death. He left in an unfinished dialogue with himself, wondering about love and death, the power of the one over the other. He would dwell on it further one day.

Few psychologists can boast of an apprenticeship in psychology as varied as Herman's years of study. It is a wide range, from the microcosms of special studies in tests and measurements—tests that measure size constancy, eye function, manual dexterity, and discrimination reaction time—to the macrocosm of Goodwin Watson's theories of personality and psychotherapy, and Harry Overstreet's social philosophy. His appetite for knowing was avaricious. His undergraduate studies took him to psychology courses in abnormal, industrial, history of, systems, social, educational, experimental, and mental hygiene, bolstered further in his graduate studies at Columbia where he worked with Robert S. Woodworth and Otto Klineberg. Yet throughout all these diverse courses he continued to seek more of the nature of man, or as he put it to me recently, "a conceptual system that can encompass not man, but the human being." Herman's justly idealized mentor and guide was Irving Lorge of Columbia, famed for his innovative work in adult psychology and adult development. It was Lorge who not only trained him additionally in the rigors of scientific methods in framing tests and measurements, but later supported him in his attempts to explore a psychology that could uncover the nature of man in his world.

In 1946, after leaving the army, he worked as a research psychologist in the Personnel Research Section of the adjutant general's office, and concurrently resumed his doctoral research until 1948, when he received his Ph.D. from Columbia University. In 1949 his friend, the eminent psychologist George Klein, urged him to join the staff at Topeka, Kansas, working out of the famed Menninger Clinic. At Topeka, he joined the staff of the Winter Veterans Administration General Hospital in 1950 as a supervisor in its clinical psychology program. It was there that he became immersed in the clinical applications of psychology, working alongside a group of psychologists who would later attain distinguished status in the larger world of psychology. His shift to clinical psychology was in keeping with his growing dissatisfaction with the narrow scope of findings gathered by many of his research cohorts: "We psychologists have become too bewitched by methodology, analysis, and operational definition at the expense of purpose, anxiety, conditions of well-being, and redemption. . . . I ask, rather, for a psychology committed to purposive and striving man: one whose scope will not be essentially derived from methods of study but rather from the functioning of human life, embodying courage, love, tragedy, will, [and] delight" (Feifel 1964, p. 418). Strange words from a man rooted in the scientific tradition. One wonders at his restiveness in his early years as a researcher, quietly disappointed that his findings did not provide more illumination to the world of pulsating life.

His unrest as a research psychologist persisted. Again, in "Death and Dying in Modern America" (1977) he was moved to observe that "we no longer command philosophic or religious conceptual creeds, except nominally, with which to transcend death. . . . Generally speaking, we are now a secular society, attempting to replace the prospect of personal immortality [with] a concern for historical immortality" (Feifel 1977, p. 6). He is here still the child who stood before the thousands of library books and wished to embrace them all in his hurry to conquer the unknown. That his path through psychology, scientific for the most part, led him at last to a wide-ranging understanding of death as an event of transcendent significance must attest to his own hunger for a transcendent view, not for himself alone, but for all people. His is a special mission to the spiritually asleep, a call to awaken to the larger tasks that life proffers us before it is taken from us. He has moved his community of psychologists from a once-held position of disavowing the scholarly merit of the meaning of death to attain international recognition. Yet the world of scientific psychology at first kept its distance from Herman's writing. When McGraw-Hill published *The Meaning of Death* (Feifel 1959), the book drew nationwide attention. But the journal *Contemporary Psychology,* a publication of the American Psychological Association wholly devoted to critiques of newly published works, refused to accept the volume for consideration. Having been reviewed in the popular press (*Time*) it had apparently "attained its allotted morbid fascination exposure" (Feifel 1990, p. 538).

In his early efforts to research attitudes among terminally ill patients he would also meet resistance from numerous physicians. "At the outset, I was met with: 'Isn't it cruel, sadistic, and traumatic to discuss death with seriously ill and terminally ill people?' [After] 'gamesmanship' of an order that would have warmed Stephen Potter . . . I was enabled to interview and test eight seriously ill patients" (Feifel 1963, pp. 9–10). Some of the patient's responses to his questions were: "'You helped me understand my feelings about death,' 'I'm grateful because I now have more control over my ideas,' 'You didn't avoid those things which concern me,' 'You cleared the cobwebs from my mind,' [and] 'Talking to you gave me a sense of relief'" (Feifel 1963, p. 10). His terminally ill patients vindicated his views of death among the dying.

As anomalous as it may seem to his professional cohorts, Herman Feifel, schooled in the traditions of science, never abandoned his enchantment with man's capacity for the spiritual life. Much of his own love and enchantment with the life of the spirit derives in great part from his early family life. His father, a devout and observant Jew, surrounded his son's life with the culture and traditions of his people. His love of music derives from his early enjoyment of *Hazzanuth,* the world of cantorial music. His love of the musical voice led him to his love of grand opera, and to a special appreciation of classical music. He treasures his memory of the renowned cantors he heard in his youth. He continues to observe the holidays and festivals in the Jewish calendar, and each year he recites the memorial prayers for his parents and some friends. He still continues to occupy positions of eminence in the educational and cultural life of the Jewish community in America.

He has been notably recognized by several of the nation's leading Jewish learning centers. He was twice invited by the University of Judaism to be its commencement speaker, once during the 1979 dedication ceremonies of its new campus, and again in 1984 when he was signally honored by the university with its Doctor of Humane Letters. He has also served on its board of governors, academic affairs, for a quarter of a century.

In 1979 he was honored with the Distinguished Human Services Award by Yeshiva University in New York. He has been a distinguished keynote speaker in Israel, and in 1985 he was asked to deliver the keynote address at the First International Conference on Grief and Bereavement, held in Jerusalem. The State of Israel also invited him to serve as a consultant on such issues as fear of death, loss, and mourning. Currently, he serves as chairman of the professional advisory board of the National Institute for Jewish Hospice.

Herman was among the prime movers in providing momentum for development of the International Work Group on Death, Dying, and Bereavement, a transdisciplinary scholarly group of clinicians, educators, and researchers. His earlier studies provided a major cutting edge to this new area of inquiry. Today these pioneers in the area of death, dying, and bereavement possess an international constituency that meets every two years. Meetings have since been held in Sweden, Portugal, the United States, Canada, Norway, England, and other world centers. His efforts at broadening the base of the new scholarship are uncommon for the professional intellectual, but it is an indication of Herman Feifel's commitment to lay bare the contents of all the books he had attempted to embrace as a youngster in the public library room.

In 1959 he was given the first research grant ever awarded by the National Institute of Mental Health to study the relation between attitudes toward death and behavior. In 1960 he was appointed senior research scientist at the Research Center for Mental Health, New York University, and worked with Robert Holt and George Klein. He was visiting professor at the University of Southern California (USC) in 1965–1966, and is now emeritus clinical professor of psychiatry and the behavioral sciences at the USC School of Medicine.

Francis Bacon once wisely observed that every professional is a debtor to his profession. The list of Herman Feifel's service to his profession appears unprecedented. Herewith and quickly are a baker's dozen of his contributions: He has served on the board of professional affairs of the American Psychological Association (APA). He served as council representative for the APA's Division 24, Theoretical and Philosophical Psychology; he also served on the APA Council for the Division of Philosophical Psychology. He has been president of the APA Division of Adult Development and Aging. His range of interests within the family of psychology reflects his talent for integrating specialty areas into a unified whole. He was elected fellow of the following divisions: Adult Development and Aging, Clinical Psychology, Consulting Psychology, Psychologists Interested in Religious Issues, Psychologists in Public Service, Psychotherapy, the Society of Personality and Social Psychology, and Theoretical and Philosophical Psychology.

His colleagues have endowed him with rich rewards of recognition. The Division of Psychologists in Public Service conferred its highly coveted Harold M. Hildreth award. Organized psychology has frequently noted his contributions to psychology as science and profession. Among his colleagues he has again and again been accorded the distinction as the psychologist who sees beyond the horizons of each limited interest area. His home community of Los Angeles, city and county, as well as the California Psychological Association, have recognized his contributions by electing him to its boards and offices and as president of the Los Angeles County Psychological Association. In addition to the notable APA award cited earlier, Herman received the state association's award for Distinguished Scientific Achievement in Psychology. It is altogether a remarkable record of honored service to his profession, which in turn honored him with their awards for exceptional service to psychology as science and psychology as a species of philosophy.

Sigma Xi, the national honorary scientific research society, named Herman Feifel national lecturer for the years 1975–1976 and 1976–1977. The *American Scientist*, the official journal of the society, characterized his work thus: "His publications on the psychological and philosophical meaning of death in contemporary society are fundamental for the subject" (Sigma Xi 1974, p. 526).

As I review this impressionistic narrative on the life and work of Herman Feifel I am drawn to the conclusion that one not only needs the requisite study and training to attain the stature of the "compleat psychologist," but far more he will need Herman Feifel's early commitment to lead his profession into a future where it may stand as a supremely humanistic calling. He has left psychology a rich legacy in his search for an enlightenment far beyond his early mastery of tests and measurements, beyond the clinician's academic view of the vicissitudes that play upon the person in all his singularity. These are skills that by themselves do not educate, nor do they lead to enlightenment.

In his own early-life commitment to seek enlightenment for himself, he has enriched the subject matter of his chosen field of psychology. He has brought a vital dimension to all of psychology and its allied professions in his courage to bring the study of death to a level of acceptance. This accomplishment can only redound to the benefit of thousands upon thousands in their search after meaning in their lives.

References

American Psychological Association (1989). Awards for distinguished professional contributions: 1988. *American Psychologist* 44:639–646.
Feifel, H., ed. (1959). *The Meaning of Death*. New York: McGraw-Hill.
Feifel, H. (1963). Death. In *Taboo Topics*, ed. N. Farberow, pp. 8–21. New York: Atherton.
——— (1964). Philosophy reconsidered. *Psychological Reports* 15: 415–420.
——— (1977). Death and dying in modern America. *Death Education* 1:5–14.
——— (1990). Death and psychology: meaningful rediscovery. *American Psychologist* 45:537–543.
Sigma Xi (1974). Sigma Xi national lecturers 1975–76. *American Scientist* 62:522–526.

PART I
Historical and Religious Perspectives

Herman Feifel's boyhood interests in history and religion had a profound shaping influence on his professional career and, consequently, on the young field of thanatology. His fascination with the origin and impact of attitudes toward death was particularly keen, and is reflected in each of the essays in this section. Robert Neimeyer and Barry Fortner start off with a historical account of the empirical study of death attitudes beginning with Feifel's first reports from the 1950s. They highlight the importance of Feifel's work in the development of methodology and in determining the kinds of hypotheses that have been tested over the past 40 years. Jeanne Quint Benoliel challenges us to see how death attitudes in contemporary Western culture were shaped by a masculine perspective that dominated the post–World War II military-industrial complex, and the development of technology in medicine. Particularly noteworthy in her account are the consequences of this perspective for the roles of doctors, nurses, patients, and their families. Florence Wald considers the place of hospice in a world that is increasingly concerned with the costs of medical care. The emergence in the 1960s and 1970s of institutions to care for the terminally ill was a triumph for the death movement, but the future of these facilities is far from clear. Wald believes that creativity, responsibility, and rexamination of health care values can pave the way for hospice's future. Elliott Dorff gives a scholarly and highly readable account of how conservative Judaism instructs and guides its followers in the realm of death, dying, and bereavement. While staying firmly within the boundaries of his religion, Rabbi Dorff nevertheless makes the wisdom and humanity of this tradition apparent to all. Concluding this section, Alan Friedman addresses attitudes toward death from the perspective of modern literature. He gives an intriguing look at the evolving image of death from the late nineteenth century to the present by linking changes with cultural and historical events, such as the advent of psychoanalysis and two world wars.

1

Death Attitudes in Contemporary Perspective

ROBERT A. NEIMEYER AND BARRY FORTNER

> Consideration of death is undoubtedly one of the foremost sources of anxiety for man. Indeed, a major task of both religion and philosophy has been to grapple with its intensity and complexity. Psychology, in coming to grips with the meaning of death for the individual, asserts its responsibility to reexamine its philosophic and humanistic heritage in the context of its generic ideal of science.
>
> Herman Feifel, 1969a, p. 292

As a prime mover in the death awareness movement from the 1950s to the present, Herman Feifel has had a defining impact on many of the facets of contemporary thanatology. Initially intoning his message as a lone voice in a discipline, and perhaps a culture, that had turned a deaf ear to death, dying, and loss, he has gradually been joined by a chorus of other voices that resonate to his concern for the role of death in human life. The result has been a reconsideration of caregiving practices toward patients with life-threatening illness, a reconceptualization of grief as a natural and healthy response to loss, a resurgence of interest in developmental aspects of death attitudes, a redefinition of the function of the helping professional when cure no longer is a feasible goal of treatment, and a refocusing of scholarly attention on the awareness of death and its implications for our lives (Feifel 1990).

Among these many contributions, Feifel's pioneering work in the area of death attitudes may be the most distinctive. Indeed, of the hundreds of authors who together have published over 1,000 articles on death anxiety since the 1950s (Neimeyer and Van Brunt 1995), Feifel is alone in having contributed seminal papers to the literature in every decade for the last 50 years. More important than his longevity as a contributor, however, is the perspicacity with which he anticipated directions in which the field would evolve, as it developed from isolated and occasional studies of fear of death to sustained programs of empirical research a half century later. This chapter outlines Feifel's methodological and substantive contributions to the study of death attitudes, and uses them as a springboard into the contemporary literature on the causes, correlates, and consequences of death anxiety. We will see that Feifel anticipated many of the major trends in subsequent research, which has confirmed, enlarged, and in a few cases called into question his pioneering conclusions. Because an understanding of methodology is foundational to a detailed consideration of substantive studies, we will begin by reviewing Feifel's contributions to the assessment of death attitudes, before progressing to an evaluation of research organized by content area.

Death Attitudes: The Problem of Measurement

The first question to confront a would-be investigator of attitudes toward death is how such attitudes can be assessed. Are thoughts, feelings, and behavioral tendencies regarding one's own death more accessible through direct questioning or indirect probing? Are death attitudes best conceived as unitary or multifaceted, and what implications does this carry for measurement? Do they require the personalism of a one-on-one interview to emerge, or are they more easily elicited through the safe anonymity of a questionnaire? Are personal meanings of death so idiosyncratic that they require narrative or free-response methods that give free rein to the respondent's self-report, or are there basic commonalities in human responses to death that permit standardization of measures? And finally, can such attitudes be formulated consciously in words at all, or are they better expressed nonconsciously in the language of imagery and metaphor, or in response to laboratory tests designed to circumvent awareness? The broad literature on death attitudes has addressed each of these questions with varying degrees of thoroughness, often using Feifel's groundbreaking efforts at measurement as a point of departure.

Direct vs. Indirect Assessment

Appropriately for a pioneer, Feifel made use of a remarkable variety of probes in his earliest research on death attitudes. For example, in his very first study of the death concerns of mentally ill persons (Feifel 1955), he asked 85 psychiatric inpatients (chiefly schizophrenic) to describe what death meant to them, draw a picture of death, detail their plans for how they would pass their last year on earth, and consider what they would return as, if reincarnated following their death. In a follow-up study on the death attitudes of older persons (Feifel 1956), he expanded this list, including inquiries about respondents' views of what happens after death, how they would prefer to die, how frequently they thought of dying, how many years they expected to live, and what personal meanings they associated with old age. As we will see in the sections to follow, some of these queries became formalized as actual research methods in subsequent work by Feifel and others, while other queries (e.g., about how one would spend one's remaining days if one had only a short time to live) evolved into values clarification exercises in the context of death education. However, one theme informing Feifel's early work had considerable relevance for the entire field of death attitudes, namely, the question of whether their study required a direct or an indirect form of assessment.

Probably as a result of the psychodynamic mind-set that then held sway over much of clinical psychology, Feifel's earliest studies betrayed a distrust of direct self-report of death fears and anxieties. For example, both his 1955 and 1956 studies required subjects to rank order the decades of life in which "people in general" were most afraid of death, in an apparent effort to circumvent participants' defensiveness about acknowledging their own death anxieties. While his later empirical research (Feifel and Branscomb 1973) shifted toward including direct questioning of subjects ("Are you afraid of death? Why?"), he never fully reconciled himself to direct self-report as an adequate measure of fear of death. Indeed, even in his more recent writings, Feifel has continued to warn of the tendency of investigators to neglect "the discrepancies that exist between conscious and nonconscious levels of death anxiety" (Feifel 1990, p. 541).

While the important question of whether it is useful to posit levels of death anxiety will be considered in more detail below, it is worth noting that the field in general has shown a shift over time, from an initial preference for more indirect forms of assessment such as projective testing (Rhudick and Dibner 1961b) to a nearly exclusive reliance upon self-report questionnaires designed to tap "conscious" death fear, threat, and anxiety (Neimeyer and Van Brunt 1995). This methodological sea change probably reflects the impact of many factors, including the greater psychometric adequacy of the latter measures, the waning impact of a psychodynamic perspective, the success of straightforward studies of attitudes in social psychology, and last but not least, the beguiling simplicity of easily administered questionnaires (Kastenbaum 1988). In evaluating this trend, the most reasonable conclusion may be that we simply do not know the extent to which death attitudes are reliably assessed by either direct or indirect means, although in general the evidence for the validity and reliability of the former are more favorable than the evidence for the latter (Neimeyer 1994a). While the characteristic distrust of people's direct reports of thoughts and feelings about death that characterized the early literature is probably insupportable, Feifel's cautions regarding the complexity of our human awareness of death serves as a continuing reminder that the contrasting assumption that people can or will report the entirety of their attitudes toward their personal mortality is likely to be equally simplistic. Thus, plenty of room remains for research that systematically compares independently validated measures of death concern that vary in their degree of directness. Attention to such methodological issues could eventually yield a more comprehensive and versatile assortment of measures for use in clinical and research contexts.

It would also be simplistic to assume that all currently available questionnaire measures are equally reliant on face valid self-report of death anxiety. For example, among those scales with significant evidence of validity, the Death Anxiety Scale (Templer 1970) directly asks for true-false responses to such statements as "I am very much afraid to die." On the other hand, other well-validated measures such as the Threat Index (Neimeyer 1994c) are more indirect, inferring a disposition to view death as threatening from the respondent's placement of the concepts of self and death in polar opposition on a variety of construct dimensions (e.g., predictable vs. random). Current evidence indicates that these measures correlate only moderately, although each has a long history of successful application in the study of death attitudes.

Conscious vs. Nonconscious Measurement

Closely related to the question of whether measurement of death attitudes should be direct or indirect is the issue of whether human beings possess different death attitudes at different levels of awareness ranging from conscious to nonconscious. This problem has been a *leitmotif* in Feifel's work, from his earliest conceptualization of the problem (Feifel 1961) to his subsequent attempts to address it empirically (Feifel 1974, Feifel and Branscomb 1973, Feifel et al. 1973, Feifel and Hermann 1973, Feifel and Nagy 1980, 1981, Feifel and Schag 1981). While not explicitly couching his approach within psychoanalytic theory, it is clear that concepts of defense, denial, and distortion permeate his early work (Feifel 1955), just as they did most nonbehavioristic clinical psychology at mid-century. This quite naturally led to a concern that "surface" reports of attitudes toward the annihilation of the self may be unreliable, and that creative means of circumventing conscious ego-defensive processes were necessary if "deeper" levels of death attitudes were to be assessed. This multilevel approach to assessment also carried another putative advantage, namely, the ability to detect intrapsychic conflict or balance between levels of awareness, to the extent that an individual displayed congruence or incongruence in responses to each.

To his credit, Feifel constructed an original battery of measures to assess the "nonunitary nature of fear of death," the component tasks of which were intended to tap death anxiety at three different levels (Feifel and Branscomb 1973). At the *conscious* level, subjects were typically asked simply, "Are you afraid of death?" and their yes/no answers were taken as evidence of conscious fear of their mortality. At a *fantasy* level, subjects were asked for the "ideas or pictures" that came to mind when they thought about death, with their replies being coded as positive, negative, or ambivalent. These images were then supplemented by ratings of death on a number of semantic differential scales. Finally, *below the level of awareness* measurement included a word association and recall task, in which the differential latency to respond between death-related and control words was taken as an index of death anxiety. A second measure of this "nonconscious" anxiety was provided by a color-word interference task requiring the respondent to name the color in which a word was printed, with the differential response time between death-related and neutral words (e.g., coffin vs. desk) interpreted as greater levels of perceptual defense against death. Later studies modified the specific tasks associated with each level, in general moving toward greater standardization of procedures, using the Collett-Lester Fear of Death of Self subscale (Lester 1994) as a conscious measure (Feifel and Schag 1981) and requiring subjects to choose among a provided list of images (e.g., death as a devouring tiger or deserved holiday) as a fantasy measure (Feifel and Nagy 1980).

Results using these measures were consistent across the early studies.[1] For example, Feifel and Branscomb (1973) studied a heterogeneous sample of 371 healthy and ill adults, and found that 71% of them reported no death fear at the conscious level, while 62% nonetheless offered ambivalent imagery at the fantasy level and showed longer mean reaction times to the death words than control words in all tasks. This pattern led the authors to conclude that "the dominant conscious response to fear of death is one of repudiation, that of the fantasy or imagery level, one of ambivalence, and at the nonconscious level, one of outright negativity" (Feifel and Branscomb 1973, p. 286). While subjects in Feifel and Nagy's (1980) study were more likely than those in earlier studies to acknowledge conscious fear of personal death, they generally replicated

---

[1]The consistency of this profile at different levels of awareness should not, however, be taken as true replication of the finding, insofar as these early studies (Feifel 1974, Feifel et al. 1973, Feifel and Hermann 1973) appear to have consisted in whole or in part of reanalyses of the Feifel and Branscomb (1973) data.

the finding of heightened anxiety at lower levels. For Feifel, this pattern
supported the provocative interpretation that subjects tend to report a
pattern of "little fear of death at the conscious level, lockstitched to one
of more pronounced fear both at the fantasy level and below the level of
awareness" (Feifel and Nagy 1980, p. 42).

Subsequent scholarship has cast doubt on this conclusion, however.
Conceptually, some critics have questioned whether response latency
assessments such as the word association or color-word interference
tasks can legitimately be interpreted as measures of perceptual defense,
noting that if they do reflect defensive processes, they are poor ones,
affording only a few fractions of a second delay in buffering the confrontation with death (Kastenbaum and Costa 1977). Moreover, the presumed
independence of conscious, fantasy, and below the level of awareness
measures has been challenged by the repeated finding that the former
two measures correlate more highly with one another than either does
with nonconscious measures (Epting et al. 1979, Feifel and Nagy 1981).
More critically, Rigdon (1983) has provided evidence that direct ratings
and imagery measures actually form a single factor, which he labeled
"conscious death fear." Thus, the critical assumption that fantasy-based
projective techniques measure fears of which the respondent is unaware
does not seem to be supported.

In a more general sense, the lack of independent construct validation of the nonconscious measures is itself a source of difficulty. While
from a psychodynamic standpoint projective and perceptual defense
tasks are plausible approaches to the measurement of "attitudes" of
which one is unaware, the actual convergence of these measures with
established instruments has received little attention. Nor have these
procedures shown much evidence of discriminant validity, in the sense
of distinguishing between groups presumed to differ in their attitudes
toward life and death. For example, fantasy images and response latency
tasks fail to differentiate mentally ill patients from normal controls (Feifel
and Hermann 1973), religious from nonreligious persons (Feifel 1974),
cancer from heart disease patients (Feifel et al. 1973), and people who
engage in life-threatening (e.g., addictive or violent) behaviors from those
who do not (Feifel and Nagy 1980). While Feifel himself acknowledged in
passing that this uniformity in findings may represent a "methodological artifact," he clearly preferred the interpretation that the apparently
universal "anxious" responses to nonconscious measures reflected the
ubiquity of fear of death stemming from our "cultural imprinting" in a
death-denying society (Feifel and Nagy 1980).

Considering Feifel's research as a whole, and the rare but occasional
use of analogous measures by other investigators, perhaps the fairest
conclusion is that the very concept of levels of death anxiety remains an

intriguing but unsubstantiated hypothesis (Neimeyer 1988, Neimeyer and Van Brunt 1995). As the hegemony of a psychodynamic perspective has waned since midcentury, and with it the conviction that opposing conscious and unconscious forces shape our fundamental attitudes toward life, investigators have increasingly concerned themselves with refining self-report measures of "conscious" death anxiety and death competencies (Neimeyer 1994a). However, it remains possible that a renaissance of interest in such tasks might occur, should a new generation of thanatologists begin to explore people's death-related schemas using such newer cognitive science measures as computer-driven implicit memory tasks, lexical decision procedures, or perceptual identification paradigms (Roediger 1990). If researchers of death attitudes develop the methodological sophistication to enter this terrain, it will be interesting to see if they bring with them their traditional reliance on notions of denial and defense, or whether they will relinquish them in favor of more contemporary conceptualizations of "nonconscious" processes as a scaffolding for, rather than antagonists to, conscious awareness.

Imaginal Assessment

Even setting aside the question of whether fantasy images of death disclose attitudes that are inaccessible by conventional verbal report, it is nonetheless the case that such images provide fascinating data in their own right. As one of the first researchers to assess death imagery systematically, Feifel contributed to a sporadic but intriguing line of research that has endured from 1955 to the present.

In his earliest study on death attitudes, Feifel (1955) asked 85 psychiatric patients to "draw a picture of death," which he then compared impressionistically to their interview-based descriptions of death, as detailed below. While viewing the content of these pictures as broadly congruent with patients' verbalized meanings of death, he noted the high frequency of traumatic death themes in the images, such as "being run over by a tractor," or "being shot." This led him to conclude that in the mentally ill, a "violent conception of death mirrors self-held feelings of aggressivity toward others as well as oneself" (p. 378).

As Feifel's research program evolved, he moved toward more reliable systems for coding unstructured responses to probes such as, "What ideas or pictures come to mind when you think about death?" In general, he found that subjects who rated themselves as more religious tended to volunteer images that were positive (e.g., resting peacefully in a garden), whereas those who reported less religious identification tended toward ambivalent or negative portrayals of death (Feifel and Branscomb 1973). In his later studies, Feifel further standardized the assessment of imagery by instructing subjects to select the death images they preferred from a fixed list of 12 (e.g., a deserved holiday, a dead-end road) (Feifel and Nagy 1980). Using this more restrictive assessment format, he discovered that subjects offering more positive death metaphors tended to be more favorable toward mercy killing and suicide, suggesting a possible link between one's cosmology and one's attitudes toward "life and death" social issues.

While Feifel's specific methods for assessing imagery have not been widely used by other investigators, it is interesting to note that some researchers have pursued the study of pictorial representations of Death using their own novel procedures. Kastenbaum and Aisenberg, for example, began by administering an open-ended probe to hundreds of subjects, asking, "If Death were a person, what sort of a person would Death be?" (Kastenbaum 1992). Respondents were encouraged to describe Death's appearance as well as personality, and types of personification were classed by the investigators for further analysis. Subsequent research in this tradition simplified the task by standardizing responses and presenting them as multiple choice alternatives to large groups of subjects. The dominant response in these studies depicted Death as an old man, typically with a monstrous or hideous appearance who stalked or overpowered its human victims. However, other images were also common, such as a gentle, comforting figure of either sex, a tempting but deceptive romantic liaison, or a faceless, emotionless automaton who indifferently cut down living beings. The most systematic follow-up to this work was conducted by Lonetto and Templer (1986), who documented the overwhelming tendency to personify Death as male, and gave careful attention to particular features of such imagery, such as the eyes, hands, clothing, and activity of the Death figure. Moreover, Lonetto and his collaborators studied the relationship between death imagery and independently assessed death anxiety scores, concluding that men and women who viewed Death as a seductive figure or in more abstract terms (as a pattern of light and color or feeling) were more likely to obtain lower scores on Templer's (1970) Death Anxiety Scale. Subsequent research on the Death personifications of health care providers suggests that imagery measures can be useful in identifying not only the positivity or negativity of a relevant sample, but also in gaining an appreciation of the subtler features of death images, such as the context of the image (indoors or outdoors), time of year (summer or winter), and so on (Tamm 1996).

An especially appropriate context for the study of death imagery is developmental research on concepts of death, insofar as straightforward questioning of children may prove unworkable or lead to more barren responses than might be elicited from a fantasy-based measure. The best work of this kind conducted to date has been reported by Tamm and Granqvist (1995), who examined drawings of death completed by a stratified sample of 431 Swedish schoolchildren ages 9 to 18. Using a sophisticated and reliable category system to code the resulting images, the authors discovered that biological concepts of death tended to permeate the drawings of younger students, whereas metaphysical conceptions emerged in the work of adolescents. Across ages, boys were more likely to portray death in violent terms, and girls were more likely to emphasize emotionality in their drawings. Interestingly, religious imagery was comparatively uncommon for both sexes, reflecting the secular orientation of Swedish society.

In sum, the study of death imagery pioneered by Feifel and extended by others has continued to provide an interesting counterbalance to the reliance on forced-choice questionnaires in the study of death attitudes. Further use of these methods is to be encouraged, particularly in cross-cultural and developmental studies, provided that investigators take care to establish the reliability of their methods and eschew unwarranted assumptions about the capacity of imagery measures to reveal unconscious attitudes or conflicts of which the person is unaware.

Personal Meanings of Death

As was true in the study of death imagery, Feifel (1955)pioneered in the investigation of personal meanings of death, analyzing responses to the question, "What does death mean to you?" in his earliest research on death attitudes. Taking care to establish adequate interjudge reliability, he coded responses into one of four categories: the end, preparation for another life, rest and peace, and "don't know." He found that conceptions of death as an ending were held by half of the psychiatric patients who constituted his sample, with slightly over 20% viewing death as the beginning of a new life. However, perhaps as a result of the influence of psychodynamic thinking on his early work, he sometimes tended to attribute patients' expressions of uncertainty to this question to their denial or avoidance of death (Feifel 1969b), which strictly speaking went beyond the data provided by his interview.

While the analysis of free-response data concerning personal philosophies of death was eclipsed until recently by a nearly exclusive reliance on forced-choice questionnaires, there has been a renaissance of interest in this way of assessing death attitudes in recent years. One example is the development of the Revised Twenty Statements Test by Durlak and his colleagues (1990), which asks subjects to give twenty open-ended responses to the question, "What does your own death mean to you?" The responses are coded into one of ten content categories, some of which parallel those used by Feifel (e.g., positive, negative, neutral, religious). Preliminary evidence supports the interrater and test-retest reliability of the measure, issues that are critical with free-response measures of this kind (Kastenbaum 1992).

Another example of a text-based method has been provided by Holcomb and colleagues (1993), who solicited narrative responses to the question, "What does death mean to you?" from over 500 respondents. Unitizing the data into discrete personal constructs (e.g., death is "fearful," it "goes beyond human understanding"), they then coded responses using a reliable twenty-five–category coding system (Neimeyer et al. 1984). Content analysis of these responses suggested that the majority of subjects (over 60%) tended to construe death in terms of its being "purposeful" and entailing some form of continued "existence," although a sizable minority (approximately 40%) of respondents interpreted death in terms of "negative emotions" or "nonexistence." Constructions of death also differed significantly as a function of the subject's sex, health status, and previous history of suicide attempts or ideation. In general, the use of content coding systems for text-based or interview data holds considerable promise in elucidating the personal meanings death holds for individuals, although the greater demands on the investigator using such systems makes it unlikely that they will displace the ubiquitous questionnaire in most studies of death attitudes.

Enhancing the Psychometric Adequacy of Death Attitude Measures

While creative advocacy for indirect, multileveled, imaginal, and interview-based measures of death attitudes are the hallmarks of Feifel's contribution to thanatological research, an important minor theme in his work concerns the empirical rigor with which death anxiety instruments are constructed. Quite early in his career, Feifel (1961) emphasized the need to check the reliability of instruments used to assess death fears, and the need for ongoing refinement of measurement tools. Thirty years later, he reiterated this concern, stressing that the perception of "fear of death" as a unitary variable, and the need for cross-validation and reliability analyses of our procedures, continued to plague psychological research in the area (Feifel 1990). This call for psychometric rigor has been echoed by generations of researchers since that time, with considerable consensus that advances in the field require the use of valid and reliable multidimensional measures of death attitudes, in combination with methodologically stronger and more practically relevant research designs (Kastenbaum and Costa 1977, Lester 1967a, Neimeyer 1988, 1994b, Neimeyer and Van Brunt 1995, Pollak 1979).

Fortunately, considerable progress has been made in the quality and precision of instrumentation in this area over the 40 years of Feifel's career. Just as he himself shifted away from early reliance on impressionistic analyses of interview responses toward more standardized assessments of conscious death attitudes, so has the field of death anxiety research as a whole moved toward the use of demonstrably valid and reliable measures. Although existing measures have their weaknesses as well as their strengths (for a full discussion, see Neimeyer 1994a, 1996), respectable instruments now exist for measuring not only anxiety, threat, and fear associated with death, but also varieties of death acceptance, coping, and self-efficacy (see Table 1–1 for a brief description of the best available measures). Thus, contemporary investigators of death attitudes can select measures that more precisely match their theoretical or practical needs, or design batteries of scales that provide a more compre-

TABLE 1–1. Best validated death attitude scales.

Scale Title	Description	References
Death Anxiety Scale	Fifteen-item true-false test measuring general fear of death and dying, sense of time passing quickly, etc.	Templer (1970) Lonetto and Templer (1986)
Revised Death Anxiety Scale	Twenty-five–Likert-item refinement of the original Death Anxiety Scale	Thorson and Powell (1994)
Threat Index	Twenty-five to forty-item versions measuring cognitive distance between self and death concepts (i.e., death threat)	Krieger et al. (1974) Neimeyer (1994b)
Multidimensional Fear of Death Scale	Forty-two–Likert-item measure of eight distinct facets of fear of death (e.g., fear of dying, the unknown, the dead, premature death)	Hoelter (1979) Neimeyer and Moore (1994)
Fear of Personal Death Scale	Thirty-one Likert items assessing personal, interpersonal, and transpersonal consequences of death	Florian and Kravetz (1983)
Death Attitude Profile-Revised	Thirty-two Likert items measuring death fear, avoidance, and neutral, approach, and escape acceptance	Wong et al. (1994)
Coping with Death Scale	Thirty Likert items assessing competencies related to death (e.g., communicating with dying, coping with loss, planning funeral)	Robbins (1994)

hensive assessment of the complex of reactions to the many aspects of death and loss in human life. In combination with progressive trends in hypothesis generation, sample selection, research design, and quantitative or qualitative analysis, the development of more subtle and reliable measures has begun to clarify the correlates and consequences of death anxiety, a topic to which we shall turn in the sections to follow.

Correlates of Death Anxiety in Adult Life

While Feifel's work touched on a remarkable range of thanatological topics over the span of his 40-year career, his contributions to the study of death attitudes cluster rather naturally into a handful of areas. We will therefore turn to five substantive areas of research sparked by his early efforts, namely death attitudes in the elderly, the relationship of death concerns to physical illness, the death anxiety of medical and nonmedical caregivers, the relationship between fear of death and psychopathology, and the association between religiosity and apprehension about death.

Death Anxiety in the Elderly

In keeping with his pioneering predilections, Feifel (1956) was the first psychologist to conduct an empirical study of the death attitudes of older persons. Lacking any standardized means of assessing death concern, he devised an ingenious set of interview probes for use with 40 white male veterans of World War I. He discovered that the group was equally divided between viewing death as "the end" versus a doorway to an afterlife (40% in each category), while smaller numbers (10% each) viewed it mainly as a release from pain or expressed uncertainty about its meaning. When asked how they would prefer to die, respondents were virtually unanimous in preferring to die in their sleep. Most professed thinking of death only "occasionally" (48%) or "rarely" (32%), although they were generally realistic in projecting a short life span for themselves. Interestingly, although Feifel did not directly question interviewees about their own death anxiety, subjects tended to believe that fear of death peaked in old age when asked to describe when "people in general" fear death.

In his later studies, Feifel more directly investigated the relation of age to death anxiety at various "levels" of awareness. At both "conscious" and "fantasy" levels, older subjects displayed less fear of death than their middle-aged and younger counterparts (Feifel and Branscomb 1973). An apparently contradictory finding that older persons were more death anxious at "nonconscious" levels cannot be considered reliable, given the failure of the study to control for the general slowing of reaction times with age, irrespective of task content. Finally, concerning retrospective reports of changes in death anxiety over the years, subjects in later research tended to report either "no change" (40%) or a decrease in death fear (44%), with only a minority reporting heightened death fears with advancing age (16%) (Feifel and Nagy 1980). However, the results of this research should be qualified by its unusual sample, which comprised a heterogeneous group of "risk-taking" men (drug users, deputy sheriffs, etc.)., Nonetheless, the results of Feifel's studies suggest that old age is not necessarily a period of morose preoccupation with personal death; indeed, the elderly may report lower levels of death fear than more youthful cohorts.

The overall picture that emerges from studies by other investigators tends to buttress this conclusion (Neimeyer and Fortner 1996). Age was not found to be a significant correlate of death anxiety in early investigations (Lester 1967a, Pollak 1979), and this may explain why it was not examined thoroughly until relatively recently. At least in the earliest research, samples used tended not to include broad ranges of age and were also inclined to ignore the poles of the age continuum, especially the elderly (Lester 1967a). But as more investigators have turned specific attention to the death attitudes of older persons, evidence has mounted against the intuitive proposition that fear of death increases with age. Indeed, well-designed large-scale surveys of ethnically diverse samples have indicated that death anxiety decreases from mid-life to old age (Bengtson et al. 1977, Kalish 1977). This finding has generally been corroborated by more fine-grained research using many of the stronger death attitude measures with diverse samples (Gesser et al. 1987, Neimeyer 1985, Robinson and Wood 1984, Stevens et al. 1980, Thorson and Powell 1989).

While most researchers have looked for linear trends in the relation between age and death concern, future investigations should consider the possibility of a curvilinear pattern. In developing the Death Attitude Profile (DAP), Gesser and colleagues (1987) administered the instrument to young (18–25), middle-aged (35–50), and elderly (60+) subjects. They found a curvilinear trend, showing that the elderly exhibited less fear of death and dying than the middle-aged but not the young.

Another consideration concerns the multidimensional nature of death anxiety, which suggests that the specific features of death that arouse fearful anticipation may differ for persons of various ages. Thorson and Powell (1994), for example, found that younger subjects feared such things as bodily decomposition, pain, helplessness, and isolation, while older subjects were more concerned about loss of control and the existence of an afterlife.

Finally, we should be cautious in reaching firm conclusions about the role of age from cross-sectional data. We are hard pressed to draw causal inferences from such designs, and it is likely that if age does exert a causal influence, it does so through mediator variables that are of more practical and theoretical interest (e.g., coping style, self-actualization, social isolation, context of early socialization). Kastenbaum (1992) aptly pointed out that elderly people differ from young people in many ways, only one of which is the time they have spent in living here on earth. Additionally, age itself may introduce some selection processes (for example, by winnowing out risk takers or the physically ill), which may restrict the range of subjects available for study in old age, thereby complicating comparisons with younger samples.

Health Status

Beginning in the late 1960s, Feifel and his colleagues published a series of studies exploring death attitudes in terminally ill, seriously ill, chronically ill, physically disabled, mentally ill, and healthy subjects. Two of these studies (Feifel et al. 1973, Feifel and Hermann 1973) included illness as a variable of analysis in relation to death anxiety. Using the multilevel approach, Feifel and colleagues (1973) found that while terminally ill subjects reported thinking of death more frequently than healthy subjects, they were no more likely to disclose conscious expressions of death concern than were their well counterparts. Nonetheless, terminally ill subjects were likely to have a "significantly more religious outlook . . . concerning personal fate after death" (p.163), a trend that has also been reported in some subsequent investigations (see below).

At putatively nonconscious levels, terminally ill subjects in the Feifel and colleagues (1973) study showed greater response latencies in the Color Word Interference Test, although it is dubious whether this finding reflected greater death anxiety, given the apparent failure to control for general slowing of reaction times to control words in this seriously ill sample. Within the terminally ill patients, no significant differences were detected at any level of measurement between heart and cancer patients. Thus, Feifel's own research fails to indicate reliable differences in fear of death as a function of medical status, the intuitive plausibility of such a link notwithstanding.

Subsequent investigations of health in relation to death anxiety have begun to clarify the conflicting findings reflected in the early literature (Pollak 1979). While some studies have found no direct relationship between levels of physical well-being and death threat or anxiety (Baum 1983, Baum and Boxley 1984, Robinson and Wood 1984, Templer 1971, Wagner and Lorion 1984), others point to higher levels of death concern among the infirm elderly (Tate 1982), people with diminished functional ability (Mullins and Lopez 1982), smokers (Kureshi and Husain 1981), and the severely ill (Viney 1984) relative to comparison groups. It is probable that much of the ambiguity in these results derives from the failure of investigators to measure relevant moderator variables that interact with health status to determine personal fear of death. A recent study by Ho and Shiu (1995) illustrates this point. Investigating the death attitudes and coping styles of Chinese cancer patients, they found that, as a group, cancer patients' mean scores on the Death Anxiety Scale (DAS) could not be distinguished from those of a comparison group of patients with hand injuries. However, the cancer patients showed much greater variability in death anxiety, with more of them falling into both high and low ranges of the DAS than control subjects. Interestingly, the high-anxiety cancer group was distinguished from the hand-injured group by their reliance on "immature" coping strategies, such as autistic fantasy and passive aggression. The authors interpreted this finding as reflecting the cultural norm among Chinese to express heightened anxieties and anger only indirectly, but it is equally possible that inadequate coping may itself contribute to heightened death concern.

The most recent investigations of death anxiety related to the AIDS pandemic also tend to measure moderator variables that can explain relationships observed between fear of death and physical threats to well-being. Catania and colleagues (1992) found that gay men with HIV infection reported greater death anxiety if they also experienced less family support. Likewise, Hintze and colleagues (1993) found that death anxiety in HIV-infected men was associated with greater deterioration and with awareness of the AIDS diagnosis by family members, perhaps leading to scapegoating or rejection. Finally, Bivens and colleagues (1995) found that HIV+ gay and bisexual men were more afraid of premature death than their noninfected counterparts. Interestingly, however, the HIV+ men also tended to report higher degrees of intrinsic religiosity, which was associated with less overall death threat, and fewer specific fears regarding an afterlife. In combination, these more complex studies suggest that while illness alone may arouse death concerns in some people, the degree of death anxiety triggered by deteriorating health is a function of both interpersonal factors (e.g., social support) and personal resources (e.g., coping styles and religious beliefs), rather than illness per se.

Finally, it is worth closing with a methodological caution for those researchers considering doing research on health status and death anxiety. If physical health does not vary sufficiently within a given sample, statistical validity is jeopardized, as any relationship will be suppressed by the uniformity of health. Myska and Pasework (1978) exemplify appropriate restraint in not analyzing state of health data given that only one person in each of their groups of institutionalized elderly acknowledged being in poor health. Whenever investigators focus on a single group design (whether ill or healthy), it is incumbent on them to demonstrate adequate variability in health to make a comparison with death attitudes statistically meaningful.

Death Anxiety among Caregivers

Early in his career, Feifel experienced repeated rebuffs by powerful physicians who blocked his access to patients whose death attitudes he wanted to study (Feifel 1963a, b). Although their objections to his research protocol were commonly phrased in terms of concerns about distressing the patients, Feifel was struck by the unwillingness of these same doctors to revise their opinions in light of evidence to the contrary. Perhaps partly as a response to this state of affairs, he developed the hypothesis that the physicians who opposed his research were acting more on the basis of their own exaggerated fears of death than out of concern for patient welfare (Feifel 1963b). This ultimately led him to conduct pilot research on a group of forty physicians, finding that while they thought less frequently about death, they had greater death anxiety than patients and other nonprofessional controls. As a result of these personal experiences and pilot data, he put forward the provocative hypothesis that "the reason certain physicians enter medicine is to govern their own above-average fears concerning death" (Feifel 1965, pp. 633–634). He soon extended this speculation to argue that the commonly encountered reluctance among physicians to inform patients of their impending deaths derived from anxieties in physicians about their own mortality, rather than any contraindication related to patients, most of whom preferred to be informed of the gravity of their condition (Feifel 1959, 1969b).

A good deal of subsequent research has been stimulated by Feifel's conjecture, focusing on the distinctive death attitudes of both medical and nonmedical caregivers. Some of these studies have supported Feifel's pilot research on physicians. For example, Neimeyer and Dingemans (1980) administered the Collett-Lester Fear of Death Scale, Threat Index, Lester Fear of Death Scale, and the Templer Death Anxiety Scale to suicide and crisis intervention workers and controls, finding that crisis intervention workers reported consistently greater threat and apprehension about their own death and dying. Similarly, DePaola and colleagues (1992) found that nursing home staff had greater concern than controls on the Fear of the Unknown factor of the Multidimensional Fear of Death Scale. However, attempts to replicate these findings using other instruments and samples have proven unsuccessful (DePaola et al. 1992, Neimeyer and Neimeyer 1984). For the most part, subsequent research has also failed to confirm the assertion that medical caregivers demonstrate greater levels of death anxiety than comparison groups. In particular, differences in death anxiety have not been found between medical students and comparable social science students (Howells and Field 1982), or between allied health professionals in death education courses and their classmates (Neimeyer et al. 1986). In fact, research on gay and bisexual men providing support to persons with AIDS indicates that they actually report *lower* degrees of death threat than gay men uninvolved in such activities (Bivens et al. 1994).

Apart from the question of whether the average helping professional experiences unusually high levels of death anxiety is the question of how variation in death anxiety among caregivers predicts, and possibly affects, their work performance. For example, Vickio and Cavanaugh (1985) found that nursing home employees with high levels of death concern tended to have more negative views toward elderly persons and aging, and were less willing to talk about death and dying, than those with low levels of death concern. This finding has been replicated by Eakes (1985) and DePaola and colleagues (1994). The latter study was useful in further specifying which facets of death anxiety were linked to devaluation of the elderly, namely those factors concerning fear of the unknown, fear of consciousness when dead, and fear for the body after death rather than global death fear per se.

Perhaps even more disturbing than the implication that death-anxious caregivers may devalue those who are close to dying are data suggesting that fear of death is associated with very conservative medical decision making. For example, Schulz and Aderman (1979) discovered that physicians having greater death anxiety were more likely to perform heroic treatment to prolong the lives of terminal patients during their final days in the hospital. And in line with Feifel's argument about why patients are not informed about the seriousness of their conditions, Eggerman and Dustin (1985) found that doctors who are highly distressed by the possibility of their own death reported considering more factors before informing terminal patients of their prognosis.

In summary, while broad group differences between caregivers and controls are not profound, the implications of elevated levels of death anxiety in some medical staff may be. Replication and extension of the research in this area is obviously indicated.

Death Anxiety and Psychopathology

Early in his career, Feifel (1955) noted that death themes were often prominent in psychopathology, and for some patients discussion of death-related issues was therapeutic. He argued that, contrary to psychoanalytic theory, death anxiety in such patients might not be secondary to some other difficulty (e.g., separation or castration anxiety), but might itself be a central force from which secondary symptomatology arose. Noting that previous studies had not involved people with psychological problems, Feifel (1955) compared the responses of open-ward patients (chiefly anxiety, depressive, character, and behavior disorders) and closed-ward patients (chiefly schizophrenics) to a variety of interview probes of death attitudes. Both groups typically viewed death as an end to a natural process, followed by the belief that death is a stage of preparation for another life. He also noted unexpected themes of violence in patients' depictions of death. However, somewhat to his surprise, degree of disturbance (closed versus open ward status) appeared to be unrelated to patients' death attitudes.

In a second study, Feifel and Hermann (1973) arranged a more focused design to determine if degree of psychological disturbance predicted higher levels of death anxiety. However, his multilevel assessment failed to disclose any differences between normal and mentally ill samples at any level. Moreover, no substantial differences between psychotic patients and neurotic patients could be identified at conscious, fantasy, or "nonconscious" levels.

Since Feifel's groundbreaking efforts, many studies have examined both general maladjustment and specific manifestations of psychopathology (e.g., depression, anxiety) in relation to death concern. However, contrary to Feifel's methodological preference for comparing patients grouped by approximate diagnosis, the majority of subsequent research has treated psychopathology as a continuous variable, which may be present in milder forms even in "normal" populations. Adopting this correlational rather than classificatory approach, a number of studies have suggested that higher levels of death anxiety are generally accompanied by elevated levels of "neuroticism" (guilt-proneness, worry, suspicion, etc.) (Howells and Field 1982, Loo 1984, Vargo and Black 1984, Westman and Brackney 1990). While this correlation of death anxious and neurotic responses is compatible with self-actualization theories that emphasize that death acceptance is both a hallmark of and contributor to psychological well-being (Tomer 1994), it is obviously impossible to infer causal relationships from simple correlational designs of this kind.

As this literature has evolved, investigators have shifted away from the study of death attitudes in relation to generalized measures of neurosis, and toward the analysis of measures of specific constructs or symptoms. Much of this work has established a link between death anxiety and general anxiety (Neimeyer 1988, Pollak 1979). More refined studies have attempted still greater specificity by comparing death concerns to both transient (state) and characterological (trait) anxiety. This research suggests that subjects who exhibit greater death anxiety (e.g., Conte et al. 1982, Gilliland and Templer 1985, Hintze et al. 1993, Lonetto et al. 1980), fear (Loo 1984), and threat (Tobacyk and Eckstein 1980) score higher on validated scales of general anxiety, especially in its more enduring or trait-like form.

A second specific expression of distress to receive attention in the death anxiety literature is depression. Lonetto and Templer (1986) review evidence that the DAS correlates positively with depression as measured by the Minnesota Multiphasic Personality Inventory (MMPI), the Zung depression scale, and other measures in samples of psychiatric patients and elderly people. Several other studies have confirmed this relationship, particularly in elderly samples (Baum 1983, Baum and Boxley 1984, Rhudick and Dibner 1961a). On the other hand, Wagner and Lorian (1984), using stepwise regression, found that depression as measured by the Self-Rating Depression Scale failed to contribute to the prediction of Death Anxiety Scale scores from five groups of elderly people (i.e., entire sample, community subjects, institutionalized subjects, subjects with sleep disturbance, and subjects without sleep disturbance), throwing into question the generalizability of this relationship.

While it is often associated with depression, suicide risk per se has received relatively little attention in studies of death anxiety, despite the intuitively plausible link between one's attitudes toward death and one's conscious selection of it as a solution to life problems. In partial support of this rationale, Lester (1967b) found that suicidal adolescents feared death less than their nonsuicidal peers. In contrast, however, a recent study by D'Attillio and Campbell (1990) discovered that scores on the Death Anxiety Scale and the Suicide Probability Scale correlated positively, indicating that subjects with greater suicide potential had higher death concern. Clearly, more research is needed in this area. Of particular importance will be future studies that go beyond global assessments of death concern (such as the DAS) and employ more multidimensional measures of death attitudes that permit a clearer identification of what facets of death attitudes inhibit or facilitate self-destructive behavior in stressful circumstances.

In summary, subsequent research has been more successful than Feifel's initial efforts in establishing an association between death anxiety and a broad band of psychopathology. While further descriptive research may be useful in filling in the outlines of this picture, it would be more valuable to construct causal models of how death fears either exacerbate or are aggravated by other forms of psychological distress. Ultimately, more research is also needed on the responsiveness of death anxiety to treatment, particularly in clinical syndromes such as panic disorder, in which an irrational fear of dying plays a central role.

Death Anxiety and Religiosity

Scholars have argued that the need to address the problem of human mortality is a driving force behind the development of virtually all world religions (Becker 1973, Choron 1974). From this perspective, one might reasonably expect that individuals who differ in their spiritual ideologies would also differ in their attitudes toward death. At least four of Feifel's published works speak directly to this question, exploring the distinctive death attitudes of religious versus nonreligious persons. The first reported only the results of pilot data on eighty-two subjects classified as religious and nonreligious. Feifel (1959) concluded that "The religious person, when compared to the nonreligious individual, is personally more afraid of death" (p. 121). This is a function of his or her compound fears of not only the cessation of earthly experience, but also concerns about an afterlife. Some evidence for this has been reported by subsequent investigators using multidimensional measures of death anxiety. Florian and Kravetz (1983), for example, found that in 178 Israeli Jews, moderately religious subjects had higher scores on certain aspects of death and lower scores on others. Moderately religious subjects were more upset about such things as the consequences of one's death on family and friends, while highly religious subjects were more concerned about such things as being punished in the afterlife.

But in general, these supportive results stand in contrast to much of the subsequent literature in this area (Neimeyer 1996). This trend is illustrated even in Feifel's later work. Feifel and Branscomb (1973) subjected ten predictor variables—age, education, intelligence, socioeconomic status, religious self-rating, recent experience with death of personal acquaintances, nearness to death, gender, marital status, number of children—to a stepwise regression in which measures of death anxiety at various levels of awareness served as the dependent variables. Of the ten predictor variables, religious self-rating was retained most often, being represented in all of the final regression equations predicting conscious reports of death anxiety, negative death imagery, and the selection of negative adjectives from bipolar pairs. Contrary to Feifel's pilot study, religious self-report predicted lower levels of death anxiety in each equation.

Using the same sample of subjects as Feifel and Branscomb (1973), Feifel (1974) improved upon his measure of religiosity by composing religious categories based on multiple dimensions of religious activity (i.e., religious creed, religious self-rating, and religious behavior). Surprisingly, considering the positive findings of Feifel and Branscomb (1973) with this same sample and the seemingly improved measure of religiosity, no significant differences between subjects classified as religious and those classified as nonreligious were found on any of the measures in either the healthy or the terminally ill patients.

Fiefel's contradictory findings, obtained through different methods of measurement and statistical analysis of the same sample, mirror the conflicting findings typical of early research in this area (Krieger et al. 1974, Neimeyer et al. 1977, Pratt et al. 1985). One early reviewer even refused to attempt an interpretation of the tangled web of diametrically opposed results available at the time (Pollak 1979). In a more positive light, Feifel's (1974) study anticipated contemporary research that has employed a more refined conceptualization and operationalization of religiosity, a movement that he explicitly encouraged (Feifel 1959).

More recent and sophisticated religiosity research has distinguished between extrinsic religiosity, which reflects a utilitarian view of religion, and intrinsic religiosity, which aims to reflect the centrality of faith to one's life. Thorson and Powell (1990) showed that of several measures related to religiosity as well as demographics, only intrinsic religiosity and age correlated negatively with death anxiety. Likewise, Bivens and his colleagues (1994) showed that intrinsic religiosity, but not extrinsic religiosity, in gay and bisexual men was negatively correlated with death threat as measured by the Threat Index. Of the Multi-Dimensional Fear of Death Scale scores, the Fear of the Unknown factor correlated negatively with intrinsic religiosity ($r = -.48$) but positively with extrinsic religious orientation ($r = .25$). These and similar results (Rigdon and Epting 1985) suggest that "deeper" or more genuine religious commitment (at least in Christian terms) ameliorates conscious fear of death, perhaps by giving meaning to an afterlife that is, by definition, beyond human experience. "Superficial" or expedient participation in a religious community, on the other hand, may actually be associated with greater death anxiety.

In 1981 Feifel and Nagy improved their methodology by including multiple measures of constructs, established scales for measurement, and more sophisticated statistical analysis. They classified groups of men who were thought to display risk-taking behavior into seven groups based on scores from the Collett-Lester Fear of Death Self Scale and Feifel's multilevel measurements of death anxiety. They then performed a factor analysis on an assortment of measures related to death attitudes, life values, religious orientation, and self-acceptance, and submitted the resulting nine factor scores obtained to stepwise discriminant analysis, predicting the variance associated with membership in the seven death anxiety groups. The final predictors selected were a semantic differential rating of concept of death, death awareness, religious orientation, and attitude toward attending funerals. These predictors accounted for 28.6% of the variance in death anxiety group membership, and reinforced the conclusion that religiosity tends to ameliorate death anxiety.

In line with Feifel and Nagy's (1981) movement toward more complex and purposively employed statistical procedures, recent work has called into question the linearity of the relationship between measures of religiosity and death concerns. For instance, Downey (1984) found that middle-aged men who were moderately religious had greater death anxiety than both believers and nonbelievers. Other studies may be interpreted as supporting this nonlinear trend (Florian and Kravetz 1983, Holcomb et al. 1993, Ingram and Leitner 1989). This suggests that if religiosity is measured across its full range (i.e., from devoutly religious through semicommitted to avowedly nonreligious or nontheistic), people with firm ideological commitments on both ends of the spectrum may be less apprehensive about death than those with more ambivalent personal philosophies.

As the above discussion suggests, the relationship between religious belief and death attitudes is far from simple. Future researchers must continue taking into account the multidimensional nature of both religiosity and death anxiety as well considering the nature of the relationship between the two constructs in terms of linearity and directionality. With respect to causality, we will be in a much better position to tease out causal arguments if researchers will work within the frameworks of theoretically driven causal models and utilize quasi-experimental designs whenever possible.

Conclusion

As a founding figure in the death awareness movement, Herman Feifel sparked a literature on the psychology of death attitudes that now numbers over 1,000 publications (Neimeyer and Van Brunt 1995). In this chapter we have tried to place Feifel's seminal contributions in the context of this subsequent work, illustrating trends in both methodology and substantive research that have derived from, paralleled, or challenged his pioneering contributions. The picture that emerges is that of a broad and intriguing, if not entirely consistent literature, characterized by competing instrumentation, diverse subject populations, and divergent research goals. Still, even in the midst of this heterogeneity, it is possible to winnow out a few themes that have characterized the study of death attitudes across time, some (but not all) of which were foreshadowed in Feifel's own work.

At a methodological level, there has been an unmistakable shift toward reliance upon psychometrically validated and reliable questionnaires for assessing death concern (Neimeyer 1994a), displacing the initial usage of imaginative, but unproven interview probes of attitudes toward death and dying. This quest for standardized and quantitative assessment of conscious attitudes has also implied an erosion of interest in more indirect methods of measuring unconscious dynamics, a trend that has been accelerated by questions regarding the validity of the latter approaches and the waning influence of psychodynamic models of personality. While this quest for scientific standing may imply some reduction in the existential richness of the data collected to assess death attitudes, there are hopeful signs that this loss will be offset by the broader utilization of reliable coding schemes for analyzing imaginal depictions of death and unstructured narratives that convey subjects' personal meanings of death in their own terms.

Substantively, the general improvement in methodology and analytic strategies has begun to clarify some of the contradictions that beset the early literature on the correlates of death attitudes. As a result, it now appears that older adults, if anything, are less death anxious than their middle-aged counterparts, although those who are infirm and socially isolated may find it more difficult to cope with some facets of their mortality, such as loss of control and concerns about an afterlife. Physical illness per se is at best a crude predictor of fear of death, insofar as death concern appears to be mediated by a number of personal resources, such as coping strategies, philosophies of life, and social integration. It is considerably clearer that death anxiety is associated with a broad band of psychological distress, although the correlational nature of this research makes it difficult to establish which is more fundamental, or whether death anxiety and other overt symptomatology (e.g., generalized anxiety) are a function of a still more basic process, such as perceived distance from one's chosen ideals, lack of identification with a culturally endorsed belief system, or other factors (Tomer 1994). Finally, genuine religious conviction seems to provide a bulwark against at least some facets of death fear, within the fairly narrow range of Christian faiths represented in the vast majority of studies. What seems needed is the formulation of more comprehensive theoretical models that would help integrate these separate factors, and clarify their joint or interactive impact on death attitudes.

In conclusion, the field of death attitudes has come a long way since Herman Feifel's inaugural research in the area 40 years ago. We are hopeful that the present encouraging trends in this literature will continue, and that the resulting understanding of the psychology of death will grow in quality as well as quantity. The willingness of future generations of researchers both to learn from and ultimately to transcend the work of its founders may prove to be the most fitting tribute to any pioneer.

References

Baum, S. K. (1983). Older people's anxiety about afterlife. *Psychological Reports* 52:895–898.

Baum, S. K., and Boxley, R. L. (1984). Age denial: death denial in the elderly. *Death Education* 8:419–423.

Becker, E. (1973). *The Denial of Death.* New York: Macmillan.

Bengtson, V. L., Cuellar, J. B., and Ragan, P. K. (1977). Stratum contrasts and similarities in attitudes toward death. *Journal of Gerontology* 32:76–88.

Bivens, A. J., Neimeyer, R. A., Kirchberg, T. M., and Moore, M. K. (1995). Death concern and religious belief among gays and bisexuals of variable proximity to AIDS. *Omega* 30:105–120.

Catania, J. A., Turner, H. A., Choi, K.-H., and Coates, T. J. (1992). Coping with death anxiety: help-seeking and social support among gay men with various HIV diagnoses. *AIDS* 6:999–1005.

Choron, J. (1974). *Death and Modern Man.* New York: Macmillan.

Conte, H. R., Weiner, M. B., and Plutchik, R. (1982). Measuring death anxiety: conceptual, psychometric and factor analytic aspects. *Journal of Personality and Social Psychology* 43:775–785.

D'Attillio, J. P., and Campbell, B. (1990). Relationship between death anxiety and suicide potential in an adolescent population. *Psychological Reports* 67:975–978.

DePaola, S. J., Neimeyer, R. A., Lupfer, M. B., and Fiedler, J. (1992). Death concern and attitudes toward the elderly in nursing home personnel. *Death Studies* 16:537–555.

DePaola, S. J., Neimeyer, R. A., and Ross, S. K. (1994). Death concern and attitudes toward the elderly in nursing home personnel as a function of training. *Omega* 29:231–248.

Downey, A. M. (1984). Relationship of religiosity to death anxiety in middle aged males. *Psychological Reports* 54:811–822.

Durlak, J. A., Horn, W., and Kass, R. A. (1990). A self-administering assessment of personal meanings of death: report on the revised Twenty Statements Test. *Omega* 21:301–309.

Eakes, G. G. (1985). The relationship between death anxiety and attitudes toward the elderly among nursing staff. *Death Studies* 9:163–172.

Eggerman, S., and Dustin, D. (1985). Death orientation and communication with the terminally ill. *Omega* 16:255–265.

Epting, F. R., Rainey, L. C., and Weiss, M. J. (1979). Constructions of death and levels of death fear. *Death Education* 3:21–30.

Feifel, H. (1955). Attitudes of mentally ill patients toward death. *Journal of Nervous and Mental Disease* 122:375–380.

—— (1956). Older persons look at death. *Geriatrics* 11:127–130.

—— (1959). Attitudes toward death in some normal and mentally ill populations. In *The Meaning of Death*, ed. H. Feifel, pp. 114–130. New York: McGraw-Hill.

—— (1961). Comments of attitudes toward death in older persons. *Journal of Gerontology* 16:61–63.

—— (1963a). Death. In *The Encyclopedia of Mental Health*, vol. 2, ed. H. Deutsch, pp. 427–450. New York: Franklin Watts, Grolier.

—— (1963b). Death. In *Taboo Topics*, ed. N. Farberow, pp. 8–21. New York: Atherton Press.

—— (1965). The function of attitudes toward death. In *Death and Dying: Attitudes of Patient and Doctor*, ed. Group for the Advancement of Psychiatry, pp. 632–641. New York: Mental Health Materials Center.

—— (1969a). Attitudes toward death: a psychological perspective. *Journal of Consulting and Clinical Psychology* 33:292–295.

—— (1969b). Perceptions of death. *Annuals of New York Academy of Sciences* 164:669–677.

———— (1974). Religious convictions and fear of death among the healthy and the terminally ill. *Journal for the Scientific Study of Religion* 13:353–360.

———— (1990). Psychology and death: meaningful rediscovery. American Psychological Association: Distinguished Professional Contributions Award Address (1988, Atlanta, Georgia). *American Psychologist* 45:537–543.

Feifel, H., and Branscomb, A. B. (1973). Who's afraid of death? *Journal of Abnormal Psychology* 81:282–288.

Feifel, H., Freilich, J., and Hermann, L. J. (1973). Fear of death in dying heart and cancer patients. *Journal of Psychosomatic Research* 17:161–166.

Feifel, H., and Hermann, L. J. (1973). Fear of death in the mentally ill. *Psychological Reports* 33:931–938.

Feifel, H., and Nagy, V. T. (1980). Death orientation and life-threatening behavior. *Journal of Abnormal Psychology* 89:38–45.

———— (1981). Another look at fear of death. *Journal of Consulting and Clinical Psychology* 49:278–286.

Feifel, H., and Schag, D. (1981). Death outlook and social issues. *Omega* 11:201–215.

Florian, V., and Kravetz, S. (1983). Fear of personal death: attribution, structure and relation to religious belief. *Journal of Personality and Social Psychology* 44:600–607.

Gesser, G., Wong, P. T. P., and Reker, G. T. (1987). Death attitudes across the life-span: the development and validation of the death attitude profile. *Omega* 18:113–128.

Gilliland, J. C., and Templer, D. I. (1985). Relationship of death anxiety scale factors to subjective states. *Omega* 16:155–167.

Hintze, J., Templer, D. I., Cappelletty, G. C., and Frederick, W. (1993). Death depression and death anxiety in HIV-infected males. *Death Studies* 17:333–341.

Ho, S. M., and Shiu, W. C. (1995). Death anxiety and coping mechanisms of Chinese cancer patients. *Omega* 31:59–65.

Hoelter, J. W. (1979). Multidimensional treatment of fear of death. *Journal of Consulting and Clinical Psychology* 47:996–999.

Holcomb, L. E., Neimeyer, R. A., and Moore, M. K. (1993). Personal meanings of death: a content analysis of free-response narratives. *Death Studies* 17:299–318.

Howells, K., and Field, D. (1982). Fear of death and dying among medical students. *Social Science and Medicine* 16:1421–1424.

Ingram, B. J., and Leitner, L. M. (1989). Death threat, religiosity, and fear of death. *International Journal of Personal Construct Psychology* 2:199–214.

Kalish, R. A. (1977). The role of age in death attitudes. *Death Education* 1:205–230.

Kastenbaum, R. (1988). Theory, research, and application: some critical issues for thanatology. *Omega* 18:397–411.

———— (1992). *The Psychology of Death*, 2nd ed. New York: Springer.

Kastenbaum, R., and Costa, P. T. (1977). Psychological perspectives on death. *Annual Review of Psychology* 28:225–249.

Krieger, S. R., Epting, F. R., and Leitner, L. M. (1974). Personal constructs, threat, and attitudes toward death. *Omega* 5:299–310.

Kureshi, A., and Husain, A. (1981). Death anxiety in intrapunitiveness among smokers and nonsmokers: a comparative study. *Journal of Psychological Research* 25: 42–45.

Lester, D. (1967a). Experimental and correlational studies of the fear of death. *Psychological Bulletin* 67:27–36.

———— (1967b). Fear of death of suicidal persons. *Psychological Reports* 20:1077–1078.

———— (1994). The Collett-Lester Fear of Death Scale. In *Death Anxiety Handbook: Research, Instrumentation, and Application,* ed. R. A. Neimeyer, pp. 45–60. New York: Taylor & Francis.

Lonetto, R., Mercer, G. W., Fleming, S., et al. (1980). Death anxiety among university students in Northern Ireland and Canada. *Journal of Psychology* 104:75–82.

Lonetto, R., and Templer, D. I. (1986). *Death Anxiety*. New York: Hemisphere.

Loo, R. (1984). Personality correlates of the Fear of Death and Dying Scale. *Journal of Clinical Psychology* 40:120–122.

Mullins, L. C., and Lopez, M. A. (1982). Death anxiety among nursing home residents: a comparison of the young-old and the old-old. *Death Education* 6:75–86.

Myska, M. J., and Pasewark, R. A. (1978). Death attitudes of residential and nonresidential rural aged persons. *Psychological Reports* 43:1235–1238.

Neimeyer, R. A. (1985). Actualization, integration and fear of death: a test of the additive model. *Death Studies* 9: 235–250.

—— (1988). Death anxiety. In *Dying: Facing the Facts,* ed. H. Wass, F. Berardo and R. A. Neimeyer, pp. 97–136. New York: Hemisphere.

—— ed. (1994a). *Death Anxiety Handbook: Research, Instrumentation, and Application.* New York: Taylor & Francis.

—— (1994b). Death attitudes in adult life: A closing coda. In *Death Anxiety Handbook: Research, Instrumentation, and Application*, ed. R. A. Neimeyer, pp. 263–277. Washington, DC: Taylor & Francis.

—— (1994c). The Threat Index and related methods. In *Death Anxiety Handbook*, ed. R. A. Neimeyer, pp. 61–101. New York: Taylor & Francis.

—— (1996). Death anxiety research: the state of the art. *Omega* in press.

Neimeyer, R. A., Bagley, K. J., and Moore, M. K. (1986). Cognitive structure and death anxiety. *Death Studies* 10:273–288.

Neimeyer, R. A., and Dingemans, P. (1980). Death orientation in the suicide intervention worker. *Omega* 11:15–23.

Neimeyer, R. A., Dingemans, P., and Epting, F. R. (1977). Convergent validity, situational stability and meaningfulness of the Threat Index. *Omega* 8:251–265.

Neimeyer, R. A., Fontana, D. J., and Gold, K. (1984). A manual for content analysis of death constructs. In *Personal Meanings of Death*, ed. F. R. Epting and R. A. Neimeyer, pp. 213–234. Washington, DC: Hemisphere.

Neimeyer, R. A., and Fortner, B. (1996). Death anxiety in the elderly. In *The Encyclopedia of Aging*, ed. G. Maddox, pp. 252–253. New York: Springer.

Neimeyer, R. A., and Moore, M. K. (1994). Validity and reliability of the Multidimensional Fear of Death Scale. In *Death Anxiety Handbook*, ed. R. A. Neimeyer, pp. 103–119. New York: Taylor & Francis.

Neimeyer, R. A., and Neimeyer, G. J. (1984). Death anxiety and counseling skill in the suicide interventionist. *Suicide and Life-Threatening Behavior* 14:126–131.

Neimeyer, R. A., and Van Brunt, D. (1995). Death anxiety. In *Dying: Facing the Facts*, ed. H. Wass and R. A. Neimeyer, pp. 49–88. Washington and London: Taylor & Francis.

Pollak, J. M. (1979). Correlates of death anxiety: a review of empirical studies. *Omega* 10:97–121.

Pratt, C. C., Hare, J., and Wright, C. (1985). Death anxiety and comfort in teaching about death among preschool teachers. *Death Studies* 9:417–425.

Rhudick, P. J., and Dibner, A. S. (1961). Age, personality, and health correlates of death concern in normal aged individuals. *Journal of Gerontology* 16: 44–49.

Rigdon, M. A. (1983). Levels of death fear: a factor analysis. *Death Education* 6:365–373.

Rigdon, M. A., and Epting, F. R. (1985). Reduction in death threat as a basis for optimal functioning. *Death Studies* 9:427–448.

Robbins, R. A. (1994). Death competency: Bugen's Coping with Death Scale and Death Self-Efficacy. In *Death Anxiety Handbook: Research, Instrumentation, and Application,* ed. R. A. Neimeyer, pp. 149–165. New York: Taylor & Francis.

Robinson, P. J., and Wood, K. (1984). Fear of death and physical illness. A personal construct approach. In *Personal Meanings of Death,* ed. F. Epting and R. A. Neimeyer, pp. 127–142. Washington, DC: Hemisphere.

Roediger, H. L. (1990). Implicit memory: retention without remembering. *American Psychologist* 45:1043–1056.

Schulz, R., and Aderman, D. (1979). Physicians' death anxiety and patient outcomes. *Omega* 9:327–332.

Stevens, S. J., Cooper, P. E., and Thomas, L. E. (1980). Age norms for the Templer's Death Anxiety Scale. *Psychological Reports* 46:205–206.

Tamm, M. E. (1996). The personification of life and death among Swedish health care professionals. *Death Studies* 20:1–22.

Tamm, M. E., and Granqvist, A. (1995). The meaning of death for children and adolescents: a phenomenographic study of drawings. *Death Studies* 19:203–222.

Tate, L. A. (1982). Life satisfaction and death anxiety in aged women. *Omega* 15:299–306.

Templer, D. I. (1970). The construction and validation of a death anxiety scale. *Journal of General Psychology* 82:165–177.

—— (1971). Death anxiety as related to depression and health of retired persons. *Journal of Gerontology* 26:521–523.

Thorson, J. A., and Powell, F. C. (1989). Death anxiety and religion in an older male sample. *Psychological Reports* 64:985–986.

—— (1990). Meanings of death and intrinsic religiosity. *Journal of Clinical Psychology* 46:379–391.

—— (1994). A Revised Death Anxiety Scale. In *Death Anxiety Handbook: Research, Instrumentation, and Application,* ed. R. A. Neimeyer, pp. 31–43. Washington, DC: Taylor & Francis.

Tobacyk, J., and Eckstein, D. (1980). Death threat and death concerns in the college student. *Omega* 11:139–155.

Tomer, A. (1994). Death anxiety in adult life: Theoretical perspectives. In *Death Anxiety Handbook: Research, Instrumentation, and Application,* ed. R. A. Neimeyer, pp. 3–28. Washington, DC: Taylor & Francis.

Vargo, M. E., and Black, W. F. (1984). Psychosocial correlates of death anxiety in a population of medical students. *Psychological Reports* 54:737–738.

Vickio, C. J., and Cavanaugh, J. C. (1985). Relationships among death anxiety, attitudes toward aging, and experience with death in nursing home employees. *Journal of Gerontology* 40:347–349.

Viney, L. L. (1984). Concerns about death among severely ill people. In *Personal Meanings of Death*, ed. F. R. Epting and R. A. Neimeyer, pp. 143–158. Washington, DC: Hemisphere.

Wagner, K. D., and Lorion, R. P. (1984). Correlates of death anxiety in elderly persons. *Journal of Clinical Psychology* 40:1235–1241.

Westman, A. S., and Brackney, B. E. (1990). Relationships between indices of neuroticism, attitudes toward and concepts of death, and religiosity. *Psychological Reports* 66:1039–1043.

Wong, P. T., Reker, G. T., and Gesser, G. (1994). Death Attitude Profile-Revised. In *Death Anxiety Handbook*, ed. R. A. Neimeyer, pp. 121–148. New York: Taylor & Francis.

2

Death, Technology, and Gender in Postmodern American Society

JEANNE QUINT BENOLIEL

In the introduction to his seminal book, *The Meaning of Death*, Herman Feifel (1959) wrote, "Denial and avoidance of the countenance of death characterize much of the American outlook" (p. xvii). Over the next two decades the silence about death was countered by a multidisciplinary human effort that fostered innovations in books and journals, therapies and organized services for the dying and their survivors, and death education for lay and professional groups (Feifel 1992). At the same time new meanings of death were being created under the influence of expanding technological innovation and a rapidly changing social environment, both changes guided by the ideals of a better life through scientific progress.

American Values and Technological Innovation

According to many social scientists, technology has been a driving force in American life, exemplified by the machine as a model of reality (Sandelowski 1993). Not surprisingly, technological innovation is a valued human activity that has been guided by the powerful influence of scientific thinking in combination with the established traditions of patriarchal power, masculine dominance, and individualism as a preferred style of being.

In Merchant's (1980) opinion, the conceptual system underlying Western technology development is built around ideas of duplicating nature and, perhaps ultimately, of controlling it. This orientation toward technology fits well with the ideology of conquest and combat that appears to lie at the core of the American masculine identity in personal, political, and cultural terms (Edwards 1990). It also matches well with the high value attached by Americans to the notion of individualism and the achievement of pragmatic goals through hard work and persistence.

This orientation can be traced to the belief systems undergirding the development of middle class American culture (Bellah et al. 1985).

The significance of conquest as a metaphor for responding to life's problems goes beyond the traditional notion of war as a means of protecting society from foreign aggression. In the United States "making war" has been the rallying cry for tackling many major social issues, for example, drug use (George Bush), poverty (Lyndon Johnson), and cancer control (Richard Nixon). The image of winning by means of conquest is commonplace in the media of current American society, illustrated by a recent newspaper item describing "video game makers in mortal combat" (Kalinske 1994).

The ideal of conquest has stimulated technological innovation throughout human history. The scientific way of thinking has expanded the power of technology over everyday human life by means of complex systems of technologies designed for achieving various societal goals. According to Max Weber (1958), these changes were manifestations of a process of rationalization that emphasized the importance of predictability and calculability and permeated all facets of social life. Characteristically, these systems produce through a division of labor, have heavy focus on efficiency and instrumental rational action, and rely on the judgments of experts.

In postwar America all aspects of daily life were altered by new technological systems and their effects on ways of thinking and being. Two systems that fostered new meanings of death were those associated with military expansion and the development of scientific medicine. The power of both systems was amplified by the incorporation of new communication and electronic technologies. Indeed, the computer was a major contributor to the expansion of both fields. However, their influence on America came through the use of expert/industrial/political power to channel societal resources to achieve two appealing postwar goals: deterrence of nuclear war and defeat of disease.

Modernization of America

Militarization and medicalization were salient forces in the modernization of American society. Modernization can be viewed as a cultural shift fueled by social/techological innovation and characterized by rising affluence, industrial expansion, and new modes of transportation and communication. This shift led to new forms of work and play and made possible a diversity of lifestyles and living arrangements.

Modernization led to a consumer society in which the purchase of material goods and services was essential to the good life. Many people benefited from these altered conditions of living. Modernization also provided the grounds for rising tensions associated with changing gender relationships and the discontents of groups marginal to the social benefits of mainstream America. It affected the options and social experiences of the dying as well.

Postmodernization of Society

The appeal of modernization was its promise of infinite progress through science and technology. Postmodernization began when people became aware of the limits of science and technology to control nature and minimize uncertainty. Examples of such limits include the failure to control cancer (Beardsley 1994) and to prevent bridge disasters because of obsolescence and poor maintenance (Dunker and Robbat 1993). Public awareness of these and other limitations affecting public health and safety was facilitated by the rise of information as the primary commodity in national and international exchange and the growing power of the communication media to control and monitor ideas in the public realm.

Postmodern society was fostered by the ending of the Cold War and the expansion of an international economy that diminished industrial output in the United States, thereby contributing to a decrease in jobs and lessened buying power for material goods (Krugman and Lawrence 1994). Population increases and competition for available resources served as grounds for violent conflict among different human groups (Homer-Dixon et al. 1993). Technological innovation continued, but disenchantment with the wonders of the computer grew as people experienced breakdowns in vital services, for example telephone availability or air travel, associated with software glitches in large complicated technological systems (W. Gibbs 1994, Littlewood and Strigini 1992).

Militarization of Society

In the aftermath of World War II, militarism in the United States developed by means of socioeconomic organization and political discourse in response to the perceived threats of the Cold War and communism. Readiness to exercise force to combat these threats was a critical assumption underlying the building of a large military machine; such buildup depended on public support despite information control and security constraints.

Postwar Militarism

Postwar militarism developed as a conjunction of high technology developments and military-based bilateral containment policies. The creation of high tech weaponry and deployment systems depended heavily on computers and automation of machines for reconnaisance, threat identification, and weapons of destruction (Edwards 1990).

According to Enloe (1983), militarization of a society occurs as a process with two dimensions. Material dimension refers to the gradual encroachment of the military into civilian arenas of life. Ideological dimension is the extent to which the public finds these changes acceptable ways of dealing with societal problems. The development and maintenance of a high technology military requires a large infrastructure that is an integral part of civil society and is part of a society committed to technological innovation.

The goal of the high tech military structure was deterrence: an idea of preventing large-scale nuclear war by having on hand massive weapons of destruction that would deter the other side from starting a major war (Cohn 1987). Since achievement of massive stores of destructive potential required massive use of federal resources, continuing economic, political, and ideological pressures were exerted on the public through effective use of communication media by the president, other elected officials, and defense experts of various kinds.

High Tech Warfare

Strategic planning for high tech warfare in modern society must take account of the reality of nuclear arms and whether or not they should or could be used. According to Edwards (1990), three major weapons systems are key elements in high tech warfare today. Totally destructive weapons, like cluster bombs and nuclear devices, reduce the role of the foot soldier to insignificance. Other weapons systems integrate human functions with sophisticated technologies, for example, fighter jets and electronic command-and-control networks. Self-controlled devices, such as cruise missiles, reach their objectives under microprocessor control.

The meaning of high tech warfare was determined by the growing power of electronics. As Edwards (1990) observed, "Vastly accelerated speed is one of the major forces shaping the high tech battlefield" (p. 113), and systems of reconnaisance and attack increasingly are managed by the almost instantaneous processes of electronic command and control. Given the destructive potential of the new weaponry, the political goal of the protagonists became the promotion of a *winning scenario* more so than a major war.

In a sense actual war became a cognitive event, and the goal of nuclear strategy was to stay in the game as long as possible—like playing a video game. The joint contributors to high tech militarism were computer science and the military as an institution. Both are structured as forms of a microworld—characterized by hierarchies of rules, strict laws of conduct, chains of command, orders, and precise jargon. Such worlds appear to have a special appeal to men who want to know the rules of the game and where they stand.

The appeal of computers to men is twofold, according to Edwards (1990). Hard masters of computers like preconceived plans, specific goals, logic, and rationality rather than spontaneity and intuitive discovery. Computer work itself can produce strong feelings of power and control over a simulated world. "In the microworld, as in children's make-believe, the power of the programmer is absolute" (p. 109).

The militarization of society was fostered by a compatibility between modes of thought in computer science and puzzle-solving strategies of military planners. Both modes contributed to a social environment in which the reality of the social goal of mass destruction could be masked behind a rhetoric of abstractions and euphemistic language. The militarization of American society brought social changes that affected many facets of civilian life.

Militarization and Social Change

The creation of a high tech military brought into being a social system controlled by a conglomerate of experts representing science, engineering, and military planners (Adler 1991). Dominance over directions and policies came from the projections of defense intellectuals who used a system of thought known as strategic analysis to manage the arms control race and to plan the deployment and use of military weapons. While attending a summer course on nuclear arms control, Cohn (1987) wondered how these military planners were able to justify the stockpiling of horrendous weapons of destruction and to consider applying them against human beings. During the following year she immersed herself in the activities of the Defense Center, using participant observation to gain insight about the language and the behaviors of these defense intellectuals.

Cohn found that the men functioned by using a special language in which the reality of death was disguised behind abstractions and euphemistic phrases. They talked about "counterforce exchanges," "clean bombs," and "countervalue attacks" with no reference to destroying cities and human beings. Human death was referred to by the abstract label, "collateral damage" (pp. 690–691). This language was also replete with sexual imagery showing weapon use to be a male prerogative and conveyor of power, with women often serving as targets. For example, devices to help bombers or missiles get past enemy defenses were known as "penetration aids," or "pen-aids" for short. Lectures about deployment of weapons included discussion of "thrust-to-weight ratios, soft lay-downs, deep penetration, and the comparative advantages of protracted versus spasm attacks" (p. 693).

Cohn also found that learning to speak the language of the defense intellectuals brought with it feelings of control and a sense of escape from thinking of oneself as victim. Despite claims of objectivity and reasoned action by these defense planners, she found their discourse to carry within it "currents of homoerotic excitement, heterosexual domination, the drive toward competency and mastery, the pleasures of membership in an elite and privileged group, the ultimate importance and meaning of membership in the priesthood, and the thrilling power of becoming Death, shatterer of worlds" (p. 717).

Although many aspects of military development were not discussed openly for security reasons, the progressive overlap of the military infrastructure with civilian life came to public awareness as established military bases were expanded and new ones came into being. Such developments made increasing demands on the economic and educational resources of nearby cities and towns. Many industries focused on production for the military, and universities expanded their research efforts in the areas of defense technology, arms control practices, and international agreements (Adler 1991). People living in parts of the midwest learned to live beside the silos that served as repositories for long-range missiles. In some plans, civilian hospitals were projected to provide services to soldiers injured in limited wars overseas, with their care taking precedence over that for civilians (Trueblood and Rapport 1984).

Blurred Social Boundaries

The expansion of electronic weaponry led to a blurring of boundaries between the front lines and rear areas of traditional war (Edwards 1990). The idea of women and children in the rear to be protected became obsolete, contributing to a breakdown in the idea of protectors and protected. Support troops no longer were "behind the lines" but became targets as much as the infantry, a fact that was brought home by television during the Gulf War when a building serving as barracks for American soldiers was hit by a missile.

The experience of war in action was brought into American homes through television, leading to growing public awareness that the real victims of war are civilians—especially children (Zwi and Ugolde 1993). Through the media the public also learned of the increased vulnerability of American troops to destruction by their own weapons systems.

During the Gulf War almost one third of the casualties suffered by the coalition forces were the result of "friendly fire" (Tilford 1993).

Although women as well as men have many of the skills needed for managing new military technologies, war continues to be perceived as a "test of manhood" and women are to be excluded from combat roles (Edwards 1990). The image of man as soldier is reinforced for the public through movies and television. As women became integral parts of the armed forces in the 1980s, the tensions over gender roles and responsibilities in the military increased. They are likely to continue in response to conflicts between rapidly changing technology demands and traditional societal values pertaining to gender definitions.

Disenchantment with War

The goal of nuclear deterrence did not prevent the United States from involvement in warfare on a limited scale, guided by the ideology of fighting communism. In the 1950s the United States entered into combat with Korea. In the 1960s the country became involved in military operations in South Vietnam and in 1965 into full-scale war against North Vietnam, under the leadership of President Lyndon Johnson (Herring 1986). In 1967 the increased demands for manpower and other resources contributed to a decline in public support for the war in Southeast Asia.

In the fateful year of 1968 public response became divisive as groups for and against the Vietnam War engaged in open argument. The Tet offensive by the Viet Cong led to increased military operations by the United States and, in turn, increased American casualties. Tensions among the fighting men as well as civilians at home rose in response to growing awareness of being in a war that could not be won. Public response to the war was heightened by news reporting that American soldiers had killed more than 200 civilians in a village known as My Lai (Herring 1986). Negativism about the war came in public demonstrations on college campuses across the country. The assassinations of Martin Luther King in April and Robert Kennedy in June reflected the violent undercurrents of divisiveness characteristic of that time.

The negative influences of the "war that could not be won" continued in the negative attitudes toward the veterans of Vietnam when they returned home. For many, homecoming brought a kind of social death in the form of posttraumatic stress disorder and an inability to fit into civilian society. For young men in particular, the war experience contributed to an identity crisis in which they asked themselves, "Who am I, what am I doing here?" (Cimons 1979, p. K4). In a sense, the entire Vietnam experience caused the American people to undergo similar concerns about the country as a whole.

Medicalization of Society

After World War II, medicine as a field increasingly was influenced by the assumptions and practices of science. Support for medical research came from the federal government through the National Institutes of Health. In time the medical/industrial/political complex came into being—a conjunction of the profession of medicine, industries focused on medical research and development, and public support by means of government funds. The biomedical model of disease became the organizing framework for scientific medicine. It fostered an ideology that emphasized disease as physical deviations from established norms and discounted personal, social, and cultural factors in the situation (Engel 1977). Ironically, the system of services through which medical care is given carries the euphemistic label *health care*, even though the bulk of medical activities center on the diagnosis and treatment of disease.

Postwar Medicine

At the heart of postwar medicine was the use of various kinds of new technologies. The immediate purpose of these innovations was to diagnose and treat diseases and potential disorders toward the long-term objective of maintaining good health and supporting and extending life. By definition, health care technology refers to the people, tools, and techniques that are organized systems designed to achieve identified human goals in relation to health-related ailments (Sandelowski 1993).

As new technologies developed, specialization of medical practice followed. Hospitals evolved into highly complex centers in which medical and support services were provided through a division of labor. In the 1960s special care units were developed to offer the specialized services needed by different populations of people, such as victims of burns, trauma, or heart attacks (Hilberman 1975). Physicians increasingly relied on technical procedures and machines to accomplish their goals, and support staff increasingly found their work involving the care of machines as well as people.

The direction of medical research and development was dominated by government influence over research funds and the directions to be taken (Ebert 1986). The goal of medicine centered on the primacy of life-saving activity. In a sense, the appearance of large medical centers was a manifestation of an industrialization of death management and medical control over dying (Benoliel and Degner 1995).

High Tech Medicine

Underlying medical technology is an assumption of the body as a machine with parts to be fixed. In time the new biomedical techniques dealt with more than disease and injury as problems to be repaired. New technologies evolved in response to the human problems of birth, reproduction, and infertility, among others.

According to Sandelowski (1993), health care technologies can be classified as information-producing or therapeutic. The former are devices for diagnosing, screening, or monitoring purposes; an example is the use of unltrasonography (ultrasound images) to search the body for evidence of pathology. Therapeutic technologies can be viewed as prosthetic, curative, and regulatory. Prosthetic technologies are those that circumvent a dysfunctional part (cardiac bypass) or replace a damaged part with a new one (total hip). Curative technologies eliminate the problem by removing or repairing it (appendectomy, herniorrhaphy). Technologies that regulate natural body processes or interfere with normal body processes include drugs of many kinds.

Sandelowski (1993) argued that Americans suffer from *technology dependency*, which in the case of health care can be defined as the "short- or long-term reliance on devices and techniques to evaluate or to satisfy or resolve health-related needs or problems" (p. 39). She argued that the use of technologies does more than the initially stated purpose. They can function to transform the preferences of consumers and providers; for example, she noted the rapid increase in use of electronic fetal monitoring despite a lack of scientific validation that its use decreased infant mortality (p. 38).

Cassell (1993) wrote that technology has great appeal to physicians because it fosters a sense of wonderment and can be applied to immediate problems. At another level, technology seems to make the ambiguous situation more clear and to enhance the drive toward certainty and power. One unfortunate side effect of this appeal is a tendency to use sophisticated technologies when they are not needed.

Sophisticated technologies also can contribute to iatrogenic physical and psychological effects—for example, interactions between drugs. Generally speaking, innovations expand the choices for professionals; but sometimes they constrain the choices of consumers—for example, spending a good portion of one's life tied to a dialysis machine. In Sandelowski's (1993) view, these technologies contribute to an objectification of persons and a fragmentation of experience. They can create an illusion of certainty even though the machines themselves add to the complexity of human interpretation.

High tech medicine affected the social organization of medical work in hospitals and created new tasks and responsibilities for the employees (Strauss et al. 1985). These investigators found that the staff had to engage in *machine work* (servicing of devices), *safety work* (judging if device helpful or harmful), *comfort work* (activities for relief of pain), *sentimental work* (interpersonal activity), and *articulation work* (coordination of multiple work activities). The requirements of specialization introduced new occupations into an already complicated social system and added to a fragmentation of experience for patients.

Medicalization and Social Change

The development of high tech medicine led to medical dominance and power over many facets of people's lives, particularly at times of high vulnerability. In other words biotechnology expanded the expert power of the physician, and the American people accepted the change as a manifestation of a commitment to science. Illich (1994) observed that this expert power made physicians responsible for peoples' lives from the "moment the egg is fertilized through the time of organ harvest" (p. 4). As well, the medicalization of society affected the social processes of dying and the work responsibilities of nurses.

History shows that all societies had organized rituals around death and dying to maintain the social order. In modern America the idea of containing death led to two rituals, according to Moller (1990). Rising out of the death-with-dignity movement, hospice was a system of services dedicated to control of discomfort during dying. Associated with hospital-based medical practice, aggressive technical management of death and dying developed with the physician in control.

The latter ritual is directed by the technocratic physician whose view of practice was shaped by technology, a stance of objectivity and life-saving at all costs, and an ideal of maintaining control over the situation. With a few exceptions, these physicians do not focus attention on dying as a personal life experience. At the actual time of death, Moller (1990) observed three types of physician response: use of lifesaving heroics, attention elsewhere, or sympathetic support that was highly individualized (and relatively infrequent). The personal and familial elements of dying were left to the individual to manage as a private matter within a techical system of care committed to life-prolonging goals. From his observations of the hospital experiences of dying patients, Moller came to believe that dying represents a weakness in the technical lifestyle of modern America and, from a moral perspective, a social evil.

The patient's experience of dying as individualized and privatized was facilitated by a hospital organization in which the needs of human beings were reduced to technologically manageable parts labeled as problems. The management of these problems took place through processes of standardization, routinization, and objectification. A major outcome is dehumanization of the person who is a patient and alienation from a communal experience in relation to the human meanings of dying (Moller 1990).

Biomedical technologies in combination with different diseases/injuries requiring treatment produced a variety of social patterns of dying in hospitals and created different caregiving needs for patients and families. Commonly recurring patterns include dead-on-arrival (DOA), produced by traumatic injuries of various kinds; hooked-to-machines in the intensive care unit (ICU), often coming at the end of chronic heart, kidney, or lung disease; and the in-and-out pattern of prolonged dying, commonly associated with cancer and involving several different types of technical treatment. These patterns contributed to variations in work problems and work-related stresses for the staff providing caregiving services for the dying and their families (Benoliel and Degner 1995).

Expansion of high tech medicine had a powerful influence on the work roles of other professionals in health care. For nurses the demands of new technologies led to new roles in combination with a perpetuation of formal medical dominance and a hierarchical pattern of work relationships. Specialization for intensive care nursing brought new responsibilities, for example, close monitoring of machine-created data and close collaboration with physicians. Families came to view nurses as important sources of medical information (Fairman 1992).

Observation of nurses at work in high tech settings showed that use of these technologies exerted a seductive pull to view oneself as godlike. Cooper (1993) noted the relative ease with which nurses could take onto themselves a sense of power over death through technology. In fact, the nurses reported that most deaths in the ICU occurred after a decision was made to "allow" death to happen. In such a context the nurses were recognized for their competence as "doctors," and the personal aspects of caregiving easily were lost or discounted.

Blurred Social Boundaries

In the beginning, high tech medicine was practiced in hospitals. A blurring of boundaries between public and private settings began when cost containment policies and regulatory practices were initiated in the 1980s. The takeover of health care by business specialists was to promote efficiency through downsizing and controlled allocation of resources. With this change came managed information systems and the concept of managed care. Unfortunately, the needs of patients in the personal sense of caregiving were not amenable to measurement in the quantitative sense of business management nor were they rewarded in the cost-accounting system (Benoliel 1993a).

Blurring of professional and private boundaries shows clearly in the tremendous expansion of high tech home care since 1985. This shift was encouraged by industrial innovations such as drug devices, changes in federal reimbursement policies, early hospital discharge, and the desires of patients and families (Arras 1994). As a result of this move, many homes now resemble hospitals, and new burdens of caregiving are experienced by families. The provision of home care for the dying was encouraged by these developments. Yet caregivers at home (the bulk of whom are women) find a great difference between the romantic image of home death and the reality of dealing with a confused and/or depressed patient, side effects of treatments, and complex family relationships (Sankar 1993).

The medicalization of society combined with population growth led to great demands for caregiving services by large numbers of people living with chronic diseases, disabling conditions, and other ailments defined as "medical problems." In postmodern society the new ills include alcoholism, drug use, mental illness, and domestic violence. The broadened definition of illness expanded the numbers of individuals in need of the benefits of technological medical treatment. Yet ill or disabled people need more than technical medical assistance. They also need personalized caregiving that centers on the humanity of each person and provides assistance in coping with difficult life transitions.

Caregiving of the person traditionally has been associated with women and women's roles. The difficult nature of this labor-intensive and demanding human relationship has not been recognized, and its benefits have been taken for granted in traditional patriarchal society (Benoliel 1992). In the world of scientific medicine, caregiving is not acknowledged with social rewards. Rather it continues to be an undervalued activity that is invisible, discounted, and assumed to be offered by the well-intentioned provider.

When management consultants were hired by hospitals to save money, they were unable to classify the activities composing bedside nursing into a neat categorization. Instead they reduced the observed work into technical and procedural tasks that could be delegated to less costly workers with the nurse serving as "manager of the case." Baer and Gordon (1994) argued that the reductionist analysis of nurses' activities failed to recognize the work of patient care as a *tapestry* that involves a complex use of interwoven skills and interrupted labor—a characteristic observed in other forms of women's work, such as teaching and mothering. Patient caregiving requires the coordinated use of technical and inter-personal skills, judgment in determining whose need has priority, and flexibility in shifting attention (often rapidly) to the concerns and demands of different patients, family members, and other providers.

The denigration of nurses' work by the management consultants reflects a gender bias that the complicated work of nursing (a form of woman's work) is not as demanding nor as valuable as the technical work associated with medicine. The images of physician as the competent and powerful saver of lives through technology and nurse as invisible non-entity whose function is to carry out medical orders are perpetuated in the culture through television narratives about hospital life.

Limits of Scientific Medicine

Despite great technological progress, signs that scientific medicine had its limits appeared in the 1980s. Perhaps the most powerful reminder of these limits was the advent of acquired immune deficiency syndrome (AIDS), a new fatal disease that struck young people in the prime of life. In addition to the many personal, interpersonal, and social problems AIDS brought into being, it shattered the illusion of control—especially in relation to infectious disease (Rosenberg 1989).

More than that, AIDS illustrated how American beliefs about disease were affected by other attitudes and beliefs, in this case those pertain-ing to sexual behaviors. The beginnings of AIDS in the homosexual com-munity fostered negative attitudes among some groups of people and delayed recognition of its seriousness. The identification of AIDS as a "gay" disease contributed to a slow political response to the new syn-drome as a public health problem, not solely a personal tragedy for the persons afflicted (Ron and Rogers 1989).

Fear of AIDS was experienced by health professionals as well as people in general. In fact, some providers refused to work with AIDS patients. As a result of the epidemic, new infection control policies and practices were adopted in all health care agencies and offices in efforts to safeguard providers from accidental infection. Despite these precau-tions, a few health care providers became infected accidentally. Pro-fessional and public concerns about the infection led to debates as to whether or not hospices were obligated to accept AIDS patients (Galazka 1987). In the communities most greatly affected, networks of private foun-dations and community organizations developed to respond to the com-plicated needs of these patients.

Because no curative treatment has been found for AIDS to date, the infection continues to spread, affecting primarily young, sexually active adults, IV drug abusers, babies born to infected mothers, and the recipients of transfusions of contaminated blood. In 1994 in the United States AIDS increased more rapidly among women than men, disproportionately so in racial/ethnic minorities living in the Northeast and South (Centers for Disease Control 1995a).

Rosenberg (1989) has called AIDS a postmodern epidemic resulting from complex interrelationships among biological, social, and interpersonal elements of human existence at the global level. It is a fatal condition that is not amenable to containment by traditional public health measures, and existing social structures are not organized to deal with its many complexities in an integrated way. In postmodern America AIDS is a powerful reminder that all human beings are potential victims of hidden environmental threats that are spread through human-to-human contact or exist in the detritus of collective human activity.

Death and Postmodern America

To my view, the defining feature of postmodern society is rapidity of change, bringing with it unending demands for human beings to adapt to uncertainty, new technologies, and unexpected events. Simon and associates (1993) argued that "intensification of the uncertain and the problematic as normal states of affairs" (p. 421) is the marker of postmodern life. In their view rapidity of change contributed to major communication gaps between generations, a decline in traditional beliefs and ways of life, and individualization of human experience as a mode of adaptation to change.

In the postmodern world there has been a shift from a theology of death to a secularized perspective in which death can be delayed through artificial prolonging of life. Concerns about the inappropriate use of life-extending capabilities led to written guidelines regarding the withdrawal of medical treatment, discontinuation of food and fluids, and decisions on resuscitation. These recommendations came from both religious groups (Kassekert 1985) and centers concerned with ethical problems in society (The Hastings Center 1987). Simon and his colleagues (1993) agree with Moller (1990) that dying increasingly has become an individualized experience, without the communal rituals that sustained individuals and families in years gone by.

At the same time new life-threatening hazards and social complexities have become part of the environment in which ordinary people live out their lives. Rapidity of change has altered the ecology of human-environment relationships, increased the risks of death from unknown hazards in the community, and contributed to moral problems and quandaries at the individual and collective levels of human existence.

Deadly Environments

Nuclear Hazards

Public disenchantment with the Vietnam War and its outcome was supplanted by growing awareness of the hazards of nuclear power. These concerns were brought to a head by an accident at the Three Mile Island nuclear power plant in Pennsylvania in 1979 (Joppke 1992–93). This event served as a kind of last straw to public confidence in nuclear power and brought an end to its development as a major energy source in the United States. A fragmentation of federal, state, and local political authority and responsibility led to conflicts over "emergency planning, utility rate regulation, and waste disposal" (p. 724). Failure to provide funds for adequate cleanup and repair of these plants meant that they remain as potential deadly and silent hazards for people in nearby communities.

In the 1980s public concern shifted from nuclear power to fear of nuclear bombs as the Reagan administration initiated a massive nuclear rearmament program (Joppke 1992–93). The threat of instant death by bombs continued throughout the Cold War. The massive buildup of nuclear devices in the 1980s led to new hazards for people in the 1990s. In 1994 a report by the U.S. Energy Department revealed that nuclear weapons factories (even though closed) continued to be public hazards because of inadequate storage of large amounts of plutonium and no corrective plans to clean up the situation or take care of long-term storage (Lippman and Smith 1994). Possible leakage of plutonium, a toxic and carcinogenic substance, creates another silent hazard for people living close to these installations.

Fatal Disease

AIDS was only the beginning of public awareness of a second deadly environmental threat, namely, microorganisms that cause fatal diseases and/or are not responsive to antibiotics and other drugs. In the 1990s previously unrecognized organisms were identified as causes of unexpected fatal illnesses, for example a new strain of hantavirus that caused acute respiratory failure in apparently healthy young adults (Grady 1993). Other diseases occurred because the causative organisms no longer responded to medication, as happened with drug-resistant pneumococcus (Centers for Disease Control and Prevention 1994a). Still other organisms, such as streptococcus A, can produce virulent strains that rapidly result in sudden death.

In postmodern society the availability of deadly organisms has been aided by human actions, for example, in the unintentional contamination of commercially prepared food. In two western states serious illness and several deaths resulted from the use of commercially prepared salami contaminated with *Escherichia coli* 0157:H7 and affecting some 500 people (Centers for Disease Control and Prevention 1995b). Also a factor, the mobility of human beings by sea and air travel has facilitated the transmission of deadly microorganisms between countries. Human travel is considered a salient factor in the movement of cholera from Asia to South America in the 1990s and the reintroduction of tuberculosis into the United States by immigrants from Southeast Asia following the Vietnam War (Lemonick 1994).

Extremely frightening for humans is the capacity of many microorganisms to adapt to human efforts to control them (as through antibiotics) and to enhance their disease-producing capabilities. Yet ironically the collective activities of humans as a species may well have aided them in their adaptive efforts to survive.

Illegal Drug Use

A third hazard in the postmodern environment is illegal drug use and the dangers associated with drug availability and addiction. Historically, drugs like marijuana have been associated in the public mind with immigrant groups and ethnic minorities, and U.S. policy on controlling drug use has centered on police enforcement efforts at national and international levels (Falco 1992). When illegal drug use became widespread in the 1960s, users were not eligible for primary and emergency health care. The free clinic movement appeared in 1967 to 1972 to respond to this need (Lewis 1992).

The war against cocaine began under President Reagan in the 1980s and was continued by President Bush, but cocaine addiction continues as a major social problem. "The Institute of Medicine estimates that 5.5 million Americans have serious drug problems that require treatment" (Falco 1992, p. 9). These figures do not account for the once-a-week recreational users of cocaine nor for the large number of cocaine and heroin overdose cases that commonly appear in hospital emergency rooms.

Effort to provide effective medical treatment for drug addiction has been handicapped by an ongoing tension between police control over illegal drugs and medical activities to treat addiction, for instance, by means of methadone programs. Much of the problem rests in federal enforcement regulations and protocols that essentially prescribe what is to be done and under what circumstances, thereby discounting clinical judgment (Lewis 1992).

The problem of illegal drug use overlaps with concerns about preventing AIDS which has increased among some addicts through the sharing of needles. Drug use is a contributor to increases in crimes and violent deaths, the latter often associated with disputes among drug dealers and sometimes resulting in the shooting deaths of innocent bystanders.

In postmodern America both AIDS and cocaine use are contributors to developmental problems and death for infants born to addicted women. Public fears about crime and public tendencies to label the women as criminals are reinforced by political statements on the media. In Lewis's (1992) view, the criminalization of women addicts is maintained by a federal policy that emphasizes a "war on drugs" more than efforts to ameliorate the social and economic conditions that foster predatory street crimes, poverty, and family disorganization.

Private and Public Violence

Concomitant with modernization, the incidence of violence and violent death in the United States increased tremendously. Over the last 20 years interpersonal violence has grown so much that leaders in the Department of Health and Human Services (DHHS) view it as an epidemic that manifests itself not only in street crimes but also in domestic abuse— including the abuse of children (Cantor 1993).

Private Violence

Death as an outcome of domestic violence between partners has received increasing attention in magazines and other media (Smolowe 1994). Recent statistics show a downward trend in deaths for both husbands and wives between 1976 and 1987 along with an increase in the deaths of women in unmarried partnerships (Browne and Williams 1993). These deaths seem to be tied to the men's needs to maintain control over the women's lives. Current information shows that women are more at risk of being killed by their male partners than by any other kind of assault (Smolowe 1994).

Violence against children increased so much in the 1980s that the U.S. Congress appointed an Advisory Board on Child Abuse and Neglect to evaluate the problem. A national study of this problem in the 1990s showed that abuse and neglect in the home had become a leading cause of death of children under 4 years of age (surpassing accidental falls, suffocation, drowning, and residential fires) (Rivera 1995). The findings show that fatalities by physical abuse most commonly "are caused by angry, extremely stressed out fathers, stepfathers, or boyfriends who unleash a torrent of rage on infants over such 'triggers' as a baby's crying, feeding difficulties, or failed toilet training" (p. A9). Mothers are most often held responsible for deaths brought about by neglect, such as starvation or bathtub drownings. Of particular concern to the board was the finding that death by child abuse is an underreported social problem that receives inconsistent attention from law-enforcement and medical professionals and is viewed by the American public as a rare and unusual event.

Violence in the workplace has increased greatly, sometimes resulting from the actions of aggrieved spouses or jilted lovers who bring their private grievances into the work setting. With increasing frequency, however, acts of violence have been performed in hospitals, offices, and industrial sites by disgruntled employees angry at the employer or by customers wanting to even a score (Toufexis 1994). All too often innocent people are among the victims of these tragic outbursts.

Public Violence

In postmodern society public violence often occurs in a context of rapid social change, including the movements of large populations of people as refugees or displaced minorities caught in the crossfire of political tensions and outright warfare (Jalali and Lipset 1992–93). The rise of ethnic conflicts is worldwide in scope, and the victims of this violence—such as children dying of malnutrition—are available for all to see through the power of television.

Movement of populations in the United States changed the character of many traditional neighborhoods, bringing into close proximity groups with different values and ways of living. Movement of ethnic and other minorities into crowded urban settings provided the grounds for conflicts over scarce social resources. Modernization of work led to affluence for educated Americans, but it eliminated opportunities for the untrained and unskilled and led to growing disparities between the lives of affluent and poor Americans.

One result of these changes was the rise of an urban underclass, a situation in which many children are growing up in fatherless homes with adults who are crack cocaine users and abusive parents. It is not surprising that young boys in these circumstanaces search for masculine role models by joining action-oriented gangs whose way of life, unfortunately, is violence and crime. This choice of lifestyle readily can lead to a life of street crime and time in prison. For some it leads to an early death, as happened to 11-year-old Yummy Sandifers who gained public fame when he was killed in a Chicago gang fracas in 1994 (N. Gibbs 1994).

The attraction of gangs to boys without strong family ties may well be a manifestation of what Marris (1974) called tribalism, a reaching out for group identity in a context of cultural disruption. He believed that the impulse to preserve continuity is critical to survival and that tribal

institutions provide individuals an organizational structure for responding to contextual and personal ambiguities resulting from social change.
Identification with a group's values and practices in response to a sense
of societal encroachment on old traditions and perceived losses provides
support and a sense of belonging.

Identification with a group has positive rewards for its members, but
it has a dark side in a tendency to view nonmembers and outsiders in
negative stereotypes. In Marris's (1974) view tribalism is a contemporary
phenomenon, a response to changes in living brought by economic development, specialization of labor, and a spread of communications. With
these developments has come "a growing intolerance of the conventions
and institutions which uphold social distance" (p. 70). A sense of tribalism is enhanced when people of different cultures live in close proximity and are expected to treat each other as equals according to the laws
and rules of the larger society. However, stereotyped views of others can
lead to racial, ethnic, and gender conflicts when contextual circumstances
exacerbate underlying tensions and perceptions of threat.

In general the victims of violence are the young more than the old.
At greatest risk for violent death are young males living in inner cities.
Recent statistics show that the homicide rate for males 15 to 19 years of
age increased 154% between 1985 and 1991, surpassing the rates for men
25 to 29 and 30 to 34 years of age (Centers for Disease Control and Prevention 1994b).

The attention given to violence on television has contributed to
people's concerns about being victims of street crimes, drug wars, or
other random events. We learn from the news that children are accidentally shooting children with guns they find at home, and others are carrying weapons to school for personal protection. Drug dealers and criminals engaged in territorial disputes increasingly use automatic combat
weapons that are massively destructive.

In many parts of the world, ethnic and racial tensions among groups
at odds with each other have produced terrorist activities to demonstrate
their claims (and also to kill innocent people in the process). In February 1993 Americans were shocked by the terrorist bombing of the World
Trade Center in New York City (Carley 1993). This event was a cogent
reminder that in a world of destructive weapons and a myriad of inter-
group tensions and strains no one is completely safe from being a victim of the violence that permeates postmodern life.

In April 1995 Americans were shocked even more by the terrorist
bombing of the federal building in Oklahoma City, killing 168 people and
injuring many more. The shock of this unexpected event was intensified
when people became aware that the likely perpetrators were disgruntled
Americans with grievances against the government (Gleick 1995). The

immediate response to the tragedy in the form of help and assistance demonstrated the great capacity of ordinary Americans to be available to others in a time of crisis and personal need (Gibbs 1995).

Moral Claims and Quandaries

The era of rationalization and new technological systems brought with it many moral complexities. The extensive development of life-prolonging capabilities focused attention on the competing ideals of preservation of life and freedom of the individual. The meaning of life was complicated by the advent of what Hewa (1994) calls "halfway technology" (p. 178) capable of keeping the comatose person alive.

Life-Prolonging Technology and Choice

Concerns about medical decisions to continue treatments despite the wishes of patients or families led to court decisions supporting the patient's right to choose. In the 1970s the courts supported the rights of the parents of Karen Ann Quinlan to serve as surrogates for her in discontinuing active medical treatments. In the 1980s the courts set limits on a nondying patient's rights to request discontinuation of fluids and nutrition, with the situation of Elizabeth Bouvia serving as an exemplar in this matter (Benoliel and Degner 1995).

Legal support for the discontinuation of life-maintaining medical treatment in comatose patients has varied from state to state. Also at issue is the question of what constitutes life-prolonging treatment. In the case of Nancy Cruzan (comatose after an automobile accident), the parents requested removal of a feeding tube that many view as ordinary treatment (Gibbs 1990). Although many search for legal answers to solve these difficult problems faced by families, many are not amenable to judicial decisions. Rather they are painful life transitions that trigger unresolved interpersonal difficulties in families and create new stresses and strains in daily living.

Patient Self-Determination

Support for the patient's right to choose was manifest in the Patient's Self Determination Act, federal legislation that required hospitals to ascertain patients' wishes on these matters. It went into effect in 1991. The courts have supported the removal of artificial feeding for the terminal patient (Miles et al. 1989). Many articles pro and con have been centered on the topic of euthanasia and what is proper in medical practice. The wide range of opinions on this matter reflects the diversity of outlook to be expected in a pluralistic society.

The issue of patients' rights to self-determination has moved to another level with the proposal that dying patients have a right to ask a physician to assist them in suicide if they so decide. Proponents of assisted suicide argue that such request is part of a person's right to self-determination. In a legal analysis of the issue, Scofield (1991) argued that, although patients have a right to request termination of medical treatment, they do not have a right to *demand* treatment, as this proposal suggests. What is striking about the idea of assisted suicide is its extension of the concept of an individual's right to self-determination into a demand on another person to take actions that in traditional society were forbidden.

Dilemmas of Postmodern Dying

Postmodern changes in family relationships make the support traditionally associated with that resource less and less certain (Simon et al. 1993). Thus dying as a social process is likely to be guided by strangers, professionals who provide the script and instruct the person on enactment of new roles. Currently such guidance is provided through many hospice programs along with various medical technologies to control distressing symptoms that interfere with personal efforts to bring closure to life.

Environments that support the autonomy of persons while they are dying depend on providers who can balance knowledge about dying as a biopsychosocial process with a capacity to respect the rights and wishes of the dying person. Such environments require movement away from patriarchal conquest-oriented work to a sense of moral community and a work ethic in which competition is replaced by creative interdependence among colleagues (Benoliel 1993b).

Although postmodern society offers multiple options for individual growth and development, the society also contains large numbers of people who are incapacitated by chronic illness, aging, or other ailments and are dependent on others for assistance in daily living. Unable often to choose freely among options, these persons are vulnerable to coercive actions by others. Decisions not to use medical treatments can be made because the patient's situation is viewed as futile (Morreim 1994). Cost containment efforts can function to coerce families into high tech home care situations that keep family caregivers (most commonly women) as prisoners at home. Such coercion raises ethical questions about whether there are limits to family obligations in the interest of justice for all members (Arras and Dubler 1994).

Currently institutional care is provided for many in nursing homes. Characteristically nursing homes in the United States have been modeled after acute care settings with caregiving provided by means of routines and standardized procedures. Collopy and associates (1991) pointed out that the major dilemma faced by nursing home residents was not a life-or-death decision but rather loss of personal control that started at the time of admission and permeated all facets of daily living. Residential models containing different levels of assisted living for elders have been provided by retirement communities, generally available to affluent Americans. A moral quandary facing the postmodern society centers on how to redefine nursing homes as communities of caring responsive to the moral personhood of both residents and staff (Collopy et al. 1991).

Some Personal Reflections

Ironically, although postmodern society has increased the lifestyle options for many individuals, these options are available only because we live in a context of technology dependency. Americans pride themselves on being independent. Yet in reality the ongoing flow of daily existence depends on the contributions of many other people to the availability of products and services that are safe and effective. Both living and dying reflect an interdependence among humans and the environments in which they live.

In recent years there has been a disenchantment with the quality of many products and services and a concern about personal safety and well-being (Harris 1981). There is growing public awareness that new technologies, such as Pentium computer chips, can have flaws traceable to human error and can result in costly mistakes (Andrews 1994). Andrews noted that the "costliest loss of life in the 1991 Gulf War was caused by a software glitch in a Patriot missile that failed to stop an Iraqi Scud missile from striking a U.S. army barracks, kllling 28 and wounding 98" (p. A16).

Distrust in the reliability of new technologies by many Americans is matched by a growing distrust of government and its ability to be responsive to local concerns and problems. As Bell (1987) pointed out some years ago, whereas the international economy has become increasingly integrated, the nation-state with its flow of power to a national political center has become ineffective in responding to the diversity and variety of local needs. In a sense, the major social institutions of America have not kept pace with the growing demands of an expanding and diversified population. As a result, many Americans experience dehumanization in their contacts with hospitals, schools, and government agencies. This mismatch between social institutions and personal human needs may well be a contributor to the discontents and perceived grievances of some groups of Americans—for example, men who experience gun control laws as efforts to take away their constitutional rights.

Yet tragically the use of military weapons to settle disputes in civilian life has been a major factor in the rise of community violence. Indeed, technological innovation and collective human activity have contributed to a pollution of air and water across the world and to an ecosystem instability that encourages new threats to public health (Epstein 1995). These forces have been at play in the proliferation of post–Cold War nuclear dangers and the growth of terrorism as a way of responding to grievances (Nuckolls 1995).

To my view, the character of the postmodern American environment has been shaped by masculine perspectives on the importance of conquest and control as ways of dealing with the world. There well may be limits in the human capacity to cope with rapid change, particularly when that change is perceived as a threat.

Perhaps the time has come to balance the powerful masculine metaphors of conquest and control, so dominant in current American society, with perspectives in which human needs and concerns are attended. Among these are feminist perspectives that value human relationships as centrally important to personal well-being and view the evils of the world—pain, separation, and death—as experiences to be lived and shared with others, not entities to be conquered and destroyed (Benoliel 1994). The extent to which such perspectives can be influential in the current political discourse of the country remains to be seen.

References

Adler, E. (1991). Arms control, disarmament, and national security: a thirty year retrospective and a new set of anticipations. *Daedalus* 120(1):1–20.

Andrews, P. (1994). Chipping away at trust in technology. *The Seattle Times*, December 22, pp. A1, A16.

Arras, J. D. (1994). The technological tether: an introduction to ethical and social issues in high-tech home care. *Hastings Center Report* 24(5):S1–S2.

Arras, J. D., and Dubler, N. N. (1994). Bringing the hospital home: ethical and social implications of high tech home care. *Hastings Center Report* 24(5):S19–S28.

Baer, E. D., and Gordon, S. (1994). Money managers are unraveling the tapestry of nursing. *American Journal of Nursing* 94(10):38–40.

Beardsley, T. (1994). A war not won. *Scientific American* 270(1):120–138.

Bell, D. (1987). The world and the United States in 2013. *Daedalus* 116(3):1–31.

Bellah, R. N., Madsen, R., Sullivan, W. N., et al. (1985). *Habits of the Heart*. Berkeley: University of California Press.

Benoliel, J. Q. (1992). Undervalued caregiving: a major issue for the thanatology community. *Loss, Grief and Care* 6:17–23.

——— (1993a). The moral context of oncology nursing. *Oncology Nursing Forum Supplement* 20(10):5–12.

——— (1993b). Personal care in an impersonal world. In *Personal Care in an Impersonal World: A Multidimensional Look at Bereavement*, ed. J. D. Morgan. Amityville, NY: Baywood.

————— (1994). Death and dying as a field of inquiry. In *Death, Dying, and Bereavement*, ed. I. B. Corless, B. B. Germino, and M. Pittman, pp. 3–13. Boston: Jones and Bartlett.

Benoliel, J. Q., and Degner, L. F. (1995). Institutional dying: a convergence of cultural values, technology, and social organization. In *Dying: Facing the Facts*, ed. H. Wass and R. A. Neimeyer, 3rd ed., pp. 117–141. Washington, DC: Taylor & Francis.

Browne, A., and Williams, K. R. (1993). Gender, intimacy, and lethal violence: trends from 1976 through 1987. *Gender and Society* 7:78–98.

Cantor, P. (1993). The roots and legacy of violence. In *Suicidology*, ed. A. A. Leenaars, pp. 63–72. Northvale, NJ: Jason Aronson.

Carley, W. M. (1993). Bombing in New York bears some hallmarks of mideast terrorists. *The Wall Street Journal*, March 1, pp. A1, A7.

Cassell, E. J. (1993). The sorcerer's broom: medicine's rampant technology. *Hastings Center Report* 23(6):32–39.

Centers for Disease Control and Prevention (1994a). Emerging infections. *Morbidity and Mortality Weekly Report*, 42(53):viii–x.

————— (1994b). Homocides among 15–19-year-old males—United States, 1963–1991. *Morbidity and Mortality Weekly Report* 43(40):725–727.

————— (1995a). Update: AIDS among women—United States 1994. *Morbidity and Mortality Weekly Report* 44(5):81–84.

————— (1995b). *Escherichia coli* 0157:H7 outbreak linked to commercially distributed dry-cured salami—Washington and California, 1994. *Morbidity and Mortality Weekly Report* 44(9):157–160.

Cimons, M. (1979). Vietnam veterans: the war is ended, but the misery lingers on. *The Seattle Times*, August 25, pp. K1, K4.

Cohn, C. (1987). Sex and death in the rational world of defense intellectuals. *Signs* 12:687–718.

Collopy, B., Boyle, P., and Jennings, B. (1991). New directions in nursing home ethics. *Hastings Center Report Special Supplement* 21(2):1–15.

Cooper, M. C. (1993). The intersection of technology and care in the ICU. *Advances in Nursing Science* 15(3):23–32.

Dunker, K. F., and Robbat, B. G. (1993). American bridges are crumbling. *Scientific American* 266(3):66–72.

Ebert, R. H. (1986). Medical education at the peak of the era of experimental medicine. *Daedalus* 115(2):55–81.

Edwards, P. N. (1990). The army and the microworld: computers and the politics of gender identity. *Signs* 16:102–127.

Engel, G. (1977). The need for a new biomedical model: a challenge for biomedicine. *Science* 196:129–136.

Enloe, C. (1983). *Does Khaki Become You? The Militarization of Women's Lives*. London: South End Press.

Epstein, P. R. (1995). Emerging diseases and ecosystem instability: new threats to public health. *American Journal of Public Health* 85:168–172.

Fairman, J. (1992). Watchful vigilance: nursing care, technology, and the development of intensive care units. *Nursing Research* 41:56–59.

Falco, M. (1992). Foreign drugs, foreign wars. *Daedalus* 121(3):1–14.

Feifel, H. (1959). *The Meaning of Death*. New York: McGraw-Hill.

————— (1992). The thanatological movement: respice, adspice, prospice. *Loss, Grief and Care* 6(1):5–16.

Galazka, M. (1987). Hospice for AIDS patients: interesting times ahead. *The American Journal of Hospice Care* 4(6):11–14.

Gibbs, N. R. (1990). Love and let die. *Time*, March 19, pp. 62–71.

———— (1994). Murder in miniature. *Time*, September 19, pp. 54–59.

———— (1995). The blood of innocents. *Time*, May 1, pp. 56–64.

Gibbs, W. W. (1994). Software's chronic crisis. *Scientific American* 271(3):86–95.

Gleick, E. (1995). Who are they? *Time*, May 1, pp. 44–51.

Grady, D. (1993). Death at the corners. *Discover* 14:82–91.

Harris, M. (1981). Why it's not the same old America. *Psychology Today*, August, pp. 23–38, 42, 51.

The Hastings Center (1987). *Guidelines on the Termination of Life-Sustaining Treatment.* Briarcliff Manor, NY: Hastings Center.

Herring, G. C. (1986). *America's Longest War: The United States and Vietnam, 1950–1975.* 2nd ed. Philadelphia: Temple University Press.

Hewa, S. (1994). Medical technology: a Pandora's box. *Journal of Medical Humanities* 15:171–181.

Hilberman, M. (1975). The evolution of intensive care units. *Critical Care Medicine* 3:159–165.

Homer-Dixon, T. F., Boutwell, J. H., and Rathjens, G. W. (1993). Environmental change and violent conflict. *Scientific American* 268(2): 38–45.

Illich, I. (1994). Brave new biocracy: health care from womb to tomb. *New Perspectives Quarterly* 11(1):4–12.

Jalali, R., and Lipset, S. M. (1992–93). Racial and ethnic conflicts: a global perspective. *Political Science Quarterly* 107:585–606.

Joppke, C. (1992–93). Decentralization of control in U.S. nuclear energy policy. *Political Science Quarterly* 107:709–725.

Kalinske, T. (1994). Video game makers in mortal combat. *The Seattle Times*, December 9, p. E6.

Kassekert, K. (1985). *Life Support Treatment Decisions: Legal and Moral Concerns.* St. Louis: The Catholic Health Association of the United States.

Krugman, P. R., and Lawrence, R. Z. (1994). Trade, jobs and wages. *Scientific American* 270(4):44–49.

Lemonick, M. D. (1994). The killers all around. *Time*, September 12, pp. 62–69.

Lewis, D. C. (1992). Medical and health perspectives on a failing drug policy. *Daedalus* 121(3):165–194.

Lippman, T. W., and Smith, R. J. (1994). Dangerous debris of the Cold War. *The Seattle Times*, December 7, p. A6.

Littlewood, B., and Strigini, L. (1992). The risks of software. *Scientific American* 267(5): 62–75.

Marris, P. (1974). *Loss and Change.* London: Routledge & Kegan Paul.

Merchant, C. (1980). *The Death of Nature: Women, Ecology and the Scientific Revolution.* San Francisco: Harper & Row.

Miles, S. H., Singer, P. A., and Siegler, M. (1989). Conflicts between patients' wishes to forego treatment and the policies of health care facilities. *New England Journal of Medicine* 321:48–50.

Moller, D. W. (1990). *On Death Without Dignity: The Human Impact of Technological Dying.* Amityville, NY: Baywood.

Morreim, E. H. (1994). Profoundly diminished life: the casualties of coercion. *Hastings Center Report* 23(1):33–42.

Nuckolls, J. H. (1995). Post–Cold War nuclear dangers: proliferation and terrorism. *Science* 267(24):1112–1114.

Rivera, C. (1995). Study says crisis reached in violence against children. *The Seattle Times*, April 26, p. A9.

Ron, A., and Rogers, D. E. (1989). AIDS in the United States: patient care and politics. *Daedalus* 118(2):41–58.

Rosenberg, C. E. (1989). What is an epidemic? AIDS in historical perspective. *Daedalus* 118(2):1–17.

Sandelowski, M. (1993). Toward a theory of technology dependency. *Nursing Outlook* 41:36–42.

Sankar, A. (1993). Images of home death and the elderly patient: romantic versus real. *Generations* 17(2): 59–63.

Scofield, G. R. (1991). Privacy (or liberty) and assisted suicide. *Journal of Pain and Symptom Management* 6:280–288.

Simon, W., Haney, C. A., and Puenteo, R. (1993). The post-modernization of death and dying. *Symbolic Interaction* 16:411–426.

Smolowe, J. (1994). When violence hits home. *Time*, July 4, pp. 18–25.

Strauss, A., Fagerhaugh, S., Suczek, B., and Wiener, C. (1985). *Social Organization of Medical Work*. Chicago: University of Chicago Press.

Tilford, E. H. (1993). The meaning of victory in operation desert storm: a review essay. *Political Science Quarterly* 108:327–331.

Toufexis, A. (1994). Workers who fight firing with fire. *Time*, April 25, pp. 35–37.

Trueblood, V., and Rapport, R. (1984). Move over. *The Seattle Times*, August 12, p. A17.

Weber, M. (1958). *The Protestant Ethic and the Spirit of Capitalism*. New York: Scribner's.

Zwi, A., and Ugolde, A. (1993). Victims of war. *World Health* 46(1):26–27.

3

Hospice's Path to the Future

FLORENCE S. WALD

Care for the terminally ill is one part of the health care system in the United States that has been transformed, beginning in the 1960s. It came into being as health care providers witnessed the neglect and suffering of those patients who do not improve with intensive scientific medical therapy. Hospice care, also called palliative care, is one of several patient-centered approaches that depends on more than medical science, visualizes the whole person, the family, social conditions, and the soul as well as the body in its scope to understand health and disease. The first of these, family-centered maternity care, began in the 1920s.

While medical care in the twentieth century has been dominated by basic science, medical science, and technology, the social sciences, ethics, the nature of man, and the nature of suffering are emerging as key issues in a counterculture.

The dominant medical sciences and the services they developed became so costly that by the final decade of the century, medical economy and decision making were taken out of the hands of professional caregivers and not-for-profit institutions and usurped by private insurance companies and commercial investors whose measure of success is tangible profit. As this came to pass, hope and plans for a national health service as a right for all United States citizens have faded.

Decisions about health care now uses business principles, but will the profit motive accommodate patient-centered aims and principles?

The changes have been swift and without consent of caregivers or receivers of care and without government regulations. Small pioneering institutions such as hospices are without power. In this unprecedented turn of events, projecting the future depends on identifying basic principles and conceptualizing a new order that can accommodate them.

Hospices are now using business strategies to survive by merging, incorporating themselves into larger health care systems, operating for profit, forming chains, and downsizing. But these are essentially battle strategies to meet the immediate economic revolution. In this chapter I propose to visualize a possible new order in which technologic medicine is separated from patient-centered health care and the knowledge coming out of these two cultures, freeing each of these two parts to function appropriately and effectively.

Rashi Fein (1980) has said:

> Health policy is a part of social policy. How nations choose to stress matters of social policy, the questions they will ask and the solutions they will elect, cannot derive from some technical model or out of multiple regressions equations. These dynamic solutions will have to take into account the nature, history, and traditions of existing institutions and relationships; the attitudes and behavioral characteristics of key actors; the sector's organic development; the climate of opinion; and the goals and values of a society and of its members. [p. 359]

Looking back on health policy in the twentieth century, dominant values were in balance with opposing values of a counterculture.

Awakening health professionals and the public to alternative ways of care for terminally ill patients and families happened suddenly and spread widely beginning in the 1960s. St. Christopher's Hospice in England opened in 1967; the first services for the terminally ill did not begin in the United States until 1974. However, groundwork was laid in the decade of the 1960s when penetrating questions and answers called for change in many institutions—government, religion, education, and medicine.

The tenor of that decade was "We shall overcome!" From one hospice in 1974, twenty years later 2,400 hospices served roughly 300,000 terminally ill (Beresford 1995). In academia there was a surge of interest following World War II in death and dying that brought the field of thanatology into being.

Health professionals became aware of the tremendous cost and suffering accompanying catastrophic and life-threatening illnesses as they faced the rise of an aging population. In an age when technology dominated mainstream medical practice there was also a call for care that recognized the whole patient, whose suffering was broader than physical suffering and whose family suffered, too. How did a call for change arise, challenge traditional medicine, and create an alternative approach?

Precursors of Change in Care of the Terminally Ill

The medical approach to diagnosis and treatment in the years after World War II focused on new technology and scientific proof. Treatment became more and more intrusive and extensive, the risks taken more and more daring. The pace in hospital and clinical research was swift, complex, constantly changing, and increasingly departmentalized. With laboratory findings to account for pathologic conditions, there was less reason for doctors to search for the patient's account of how his illness began.

Beyond the great success of the new-age treatments, there were still those patients for whom treatment did not alter the disease process. Doctors and nurses were unskilled in dealing with death and dying and thus avoided the dying patients whose situation baffled them. Health professionals searched in vain for mentors to show them how to help (Quint 1967).

Dame Cicely Saunders was first struck by the physical pain patients had, Elisabeth Kübler-Ross by the student caregivers who wanted to help but were afraid to try. What Jung wrote in 1959 rang true:

> When death confronts us, life always seems like a downward flow or like a clock that has been wound up and whose eventual "running down" is taken for granted. We are never more convinced of this "running down" than when a human life comes to its end before our eyes, and the question of the meaning and worth of life never becomes more urgent or more agonizing than when we see the final breath leave a body which a moment before was living. [p. 3]

Although it was technology that dominated the medical world after World War II and attracted the majority of caregivers, nevertheless there was a significant minority whose focus was on the whole person, in whom psyche and soma interact, whose health affects and is affected by family, whose coping skills were determined by lifestyle and one's place in community. There was a counterculture that thought of the patient and family first and then adapting medical intervention to it.

While hospitals' rules, regulations, schedules, and environment were composed to make the work of doctors and nurses run smoothly, after World War II dissident caregivers called for space and services to include family and put patients' needs first. Changes came first in obstetrics, psychiatry, and pediatrics. These services preceded changes hospices and palliative care units would make as St. Christopher's Hospice did in 1967 in England and the Connecticut Hospice did in 1974. They were strengthened by war experiences and assisted by English and American practitioners, midwives, psychiatrists, obstetricians, and pediatricians.

The struggle for family-centered maternity practice in the United States dated back to the 1920s when a small group of nurses and a handful of obstetricians proposed education and credentialing for professional nurse-midwives to care for mothers during pregnancy. They proposed antepartal care for mothers, normal deliveries without the use of forceps, home deliveries as it was practiced in Great Britain and Europe, and education in infant care. The opposition from the new specialists-obstetricians and the hospitals was so strong that these efforts were not successful. After the war credentialed English midwives and the English obstetrician G. D. Read played a major role in making natural childbirth accepted in the United States.

While home deliveries were not yet sanctioned, a demonstration project in Yale New Haven Hospital was given space for "rooming in." In 1946 the pediatrician Edith B. Jackson saw that modern clinical training in pediatrics was almost wholly within hospital walls and focused on the recognition and treatment of disease—they had no direct experience with the family situation and the mothers felt that if they had had more experience with their babies in the hospital, they would not have felt so frightened to care for their babies at home (Silberman 1990). Here, mother and baby were kept together during hospitalization. Fathers were included in education during pregnancy, assisted in labor and delivery, and took part in the care of the newborn baby. It signaled family-centered maternity care and preceded natural childbirth practiced by midwives.

Educating nurse midwives in universities began in 1947; by 1965 nine universities prepared midwives, but until the early 1960s midwives were limited by state licensure to practice. Education and credentialing accelerated in the late 1960s and early 1970s, when nurse-midwifery was not just acceptable, but inundated with requests for practitioners. The women's movement, consumer demand, federal funding, and at last, willingness of obstetricians to practice jointly with nurse-midwives contributed to the speed and strength of its growth. Official recognition finally came from the College of Obstetricians and Gynecologists in 1971. By 1982 there were 1584 nurse-midwives, 67 percent of them were practicing nurse-midwifery, and by 1984 they practiced in all fifty states.

Varney-Burst (1983) attributes a call for change to the childbearing consumer:

> The right to know all there is to know about what is happening to her, to participate in decision making, to assume responsibility for her own care, to involve whoever is important and significant to her and to have those people treated with respect, to maintain self-worth and dignity, and to maintain control over what her childbearing experience will be within the realities of her condition and situation. The

consumer movement in childbirth had its origins in the fact that these rights almost universally were not being respected. Fear, pain, and the use of anesthesia were rampant; care was physician centered or hospital centered rather than family centered; and the mother was physically separated from her family and, except for feeding every four hours, from her infant. [p. 42]

Hospital services for children in pediatric wards also changed because of experiences in World War II with children who were separated from their parents. English child psychiatrists, John Bowlby, Anna Freud, and Dorothy Burlingame observed children who were evacuated from their homes in cities likely to be bombed. Children separated from their families were far more fearful, did less well in school, and craved affection (Bowlby 1952). Renee Spitz (1945) photographed grieving children separated from their mothers. Ultimately, pediatric nurses and pediatricians became, at least reconciled, if not convinced, that the hospitalized child's need for the mother outweighed the risk of infection or the fear that the parent's presence would disrupt caregiving routine.

A wartime episode in Newcastle on Tyne, England, gave added cause for change. Short of nurses, hospital staff had to ask the children's parents to help with care. To the staff's surprise, the children fared better (Hunt and Trussell 1955). Report of that experience in time prompted hospitals to change their rules and allow, and even encourage, a parent to stay with the hospitalized child as much as possible, including overnight. The risk of infection became less of an issue when antibiotics came into use.

Ida Martinson (1976), a pediatric nurse practitioner demonstrated that parents were able to and preferred to care for the dying child themselves at home. They did this with assistance from the nurse in visits to the home, by telephone, and by closed-circuit television contacts.

Care for psychiatric patients changed most. Before World War II, most patients were in large, remote state, or privately owned hospitals. Some academic medical centers had psychiatric institutes, but while geographically near they were organizationally separate.

Doctor–patient therapy, one on one, came into being as practiced by Freud, his protégés, and colleagues whose theoretical knowledge base was similar. While such treatment concerned itself with a patient's perceptions and was acknowledged to be effective, its cost was high and access was limited, with psychiatric patients far outnumbering psychotherapists.

Approaches to the mentally ill and patients handicapped by stress changed by World War II, beginning with an influx of European psychiatrists such as Erik Erikson, Bruno Bettelheim, Fritz Redlich, and Erich

Fromm, who were refugees. Their earlier Freudian concepts changed over time.

Tranquilizers, introduced in the early 1950s, helped agitated and combative patients become amenable to therapeutic human relationships. One-on-one psychotherapy was possible for those who could afford it (Hollingshead and Redlich 1958).

Several remarkable clinicians and educators in the nursing profession, especially Hildegard Peplau (1952) and Ida Orlando (1961) developed conceptual framework and skills in interpersonal relations that opened the way for therapists to perceive how patients experienced their situations.

Nurses, psychiatrists, and social workers found ways to augment their skills working in interdisciplinary teams, dovetailing one to one, and group encounters. Community mental health centers and psychiatric units in general hospitals began to include the patient's family and recognize how lifestyle is molded by the community in which a patient lives.

Teams learned to collaborate and lower the walls of stratification between doctors, nurses, and social workers. When the need to transfer unmanageable patients to remote asylums diminished, general hospitals opened psychiatric units with inpatient beds. Now it was possible for family members to contribute to the rehabilitation of the patient and amend dysfunction in family life. Family-centered psychiatric care emerged.

In academia social scientists and psychiatrists jointly studied the relationship of social class, to mental illness in incidence and treatment (Hollingshead and Redlich 1958, Langner and Michael 1963, Srole et al. 1961).

As large state hospitals gave way to community mental health centers it helped caregivers to visualize the limits and contributions of the environment on the individual.

Finally, it was in large psychiatric hospitals in England where Maxwell Jones helped patients take an active role in patient governance. This was a first step in defining patients' rights, a movement that would permeate increasingly the other special care areas in medicine.

From the changing relationship of patients and caregivers, the issue of rights of patients arose. Physicians in a position of power gave much thought to what and who influenced the choice of treatment; Edmund D. Pelligrino, H. Tristram Englehardt, Jr., Robert Veatch, Jay Katz, Ray Duff, and Daniel Callahan worked in academia and helped form societies such as the Society for Health and Human Values in 1965 and the Hastings Center in 1969.

Putting medical ethics into practice proved daunting. The pediatrician Ray Duff (1987) reflected on how he helps families decide which way to go in caring for infants with poor prognosis. He uses two terms for these processes: "close-up" versus "distant" ethics:

> Close-up ethics directs attention toward what Tocqueville called "habits of the heart," that is, specific family, religious, philosophical, or social conditions or orientations that commonly serve as the foundation for individual and family life in particular situations. It requires active participation of patients and families as well as health professionals in deciding and providing care. Since it is patient- and family-centered, it may direct attention away from organized religious, philosophical, legal, or even health codes. Implicitly, close-up ethics within reasonable limits asserts the freedom to express individual and family conscience. [p. 244]

Ethics committees were formed in hospitals with physicians, nurses, ethicists, and lawyers participating to consider the options in a particular case. What are the treatment alternatives? What does the patient know and want? What impact will it have on the patient/family quality of life? These discussions gave a picture of the whole person in the context of his relationships with family and other important people in his/her life.

The 1960s saw the rising tide of alternative therapies. In the spirit of challenge to tradition and open-mindedness, the public became interested in Eastern medicine, herbal and homeopathic medicine, meditation, prayer, therapeutic touch, hypnosis, and vitamins as preventatives.

The medical profession took a long time to integrate the relationship of soma and psyche. Flanders Dunbar (1954) traces that history from 1910 to 1953. Experiences of doctors and nurses with battle fatigue in World War II made them more receptive to the effect of stress.

Nursing took the body and soul or mind seriously, although it was a difficult relationship to trace in scientific inquiry. Doris Krieger (1981) did so in the use of therapeutic touch. Outside the constraints of academic settings, Ram Dass, Dr. Elisabeth Kubler-Ross, Dr. Bernie Siegal, and Dr. Larry and Barbara Dossey (a nurse) gave seminars and held workshops and retreats for professionals and the public.

Experiential accounts by patients published in trade books were read by health professionals and were given credence. Norman Cousins (1981) was not only read by physicians but was appointed to the Medical School faculty of the University of Southern California.

Lawrence LeShan (1989), a psychologist, persisted twenty years in developing his ideas from his private practice with patients whose cancer was far advanced. These patients demonstrated that changing one's lifestyle to accommodate one's dreams and ambitions led to remission.

Larry Dossey (1993), once chief of staff of Humana Medical Center with a practice in internal medicine, spent ten years studying the power of prayer evidenced in patient's quality of life and recovery. This changed his professional point of view from a belief in Western medicine and agnosticism to respect for and use of the patient's style of prayer in balance with traditional medicine. By 1993 there was an office of alternative medicine in the National Institutes of Health. Dr. Dossey cochairs its panel on mind–body interventions, which can be seen as a first step toward acceptance in established practice.

Spiritual support in illness that had disappeared in the age of enlightenment in the eighteenth and nineteenth century returned with the active role that church and divinity schools played in the community in the early 1960s. Departments of religious ministries were established in hospitals, and divinity students learned to give spiritual support.

This was only the beginning of the prominent part religious spiritual support would come to have in hospice care. The religious component in the founding and operating of St. Christopher's Hospice went far beyond that. Legally St. Christopher's is both a religious and medical foundation; while Dame Cicely is Anglican, the hospice's foundation is "ecumenical Christian" (du Boulay 1984).

Spiritual support and transcendence through the arts, such as writing and music, plays a larger role in the United States. Sally Bailey (1994), responsible for much of this trend, writes that the arts and creativity, "reflect and express our engagement with our environment" and "connect us to the energy and breath of life" (p. 329).

To summarize: new ways to conceptualize suffering and changes in the way medical care was given preceded and continued to change as that movement came into being. Doctors, lawyers, nurses, ethicists studied and revamped the roles of patients and caregivers in terms of moral responsibility and patient rights. Patients became partners in being and getting informed and deciding the course of action.

The effect of illness on the whole family became a significant issue in planning care. A broader view of healing and the value of spiritual support brought other disciplines into the caregiving team. Medical science and medical models of care are no longer the only perspective. The patient has become the whole person in sickness or good health. The physician is a member of an interdisciplinary team.

Changing Care of the Terminally Ill

Changes in terminal care had other derivations. Herman Feifel (1994) writes that the shock of the bombing of Hiroshima and Nagasaki in August 1945 and the death of his mother in 1952 "brought death truly in my gut." His first published paper on death dealt with the attitudes of mentally ill patients (Feifel 1955). The conference of many disciplines he organized at the 1956 Meetings of the American Psychological Association was, in Gardner Murphy's (1959) review, "an event epitomizing a boldness, scope and realism for which official American psychology may be grateful" (p. 317).

The high degree and broad exposure to suffering and dying that came with World War II had touched the personal lives and professional careers of social scientists and health professionals, beginning with Viktor Frankl's (1962) account of his own survival in a death camp. His book, *Man's Search for Meaning* was published in German in 1946, virtually upon his release from a concentration camp.

Feifel's conference had two significant characteristics that molded the thanatology movement. The people he called on for papers came from a wide range of professions, including both academicians and practitioners. In *The Meaning of Death*, produced as an anthology of essays written by social scientists, clergy, theologians, philosophers, and caregivers, Jung's (1959) description of life's end rang true in caregivers' ears: "When a human life comes to an end before our eyes, . . . when we see the final breath leaving a body which a moment before was living" (p. 3). This was what many nurses and clergy and a few doctors faced but felt helpless in changing because of the rapid pace of medical care, the fragmentation, and the attention required to technical detail and nuances. Yet they witnessed the exhaustion brought on by the disease and amplified by treatment. This passage spoke for them.

Feifel's (1994) conviction that "vital psychology must be rooted in people, not in a mathematical physics paradigm, and that psychology was neglecting the existential richness of life" (p. 60) was the spirit in the air when practitioners and academicians began to exchange ideas comparing what was experienced with what was formulated in reflective thought. In hospitals in the 1960s, traditional medical and surgical care for adults prevailed, curative treatment was pursued even when the hoped-for recovery was not achieved, and the patient's suffering continued. The patient who wanted to cease treatment had to accept discharge from the hospital. It was difficult to change course, even in shifting from one form of therapy to another, such as surgery, radiation, and/or chemotherapy for patients with cancer. Seeking a second opinion took courage on the part of a patient, and doctors did not feel obligated to fully explain what medical problem they found, what options there were to correct it, or to engage the patient and family in deciding what to do. In 1970 Oliver Cope, emeritus professor of surgery at Harvard Medical School, urged breast surgeons to hear their patients' thoughts and feelings when a cancer was found. He urged the specialists, pathologists, surgeons, radiologists, and chemotherapists to confer with one another in order to inform the patient of the options and allow the patient to decide. Despite Cope's illustrious background and high regard by colleagues, the *New England Journal of Medicine* refused to publish a paper presenting this idea. Rebuffed, he wrote a book for professionals and the public alike, entitled *The Breast* (Cope 1977). He encouraged women with breast cancer to discuss the options and be involved in the decision.

The cost of catastrophic illness was publicized by 1970, by which time medical economists were alarmed by the precipitous rise of health care expenditures. In 1983, I. S. Falk, who had been following medical care for 50 years, remarked that

> Total national health expenditures had moved up from $18 billion in 1955 to $42 billion in 1965, and they were continuing to grow much faster than the economy or than spendable income. By July 1969, when they reached $66 billion, even the conservative President Nixon was constrained to say the "system" faced "a massive crisis," expecially from the discovery that there was no end in sight for such escalation, and that it was being defended by personal providers and by the hospitals and related institutions as unavoidable in meeting the obligations for good quality of care. [p. 148]

The accumulation of new knowledge and new technology in diagnosis and treatment that took place in the years following World War II came with an expensive price tag. Many patients with limited incomes had their assets wiped out by medical expenses. There was no Medicare or Medicaid, although those who believed in a national health service anticipated it would come with President Lyndon Johnson's "Good Society."

Nurses and doctors became increasingly uncomfortable in seeing patients exhausted, depleted, in pain, and frightened. But patients' questions about prognosis were evaded by the doctors (Duff and Hollingshead 1968). Some nurses wanted to answer patients' questions, but were unable to get the doctors' permission. Doctors and nurses moved in parallel tracks rather than collaboratively in teams. The dissatisfactions with each other were usually unspoken.

Answering the Call for Change

Two charismatic leaders came to the fore in the early 1960s; both were doctors and both were women, but they differed in philosophy and approach. Cicely Saunders had found her professional path as early as 1947. She was educated as a nurse and almoner (social worker). She knew she needed the best that medicine offered and she believed a new way of caring for terminally ill had to be accepted by the medical hierarchy. So she went to medical school, and after she became a physician she carefully studied symptom control.

She was a Christian and needed the support of the Anglican Church in the services she envisioned, as she felt a Christian foundation was essential for her. So in creating new services and a new kind of institution, she made sure those two establishments accepted the hospice concept (du Boulay 1984). In both her speaking and writing, she has always been clear and convincing to many professionals and the public.

Elisabeth Kübler-Ross has a different style and took a different route. When World War II ended, she left Switzerland and went to Poland and Germany where displaced civilians were stranded and needed help. She later attended medical school. She is a free spirit who trusts her intuition and urges nurses, doctors, and clergy to act upon their spontaneous ideas when caregiving. She has boundless energy and is undaunted by critics. She has the power to spellbind an audience and convince the doubtful. When her colleagues at the University of Chicago Medical School failed to renew her faculty appointment because they found her book *On Death and Dying* (1969) professionally unacceptable, she created a roving school without academic sponsorship, and held workshops in the United States and abroad. She created her own organization based first in California and later in Virginia where she offered workshops for caregivers, patients, and families, assembling vast numbers of followers in the United States and abroad.

These two charismatic leaders came upon the scene during the social changes of the 1960s. On March 8, 1963, the civil rights movement culminated in a march from Montgomery to Selma, Alabama. The central issue was voting rights for blacks. Most of the whites active in the civil rights movement were clergy, but other professionals soon joined including doctors, lawyers, and medical students. These protest marches began in the South, and later from various parts of the United States to Washington.

Two months after the first march, Cicely Saunders gave her first lecture in the United States. From her first lecture to a class of medical students at Yale University, and a second one to Yale's Nursing School, she became a much sought after speaker throughout this country for the next two decades. Within the health care system there was increasing concern about the costs of medical technology and of keeping patients alive, which often ended in a long period of recovery and compromised well-being.

It was not only the profession of medicine being challenged by patients, but clergy were also challenged by parishioners for a more active role in the rituals and liturgy in church and synagogue; teachers were challenged by students, and government by its citizens.

The presidencies of Lyndon B. Johnson (1963–1969) and Richard Nixon (1969–1974) were shaken by populist pressure to end our participation in the Vietnam War. The song of marches and demonstrations, "We Shall Overcome," reflected the will and empowerment of the people to speak out and follow through. It cleared the caregivers' path to patients' rights and a changed doctor–patient relationship that respected patient autonomy. The methods of involving a patient in clinical research were stipulated and regulated by an interdisciplinary ethics research committee. In this era of challenge to the establishment, doctors could no longer withhold information or exclude the patient from decision making (Katz 1984). For many doctors who conceive of their role as paternalistic protector, this remains a difficult adjustment.

When awakened to the possibility of providing comfort, care, and support, a substantial number of health professionals and the public thirsted for ideas and expertise in practice. After St. Christopher's Hospice in London opened its doors in 1967, a few professionals from the United States and Canada gathered work experience there. Professional practitioners and academicians of various disciplines met in conferences. Among the first of these was Cicely Saunder's 1968 conference "The Moment of Truth—Care of the Dying Person," at Yale University Medical Center, and "Nature and Management of Terminal Pain," the Cancer Care Fourth National Symposium in New York City (Saunders 1971).

By the mid-1960s, there was a growing number of health professionals examining health and human values. In 1969 the Society for Health and Human Values took on the task of fostering education in human values in medical and other health professional schools. The society's annual meetings became a nurturing environment for professional schools of health in the United States to learn from one another. For those who were concerned with death, dying, and bereavement, new organizations were founded, such as Ars Moriendi in Philadelphia and the Foundation of Thanatology in New York City.

Luminaries in theory building and/or in practice, in addition to Cicely Saunders and Elisabeth Kübler-Ross, surfaced. Having worked independently of one another, they welcomed kindred spirits. Books and articles began to flood the literature.

Eventually, the professionals needed a different kind of forum, (ne in which they could collaborate on a common problem. In 1974 the International Work Group on Death, Dying, and Bereavement came into being. At its first meeting members gravitated into two groups. One called itself the "feelies," the other the "doers." The feelies had Elisabeth Kübler-Ross at its center; the doers worked with Cicely Saunders. The feelies were already involved as caregivers and exposed to the intense and profound emotions in tending to the end of the life cycle. They found common ground in their experience and exchanged ways to cope. This remains a strong support group.

The doers worked on the nuts and bolts of setting up services, finding ways to link with other parts of the health care systems, and defining principles for palliative and hospice care and the underlying assumptions. The spirit was invigorating from the beginning. Finding colleagues with common problems and different ways to solve them made it hard to bring sessions to a close. Conversations continue through the night. The luminaries were as good at listening as the neophytes.

Meanwhile, the public became so enthused about the concepts of palliative and holistic care that new ventures began services and accepted volunteers.

The broader concept of suffering of the dying patient/family infiltrated the medical model. Strategies borrowed from the best of traditional modern medicine, as Saunders emphasized from the beginning, blended with other ways of healing and reducing stress. However, Saunders's position was to maintain and sustain a firm footing in established medicine, and established religion.

In the United States nurses were attracted to and promoted hospice care sooner and more enthusiastically than doctors. Nurses had developed their role as being perceptive of patients' wants and skilled in helping them to express it. Their focus was on the human being with an illness.

The balance between traditional and holistic practitioners in each palliative care/hospice institution shapes the therapeutic thrust. The ability and willingness of doctors and nurses to learn from one another and negotiate determine how much the process moves forward.

A World Slow to Change

Those who changed the care given in terminal illness in the 1970s anticipated that changes in the health care system and their availability would be slow to materialize in the United States. The reluctance of a democracy to offer national health service can be traced back to the 1930s.

To Franz Goldmann, an émigré physician in the 1930s who came to teach medical care at Yale, the absence of a national health service in the United States was appalling. In Germany, where he came from, it had been established nearly one hundred years before.

I. S. Falk (1983) traced the fifty years of the study, proposals, and enactments for medical care and health services in the United States. It began with the creation of a Committee on the Costs of Medical Care and the five-year study it prepared from 1927–1932. Its recommendations were for basic public health services for the entire population, its costs on a group basis to be provided through insurance, taxation, and/or both. Strong objections from the medical profession impeded development and the beginning of a severe depression, followed by World War II, stopped further progress although at least the federal government saw the issues. Meanwhile, private insurance companies expanded in the health insurance programs.

Roosevelt prepared for strengthening the national health care program and in November 1945 Truman proposed to Congress a comprehensive national system for the prepayment of medical care costs. It would take twenty years still until Medicare and Medicaid were established in 1965. Yet there was increasing expectation that national health service was not far behind. Goldmann (1946) lauded President Truman's first full-length presidential message on health, the first ever submitted by a president to Congress, on November 19, 1945, and urged the representatives of the American people to give careful consideration to Truman's proposal for the establishment of a national health program. Truman listed five important problems "which must be solved, if we hope to attain our objective of adequate medical care, good health, and protection from the economic fears of sickness and disability." The problems he cited were better distribution of both professional personnel and medical care facilities, improvement of public health services, promotion of medical research and professional education, development of organized payment for medical care, and protection against the economic risks of disabling illness.

Have health planners been naive in thinking health care can and should be a right in a capitalist society because it is also a democracy? Controlling cost had to happen. The question is: how. Should and will private enterprise fill the void?

Federal, state, and municipal monies are insufficient for care of the underinsured and uninsured. Large city hospitals face closing, and their services have become substandard. Knickman (1995) predicted 40 percent would close by the end of 1995. Will private hospitals accept inadequately insured patients?

Strategies come from the business world and its principles. The larger the system, the higher the profits. The faster the pace, the lower the cost. The more people involved, the more it costs. The fewer the competitors, the greater the control.

Mergers, consolidation, horizontal and vertical alliances, decision making by the payer, and amassing capital for new ventures are the means. Chains spread across the country, or in a state, and megacenters in a region have revised the way hospitals, health maintenance organizations, hospices, and home care agencies function.

Present health care reform is economic in purpose. The expectation is that recovery and healing can take place in the home. Professional caregivers are being replaced by nonprofessionals. The numbers of caregivers per patient is reduced. The new system of corporate health care is emerging with a loose framework of rights and obligations.

State licensure and certificates of need are loosely reined in and dissimilar in the states. Accreditation and credentialing are in the hands of private professional organizations. Changes are coming so fast and are so erratic that making sense of them is difficult and the outcomes are elusive. Also, it isn't possible to compare health care systems with other business systems. Television stations merge with manufacturers of electronic equipment. A United States pharmaceutical company merges with a Swiss one. A single owner of a newspaper buys out other newspapers as if there are no restraint of trade or antitrust laws. While most business ventures move toward becoming larger to be more profitable, American Telephone and Telegraph divided its one structure that combined telecommunications and computers into three. Information technology has been exploding so quickly and so widely that the global information solutions arm was incompatible with the long-distance services and with the manufacture of communications equipment. Changes so mercurial make the future uncertain, except that control of economic resources and power is going into the hands of fewer and fewer and that resources are diminishing.

The United States has two contradictory natures as a democracy and a capitalist society. One values health care as a right, the other as an earned reward. One requires government management, the other private enterprise. One measures success in the common good, the other in economic success.

What will managed health care be like in 5 years? Are the medical professions ready to accept reduced incomes? Is a society that believed "We Shall Overcome" able now to shake off the sense of being overcome?

John Galbraith (1996) comments on "the tragic gap between the needful and the fortunate" (p. 1); he proposes the reformer recognize what is achievable. While not tolerating the unacceptable, reaching for the ideal may generate resistance that defeats. Such is human nature. The Clinton Health Plan and the response in Congress to it illustrates his point. The Congressional Record of November 20, 1993 contains the purpose of the bill: "To ensure individual and family security through health care coverage for all Americans in a manner that contains the rate of growth in health care costs and promotes responsible health insurance practices, to promote choice in health care, and to ensure and protect the health care of all Americans" (p. 1).

Protagonists in Congress blocked its passage and a lasting stalemate is, at this writing, still in effect.

Hope for the Future

If one reviews the problems solved and the emerging new solutions of the twentieth century, health professionals can reshape and restructure approaches based on knowing what works and what doesn't. This is a substantive but difficult revolution. At the Catastrophic-Illness Conference that Cancer Care Inc. conducted in 1970, Jerome Pollack (1971) said:

> There probably are no clearer examples than those in the health-care field of the subordination of people to programs, of a stubborn adherence to territorial imperatives, of the process by which social institutions are bogged down in geological, glacial deposits corresponding to the time when each program was started, rather than their subsequent realities and capabilities. This incidently should caution and guide us. When we embark on new programs, let us call for a basic reexamination of what we have done with the old. [p. 22]

In the years of waiting for socialized medicine, it was not only medical science and medical care that emerged. The new ways to maintain health emerged to help the consumer in life cycle events such as natural childbirth, family planning, coping with stress, aging, dying, and grieving. Most took place in the community. Maintaining health costs less than curing illness. While this change evolved in different ways and separate services, put together they can form a cohesive counterculture.

A parting of the ways presents an obvious solution. The medical model founded on medical science and a health support system would emerge as separate entities. The medical model would still engage in diagnoses, complex treatments and scientific inquiry with its own space, order, and ethos. Its domain would be smaller, but designed for an ever changing technology. The health support system would have its base in the community, helping patients cope with their own and family illness and keeping well. A bridge between these two is essential to its function: people caring for themselves and for each other to sustain health through the life cycle.

The idea is not new. One hundred years ago, Lillian Wald and a nursing colleague moved into a tenement area of New York City to help the working poor tenants manage illness at home. Two years later, the Henry Street Settlement built its own house. Wald (1934) knew that hospitals at that time were staggering under heavy deficits and that most illnesses could be checked in early stages. She found an ingenious way to pay for this. She convinced the Metropolitan Life Insurance Company to add home nursing services in its contracts, most of which were very small and meant for burial costs.

The other purposes of the settlement house at the turn of the century in New York City were to empower the newly arrived immigrants from Europe, help them learn the language, enable neighbors to help each other, use political action, and encourage expression through the arts. It opened a path for upward mobility.

Health needs of the poor in large cities are still unmet. Cities by nature decay; old housing becomes slums. The flow of immigrants continues, although from different geographic areas. Disconnectedness is amplified by the presence of machines in the workplace. Fear of crime keeps people locked in city apartments and even in suburban houses.

A second organizational form to consider is health maintenance organizations (HMO) in the original form that I. S. Falk proposed to President Franklin Roosevelt. They were first connected to labor unions and industry, such as the Kaiser Permanante Foundation, begun in 1941, to give comprehensive health care for workers and families. Nelson (1987) recalls "the overt opposition of organized medicine to contractual medical care. . . . Founders of the pioneer plan were expelled from their local medical societies." The Mayo Clinic, a prepaid medical group practice founded by doctors, was accepted.

It took until 1970 before medical centers, universities, and labor unions succeeded in developing HMOs. It was in Nixon's presidency that it moved forward. HMO structures were created by venture capitalists to provide for-profit managed care; doctors were owners, not paid staff. By 1995 the original concept of HMO became mixed with the HMO as conceived by doctor entrepreneurs. In the original concept of an HMO, all events in the life cycle requiring assistance from an interdisciplinary team, such as birth, growth and development, aging, dying, death, and bereavement, could be served. The original concept of HMOs gave its services to families and worked in interdisciplinary teams to provide life-cycle services, but not every HMO takes that original form.

A Proposal for the Future

Considering the precursors and contemporary developments of the hospice movement and the like-minded approaches presented at the beginning of this chapter, a future community service emerges with principles of family-centered care, patients' rights to know and decide, suffering redefined, psychosocial elements of health and disease considered, and empowerment of people throughout the life cycle as its base, with its caregivers interdisciplinary. Ira Byock, hospice medical director of Partners in Home Care, Missoula, Montana, sees this happening with a developmental approach. Even in the final stage of life the patient and family can grow and develop, he notes. He proposes, "a model of life long growth and development. Medicine approaches dying as a series of medical problems to be solved, even though the nature of dying is not medical but profoundly personal" (Byock 1995). To make his concept explicit, he has developed a tool to assess quality of life in the terminally ill with a working set of milestones and tasks at the end of life (Byock and Pratt 1994). These revolve around the patient as a whole person connected with family and social relationships in work and community. They look at the meaning of life and the ability to surrender to the transcendent, to the unknown, making it possible to let go.

Interim Response to a Changed Health Care System

It is uncertain what managed care will be like in the year 2000. Some hospices have responded by becoming part of a health care system, not always by choice but because of coercion and competition by the larger system. Others have fortified themselves by merging with other hospices, some resulting in hospice chains or becoming mega-hospices. In 1994 88% of hospices were not-for-profit, 5% proprietary, and 6.7% government (National Center for Health Statistics 1994). Beresford (1995) assesses it this way: "The bottom-line challenge for hospice now may be just to survive, to learn new skills, to forge the productive relationships and negotiate the best deals and to operate as leanly as possible until managed care systems finally start valuing quality over cost" (p. 4). The hospice movement still has weaknesses. Its wildfire spread fanned by an eager public and zealous founders bypassed careful study of need and existing resources. Not every state requires certificates of need, and those that do have different stipulations.

Organizational forms vary. There are free-standing hospices, palliative care units in hospitals, home care agencies, skilled nursing facilities, hospice teams serving dying nursing home clients, AIDS hospices, residences and services to the homeless in the community, and hospice day care (NHO 1993). Interagency relations have taken a variety of forms.

The patients admitted initially were primarily cancer patients. Now there are patients with other diagnoses. Patients with AIDS have an extended trajectory and uneven course. A patient whose crises are severe may unexpectedly go into remission.

Home care in theory makes sense, but for the patient who lives alone or whose helpmate is at work, it is inadequate.

Jay Mahoney, president of the National Hospice Organization, points out that Medicare is still the largest payer for hospice care, since most terminally ill patients are over 65, and managed care does not yet dominate the Medicare market. But in any case, hospices need to ask themselves, "Where are our patients coming from?" The hospitals and physicians that could refer Medicare patients may end up locked into networks with exclusive referral policies (Beresford 1995).

While revenues come from multiple sources—government, private insurance, patient, private foundations, contributions, community fund raising, and corporations—deficits and operational costs are a common problem. How many not-for-profit hospices are able to put aside capital funds to guarantee the institutions' security and independence?

Educating and credentialing caregivers has just begun. The impetus for assessing quality of care and measuring outcomes comes from the National Hospice Organization and the Commission on Joint Accreditation of Health Care. These proofs of quality are precisely what managed care needs to assure the components of its unique philosophy and delivery system.

How will managed care and corporate systems last? Can society depend on the world of business with its values of efficiency, speed, and shifting organizational form and revenue base? Charles Siebert (1995) comments, "When the excitement of all the science, all the new genetic discoveries has died down, you have to get back to the particulars of the human being" (p. 74).

Given the knowledge now available about the nature of suffering and holistic care, will government and the society it serves recognize and choose basic health care for all as a right? Can our society strike an equitable balance in its democratic and capitalist values?

References

Bailey, S. (1994). Creativity and the close of life. In *Dying, Death, and Bereavement. Theoretical Perspectives and Other Ways of Knowing*, ed. I. B. Corless, B. Germino, and M. Pittman, p. 329. Boston: Jones & Bartlett.

Beresford, L., ed. (1995). *Idealistic Hospice Industry Confronts Managed Care Era. Medicine and Health Perspectives*. Washington, DC: Healthcare Information Center.

Bowlby, J. (1952). *Maternal Care and Mental Health*. Geneva: World Health Organization Monograph Series.

Byock, I. R. (1995). The core of the problem: assumptions and cognitive models of dying. *Symposium: Project on Death in America*. New York: Soros Foundation, January, pp. 12–13 (unpublished).

Byock, I. R., and Pratt, M. (1994). Assessing quality of life in the terminally ill: a developmental approach. *The National Hospice Organization's 16th Annual Symposium and Exposition Session*, Washington, DC (unpublished).

Congressional Record (1993). November 20. Washington, DC: US Government Printing Office.

Cope, O. (1977). *The Breast*. Boston: Houghton Mifflin.

Cousins, N. (1981). *The Anatomy of an Illness*. New York: Norton.

Dossey, L. (1993). *Healing Words: The Power of Prayer and the Practice of Medicine*. San Francisco: HarperCollins.

du Boulay, S. (1984). *Cicely Saunders. The Founder of the Modern Hospice Movement*. London: Hodder and Stoughton.

Duff, R. S. (1987). "Close-up" versus "distant" ethics: deciding the care of infants with poor prognosis. *Seminars in Perinatology* 2(3):244–253.

Duff, R. S., and Hollingshead, A. (1968). *Sickness and Society.* New York: Harper & Row.

Dunbar, H. F., ed. (1954). *Emotions and Bodily Changes: A Survey of Literature on Psychosomatic Interrelationships, 1910–1953.* New York: Columbia University Press.

Falk, I. S. (1983). Some lessons from the fifty years since the CCMC final report, 1932. *Journal of Public Health Policy,* June, p. 148.

Feifel, H. (1955). Attitudes of mentally ill patients toward death. *Journal of Nervous and Mental Disease* 122:375–380.

——— (1994). Attitudes toward death: a personal perspective. An interview with Herman Feifel conducted by Inge Corless, 1991. In *Dying, Death, and Bereavement,* ed. I. B. Corless, B. Germino, and M. Pittman, p. 60. Boston: Jones & Bartlett.

Fein, R. (1980). Social and economic attitudes shaping American health policy. *Milbank Memorial Fund Quarterly/Health and Society* 58:359–385.

Frankl, V. E. (1962). *Man's Search for Meaning.* Boston: Beacon.

Galbraith, J. K. (1996). *The Good Society: The Humane Agenda.* Boston: Houghton Mifflin.

Goldmann, F. (1946). The right to medical care. *Social Service Review* 20:18–26.

Hollingshead, A. B., and Redlich, F. (1958). *Social Class and Mental Illness.* New York: Wiley.

Hunt, A. D., Jr., and Trussell, R. E. (1955). They let parents help in children's care. *Modern Hospital* 85(3):89–91.

Jung, C. G. (1959). The soul and death. In *The Meaning of Death,* ed. H. Feifel, pp. 1, 3. New York: McGraw-Hill.

Katz, J. (1984). *The Silent World of Doctor and Patient.* New York: Free Press.

Knickman, J. (1995). Public hospitals cutting as pressure increases. *The New York Times,* August 20, p. 24.

Krieger, D. (1981). *Foundations of Holistic Health: Nursing Practices.* Philadelphia: J. P. Lippincott.

Kubler-Ross, E. (1969). *On Death and Dying.* London: Macmillan.

Langner, T. S., and Michael, S. T. (1963). *Life Stress and Mental Health. Thomas C. Rennie Series in Social Psychiatry,* vol. 2. London: Free Press of Glencoe.

LeShan, L. (1989). *Cancer as a Turning Point.* New York: NAL Penguin.

Martinson, I. M. (1976). *Home Care For the Dying Child. Professional and Family Perspectives.* New York: Appleton-Century-Crofts.

Murphy, G. (1959). Discussion. In *The Meaning of Death,* ed. H. Feifel, p. 317. New York: McGraw-Hill.

National Center for Health Statistics (1994). *Hospices and Home Health Agencies: Data from the 1991 National Health Provider Inventory,* #257. Hyattsville, MD: National Health Provider Inventory.

National Hospice Organization (1993). *Managed Care Monograph,* p. 6. Arlington, VA: NHO.

Nelson, J. A. (1987). The history and spirit of the H.M.O. movement. *H.M.O. Practice* 1(2).

Orlando, I. J. (1961). *The Dynamic Nurse-Patient Relationship. Function, Process, and Principles.* New York: Putnam.

Peplau, H. (1952). *Interpersonal Relations in Nursing.* New York: Putnam.

Pollack, J. (1971). Observations on the economics of illness. In *Catastrophic Illness in the Seventies: Critical Issues and Complex Decisions.* Cancer Care, Inc. of the National Cancer Foundation proceedings of the Fourth National Symposium, 1970, p. 21. New York: Cancer Care Inc.

Quint, J. (1967). *The Nurse and the Dying Patient.* New York: Macmillan.

Saunders, C. (1971). The patient's response to treatment. In *Catastrophic Illness in the Seventies: Critical Issues and Complex Decisions.* Cancer Care, Inc. of the National Cancer

Foundation Proceedings of the Fourth National Symposium, 1970, pp. 33–46. New York: Cancer Care Inc.

Siebert, C. (1995). The DNA we've been dealt. *The New York Times Magazine*, September 17, pp. 50–74.

Silberman, S. (1990). Pioneering in family-centered maternity and infant care. Edith B. Jackson and the Yale Rooming-In Project. *Bulletin of the History of Medicine* 64: 262–287.

Spitz, R. (1945). Hospitalism: An inquiry into the genesis of psychiatric conditions in early childhood [II]. *Psychoanalytic Study of the Child* 1:53. New York: International Universities Press.

Srole, L., et al. (1961). *Mental Health in the Metropolis*, vol 1. The Thomas A. C. Rennie Series in Social Psychiatry. New York: McGraw-Hill.

Varney-Burst, H. (1983). The influence of consumers on the birthing movement. *Topics in Clinical Nursing: Rehumanizing the Acute Care Setting* 5:42–54.

Wald, L. D.(1934). *Windows on Henry Street*. Boston: Little, Brown.

4

Judaism's Import for End-of-Life Issues*

ELLIOT N. DORFF

The Jewish tradition, spanning over three thousand years, is based on the Torah (the five books of Moses) and the way that it was interpreted by rabbis and practiced by Jews through the centuries. The Torah includes, according to the traditional count, 613 of God's commandments, and, in a summary statement, it demands that we "do the right and the good in the eyes of the Lord" (Deuteronomy 6:18). Judaism is therefore profoundly normative: we do not exist, for the Jewish tradition, simply to live out our lives however we wish; we instead have a divine mission to follow God's commands so that we might be, in the words of Exodus, "a kingdom of priests and a holy nation."[1] The Jewish tradition is thus keenly aware of divine demands for our lives, it spends considerable time and effort to articulate exactly what those demands are, and it strives to motivate us to fulfill them.

The commandments deal not only with matters of ritual, but with family law, commerce, criminal law, interpersonal relations—indeed, with the entirety of life. It thus should not be surprising that Jewish law and tradition are concerned with how we face the end of life as well. Moreover, the Jewish tradition places great emphasis on the preservation of life and on each person's membership within the community, and so

---

*In the following, M. = Mishnah (edited c. 200 C.E.); J. = Jerusalem (Palestinian) Talmud (edited c. 400 C.E.); B. = Babylonian Talmud (edited c. 500 C.E.); M.T. = Maimonides' *Mishneh Torah* (completed 1177 C.E.); and S.A. = Joseph Karo's *Shulhan Arukh* (completed 1565 C.E.).

[1]Exodus 19:6. Non-Jews fulfill God's demands by obeying the seven commandments that, according to rabbinic tradition, were given to all descendants of Noah; cf. T. *Avodah Zarah* 8:4; B. *Sanhedrin* 56a, 60a. Jews, however, are subject to all 613 of the Torah's commandments and to their rabbinic extensions. For more on this, see Dorff 1982.

parts of the tradition concern our obligation to preserve life and the duties of the community to prevent pain and loneliness.

I shall discuss two of Judaism's fundamental assumptions that govern its responses to many issues in health care. I will also address issues that face the dying, such as euthanasia, hospices, and living wills, and issues that occur after death, such as cremation, autopsy, and organ donation. I will also address the social context in which people face death, and describe the ways in which Judaism would have us as a community not only cure when we can, but care for the people suffering illness. That, in this context, is at the core of what it means to be holy.

Other religions and philosophies share some of Judaism's views and directives. In exploring Judaism's views on these issues, I will show how one religion guides its adherents in these matters. We do not face death in a vacuum; all of our views and values impinge on what we do when confronted with the dying. This description of Judaism's import for end-of-life issues, then, will suggest to the reader some specific courses of action to help the dying and those attending to them, and will guide the reader in the process of probing one's own traditions for the guidance they offer on these matters.

Two of Judaism's Fundamental Assumptions on Health Care

Dr. Herman Feifel (1977) has noted several reasons why "Americans approach death warily and gingerly." "Foremost among these," he says, "is the fact that many of us no longer command, except nominally, conceptual creeds or philosophic-religious views with which to transcend death" (p. 4). Also, our disintegrated families and our materialism make it difficult for us to integrate death into our understanding of our lives, or to give it meaning.

Judaism is the kind of "philosophic-religious view" of which Dr. Feifel speaks. In contrast to Christianity, whose central symbol of the crucified and risen Christ puts concerns of the afterlife at the very heart of Christian consciousness, Judaism, through its core symbols of the Exodus and God's revelation on Mt. Sinai, focuses instead on God's redemptive role in our lives in the here and now. Judaism's principal symbols also highlight the life of the community more than the individual, for it was the entire people of Israel who were redeemed from Egypt and stood at Mt. Sinai, in contrast to the single figure of Christ. Goldberg (1985) discusses how the central stories of Judaism and Christianity lead its followers to have significantly different conceptions of the meaning of life and death. Despite these differences, Judaism has much to say to Jews about how to conceive of life and death.

Judaism's positions on issues in health care generally, and on end-of-life issues in particular, stem from two of its underlying principles, i.e., that the body belongs to God, and that human beings have both the permission and the obligation to heal.

The Body Belongs to God

For Judaism, God owns everything, including our bodies.[2] God loans them to us for the duration of our lives, and they are returned to God when we die. The immediate implication of this principle is that we do not have the right to govern our bodies as we will; since God created our bodies and owns them, God asserts the right to restrict the use of our bodies according to the rules articulated in Jewish law.

One set of rules requires us to take reasonable care of our bodies. It is as if we had the use of an apartment on loan to us; just as we would have the obligation to take reasonable care of the apartment while using it, so too we have the duty to take care of our bodies. That is the reason why a Jew may not live in a city where there is no physician.[3] It is also the reason why rules of good hygiene, sleep, exercise, and diet are commanded acts that we owe God. So, for example, bathing is a commandment (*mitzvah*) according to Hillel, and Maimonides includes his directives for good health in his code of law, making them just as obligatory as other positive duties like caring for the poor.[4]

Just as we are commanded to take positive steps to maintain good health, so are we obligated to avoid danger and injury.[5] Indeed, Jewish law views endangering one's health as worse than violating a ritual prohibition.[6] So, for example, anyone who cannot subsist except by taking charity but refuses to do so out of pride is shedding blood and is guilty of a mortal offense.[7] Similarly, Conservative, Reform, and some Orthodox authorities have prohibited smoking as an unacceptable risk to our God-owned bodies (Dorff and Rosett 1988).

Ultimately, human beings do not, according to Judaism, have the right to dispose of their bodies at will (i.e., commit suicide), for that would

---

[2]See, for example, Deuteronomy 10:14; Psalms 24:1.

[3]J. *Kiddushin* 66d; cf. B. *Sanhedrin* 17b.

[4]Bathing is a commandment, according to Hillel: *Leviticus Rabbah* 34:3. Maimonides' codified rules requiring proper care of the body: M.T. *Laws of Ethics* (*De'ot*), chs. 3–5.

[5]B. *Shabbat* 32a; B. *Bava Kamma* 15b, 80a, 91b; M.T. *Laws of Murder* 11:4–5; S.A. *Yoreh De'ah* 116:5 gloss; S.A. *Hoshen Mishpat* 427:8–10.

[6]B. *Hullin* 10a; S.A. *Orah Hayyim* 173:2; S.A. *Yoreh De'ah* 116:5 gloss.

[7]S.A. *Yoreh De'ah* 255:2.

be a total obliteration of that which does not belong to them but rather belongs to God.[8] In the laws of most American states, suicide is not prohibited, but abetting a suicide is. It is difficult to construct a cogent argument that it is in the state's interest to prohibit suicide, especially if the person is not leaving dependents behind. In Judaism the theoretical basis for this prohibition is clear; we do not have the right to destroy what is not ours.

The Permission and Obligation to Heal

God's ownership of our bodies is also behind our obligation to help other people escape sickness, injury, and death.[9] It is not for some general (and vague) humanitarian reason or for reasons of anticipated reciprocity. Even the duty of physicians to heal the sick is not a function of a special oath they take, an obligation to the society that trained them, or a contractual promise that they make in return for remuneration. It is because all creatures of God are under the divine imperative to help God preserve and protect what is His.

That is neither the sole, nor an obvious, conclusion from the Bible. Since God announces Himself as our healer in many places in the Bible,[10] perhaps medicine is an improper human intervention in God's decision to inflict illness.

The Rabbis were aware of this line of reasoning, but they counteracted it by pointing out that God Himself authorizes us to heal. In fact, He requires us to heal. They found that authorization and that imperative in two biblical verses, i.e., Exodus 21:19–20, according to which one who assaults another must provide for his victim to be "thoroughly healed," presumably by paying for his/her medical care, and Deuteronomy 22:2 ("And you shall restore the lost property to him"). The Talmud understands the Exodus verse as giving *permission* for the physician to cure, whether hired by an assailant, as in the Bible's case, or not. On the basis of an extra letter in the Hebrew text of the Deuteronomy passage, the Talmud declares that that verse includes the *obli-*

---

[8]Genesis 9:5; M. *Semahot* 2:2; B. *Bava Kamma* 91b; *Genesis Rabbah* 34:19 states that the ban against suicide includes not only cases where blood was shed, but also self-inflicted death through strangulation and the like; M.T. *Laws of Murder* 2:3; M.T. *Laws of Injury and Damage* 5:1; S.A. *Yoreh De'ah* 345:1–3. Cf. Bleich 1981, Ch. 26.

[9]*Sifra* on Leviticus 19:16; B. *Sanhedrin* 73a; M.T. *Laws of Murder* 1:14; S.A. *Hoshen Mishpat* 426.

[10]E.g., Exodus 15:26; Deuteronomy 32:39; Isaiah 19:22; 57:18–19; Jeremiah 30:17; 33:6; Hosea 6:1; Psalms 103:2–3; 107:20; Job 5:18; etc.

gation to restore another person's body as well as his/her property, and hence there is an obligation to come to the aid of someone else in a life-threatening situation. On the basis of Leviticus 19:16 ("Nor shall you stand idly by the blood of your fellow"), the Talmud expands the obligation to provide medical aid to encompass expenditure of financial resources for this purpose. And Nahmanides (fourteenth century) understands the obligation to care for others through medicine as one of many applications of the Torah's principle, "And you shall love your neighbor as yourself" (Leviticus 19:18).[11]

While each Jew must come to the aid of a person in distress, and while the assailant has the direct duty to cure his victim, Jewish law recognized the expertise involved in medical care and thus here, as in other similar cases, the layman may hire the expert to carry out his obligations. The Talmud reflects some ambivalence about the level of expertise of physicians of its time (most explicitly in comments like "The best of physicians deserves to go to Hell!"), and some later Jewish authorities were particularly wary of physicians' abilities to practice internal medicine (in contrast to surgery and healing external wounds and diseases); but, in the end, the Talmud prohibits Jews from living in a community in which there is no physician. This returns us to the first principle described above, for only if a physician is available can one carry out one's duty to preserve that part of God's property which is our bodies.[12]

The expert, in turn, has special obligations because of his expertise. Thus Rabbi Joseph Caro (1488–1575), the author of one of the most important Jewish codes, says this:

---

[11]B. *Bava Kamma* 85a, 81b; B. *Sanhedrin* 73a, 84b (with Rashi's commentary there). See also *Sifrei Deuteronomy* on Deuteronomy 22:2 and *Leviticus Rabbah* 34:3. Nahmanides (=Rabbi Moses ben Nahman, or "Ramban"), *Kitvei Haramban*, Bernard Chavel, ed. (Jerusalem: Mosad Harav Kook, 1963 [Hebrew]), Vol. 2, p. 43; this passage comes from Nahmanides' *Torat Ha'adam* (*The Instruction of Man*), *Sh'ar Sakkanah* (*Section on Danger*) on B. *Bava Kamma*, Chapter 8, and is cited by Joseph Karo in his commentary to the *Tur, Bet Yosef, Yoreh De'ah* 336. Nahmanides bases himself on similar reasoning in B. *Sanhedrin* 84b.

[12]The best of physicians deserves to go to Hell: B. *Kiddushin* 82a. Abraham ibn Ezra, Bahya ibn Pakuda, and Jonathan Eybeschuetz all restricted the physician's mandate to external injuries: see Ibn Ezra's commentary on Exodus 21:19 and cf. his comments on Exodus 15:26 and 23:25, where he cites Job 5:18 and II Chronicles 16:12 in support of his view; Bahya's commentary on Exodus 21:19; and Eybeschuetz, *Kereti U'pleti* on S.A. *Yoreh De'ah* 188:5. See Jakobovits 1959, pp. 5–6. That a Jew may not live in a city without a physician: J. *Kiddushin* 66d; see also B. *Sanhedrin* 17b, where this requirement is applied only to "the students of the Sages."

The Torah gave permission to the physician to heal; moreover, this is a religious precept and is included in the category of saving life, and if the physician withholds his services, it is considered as shedding blood.[13]

The following Rabbinic story indicates that the Rabbis recognized the theological issue involved in medical care, but it also indicates the clear assertion of the Jewish tradition that the physician's work is legitimate and, in fact, obligatory:

> It once happened that Rabbi Ishmael and Rabbi Akiva were strolling in the streets of Jerusalem accompanied by another person. They were met by a sick person. He said to them, "My masters, tell me by what means I may be cured." They told him, "Do thus and so until you are cured." The sick man asked them, "And who afflicted me?" They replied, "The Holy One, blessed be He." The sick man responded, "You have entered into a matter which does not pertain to you. God has afflicted, and you seek to cure! Are you not transgressing His will?"
>
> Rabbi Akiva and Rabbi Ishmael asked him, "What is your occupation?" The sick man answered, "I am a tiller of the soil, and here is the sickle in my hand." They asked him, "Who created the vineyard?" "The Holy One, blessed be He," he answered. Rabbi Akiva and Rabbi Ishmael said to him, "You enter into a matter which does not pertain to you! God created the vineyard, and you cut fruits from it."
>
> He said to them, "Do you not see the sickle in my hand? If I did not plow, sow, fertilize, and weed, nothing would sprout."
>
> Rabbi Akiva and Rabbi Ishmael said to him, "Foolish man! . . . Just as if one does not weed, fertilize, and plow, the trees will not produce fruit, and if fruit is produced but is not watered or fertilized, it will not live but die, so with regard to the body. Drugs and medicaments are the fertilizer, and the physician is the tiller of the soil."[14]

This is a remarkable concept, for it declares that God does not bring about all healing or creativity on His own, but rather depends upon us to aid in the process and commands us to try. We are, in the talmudic phrase, God's partners in the ongoing act of creation.[15]

---

[13]S.A. *Yoreh De'ah* 336:1.

[14]*Midrash Temurrah* as cited in Eisenstein, J. D., ed., *Otzar Midrashim* (New York: Hebrew Publishing Company, 1915 [Hebrew]), II, pp. 580–581.

[15]B. *Shabbat* 10a, 119b. The Talmud in B. *Sanhedrin* 38a specifically wanted the Sadducees *not* to be able to say that angels or any being other than humans participate with God in creation.

Euthanasia, Hospices, and Living Wills

Active and Passive Euthanasia

When we consider issues at the end of life, a few definitions are needed. *Murder* is the malicious taking of another's life without a legal excuse (such as self-defense). *Active euthanasia* is a positive act with the intention of taking another's life, but for benign purpose (e.g., to relieve the person from agonizing and incurable pain). *Passive euthanasia* is a refusal to intervene in the process of a person's natural demise.

Judaism prohibits murder in all circumstances, and it views all forms of active euthanasia as the equivalent of murder.[16] That is true even if the patient asks to be killed. Because each person's body belongs to God, the patient does not have the right either to commit suicide or to enlist the aid of others in the act, and anybody who does aid in this plan commits murder. No human being has the right to destroy or even damage God's property.[17]

The patient does have the right, however, to pray to God to permit death to come,[18] for God, unlike human beings, has the right to destroy His own property. Moreover, Judaism does permit passive euthanasia in specific circumstances, and in our day it is those circumstances that are of extreme medical interest.

Unfortunately the sources on this issue are sparse. This should not be surprising. Until the advent of antibiotics in 1938, physicians could do very little to impede the process of dying unless the problem could be cut out of the patient. Even when a gangrenous leg, for example, could be amputated, the patient stood a very good chance of dying from the surgery itself or from the infections that almost inevitably followed it. There are therefore only a few sources from the past that reflect circumstances in which people thought they had an effective choice of whether to delay death or not. This will mean that contemporary Jews seeking

---

[16]M. *Semahot* 1:1–2; M. *Shabbat* 23:5 and B. *Shabbat* 151b; B. *Sanhedrin* 78a; M.T. *Laws of Murder* 2:7; S.A. *Yoreh De'ah* 339:2 and the comments of the Shakh and Rama there.

[17]This includes even inanimate property that "belongs" to us, for God is the ultimate owner. Cf. Deuteronomy 20:19; B. *Bava Kamma* 8:6, 7; B. *Bava Kamma* 92a, 93a; S.A. *Hoshen Mishpat* 420:1, 31.

[18]Cf. RaN, B. *Nedarim* 40a. The Talmud records such prayers: B. *Ketubbot* 104a, B. *Bava Mezia* 84a, and B. *Ta'anit* 23a. Note that this is not a form of passive euthanasia, in that people refrain from acting, but here God is asked to act.

moral guidance from their tradition must place a heavy legal burden on those few sources.[19]

One such source is the account of the tragic death of Rabbi Haninah ben Teradyon. When the Romans burned him at the stake for teaching Torah, they put wool soaked with water around his chest to retard the effectiveness of the fire and thus prolong his agony. According to the talmudic story, when urged by his students to open his mouth to enable the fire to penetrate within and kill him more speedily, he refused, saying, "Let Him who gave me my life take it away, but no one should injure himself." But when the executioner asked Rabbi Haninah whether the rabbi would guarantee him entrance into the World to Come if he raised the flames and removed the tufts of wool, Rabbi Haninah said he would; and when the executioner carried out the plan, a voice from heaven (*bat kol*) proclaimed that both Rabbi Haninah and the executioner had been assigned to the World to Come.[20] Notice that Rabbi Haninah permitted the removal of an agency that he knew to be beneficial in maintaining his life even after it had already been applied, and notice too that his decision is not just one opinion but rather it has the approval of God Himself.

Another talmudic story relates the story of the death of Rabbi Judah, the Prince. Upon seeing the extent of his agony, his handmaid threw a jar from the roof to the ground so that his students' prayers would be interrupted and he could die. The Talmud records without objection this action of removing an impediment to dying (in this case, prayer).[21]

A third source is the comment of Rabbi Moses Isserles on an authoritative code, the *Shulhan Arukh*:

> It is forbidden to do anything to hasten the death of one who is in a dying condition. . . . If, however, there is something that causes a delay in the exit of the soul, as, for example, if near to this house there is a sound of pounding as one who is chopping wood, or there is salt on his tongue, and these delay the soul's leaving the body, it is permitted to remove these because there is no direct act involved here, only the removal of an obstacle.[22]

Here again impediments to death may be removed. *Sefer Hasidim*, the thirteenth century source on which Isserles' ruling is based, *prohibits* any action that may lengthen the patient's agony by preventing his quick

---

[19]For a discussion of the methodological issues involved in deriving legal guidance from such stories, see the articles by David Ellenson, Louis Newman, Elliot Dorff, and Aaron Mackler in Dorff and Newman (1995, pp. 129–193).

[20]B. *Avodah Zarah* 18a.

[21]B. *Ketubbot* 104a. For a sensitive analysis of this story, see Cutter (1995).

[22]S.A. *Yoreh De'ah* 339:2 gloss.

death, and it forbids those attending at the moment of death to cry, lest the noise restore the soul to the deceased.[23] According to some authorities even medicines must not be used to "delay the departure of the soul."[24]

The Point When Passive Euthanasia is Permissible

In former ages these precedents caused little difficulty because the number of ways in which people could impede death was extremely limited. Nowadays that is not true. Current technology enables us to maintain heart, lung, and kidney function totally by machine, at least for a time. The crucial question that arises, then, is, When does our obligation to cure end, and when does our permission (or, according to some, our obligation) to let nature take its course begin?

Authorities differ. All agree that one may allow nature to take its course once the person becomes a *goses*, a moribund person. But when does that state begin? Not surprisingly, definitions among the rabbis who have written about this vary. Rabbi J. David Bleich (1981) restricts it to situations when all possible medical means are being used in an effort to save the patient and nevertheless the physicians assume that he or she will die within 72 hours. Others define the state of *goses* more flexibly and therefore apply more broadly the permission to withhold or withdraw machines and medications during that time, noting that while the sources all speak about cases where death is imminent, they leave open the applicability of the permission to withhold or withdraw medical procedures to other cases as well (Jakobovits 1975, Reisner 1991a).

In a rabbinic ruling approved by the Conservative Movement's Committee on Jewish Law and Standards, I noted (Dorff 1991a,b) that Jewish sources describe a *goses* as if the person were "a flickering candle," so that he or she may not even be moved for fear of inducing death. That description and that medical therapy only apply to people within the last hours of life (not even the last three days). Consequently, I argued, the appropriate Jewish legal category to describe people with terminal, incurable diseases, who may live for months and even years, is, instead, *terefah*. Permission to withhold or withdraw medications and machines would then apply to people as soon as they are in the state of being a *terefah*, that is, as soon as they are diagnosed with a terminal, incurable illness.

---

[23]Rabbi Judah the Pious, *Sefer Hasidim* nos. 723, 234.

[24]*Bet Ya'akov*, no. 59 and *Gilyon MaHaRSHA* on S.A. *Yoreh De'ah* 339:1. Cf. also Moshe Feinstein, *Iggrot Mosheh, Yoreh De'ah*, II, no. 174.

One important principle in these matters is that since Jewish law does not presume that human beings are omniscient, it is only the best judgment of the attending physicians that counts in these decisions. Even if some cure is imminent, we are not responsible for knowing that. We must proceed on the best knowledge available at the time. If that means that the person is currently incurable, then machines and medications may be withdrawn and palliative care administered.

Artificial Nutrition and Hydration

Physicians initially use the least invasive way to intubate patients in comas—the nasogastric tube, which is inserted into the nose and down the throat. Patients in comas have lost the functioning of their upper cortex, but their brain stem may be unimpaired. The brain stem controls instinctual activity, and because of our instinct to cough, comatose patients sometimes try to cough up the tube or pull it out; they then have to have their hands restrained. When the nasogastric tube is no longer usable, physicians insert tubes into the patient's veins. The veins, however, can collapse or develop infections at the point of the tube's entry, and so various veins must be successively used. Finally, when all else fails, physicians use a gastrointestinal tube, which requires surgery to insert the tube directly into the stomach. Clearly, all of these available forms of intubation are uncomfortable and pose some risk of infection, but they are commonly used to give comatose patients the fluids and nutrients they need.

If the patient has been comatose for a number of months, however, and there seems to be little, if any, hope of recovery, may one remove such tubes? On the one hand, in contrast to medical interventions needed only by the sick, the nutrition and hydration delivered through tubes supply liquids and nutrients that any person needs to survive. Consequently, many (e.g., Reisner 1991a) maintain that while we may withhold or withdraw medications and machines, we may not withhold or withdraw artificial nutrition and hydration.

On the other hand, the nutrients that enter the body through tubes look exactly like medications administered that way and, more to the point, the Talmud specifically defines "food" as that which is ingested through the mouth and swallowed. Consequently, the Conservative Movement's Committee on Jewish Law and Standards has endorsed my ruling that while we must go through the motions of bringing in a food tray at mealtimes to a comatose patient, we need not administer nutrition and hydration artificially. We should do so as long as there is a reasonable chance that the patient may recover. Otherwise the artificial nutrition and hydration are just prolonging the dying process, and they may be removed (Dorff 1991a).

Curing the Patient, Not the Disease

There is general agreement that a Jew need not use heroic measures to maintain his or her life but only those medicines and procedures that are commonly available. We are, after all, commanded to *cure* based on the verse in Exodus 21:19, "and he shall surely cure him." We are not commanded to sustain life per se.[25] Thus, on the one hand, as long as there is some hope of cure, heroic measures and untested drugs *may* be employed, even though this involves an elevated level of risk. On the other hand, physicians, patients, and families who are making such critical care decisions are *not* duty-bound by Jewish law to invoke such therapies.

This should help us deal with a common phenomenon. A person is suffering from multiple, incurable illnesses, one of which is bound to cause death soon. The person develops pneumonia, and doctors are then in a quandary. A generally healthy person who contracts pneumonia would be treated with antibiotics, and often the drugs would bring cure. In those situations both the physician and the patient would be required to use antibiotics according to Jewish law, and few would need Jewish law to convince them to do so. But what happens in this case? The physician can probably cure the pneumonia, but that would only restore the patient to the pain and suffering caused by his/her other terminal illnesses. The alternative would be to let the patient die of the pneumonia so that death would come more quickly.

From the perspective of Jewish law, the question is whether our inability totally to cure the person gives us the right to refrain from curing what we can. Normally we do not have this right. So, for example, we must try to cure the pneumonia of a child who has Down's syndrome, even though we cannot cure Down's syndrome. If a person has a terminal illness, however, we would not need to intervene; rather, we may let nature take its course. We must view the person as a whole rather than consider each disease separately. Therefore, even though we could probably cure the pneumonia, the *person* cannot be cured, and therefore we may refrain from treating the pneumonia if that will enable the patient to die less painfully.

This resolution would be in line with the strain in Jewish law that does not automatically assume that preservation of life trumps all other considerations, but rather judges according to the best interests of the patient.[26] This principle does not extend so far as to permit mercy killing

---

[25]Thus the Talmud specifically says, "We do not worry about mere hours of life" (B. *Avodah Zarah* 27b).

[26]Tosafot, B. *Avodah Zarah* 27b, s.v., *lehayyei sha'ah lo hyyshenan*. See Dorff (1991a); for a contrasting interpretation of this source, see Reisner (1991a).

(active euthanasia), but it does make it permissible to refrain from administering the antibiotic so that the patient can die of the other diseases.

Hospice Care

The fact that Jewish law does not require the use of heroic measures means that a Jew may enroll in a hospice program in good conscience and that rabbis may suggest this. Hospice care typically does not take place in a special facility, at least until the very last hours or days of life (and not necessarily even then); rather, the patient lives at home as long as possible, doing whatever he or she can do. The word *hospice* thus designates a form of care. In hospice care, the goal is not to cure the disease, for that has been diagnosed as incurable, a diagnosis usually confirmed by tests and by a second opinion, but rather to make the patient as comfortable as possible.

This is accomplished, in part, through pain medication. Even in the last stages of life, when the dosage of pain medication needed may actually hasten the patient's death, that is permissible as long as the intent is not to kill the person but rather to alleviate his or her pain. Rabbi Reisner (1991a) does not accept this "double effect" argument, but he would agree that pain should be alleviated as much as possible up to, but not including, the dosage that would have the inevitable effect of hastening the person's death, even if not intended for that purpose. (See, in contrast, Dorff (1991a) and Reisner's (1991b) summary of the differences between the Dorff and Reisner positions.)

Hospice care also includes all the nonmedical ways in which people are supported when they go through crises, such as the forms of care provided by family and friends who keep the patient company and make the patient feel that he or she is still part of their world and not simply a locale of illness and pain. Nurses, social workers, and rabbis may also be involved at various points in the patient's care. The patient still seeks medical help, as Jewish law demands, but the object of the medication has now shifted from cure to comfort.

Hospice care has the distinct advantage of making it clear to all involved that death is approaching and that that fact is acknowledged. This clears the way for the patient to speak openly with relatives and friends about his/her feelings about what is happening. In non-hospice settings, visitors are often afraid to mention death, both because they themselves are afraid of it and because they do not want to diminish the will of the patient to live. When it is clear to all concerned, though, that cure is not possible, then visitors can help patients most by permitting them to speak honestly about their pains and desires, their fears and hopes. As Feifel (1959) noted,

> I think one of the serious mistakes we commit in treating terminally
> ill patients is the erection of a psychological barrier between the liv-
> ing and the dying. Some think and say that it is cruel and traumatic to
> talk to dying patients about death. Actually, my findings indicate that
> patients want very much to talk about their feelings and thoughts
> about death but feel that we, the living, close off the avenues for their
> accomplishing this. [p. 123]

Hospice care, then, is a valid Jewish option for patients afflicted with a
terminal, incurable disease, and it is often the more comfortable, meaningful, and humane method to live one's last days or months.

Moreover, if the doctors can use extraordinary means but only at
great cost and by inflicting great pain and even then with only a slight
possibility of cure, Jewish law would permit such action but would not
require it. Consequently, a Jew may legitimately refuse supererogatory
medical ministrations and may sign an advance directive for health care
(sometimes called a "living will") indicating his/her desire to decline such
care, choosing instead only to alleviate whatever pain is involved in dying.
When cure is not possible, both the patient and the physician cease to
have an obligation to do more medically than ease pain. Similarly, family and friends should not pressure the patient or physician to employ
extraordinary or futile measures; they should instead focus on their
continuing duties to visit the sick and provide all forms of nonphysical
comfort they can, as I shall describe in the section on social support
below. All four movements in American Judaism—Conservative, Orthodox, Reconstructionist, and Reform—have produced their own versions
of a Jewish advance directive, each according to its own understanding
of Jewish law, and while they differ in tone and substance, they all permit hospice care.

Cremation, Autopsy, and Organ Donation

The treatment of these topics in Jewish law depends on two primary
principles. The general tenet that governs treatment of the body after
death is *kavod ha-met*, i.e., we should render honor to the dead body.
This is not only demanded by respect for the deceased person; it also
derives from the theological tenet that the body, even in death, remains
God's property. Honor of the corpse, then, underlies Jewish burial customs—closing the eyes of the deceased, preserving modesty even in
death by having women prepare a female body for burial and men a male
body, washing the body before burial, clothing it in burial shrouds, bury-
ing the body as soon after death as possible in a closed coffin so that
onlookers will not notice its disintegration, and convening family and
friends to utter memorial prayers and to eulogize the deceased.

The other principle is that of *pikkuah nefesh*, the obligation to save people's lives. When interpreting Leviticus 18:5, which says that we should obey God's commands "and live by them," the Rabbis deduce that this means that we should not die as a result of observing them. The tenet of *pikkuah nefesh* is so deeply embedded in Jewish law that, according to the rabbis, it takes precedence over all other commandments except murder, idolatry, and incestuous or adulterous sexual intercourse. That is, if one's choice is to murder someone else or give up one's own life, one must give up one's own life. Similarly, if, as in the case of the Greek king Antiochus of the Hanukkah story, a king forced a Jew to bow down to idols, one must choose instead to give up one's life, and the same would be true if, as in the case of the Nazis, Jews were forced to commit acts of incest or adultery (although rabbis living in the death camps found ways retroactively to excuse women who were raped by the Nazis on the grounds that these women often were not even given the choice of dying instead).

If, however, one needed to violate the Sabbath laws or steal something to save one's own life, then one is not only permitted but in fact commanded to violate the laws in question to save a life. If one stole something (that is, if one violated a law regarding the relationships between one person and another), one would have to restore the lost object or its equivalent when one could; but there would be no culpability, and therefore none of the usual fines involved if one had stolen in a medical emergency for the sake of saving a life.[27] If one violated the Sabbath (that is, if one violated a law governing the relationship between Jews and God), God would forgive the transgression, for, as the rabbis say, "better that he should violate one Sabbath so that he can observe many Sabbaths [once his life has been saved]."[28]

Jews are commanded not only to do virtually anything necessary to save their own lives; they are also bound by the positive obligation to take steps to save the lives of others. The imperative to do so is derived from the biblical command, "Do not stand idly by the blood of your neighbor" (Leviticus 19:16). This means, for example, that if you see someone drowning, you may not ignore him or her but must do what you can to save that person's life.[29]

What happens, though, when you can save only one life—yours or someone else's? Whose life takes precedence? The Talmud[30] tells the

---

[27]S.A. *Hoshen Mishpat* 359:4; 380:3. Cf. Jakobovits (1975).

[28]B. *Yoma* 85a–b (with Rashi there); B. *Sanhedrin* 74a-b; *Mekhilta* on Exodus 31:13. For a general discussion of this topic, see Jakobovits (1975).

[29]B. *Sanhedrin* 73a.

[30]B. *Bava Metzia* 62a.

story of two men in a desert who discover that they only have enough water for one of them to reach civilization alive. Should they divide the water between them, acting on a principle of human equality, even though they know that then both of them will die? Should the decision be made on the basis of property rights, such that whoever owns the water should claim it (and if they own it jointly, they should divide it accordingly)? Or should they leave the matter at its status quo position so that whoever has possession of the water when they discover the shortage should retain it?

The opinion that ultimately prevails in Jewish legal literature is that of Rabbi Akiba, who takes the last of these positions. He argues on the basis of textual analysis and moral concerns. The Torah says that one should not exact interest from a fellow Jew "so that your brother may live with you" (Leviticus 25:36). That requires, though, that you must be alive before you care for your brother, for otherwise he cannot possibly live *with you*. Consequently, according to Rabbi Akiba, "your life takes precedence (*hayyekha kodemim*)."

On a moral plane, this means that the two men should leave the water with whomever has it at the time they discover their shortage, for to do otherwise would involve both of them in either suicide or murder. One or both of them may die if they follow Rabbi Akiba's ruling, too, but at least it will be nature that determined this outcome rather than their voluntary choice. In other words, under morally impossible circumstances, when an untoward result will happen no matter what one does, Rabbi Akiba directs us to remain passive and let nature take its course.

The principle is established, then, that your life takes precedence. In the case of the drowning person, therefore, one must not immediately jump into the water to save him or her; indeed, if you are not trained as a lifesaver, you must not do so. You should instead seek the help of others or do what you can from the shore. Even if you have lifesaving training, Red Cross lifesaving procedures demand that you first try to save the person's life by staying out of the water, for example, by throwing a rope and pulling the victim in, so as not to endanger your life—and Jewish law would concur. Protecting your life comes first.

Cremation

Jewish law prohibits cremation as it is the ultimate form of dishonor of the dead. Cremation also represents the active destruction of God's property, and it is improper for that reason as well. In the generations after Hitler's gas chambers, burning the bodies of our own deceased seems especially inappropriate.

Autopsies

The two procedures that are permitted to interrupt the normal Jewish burial process are autopsies and organ transplants. Autopsies were known in the ancient world, but Jewish sources largely looked askance at them as a violation of human dignity. In the nineteenth and especially the twentieth centuries, however, as the prospects of gaining medical knowledge from autopsies improved considerably, many rabbis have become more sanguine toward them. One even suggested a popular campaign to persuade people to grant their written consent to an autopsy as a service to medicine.[31]

A definitive position, however, was enunciated by Israeli Chief Rabbi Isaac Herzog in his 1949 agreement with Hadassah Hospital. Under that agreement, autopsies would be sanctioned only when one of the following conditions obtain:

1. The autopsy is legally required.
2. In the opinion of three physicians, the cause of death cannot otherwise be ascertained.
3. Three physicians attest that the autopsy might help save the lives of others suffering from an illness similar to the patient's.
4. Where a hereditary illness is involved, performing the autopsy might safeguard surviving relatives.

In each case, those who perform the autopsy must do so with due reverence for the dead and, upon completion of the autopsy, they must deliver the corpse and all of its parts to the burial society for interment. This agreement was incorporated into Israeli law four years later.

Whether an autopsy is justified for legal or medical reasons, it is construed not as a dishonor of the body, but, on the contrary, as an honorable use of the body to help the living. Indeed, it is assumed that the deceased would, if asked, want the autopsy to take place if it could accomplish one of these two purposes. That is, this is not so much a preference of the principle of saving a life (*pikkuah nefesh*) over that of the honor due the dead (*kavod ha-met*), but rather a different form of preserving the honor of the deceased in contexts where saving other people's lives is possible.

In recent years there has been considerable controversy over autopsies in Israel because they have become routine, and so, to the consternation of Israeli medical researchers, Israeli law changed in 1980 to make autopsies more difficult to justify. Demonstrations, street riots, and intermittent government crises have periodically occurred over the issue.

---

[31]Hillel Posek, *Haposek*, vol. 9 (1949; *Av* 5709), no. 111.

It was a major factor in the failure of the traditional coalition between the Labor and National Religious parties to form a government in 1977, in the resultant concessions on this issue promised by Menahem Begin to the religious parties, and ultimately, on December 2, 1980, in the revision of the anatomy and pathology law making autopsies subject to family agreement, thus diminishing their number considerably. The new legislation did not prevent further disturbances over this issue, though, as evidenced by the Jewish Telegraphic Agency report of August 27, 1981 that police had to fire tear gas to disperse a crowd of ultra-Orthodox Jews in Jerusalem on the previous day when they tried to prevent police from removing the body of a suspected murder victim (Margalit Cohen) lest an autopsy be performed on her body.[32]

New procedures, such as a needle biopsy of a palpable mass, or a peritoneoscopy with biopsy, may soon accomplish most of the same medical objectives as autopsies do without invading the corpse to the same degree, and that would clearly be preferable from a Jewish point of view. Jakobovits (1975) discusses the history of Jewish attitudes toward autopsies and dissection against their non-Jewish background. The Chief Rabbinate's ruling and the Israeli Anatomy and Pathology Act of 1953 are also discussed.

Organ Transplantation

The other procedure that may interrupt the usual process of burial is organ transplantation. Once again, the overriding principles of honoring the dead (*kavod ha-met*) and saving people's lives (*pikkuah nefesh*) work in tandem. That is, saving a person's life is so sacred a value in Judaism that if a person's organ can be used to save someone else's life, it is an honor to the deceased person to donate the organ. That is certainly the case if the person completed an advanced directive, either orally or in writing, indicating willingness to donate portions of his or her body, but even if not, the default assumption is that a person would be honored to help another live.

Living Donors. Because one's own life takes precedence over helping someone else live, one should provide whatever medical care one can for others, but not that which threatens one's own life. In line with this, since every organ donation from a living person involves surgery

---

[32]See, for example, the following articles in *The Jerusalem Post*: "A Matter of Life and Death," June 24, 1977, p. 6 of the Magazine; "Medical Progress Must Not Be Prejudiced," August 21, 1977; and several articles and editorials on this topic (all negative!) in the issues of November 13, December 1, 2, and 3, 1980, surrounding the passage of the amendment.

and therefore at least some risk, contemporary rabbis have generally permitted, but not required, such donations, but their permission extends only to those cases where the donation can be accomplished without a major risk to the life or health of the donor. For example, Rabbi Immanuel Jakobovits (1975), former Chief Rabbi of the British Commonwealth and author of the first comprehensive book on Jewish medical ethics, has ruled that a donor may endanger his or her life or health to supply a "spare" organ to a recipient whose life would thereby be saved as long as the probability of saving the recipient's life is substantially greater than the risk to the donor's life or health. "Since the mortality risk to kidney donors is estimated to be only 0.24% and no greater than is involved in any amputation, the generally prevailing view is to permit such donations as acts of supreme charity but not as an obligation."[33]

Cadaveric Donors. Once a person has died, all questions of risk to the donor disappear. Nevertheless, because of concerns for honoring the dead body, some rabbis have imposed restrictions on cadaveric donations. The most restrictive opinion would limit donations to cases in which there is a specific patient before us (*lefaneinu*) and that person's life or an entire physical faculty of the person is at stake. So, for example, if the person can see out of one eye, a cornea may not be removed from a dead person, according to this opinion, to restore vision in the other eye. Only if both eyes are failing, such that the potential recipient would lose all vision and therefore incur increased danger to life and limb, may a transplant be performed. Moreover, the patient for whom the organ is intended must be known and present; donation to organ banks is not permitted (Bleich 1981).

That is definitely an extreme position. Most rabbis, including Orthodox ones, would expand both the eligibility of potential recipients and the causes for which an organ may be taken. For reasons I shall delineate in the next section, all authorities would insist that the family agree to the use of their loved one's body for this purpose. Assuming such agreement, most rabbis would permit the transplantation of a cornea into a person with vision in only one eye on the grounds that impaired vision poses enough of a risk to the potential recipient to justify the surgical

---

[33]This is the generally held opinion regarding living donors not only for Orthodox rabbis but also for Conservative and Reform rabbis. For Orthodox opinions, see Moshe Feinstein, *Igrot Moshe, Yoreh De'ah* 229 and 230 (Hebrew); Eliezer Waldenberg, *Tzitz Eliezer*, Vol. IX, #45; Vol. X, #25 (Hebrew); Obadiah Yosef, *Dinei Yisrael*, Vol. 7 (Hebrew). For a Conservative position (the only one I know of to date on living donors), see Dorff (1985). For Reform positions, see Freehof (1969, 1980) and Jacob (1987).

intrusion of the corpse necessary to provide the cornea. Some would also not insist that the recipient be immediately present, and some would require that a specific person for whom the organ is appropriate be identified before the transplantation may take place, even if that person is not nearby and ready for transplantation. In these days of organ banks, however, most rabbis would be satisfied that there is sufficient demand for the organ that it is known that it will eventually, but definitely, be used for purposes of transplantation. So, for example, the Rabbinical Assembly, the organization of Conservative rabbis, approved a resolution in 1990 to "encourage all Jews to become enrolled as organ and tissue donors by signing and carrying cards or drivers' licenses attesting to their commitment of such organs and tissues upon their deaths to those in need" (*Proceedings of the Rabbinical Assembly* 1990, p. 279). Although somewhat dated, a good summary of the positions of all three movements, with relevant quotations from responsa and other official position statements, can be found in Goldman (1978). Included are quotations from two responsa approved by the Conservative movement's Committee on Jewish Law and Standards. A similar stance can be found in the work of two other Conservative rabbis, Klein (1975) and Feldman (1986). For a summary of Orthodox positions, see Jakobovits (1975) and Rosner (1979). For a Reform position, see Freehof (1956, 1960, 1968, 1974). In a March 1986 responsum, the Central Conference of American Rabbis officially affirmed the practice of organ donation, and the synagogue arm of the Reform movement, through its Committee on the Synagogue as a Caring Community and Bio-Medical Ethics, just published a manual for preparing for death, which specifically includes provisions for donation of one's entire body or of particular organs to a specified person, hospital, or organ bank for transplantation and/or for research, medical education, therapy of another person, or any purpose authorized by law (Address 1992).

Transplanting vital organs, however, introduces another consideration, namely, the moment of death. We need, after all, to guard against the possibility that the physician will murder the donor while trying to save the life of the recipient through the transplant of the vital organ. The recipient's life does not take precedence over the donor's. A physician would effectively murder the donor in the process of transplanting a vital organ only if the donor were alive at the time of the transplant, and consequently the definition of death becomes crucial in matters of organ donation.

Classical Jewish sources use two criteria for death. One is the breath test, in which a feather is placed beneath the nostrils of the patient to see if it moves. The exegetical bases for this test are the verses in Genesis according to which "God breathes life into Adam" (2:6) and the Flood kills "all in whose nostrils is the breath of the spirit of life" (7:22),[34] but there clearly is also a cogent, practical reason for using the breath test— it is easy to administer. A minority view in the Talmud maintains that those rescuing someone buried by a pile of rubble on the Sabbath must dig out enough to expose both the head and chest of the victim in order to determine if there is still breath or heartbeat, even though the extra digging entails further violation of the Sabbath.[35]

Later codifiers embraced the approach of insisting on both respiratory and cardiac manifestations of death. Some even held that the breath test is only sanctioned by the Talmud because it normally is a good indication of the existence of heartbeat, but actually it is the cessation of heartbeat that forms the core of the Jewish definition of death.[36] Moreover, in the sixteenth century Rabbi Moses Isserles ruled that there was no way then to distinguish death with accuracy from a fainting spell, and consequently even after the cessation of breath and heartbeat one should wait a period of time before assuming that the person is dead. Some contemporary rabbis claim that we should still wait 20 or 30 minutes after observing these signs, but others claim that the availability of the sphygmomanometer and electrocardiogram permit us to revert to the traditional mode of defining death as cessation of breath and heartbeat.[37]

Even waiting that long, however, would generally be too long if doctors are to be able to use the dying person's heart. Consequently Conservative rabbis Daniel C. Goldfarb (1976) and Seymour Siegel (1976a) suggested that a flat electroencephalogram, indicating cessation of spontaneous brain activity, be sufficient on the grounds that this would conform to the medical practice of our time just as our ancestors determined Jewish law in light of the medical practice of their time. In 1988 the Chief Rabbinate of the State of Israel approved heart transplantation, effectively accepting that a flat electroencephalogram guarantees that the patient no longer can independently breathe or produce heartbeat, and that has become the accepted opinion of virtually all Jews, with the exception of a few Orthodox rabbis. The same considerations would apply to transplanting any other organ from a dying person, namely, whether the doctor is accelerating the death of the donor by removing the organ. If a flat electroencephalogram is confirmed, however, that concern is allayed, and the transplantation is permissible. For a summary of some of the varying Orthodox opinions on this subject up to 1978 in America, England,

---

[34]B. *Yoma* 85a; *Pirkei de-Rabbi Eliezer*, Ch. 52; *Yalkut Shim'oni*, "Lekh Lekha," no. 72.

[35]B. *Yoma* 85a.

[36]Cf. Rashi on B. *Yoma* 85a; Rabbi Tzevi Ashkenazi, *Hakham Tzevi*, no. 77; Rabbi Moses Sofer, *Teshuvot Hatam Sofer, Yoreh De'ah*, no. 338.

[37]Cf. Isserles, S. A. *Yoreh De'ah* 338; see also Bleich (1981).

and Israel, see Goldman (1978). Rabbi Immanuel Jakobovits, immediate past Chief Rabbi of the British Commonwealth, began to accept heart transplants in 1966. In Israel, Ashkenazic Chief Rabbi Issar Yehudah Unterman (1968) permitted heart transplants in 1968 (Rosner 1979, Unterman 1970). The Sephardic Chief Rabbi at that time, Rabbi Yitzhak Nissim, endorsed that responsum.

On the other hand, Rabbi Moses Feinstein, President of Agudat Harabanim, the Union of Orthodox Rabbis of America, and the rabbi whose responsa shaped right-wing Orthodox practice in North America throughout his life, issued a strong prohibition against heart transplants, claiming that they involve a double murder (the donor and the recipient) and that physicians who perform them are "evil" (*Hapardes* 43:6 [March–April, 1969], p. 4). His son-in-law, Rabbi Moses Tendler, however, and Dr. Fred Rosner report subsequent conversations with him in which Rabbi Feinstein "clarified" his position such that if the donor is absolutely dead by all medical and Jewish legal criteria, then heart transplantation would be permissible, a view that he seems to take in his responsum concerning the signs of death (Rosner 1979). Bleich (1981) categorically denies the acceptability of brain death criteria to determine death. Bleich (1977b) claims that in oral communications with him Rabbi Feinstein "in no way is prepared to accept any form of 'brain death' as compatible with the provisions of Halakhah" (p. 133).

The Chief Rabbinical Council of the State of Israel reaffirmed the acceptability of heart transplants in a responsum issued in 1987 (Jakobovits 1989). For yet other Orthodox opinions, see Rosner (1979) and Goldman (1978). For Conservative positions, see Segal (1969), quoted in Goldman (1978), Siegel (1975, 1976a), and Goldfarb (1976). The first official endorsement of the new criteria for the Conservative movement came in the approval of the movement's Committee on Jewish Law and Standards in December 1990 of the responsa by Rabbis Elliot N. Dorff (1991a) and Avram Reisner (1991a), both of which assume and explicitly invoke the new medical definition. The Reform movement officially adopted the Harvard criteria (presumably, as modified by the medical community) in 1980 (Jacob 1983).

All of these positions permit organ transplantation in at least some circumstances and even applaud it as a great gift. In 1995, however, the Conservative movement's Committee on Jewish Law and Standards endorsed a ruling by Rabbi Joseph Prouser according to which it is a laudable act of generosity to provide for the donation of one's bodily parts after death as well as a positive obligation. Rabbi Prouser pointed out that because of the shortage of organs available for transplant, cadaveric organ donation not only saves the lives of recipients but also saves family members who might otherwise be called upon to be living donors (e.g., of a kidney) from the risk of doing so. Organ donation, then, comes under the Torah's demand that we not stand idly by the blood of our neighbors (Leviticus 19:16) but rather come to their aid.

According to the rulings of the vast majority of rabbis who have written on this, then, cadaveric donations of skin, corneas, kidneys, lungs, colon, liver, pancreas, ovaries, testicles, heart, tissue, and, in general, any body part would be permissible, an act of special kindness (*hesed*) and perhaps even a positive obligation, since using the body to enable someone else to live with full use of one's faculties is not a desecration of the body but rather a consecration of it. The only concern is to make sure that the donor is indeed dead before the donation takes place. For most rabbis, including the Chief Rabbinate of the State of Israel, that means, in the age of modern technology, the cessation of all brain wave activity; for a few, it still requires cessation of breath and heartbeat. The prohibitions against desecration of the dead, deriving benefit from the dead, and delaying the burial of the dead are suspended for the greater consideration of saving the recipient's life or restoring his or her health, thus giving even greater honor to the deceased.[38]

The Use of Animal or Artificial Organs

Because donated organs are in short supply, physicians have recently tried to use animal or artificial organs. The use of such organs would afford a reliable, relatively inexpensive supply for transplant, and it would also obviate the need to make precise determinations of the moment of death so that a vital organ might be transplanted. From a Jewish perspective, these are great advantages.

Although some have raised questions about the use of animal parts for direct transplant or for making artificial organs, it is not a problem in Jewish law or ethics. Judaism, after all, does not demand vegetarianism, and, if we may eat the flesh of animals under Judaism's dietary rules (*kashrut*), then we may use animal parts for saving a life. Indeed, as we have seen, Jewish sources, in fact, go further; they hold that if the use of animal parts can save a human life, we have a moral and religious obligation to use them, and they do not even have to be from a kosher animal, for saving a human life takes precedence over the dietary laws. Consequently those Jews who choose to be vegetarians (and there is support for this within the tradition) would nevertheless be obliged to use animal parts for medical purposes if that was the method that held the greatest promise for curing a person or saving a life.

---

[38]See also Feldman and Rosner (1984), Goldman (1978).

At present the use of animal or artificial organs is in an early, experimental stage. Patients who have undergone such operations have not been cured, and in the process they have given up what could have been several months of life. Even so, if there is no known cure for a disease and an experimental drug or surgical procedure offers any chance for cure, Jews *may* choose to use the drug or undergo the operation, although they are not obligated to do so.[39]

Donation of One's Body to Science

May one donate one's entire body to science for purposes of dissection by a medical student as part of his or her medical education? Objections to this center round the desecration of the body involved in tearing it apart and the delay in its burial until after the dissection. Rabbi Bleich (1981) and others take a very hard line on this, claiming that any invasion of the corpse for purposes of autopsy or transplant is warranted only if there is a *holeh le'faneinu*, a patient who will benefit immediately thereby. In contrast, Israeli Chief Rabbi Herzog issued the following statement in 1949:

> The Plenary Council of the Chief Rabbinate of Israel . . . do not object to the use of bodies of persons who gave their consent in writing of their own free will during their lifetime for anatomical dissections as required for medical studies, provided the dissected parts are carefully preserved so as to be eventually buried with due respect according to Jewish law. [Jakobovits 1975, p. 150]

This seems to me to be a much more sensible reading of the sources and the process of medical research than that of Bleich. Dissection is crucial to the preparation of physicians. Consequently participating in medical education in this way is an honor to the deceased and a real kindness in that it helps the living. The levity that sometimes accompanies dissection is not because medical students find dissection funny, but it is rather a way for them to dissipate their discomfort in handling a corpse. No disrespect is intended, and therefore dissection is not objectionable on that ground.

Rabbi Isaac Klein (1975) cites yet another argument to permit the donation of one's body to science:

> In a country where the Jews enjoy freedom, if the rabbis should refuse to allow the Jewish dead to be used for medical study, their action

---

[39]B. *Avodah Zarah* 27b; Jakobovits (1975), Bleich (1981).

will result in *hillul ha-shem* (a desecration of God's Name), for it will
be said that the Jews are not interested in saving lives; there is (therefore) reason to permit it. [p. 41]

These arguments would not apply, however, if there are ample bodies available for dissection. Then there would be no special gift being
given by the donor to future physicians and their patients, and there
would be no particular taint involved if Jews do not generally donate their
bodies to science. Since medical schools currently have more than
enough bodies from county morgues, largely bodies of unknown people
that have been abandoned, Jews need not and therefore should not offer
to have their bodies dissected, for there is no medical necessity to set
aside the honor due a corpse according to the Jewish concept of *kavod
ha-met*.

In sum, then, most Jewish authorities would not only permit but
would encourage people to arrange to donate their organs to others upon
their demise, and some would even permit donating one's entire body
to medical science. The only restrictions are that the remains are ultimately buried according to Jewish law and custom and that the family
of the deceased agrees. Permission of the donor or his family must be
procured so that the transplant does not constitute a theft according to
Chief Rabbi Unterman's responsum in Goldman (1978). Feldman and
Rosner (1984) say that the family's permission is advisable in Jewish law
and mandatory in American law. See also Klein (1975). The thought of a
relative being cut up after death may be abhorrent to family members,
even if it is for the best of purposes. If the entire body is to be donated
to science, the family has an even greater stake in the decision for that
will force them to forgo a timely burial. After a person's death, relatives
and friends must separate themselves psychologically from the deceased
if they are to be able to resume their normal lives. By graphically indicating that the person has died, burial helps people gain the emotional
catharsis and closure that they need. Therefore, the permission of the
family is necessary not only in accord with American law, but also to
assure that even without burial relatives of the deceased can effectively
carry out the mourning process so that they can have psychological closure and return to their lives in full. If that is not possible, families may
refuse to give permission for organ donation or dissection, and they
should not be made to feel guilty for not doing so.

Social Support

Caring for a person is not a matter of physical ministrations alone.
The Jewish tradition was well aware that recovery is often dependent

on the social and psychological support that family and friends provide. Indeed, in cases where people ask to die, it is often because nobody is around to support them.

A personal anecdote may illustrate just how critical this is. My mother had polycythemia, which means that she had thick blood and thin veins. That required a series of amputations of parts of her leg that had turned gangrenous. Each time it would be a stay in the hospital, more time in a nursing home, and then home again until the next amputation was required. During one stay in the nursing home, her roommate was a woman who was never visited by family or friends. Her children lived thousands of miles away, and she had not been living in the area long enough to develop close friendships. She consequently had no visitors. Moreover, some of her belongings, along with some of my mother's and those of other residents, were stolen one day. It is never easy to cope with such an attack on one's sense of security, but without family and friends it is even harder. This woman at least had my mother for company and commiseration, but one can imagine that without that human contact, a patient might well think that there is no reason to get up in the morning, that it would just be better to die.

Part of the reason why my mother's roommate and many others like her have nobody to visit them is, as Feifel (1959) has pointed out, because our culture trains us to avoid instances of illness and death lest we too be tainted by them. Illness reminds us of our frailty and ultimate death. Thus, even though "death is one of the essential realities of life, . . . camouflage and unhealthy avoidance of its inexorableness permeate a good deal of our thinking and action in Western culture" (p. 115). We use euphemisms to describe it, we valorize the young and vigorous in our literature, movies, television programs, and commercials, and we shunt off the ill to hospitals where people in antiseptic white coats deal with them so that we do not have to get personally involved.

In sharp contrast to this, the Jewish tradition imposes the obligation on us of *biqqur holim*, visiting the sick. That is a *mitzvah* for all Jews. We must deal with illness as forthrightly as we appreciate and promote health, and our efforts must include the personal and interactive needs of the patient as well as the physical.

In response to this duty, synagogues and Jewish social groups have created a *biqqur holim* society, a group of people who make sure that members of the congregation or group are visited when sick, whether in the hospital or at home. Rabbis, psychologists, and social workers might train the members of the society on how to visit a bedridden person. This should include simple techniques like not standing over the bed but rather sitting down next to the patient so that the two of you are on the same plane, and it should also include more complex matters, like how to engage the patient in conversation about matters beyond the food served for lunch that day.

Such *biqqur holim* societies ideally should include not only older people, but people of all ages. In particular, teenagers and college students should be involved in this. It appeals to their sense of idealism, and it demonstrates that Judaism as we understand it is not only about study and rituals, as important as they are, but also about caring. Moreover, older people in hospitals and nursing homes love the intergenerational interaction, and the younger people, much to their surprise, do, too. In fact, they often will listen to the patients more than they listen to their parents.

Once death has occurred, Jewish tradition prescribes a period of seven days (*shivah*) after the burial of a person when close relatives of the deceased (parent, child, sibling, or spouse) must take off from work, stay at home, and mourn their dead. The community is duty-bound to visit them during this time, to supply their physical needs (shop for their groceries, help with their young children, etc.), provide a prayer quorum for worship in the morning, afternoon, and evening, and, most especially, to help them remember their loved one and express the many different emotions that one has when doing so. This is not only a recognition of the death and a mark of respect for the dead, but an aid to the mourners to acknowledge the death, mourn it, be comforted by one's community in the process, and, after the *shiva* period, integrate oneself once again in the activities of life. Memories of the dead person will continue on, especially if that person played an important role in one's life, but the *shiva* period enables mourners to mourn unashamedly with the support of the community for a period of time so that the person and his/her death are duly noted in the life of the community and so that the mourners can gain the strength to become part of life once again after *shiva* is over. Like illness, death, according to the Jewish tradition, must not be avoided but must rather be seen for the real part of life that it is and treated accordingly.

The Jewish tradition, then, not only obligates us to cure, but to care. Our medical facilities and our residence homes need to be not only medically sound, but warm, caring places. Moreover, our communities must consist of caring people who know that the Torah is serious when it says, "Love your neighbor as yourself" (Leviticus 19:18). Just as we would want the support of our family and friends if we were sick or if a relative has died, so too we must provide that support for others, and just as we would want good medical care if we were sick, so too we must provide that for others as well. Jewish law on medical issues in general, and its requirements for visiting the sick and mourners in particular, beckon us to be a warm, caring community in which we indeed do love our neighbors as ourselves.

Conclusion

The key to understanding issues at the end of life and to facing them wisely, for the Jewish tradition, is to recognize that dying people are not just bodies that need fixing, but human beings created in the image of God. Similarly, healthy people are not just animals put on this earth to procreate and to live out their lives as they may, but people created in the image of God with a divine mandate to make this a better world. As a result, both the dying and those who care for them must not let disease diminish the respect that people have for themselves or for each other.

We must cure whenever we can, and the health care professionals who enable us to do that ever more effectively are nothing less than God's partners in God's ongoing acts of creation. At the same time, we must recognize that we are not God, that we are, by nature and by definition, mortal, and so it is not always either theologically required or morally right to seek to extend life per se when there is no hope for recovery.

At least as importantly, we must remember that medical care for people at the end of life is a matter of attending not only to the physical aspects of the dying person, but also to the mental, emotional, and spiritual aspects of his or her being as well. The degree of both care and compassion we muster for those of our numbers who are in the process of dying is an accurate measure of our character and our moral mettle as individuals and as a community.

References

Address, R., ed. (1992). *A Time to Prepare: A Practical Guide for Individuals and Families in Determining One's Wishes for Extraordinary Medical Treatment and Financial Arrangements.* Philadelphia: Union of American Hebrew Congregations Committee on Bio-Medical Ethics.

Bleich, J. D. (1977a). Smoking. *Tradition* 16(4):130–133 (reprinted in Dorff and Rosett [1988], pp. 337–362).

—— (1977b). Time of death legislation. *Tradition* 16(4):133.

—— (1981). *Judaism and Healing.* New York: KTAV.

Cutter, W. (1995). Rabbi Judah's handmaid: narrative influence on life's important decisions. In *Death and Euthanasia in Jewish Law: Essays in Responsa*, ed. W. Jacob, and M. Zemer, pp. 61–87. Pittsburgh and Tel Aviv: Freehof Institute for Progressive Halakhah.

Dorff, E. N. (1982). The Covenant: how Jews understand themselves and others. *Anglican Theological Review* 64(4):481–501.

——— (1985). *"Choose Life:" A Jewish Perspective on Medical Ethics*. Los Angeles: University of Judaism.

——— (1991a). A Jewish approach to end-stage medical care. *Conservative Judaism* 43(3):3–51.

——— (1991b). A time to live and a time to die. *United Synagogue Review* 44(1):21–22.

Dorff, E. N., and Newman, L. E., eds. (1995). *Contemporary Jewish Ethics and Morality: A Reader*. New York: Oxford.

Dorff, E. N., and Rosett, A. (1988). *A Living Tree: The Roots and Growth of Jewish Law*. New York: State University of New York Press.

Feifel, H. (1959). Attitudes toward death in some normal and mentally ill populations. In *The Meaning of Death*, ed. H. Feifel, pp. 114–130. New York: McGraw-Hill.

——— (1977). Death in contemporary America. In *New Meanings of Death*, ed. H. Feifel, pp. 3–12. New York: McGraw-Hill.

Feldman, D. M. (1986). *Health and Medicine in the Jewish Tradition*. New York: Crossroad.

Feldman, D. M., and Rosner, F. (1984). *Compendium on Medical Ethics*. New York: Federation of Jewish Philanthropies of New York.

Freehof, S. B. (1956). The use of the cornea of the dead. *C.C.A.R. Yearbook* 66:104–107. New York: Central Conference of American Rabbis.

——— (1960). Donating a body to science. In *Reform Responsa*, pp. 130–131. Cincinnati: Hebrew Union College Press.

——— (1968). Surgical transplants. *C.C.A.R. Yearbook* 78:118–121. New York: Central Conference of American Rabbis.

——— (1969). *Current Reform Responsa*. Cincinnati: Hebrew Union College Press.

——— (1974). Bequeathing parts of the body. In *Contemporary Reform Responsa*, pp. 216–223. Cincinnati: Hebrew Union College Press.

——— (1980). *New Reform Responsa*. Cincinnati: Hebrew Union College Press.

Goldberg, M. (1985). *Jews and Christians. Getting Our Stories Straight*. Nashville: Abingdon.

Goldfarb, D. C. (1976). The definition of death. *Conservative Judaism* 30(2):10–22.

Goldman, A. J. (1978). *Judaism Confronts Contemporary Issues*. New York: Shengold.

Jacob, W., ed. (1983). *American Reform Responsa*. New York: Central Conference of American Rabbis.

——— (1987). *Contemporary American Reform Responsa*. New York: Central Conference of American Rabbis.

Jakobovits, I. (1975). *Jewish Medical Ethics*. New York: Bloch.

Jakobovits, Y. (1989). [Brain death and] heart transplants: The [Israeli] Chief Rabbinate's directives. *Tradition* 24(4):1–14.

Katz, J. (1961). *Exclusiveness and Tolerance*. New York: Schocken.

Klein, I. (1975). *Responsa and Halakhic Studies*. New York: KTAV.

Proceedings of the Rabbinical Assembly (1990). Vol. 52. New York: Rabbinical Assembly.

Reisner, A. I. (1991a). A Halakhic ethic of care for the terminally ill. *Conservative Judaism* 43(3):52–89.

——— (1991b). Mai Beinaiyhu. *Conservative Judaism* 43(3):90–91.

Rosner, F. (1979). Organ transplantation in Jewish law. In *Jewish Bioethics*, ed. F. Rosner and J. D. Bleich, pp. 387–400. New York: Sanhedrin.

Rosner, F., and Bleich, J. D., eds. (1979). *Jewish Bioethics*. New York: Sanhedrin.

Siegel, S. (1975). Fetal experimentation. *Conservative Judaism* 29(4):39–48.

——— (1976a). Updating the criteria of death. *Conservative Judaism* 30(2):23–30.

———— (1976b). The ethical dimensions of modern medicine: a Jewish approach. *United Synagogue Review* Fall:4.

Unterman, I. Y. (1968). Points of Halakhah in the question of heart transplantation, from an address to the Congress of Oral Law, Jerusalem, August. Cited in Organ transplantation, by F. Rosner. In *Jewish Bioethics*, ed. F. Rosner and J. D. Bleich, pp. 367–371. New York: Sanhedrin.

———— (1970). The problem of heart transplantation from the viewpoint of Halakhah. *No'am* 13:1–9.

5

Modernist Attitudes toward Death

ALAN W. FRIEDMAN

This chapter discusses Western attitudes toward death as represented in our literature and culture. Death pervades the narratives we tell and live, although its forms have changed radically with changing cultural circumstances. Specifically, Western literature of the late nineteenth century and the first half of the twentieth century (coincident with what literary critics call modernism) reflects a historical shift from Victorian familiarity with and aestheticizing of death to a period of fearful denial, when death became our "dirty little secret." A second radical shift occurred beginning in the 1950s (coinciding with the onset of literary critical postmodernism), when death again began to be confronted and accepted by investigators in a new discipline that came to be called thanatology.

Death as Literature and History

Every story continued far enough ends in death (Hemingway 1932), yet every recounting suspends finality. In *The Thousand and One Nights*, Scheherazade's narrative simultaneously foregrounds and forestalls the impending death that inspires and requires it, and thereby exercises shaping authority that exceeds ordinary mortal limits.[1] Fictional titles often proclaim death's centrality to their storytelling: Tolstoy's *The Death of Ivan Ilyich*, Mann's *Death in Venice*, Joyce's *The Dead* and *Finnegans Wake*, Lawrence's *The Man Who Died*, Faulkner's *As I Lay Dying* and *Requiem for a Nun*, Hemingway's *For Whom the Bell Tolls*, Beckett's *Malone*

---

[1]For Scheherazadean narrative as mediating and meditating on death, see Faris 1982, pp. 829–830.

Dies, for example. Other titles—Forster's *The Longest Journey* and *A Passage to India*, Lawrence's *The Woman Who Rode Away*, Woolf's *The Voyage Out*, Ford's *The Rash Act*, Beckett's *The Unnamable*—reveal their thanatological meaning only after we have read the texts they subtend. Like history, death is both narrative and event: a process created, ordered, and performed by survivors or, sometimes, as in *As I Lay Dying*, by nonsurvivors.

In "Four Quartets" T.S. Eliot writes, "human kind/Cannot bear very much reality." But we can and we do: only reality must be sanctioned, "naturalized," by history, culture, and storytelling. For Gil Elliot (1972) "The manner in which people die reflects more than any other fact the value of a society" (p. 10). The anthropologists Richard Huntington and Peter Metcalf (1979) similarly maintain that in all societies "Life becomes transparent against the background of death, and fundamental social and cultural issues are revealed" (p. 2). More than any other manifestation, narratives of death and dying reflect a culture's symbolic and mythic truths. Artifacts of death—rituals of dying and funeral, graveyards and tombs, wills and death certificates, the corpse itself—are as much communal constructs, dramatic and narrative performance, as are the texts that contain them.

In 1977 Herman Feifel, suggesting that "in the last analysis all human behavior of consequence is a response to the problem of death," quoted Hegel's defining of history as the record of "what man does with death" (p. xiii). Prior to Philippe Ariès (1981), however, historians generally assumed that death "has no history." Unlike battles and reigns, cultural changes—what Robert Darnton (1990) calls "the history of mentalities"— are nebulous and difficult to document, so historians preferred "dramatic events to the great constants of the human condition" (p. 269). Since Ariès, death's history has become a major thanatological concern. For all its haphazardness, Ariès maintains, death prior to the twentieth century was an ordering principle, a force and form of moral and aesthetic meaning; in turn, it lent itself to appropriation by ritual and narrative, in which it served a climactic, shaping function. Medieval death, Ariès argues, was integral to everyday experience; in literature and in society death and dying were foreknown, expected, and accepted—or so the record suggests since those who survived a "foreseen" death were unlikely to document their mistake. Ariès' historiographical reconstruction is, therefore, unlikely to be a full account of the past, yet such reenvisioning of culture—like studies of the Western family and sexuality by Lawrence Stone, Michel Foucault, and Stephen Heath, and the pioneering thanatological investigations by Herman Feifel, Geoffrey Gorer, Robert Fulton, Avery Weisman, and then Elisabeth Kübler-Ross, Robert Kastenbaum, and Edwin Shneidman—convincingly argue that there is nothing "natural" about how a people experience and recount their stories of sex or death. Both are products of culture: mediated, made, symbolic.

Death Prior to the Twentieth Century

Enlightenment faith in progress and in our increasing comprehension of life and death retained potency throughout the nineteenth century. According to Jürgen Habermas (in Foster 1983) Enlightenment thinkers expected "that the arts and sciences would promote not only the control of natural forces but also understanding of the world and of the self, moral progress, the justice of institutions and even the happiness of human beings" (p. 9). The Newtonian Pierre Laplace (1749–1827) conflated theology, philosophy, and mathematics when he posited a powerful intelligence capable of embracing "in the same formula the movements of the greatest bodies of the universe and those of the lightest atom; for it, nothing would be uncertain and the future, as the past, would be present to its eyes" (in Gleick 1987, p. 14).[2] Laplace, who supposedly told Napoleon "Give me the initial details and I will tell you the whole story of the world" (p. 3) maintained that all events follow nature's laws as necessarily as the sun's revolutions. Those were the heady days when one could believe that the whole story of anything, even the world, could be told.

Modern Revisionism

Like anthropologists and historians who repudiate the notion that civilizations evolve, Gleick (1987) argues, Thomas Kuhn destroyed "the traditional view that science progresses by the accretion of knowledge, each discovery adding to the last, and that new theories emerge when new experimental facts require them. He deflated the view of science as an orderly process of asking questions and finding their answers" (p. 36). Once the envy of the social sciences, scientific research now depends greatly on preconceptions and accidents (Kuhn 1962). Not only is scientific "progress" discontinuous and disorderly, but it seems increasingly likely to produce Chernobyl or ozone depletion or AIDS rather than to cure tuberculosis. Where both life and death had once seemed susceptible to scientific control, its promises and threats have become inextricable from each other.

Ariès (1981) suggests that the centuries-old clerical control of dying, which began to weaken during the Reformation, ended at the beginning

---

[2]Ian Stewart (1989) also quotes this statement, and calls it "awe-inspiring."

of the twentieth century. When dying was viewed as a spiritual transition to final judgment, it was deemed tame, climactic, and appropriate. Occupying a privileged place in the life cycle, such death deemphasized all that preceded the final moment. Ariès regrets modernist secularization because it downgraded death's impact and uniqueness, diluting and distributing it over the whole of life: "This life in which death was removed to a prudent distance seems less loving of things and people than the life in which death was the center" (pp. 314–315). Nostalgic for death's climactic function, Ariès mourns its reduction to "an intrinsic part of the fragile and empty existence of things" (p. 332).

The major precursors of European modernism—Marx, Darwin, Nietzsche, and Kierkegaard in the latter part of the nineteenth century; Einstein, Arnold van Gennep, and Freud after the turn of the century—radically reformulated earlier paradigms of humankind and the universe, and thus of the meaning of death. Reorientations in physics, anthropology, and psychoanalysis provided cultural and historical contexts for modernist death. As Heisenberg noted, "Changes in the foundations of modern science may perhaps be viewed as symptoms of shifts in the fundamentals of our existence which then express themselves simultaneously in many places, be it in changes in our way of life or in our usual thought forms" (in Holton 1973, p. 210). Decaying religious faith, waning belief in progress, changed perceptions of human existence after Darwin, Freud, and Einstein, and the trauma of the Great War destabilized traditional views of death's place in the cycle of mortality and immortality. Modernist fictional death, no longer tragic and consummatory, the ultimate and timely form of closure, became unpredictable, incoherent, often initiatory and pervasive. What was once solidly anchored was suddenly cast adrift: nothing, it seemed, was possible without God, and God had become impossible.

Dating modernism from England's 1916 Military Service Act, Paul Fussell (1977) argues that the world was different before the war: "The certainties were intact. . . . the Great War was perhaps the last to be conceived as taking place within a seamless, purposeful 'history' involving a coherent stream of time running from past through present to future . . . where the values appeared stable and where the meanings of abstractions seemed permanent and reliable" (p. 21). The rupture, at first misread as continuity or historically sanctioned change, was widely welcomed as ending a complacent, stultifying culture and providing opportunity to sacrifice for an ideal. But far more was at stake, and lost. Fussell argues for the uniqueness of the Great War: "Every war is ironic because every war is worse than expected. . . . But the Great War was more ironic than any before or since. It was a hideous embarrassment to the prevailing Meliorist myth which had dominated the public consciousness for a century. It reversed the Idea of Progress" (pp. 7–8). J. B. Bury (1932) examines "progress" from the early eighteenth century; Robert Nisbet (1980) shows how millions died because some people eagerly increased misery in order to impose their vision of progress.

Inaugurating what Lawrence Langer in his study of death in modern literature calls "the age of atrocity," the Great War provoked fundamental changes in Western attitudes toward death. The war that was to be over by Christmas, and was to end all wars, metastasized like cancer and made continuing mass death a central feature of Western civilization. Olivia Bland (1986) suggests that the war ended lingering Victorian sentiment about death and dying, for people were finally unable to cope "with the very thought of death. Death and its trappings, mourning and elaborate funerals were pushed under the carpet and ignored" (p. 13). Even when ritual was enacted, it was drained of meaning and authority; often it was elided as impossible or irrelevant.

World War One's casualties, Fussell (1977) maintains, included the "system of 'high' diction" (p. 22). In 1908 Conrad could write unironically,

> You cannot fail to see the power of mere words; such words as Glory, for instance, or Pity. . . . Shouted with perseverance, with ardour, with conviction, these two by their sound alone have set whole nations in motion and upheaved the dry, hard ground on which rests our whole social fabric. . . . Give me the right word and the right accent and I will move the world" (p. 6).

The linguistic transformation is enacted in Ford Madox Ford's *The Good Soldier* (1915), which is set before (but written during) the war. Ford's emasculated narrator unintentionally caricatures the lecherous Edward Ashburnham, whom he absurdly projects as his alter ego and eponymous hero: "For all good soldiers are sentimentalists—all good soldiers of that type. Their profession, for one thing, is full of the big words—'courage,' 'loyalty,' 'honor,' 'constancy'" (pp. 26–27).

Hemingway, who believed in the war as a "crusade for democracy" and anticipated that it would serve his writing, eagerly sought martial action and felt only contempt for "military politicians of the rear." As he subsequently wrote, "any experience of war is invaluable to a writer" (1952; see 1981, p. 765). He also liked the way he looked in uniform and the status it conferred: "Our uniforms are regular United States Army officers' and look like a million dollars. Privates and non-coms must salute us" (1918; see 1981, p. 6). The wound he received within a week of arriving at the front, and which remained psychically significant all his life, fulfilled a juvenile fantasy. He reveled in his medals and promotion and his sense of being newly appreciated: "It's the next best thing to getting killed and reading your own obituary" (1918, see 1981, p. 13). His good fortune at being alive "conclusively proved that I can't be killed" (1918; see 1981, p. 18); and, undeterred, he went subsequently to the Greco-Turk war, the Spanish Civil War, and World War Two.

Yet the wars and wounds that inspired Hemingway, maimed, un-manned, and destroyed many of his protagonists. The autobiographical Nick Adams returns home shell-shocked in "Big Two-Hearted River"; Jake Barnes's wound renders him impotent, an embodiment of the spiritual wasteland, and he can find no way to shore his fragments against his ruin. Lt. Henry, seeking to escape a similar fate in *A Farewell to Arms*, finds death pursuing him like an avenging fury and assailing the "separate peace" that he and Catherine seek away from the world's self-destruction. And in *For Whom the Bell Tolls*, Robert Jordan can find meaning only in fighting and dying bravely for another's hopeless cause.

Retrospectively, Hemingway characterized himself as "not . . . at all hard boiled since July 8 1918—on the night of which I discovered that that also was Vanity" (1926; see 1981, p. 240). And he came to see the war as having debased Conrad's rhetoric of bravado: "There were many words that you could not stand to hear and finally only the names of places had dignity. . . . Abstract words such as glory, honor, courage, or hallow were obscene beside the concrete names of villages, the numbers of roads, the names of rivers, the numbers of regiments and the dates" (Hemingway 1919, p. 185). In *Across the River and Into the Trees* (1950), Richard Cantwell, like Hemingway before him, revisits the scene of his wounding at the Italian front thirty years earlier. He "relieved himself in the exact place," and then completes "the monument" by digging a hole in which to bury his excrement and a 10,000 lira note, the amount that came with his medals: "It's fine now, he thought. It has merde, money, blood. . . . It's a wonderful monument. It has everything. Fertility, money, blood and iron. Sounds like a nation. Where fertility, money, blood and iron is, there is the fatherland" (pp. 18–19). In this extraordinary passage in an otherwise inferior novel, a passage that echoes Bismark's "blood and iron" and Marx's conflating of death and money, Hemingway erects the perfect memorial to war's masculinist values.

During this same war, however, in a country as yet uninvolved and that was never bombed or invaded, the "big words" were being enacted unironically. Determined to eradicate mourning, Hubert Eaton created Forest Lawn, that monument to American nostalgia for Victorian taste and belief in progress (Oring 1986), as if he inhabited a planet devoid of suffering and linguistic decay. Forest Lawn replaced vertical tombstones with tablets flush with vast grassy expanses, and thanatological statu-ary and edifices with copies of Old World art and architecture grander, better made, more permanent than the originals. Eaton's 1917 "Builder's Creed" proclaimed his intent to create a cemetery

> as unlike other cemeteries as sunshine is unlike darkness, as eternal life is unlike death. I shall try to build at Forest Lawn a great park, devoid of misshapen monuments and other customary signs of earthly death, but filled with towering trees, sweeping lawns, splashing fountains, singing birds, beautiful statuary, cheerful flowers, noble memorial architecture with interiors full of light and color, and redolent of the world's best history and romances. [Cited in Anonymous 1977]

Espousing faith in divine benevolence that was cleanly, like muscular Christianity, Eaton built his California cemetery as a monument to "love, patriotism, and beauty," and all the other virtues that the United States means to embody: "Tolerance, faith, humility, reverence, trust, truth, courage, vision, and determination—these are the virtues . . . evoked . . . throughout Forest Lawn" (Oring 1986, p. 68).

Forest Lawn, Elliott Oring (1986) writes, "is dedicated to the stirring of national as well as domestic sentiments. . . . Besides love, patriotism, and beauty . . . Forest Lawn is clearly committed . . . to the formation of what might be called 'good character'" (p. 68). Forest Lawn promulgates virtues central to the national mythos: tolerance, faith, humility, reverence, trust, truth, courage, vision, and determination. The religious message is represented by "a smiling Christ, a Christ that 'loved you and me,' what Eaton called an 'American Christ'" (p. 68). The afterlife is also American: material yet asexual, even puritanical. Glorifying a stylized body, scores of statues depict the beauty of imitation flesh: "Forest Lawn acknowledges the physical beauty of its statuary, it does not entertain the notion of its sensuality. Beautiful, yes; erotic, no" (p. 68). The most famous statue, *The Mystery of Life*, represents all the stages of human existence as somehow occurring asexually (Figure 5–1). Forest Lawn's popularity (500,000 visitors annually, Southern California's most popular tourist site prior to Disneyland's opening) and appeal as a marriage site (25,000 weddings performed there by the mid-1980s) attest to Eaton's commercial perspicacity.

Eaton's rhetoric and faith are echoed in William Faulkner's (1985) famous Nobel Prize speech (1950), in which he extols "the old verities and truths of the heart . . . the courage and honor and hope and pride and compassion and pity and sacrifice which have been the glory of [man's] past" (pp. 723–724). But Eaton and Faulkner, unlike Hemingway, were untouched by the horrors of European wars; they could, therefore, sustain a faith in progress and a rhetoric of abstract values that sounds anachronistically hollow east of the Atlantic Ocean.

FIGURE 5–1. *The Mystery of Life*, **statue by Ernesto Gazzeri. Reproduced by permission of Forest Lawn Memorial-Park Association. All rights reserved.**

The peaceful, nurtured settings of modern cemeteries (a revival of ancient Greco-Roman practice) follow Eaton's model of excluding both passion and the surrounding world. They are usually located in urban settings (largely because towns have overtaken and surrounded them), but prettified and distinct: in a curious historic reversal, the city of the dead is now protected from everyday pollution. The cemetery's death- (and therefore life-) denying message dates from the Great War, which, Michel Ragon (1983) writes,

> Brought about the creation of specifically military cemeteries, with their endless rows of identical crosses. . . . In their impeccable symmetry of identical graves they . . . suggest the discipline of the serried ranks of the army. [Before the nineteenth century,] all great battles that left a region littered with dead sowed terror all around, for, very often, plague or cholera followed. The soldiers, stripped of their uniforms, were buried on the spot in common graves, and the officers were buried in the nearest church. [pp. 110–111]

Cemeteries of the Great War simultaneously assert and subvert the individual identity and meaning of lives both raised to heroic stature and reduced to pieces of an endlessly repeating pattern. Although first employed during medieval plagues, mass graves, Fussell (1977) writes, "pertain especially to the twentieth century. There are 2500 British war cemeteries in France and Belgium." The bodies below the rows of headstones, he suggests, are often "buried in mass graves, with the headstones disposed in rows to convey the illusion that each soldier has his individual place" (Figure 5–2). What changed was perhaps less substance (below ground) than appearance (rows of crosses). These cemeteries, Fussell adds, are also peculiar sign systems that, "both pretty and bizarre, fertile with roses, [project] an almost unendurably ironic peacefulness. They memorialize not just the men buried in them, but the talents for weighty public rhetoric of Rudyard Kipling. He was called on to devise almost all the verbal formulas employed by the Imperial War Graves Commission" (pp. 6, 70). The choice of Kipling was one that Eaton would have approved.

FIGURE 5–2.   Meuse-Argonne World War I cemetery, France. Photograph by Herman Manasse. Reproduced by permission of the American Battle Monuments Commission, Washington, DC. All rights reserved.

For Evelyn Waugh, writing shortly after his experience of World War II, such rhetoric and architecture are appropriate targets of satire and ridicule. His Whispering Glades, the "great necropolis" of *The Loved One*, is based on Forest Lawn, and its self-reflexive boast echoes Eaton's credo: "This is more than a replica, it is a reconstruction. A building-again of what those old craftsmen sought to do with their rude implements of bygone ages. Time has worked its mischief on the beautiful original. Here you see it as the first builders dreamed of it long ago." Yet, Dennis Barlow notes, movie sets seem solider than Whispering Glades' buildings, which are as deceptive as World War One cemeteries. At Whispering Glades' trysting-place, which is modeled on Yeats' "Lake Isle of Innisfree," nature, like death, is transmogrified into artifact: the boatman who carries Dennis across says, "They got bee-hives," but no bees: "Once they had bees, too, but folks was always getting stung so now it's done mechanical and scientific; no sore fannies and plenty of poetry" (Waugh 1948, pp. 78, 82).

Even as World War I denied worth to individual life and death, civilian dying, increasingly the domain of medical personnel and hospitals, was becoming clinical, remote, and clandestine. Accompanying the decline in traditional faith, the loss or hollowing of ritual created social and cultural gaps as death became unnameable and unknowable. R. W. B. Lewis (1961) asserts that twentieth-century literature "began on the note of death" (p. 17)[3] but modernist fiction reflected society's refusal to countenance death's quotidian presence: deathbeds and dying were elided; death was past or future but rarely present, confronted, and mourned. When they were formally enacted, death's processes shifted from Victorian aestheticization (the death of Little Nell) to decaying material (Kafka's "A Hunger Artist"; Hemingway's "Snows of Kilimanjaro"), from what Ariès (1981) calls the "beautiful death" to the elided or the "dirty death."

For all our veneer of civilization, Freud (1919) saw Western attitudes toward death as essentially "primitive":

> There is scarcely any other matter . . . upon which our thoughts and feelings have changed so little since the very earliest times, and in which discarded forms have been so completely preserved . . . as our relation to death. Two things account for our conservatism: the strength of our original emotional reaction to death and the insufficiency of our scientific knowledge about it. [pp. 241–242]

What, Freud (1915) had asked, "is the attitude of our unconscious towards the problem of death? The answer must be: almost exactly the

---

[3]Ziolkowski (1969), who quotes this line of Lewis's, adds that "The last years of the nineteenth century also resounded with its knell" (p. 217).

same as that of primaeval man. In this respect, as in many others, the man of prehistoric times survives unchanged in our unconscious, [manifested, for example, as] the doctrine of primal guilt, of original sin" (pp. 296, 292). Proclaiming an acultural determinism, Freud (1920) saw self-destructiveness and the desire for pleasure as equally fundamental to the "vacillating rhythm" (p. 41) of life or, rather, the pleasure principle "seems actually to serve the death instincts" (p. 63). He conceptualizes the desire to move beyond the pleasure principle as "*an urge inherent in organic life to restore an earlier* [inorganic] *state of things* [because] of the *conservative* nature of living substance" (p. 36). Seeking his own key "to a universal logic of human social life," Freud formulated his theory of "death instincts," pronouncing that "*the aim of all life is death*" (p. 38).

According to both Ernest Jones, Freud's biographer, and the psychoanalyst Erich Fromm (1973), Freud derived the theory of the death instinct from obsessive self-absorption: "He thought of dying every day, after he was forty. . . . To assume that man needs to die because death is the hidden goal of his life might be considered a kind of comfort destined to alleviate his fear of death" (p. 498; Fromm credits Jones with first proposing this idea). But the proximate, larger cause of Freud's (1920) postulating the death instinct was that extraordinary manifestation of man's destructiveness, the "terrible war which has just ended" (p. 12). The optimistic vision characteristic of Europe's middle class, which Freud had shared, seemed irreconcilable with the hatred and destruction unleashed by the Great War. As the underlying mechanism of Western society's tragedy, the repression theory underlies the death instinct, for Freud saw repression as creating civilization *and* its discontents. Hence, although he valorized both civilization and repression, Freud saw self-destructive contradictions within them.

Freud evinces his own contradictions in his correspondence with Einstein, *Why War?*, written shortly before Hitler's accession to power in 1933; he reaffirmed his belief in death instincts even as he sought to resuscitate the meliorist view of history. Maintaining that organic reasons oblige us to be pacifists who "have a *constitutional* intolerance of war," he prophesies "an end to the waging of war. By what paths or by what side-tracks this will come about we cannot guess. But one thing we *can* say: whatever fosters the growth of civilization works . . . against war" (pp. 214–215). Freud's writings about war and death, which are more suggestive and problematic than definitive and conclusive, are amenable to multiple interpretations. For Fromm (1973), "Freud's reliance on a 'constitutional' intolerance to war was . . . an attempt to transcend the tragic perspective of his death instinct" (p. 516), while René Girard (1972), who links Freud to early ethnologists in seeking "to fathom the hidden meaning of primitive religions and to establish their essential unity," argues that the death wish is "a last surrender to mythological thinking, a final manifestation of that ancient belief that human violence can be attributed to some outside influence—to gods, to Fate, to some force men can hardly be expected to control. . . . It is an act of evasion, an attempt to 'pass the buck'" (pp. 145, 197). Freud's "mythological thinking" also contains a gendered quality; unlike the generative process that culminates in childbirth, the death wish expresses patriarchal thinking that climaxed in what Europeans still commonly call the Great War and that has continued to perpetrate catastrophic conflicts ever since.

In contradistinction to Freud, Fromm (1973) maintains that "aggression and destructiveness are not biologically given and spontaneously flowing impulses" (p. 37), and that Freud's elegantly simple vision contravenes historical reality. Yet Freud (1915) himself sometimes writes against both essentialism and the meliorist view of ethical progress:

> When the furious struggle of the present war has been decided, each one of the victorious fighters will return home joyfully to his wife and children, unchecked and undisturbed by thoughts of the enemies he has killed. . . . Primitive races . . . act differently in this respect, or did until they came under the influence of our civilization. . . . When [savages] return victorious from the war-path they may not set foot in their villages or touch their wives till they have atoned for the murders they committed in war by penances which are often long and tedious. . . . Behind this superstition there lies concealed a vein of ethical sensitiveness which has been lost by us civilized men. [p. 295]

Still, the "primitive" rituals Freud describes may have been for purification rather than atonement: cleansing rather than penance is required if warriors are to resume social life without becoming a threat to communal health and stability. Susceptible to multiple interpretations, the evidence may serve various historical reconstructions.

Epistemological and religious incertitude, Freud's repression theory, and extraordinary technological breakthroughs unaccompanied by moral advance—all help to explain modernism's turn from stable rituals and beliefs associated with Victorian dying. The result was cultural doublethink regarding death: denial on a personal level and orchestrated mass killing. Gil Elliot (1972) sees the vast scale of man-made death as "the central moral as well as material fact of our time"; our "century of death" is distinguished by a public commitment "to the preservation and care of life" but also to the replacement of disease and plague, which (prior to AIDS and the return of tuberculosis) seemed increasingly amenable to control, by extraordinary slaughter. The apparent paradox results from the fact "that one area of public death has been tackled and secured by the forces of reason; the other has not" (pp. 6–10). Foucault (1976) writes, "For millennia, man remained what he was for Aristotle: a living animal with the additional capacity for a political existence; modern man is an animal whose politics places his existence . . . in question" (vol. I, p. 143). Hence, Shneidman (1976) speaks of our "oxymoronic century"; great efforts are expended in saving individual lives and increasing mortality, at least for some. Yet "brutish wars, deliberate famines, planned starvations, police and government executions" (p. 2) have wiped out vast populations; the estimates range from 150 to 200 million.

Instead of opposing each other, killing and curing are complementary: each requires and sustains the other. Modern war-makers harnessed healing to serve killing so as to guarantee sufficient participants. The *Herald* of January 25, 1890 editorialized on the irony:

> The epidemic of influenza has the one advantage that it is a preserver of the public peace. War is out of the question when armies are suffering from the prostrating effects of the grippe. We can fancy an army, say, of 200,000 men receiving orders to march to attack. The attacking army would have to leave at least 150,000 men in the hospital, and the sneezing of the remaining 50,000 would warn the enemy of their approach. We may be quite sure that no European war will break out until the influenza has vanished, especially as the disease has shown a marked fondness for soldiers.[*International Herald Tribune* reprint January 25, 1990, p. 4][4]

History's worst plague for the most people dead in the shortest time was probably the pandemic that began, apparently at a United States military base, as the Great War was ending and medical science was coming into its own. In one-third the time, the 1918–19 influenza killed double or triple the estimated nine to ten million claimed by the war. Beveridge (1977) estimates that "between 15–25 million—the greatest visitation ever experienced by the human race" (p. 32)—were killed. Such estimates vary widely: Craig and Egan (1979) propose 41,435,000 as the number of World War One dead. Although influenza still lacks a cure, war-related research produced many of the century's great medical advances; "wonder" drugs, for example, were fortuitous by-products of political and military necessity. Bertrand Russell (1954) dryly commented that atomic energy, which "has already proved itself very useful in medicine . . . may in time cure nearly as many people as it will kill" (p. 208).

Whether hiding and forestalling death in hospitals or enacting it massively in wars, modern technology removed death from the home and rendered it artificial, arranged, civilization's chief product; its dehuman-

---

[4]See also Frederick Cartwright (1972).

ized subjects were distanced from what had long seemed the "natural" site and processes of living and dying. Usurping nature's role, man's efficient machinery became so pervasive as to seem a fixture of the human condition, immune from interrogation. Foucault (1975) sees that control personified by the doctor who supervises executions (as is now required by about half the states, a practice condemned by the American Medical Association as unethical), "thus juxtaposing himself as the agent of welfare, as the alleviator of pain, with the official whose task it is to end life" (p. 11). In a logical extension, many states now perform executions by injection. Soldiers assail the "enemies" of the body politic; doctors "cure" it by extirpating virulent criminals. Lisa Belkin's (1993) *First, Do No Harm*—whose title derives from the still apt physician's adage: "There are some patients whom we cannot help; there are none whom we cannot harm"—describes how hospital medical committees now decide on extraordinary life-prolonging measures. Douglas Black and colleagues (1992) examine doctors' role in torture and executions. Extreme but hardly unique were Nazi Germany's health care system and scientific community, much of whose resources were dedicated to so-called racial hygiene. (See also Robert Lifton [1986].)

No moral reformation accompanied nineteenth-century technological advances. Producing both massive wealth and the living death of grinding poverty, the Industrial Revolution had a class-based impact on urban mortality rates. Although reliable demographic evidence is scanty and deceptive (Drake 1969), Walt Rostow (1978) notes that "Infant mortality and the ravages of infectious disease remained powerful forces in the industrializing West [and even worsened for urban dwellers crowded in squalid tenements]; but improvements in food, shelter, clothing, water supply, and sanitation gradually brought down death rates" (p. 9)—an early version of trickle-down economics. M. C. Buer, William Frazer, and Bruce Haley also examine nineteenth-century mortality and health. By 1900 unchecked inventiveness, industrialization, and greed had produced healing and killing machines that gave those who were rich, white, and privileged greater control of their own lives and others' deaths than ever before. Marx, who had seen such contradictions as inherent in capitalism, would not have been surprised. Fromm (1975) writes, "Capital for him was the manifestation of the past, of labor transformed and amassed into things; labor was the manifestation of *life*, of human energy applied to nature in the process of transforming it. . . . Who (what) was to rule over what (whom)? What is dead over what is alive, or what is alive over what is dead?" Paralleling Marx's thinking with Freud's death instinct, Fromm defines the "necrophilous" person as someone for whom "only the past is experienced as quite real, not the present or the future. What has been, i.e., what is dead, rules his life: institutions, laws, property, traditions, and possessions. Briefly, *things* rule *man*; *having* rules *being*; *the dead* rule *the living*" (p. 377). What inevitably follows is war, both between nations and within them.

Modern fiction is replete with characters of uncertain mortal (as well as moral) status, "grave" voices, revenants. No longer natural and culturally acceptable, fictional death became attenuated, denied, or horrific: initiatory or evaded rather than, as it had previously been, climactic. Subverting suspense, modern novels became circular and self-reflexive, returning repeatedly and ultimately to terminal events that they rarely confront or transcend. Machado de Assis's *Epitaph of a Small Winner* (1880), *The Death of Ivan Ilyich*, *The Man Who Died*, *As I Lay Dying*, and *Finnegans Wake* all begin after the protagonist's death, an event to which they repeatedly return in search of lost meaning. Set in Gravesend, *Heart of Darkness* begins and ends with England, now, as in Roman times, "one of the dark places of the earth." After opening with a discussion of marriage as impossible, *Women in Love* depicts a trek through a Dantesque "country in an underworld . . . a ghoulish replica of the real world" (Lawrence 1920, p. 11), and it ends with Rupert Birkin mourning the death of Gerald Crich, the god of that Hadean darkness. Yet modern novels usually elide the dying process (Woolf's *To the Lighthouse*, and Forster's *Howards End* and *Passage to India*); refract it through untrustworthy memory (Marlow in *Heart of Darkness*, Stephen in *Ulysses*); base it in rediscovered materiality (*Women in Love*, *As I Lay Dying*, "Snows of Kilimanjaro"); or foreground the complementarity of eros and thanatos (Lawrence's *The Woman Who Rode Away* and *The Man Who Died*; the "Hades" chapter of *Ulysses*). Sheldon Brivic's (1980) notion of "The Dead" as "a Gothic story of walking corpses" (p. 88) fits all these texts.

In *A Streetcar Named Desire* Blanche du Bois says that "funerals are pretty compared to deaths. . . . Unless you were there at the bed when they cried out, 'Hold me!' you'd never suspect there was the struggle for breath and bleeding" (Williams 1947, pp. 21–22). Yet like other death rituals, modern funerals were often elided (as in Forster's *Howards End* and Woolf's *To the Lighthouse*), or emptied of traditional meaning, or transformed into horrific parody of communal ritual during which corpses fail to fill the coffin-shaped holes, like the one Faulkner outlines in *As I Lay Dying*, at the center of survivors' lives. Modernist texts are generally skeptical of dying and its product, the material object needing disposal. No bodies remain after the elided deaths of Forster's Mrs. Wilcox and Woolf's Mrs. Ramsay. In *Heart of Darkness* Marlow links the emptiness of Kurtz's life with his absence at his own death: "The voice was gone. What else had been there? But I am of course aware that next day the pilgrims buried *something* in a muddy hole" (Conrad 1898–99, p. 86; my emphasis). Marlow's "of course" asserts more than he knows. In *Absalom,*

Absalom! Faulkner (1936) literalizes such retrospective emptying out
when Rosa Coldfield tries to explicate her relationship with Charles Bon:

> *I never saw him. I never even saw him dead. I heard an echo, but not the
> shot; I saw a closed door but did not enter it. . . . One day he was not.
> Then he was. Then he was not. . . . For all I was allowed to know, we
> had no corpse. . . . He was absent, and he was; he returned, and he was
> not; three women put something into the earth and covered it, and he
> had never been.* [pp. 150–153]

Never fully accepted when alive, Bon in death compels no satisfactory
ritual of closure; his unlived life leaves no corpse. A gap, what Ariès (1981)
calls the "empty space that death has created in the heart of life, the love
of life, and the things and creatures of life" (p. 327), remains in such texts.
Repressed or inadequately represented in its appropriate place, death
leaks into language everywhere, displacing life, or else death and life seem
to become interchangeable as in Ambrose Bierce's "An Occurrence at
Owl Creek Bridge," Joyce's "The Dead," and many of Forster's, Woolf's,
and Lawrence's novels.[5]

World War II and the End of Modernism

Fussell's books on the world wars, *The Great War and Modern Memory*
and *Wartime*, help to contextualize and frame the modern period. Fussell
sees the wars enacting Marx's vision of history as repetition with a difference: first tragedy, then farce; or modernism and then postmodernism.
Those like Fussell who fought in World War II experienced "an unroman-
tic and demoralizing sense that it had all been gone through before" (1989,
p. 132). World War I was tragic in destroying innocence, certainty, the
sense of history as seamless and purposeful (Fussell 1975). World War
II, Fussell argues, played as deadly farce: numerous strategic blunders,
with many on both sides killed by what is now called "friendly fire";
rumors, mostly false (although the most horrific, that concerning the
slaughter of Europe's Jews, proved true); and "chickenshit" (behavior
that makes military life worse than it need be and that has nothing to do
with winning the war) (Fussell 1989). The total madness of World War II
made the "social and ethical norms" (p. 132) of the Great War seem retrospectively Victorian. European monuments to the two wars materially
enact Fussell's paradigm: set in French town squares, those for the Great
War are stone edifices occupying places of honor; those for the second,
like self-reflexive postscripts or afterthoughts, are merely plaques stuck

---

[5]See Garrett Stewart (1984). See also Ronald Schleifer's (1990) notion of "the negative
materiality of death," especially in the rhetoric of modernism.

on to the World War I structures. Because of its quick surrender in World War II, France suffered far fewer casualties than it did in World War I. Hence, it is World War I that France mainly remembers; even the War of 1870 became a postscript to it. Only in the 1990s has France candidly begun to confront its World War II role.

Trench warfare's lunacy seemed almost reasonable after the Holocaust—Germany's systematic destruction of much of its own population while it was fighting to conquer the world. Not only were German Jews unusually assimilated (and therefore likely to have supported the war effort if given the chance), but vast resources were deployed in their annihilation. So outrageous was this action and so little sense did it seem to make from even a Nazi perspective that many then and since have refused to believe it, have denied its historical status. Fussell himself is susceptible to such amnesia. *The Great War* builds on the power of shaping retrospection, both Fussell's and that of its participants. *Wartime*, however, marginalizes what, especially in hindsight, was central to World War II: concentration camps and genocide. It occludes what it should remember.

The rhetorical shift that Fussell associates with World War I seems especially germane to Holocaust writings. Discussing Raymond Federman's postmodern novel, *Take It or Leave It*, Brian McHale (1987) answers Adorno's question of how Holocaust survivors can write about the mass death they narrowly escaped: "One of Federman's solutions is *not* to write about it at all, but to let the blank spaces in the text . . . speak for him. . . . It is the gaps that convey the meaning here, in a way that the shattered words *juif, cremation, lampshade, Auschwitz, responsabilité* . . . could never have done had they been completed and integrated into some syntactical continuity."[6] In a sense, the second revolution in twentieth-century Western attitudes toward death, which began after World War II, sought to speak what had become the unsayable.

Postmodernism

A central tenet of postmodern texts is again saying the unsayable. Unlike modernism, postmodernism's rhetorical strategy is to foreground fictional seams and scaffolding, rather than hiding them, make author and character interchangeable, and freely juxtapose irreconcilable realities inhabited by the living and dead, new characters and intertextual ones, the fictive and historical—without, as was once common practice, privileging the first term in each of these pairings. Linda Hutcheon (1988) writes, "There is no dialectic in the postmodern" (p. x)—mutually exclu-

---

[6]See also Berel Lang (1988), Lawrence Langer (1975), and James Young (1988).

sive worlds and conditions exist side by side without qualifying each
other. In the writings of Carlos Fuentes, Thomas Pynchon, Günter Grass,
Robert Coover, Ishmael Reed, E. L. Doctorow, D. M. Thomas, and Salmon
Rushdie, dead, borrowed, and historical personages, no more circum-
scribed than other characters, participate in all levels of action. Postmodernist writers themselves commonly intrude into their characters'
worlds and fates. In *The Exaggerations of Peter Prince*, for example, Steve
Katz's (1968) narrator says that his character "knew he was going to die,
no doubt about it, and he tossed my way such an immense glare of hate
that if I wasn't sure of what was happening I might have turned away in
shame" (p. 257). Brian McHale (1987) comments on Prince's awareness
of his doubly unstable existence: "A character's knowledge of his own
fictionality often functions as a kind of master-trope for determinism—
cultural, historical, psychological determinism, but especially the inevitability of death" (p. 123). Postmodernist texts undermine categorical
barriers between levels of fictional realities.

Characters in such fictions need never die, or their deaths need not
be final. Such representation can trivialize death (as well as history and
fiction), as in Lawrence Durrell's *Avignon Quintet*, or reconfigure it as a
powerful refusal to release a fictional or even an historic character to
death until opportunity is afforded to confront the past. Crossing "the
ultimate ontological boundary," postmodernist fiction often enacts "the
venerable *topos* of the 'world to come'": Flann O'Brien's *The Third Police-
man*, Pynchon's *Gravity's Rainbow*, Stanley Elkin's *The Living End*, Alasdair
Gray's *Lanark* (McHale 1987, p. 65). To paraphrase *The Communist Mani-
festo*, history and death are specters haunting postmodernist fiction; the
imagined, dead, or unborn inhabit texts that reconceive their lives.
Civilization's carnage—man's assault on planet, species, and self—has
become so prevalent as to render life often impossible, and history sur-
real; fiction has had to devise strategies for keeping pace. Slavery, colo-
nial exploitation, genocide, mass slaughter and warfare, the threat of
annihilation, urban terror, and the social institutions that sustain them
not only refused to disappear after the modernist attempt to elide them,
but became increasingly foregrounded in twentieth-century life and
literature.

The Cold War's technology of killing seemed likely to climax in
nuclear cataclysm, so modernism's metaphoric apocalypse is literalized
in fictions of macrocosmic devastation like Nevil Shute's *On the Beach*
(1957), Kurt Vonnegut's *Cat's Cradle* (1963), Angela Carter's *Heroes and
Villains* (1969) and *The Passion of New Eve* (1977), and Bernard Malamud's
God's Grace (1982). Fuentes's *Terra Nostra* (1975) represents the end of
the world as a monstrous Parisian carnival. In *Dying, in Other Words* (1981)
Maggie Gee writes her own death into the text, and then her world's

nuclear destruction. Postmodernist fictions like Philip Roth's *The Ghost Writer* and *The Counterlife*, D. M. Thomas's *The White Hotel*, Graham Swift's *Waterland*, Toni Morrison's *Beloved*, and Leslie Silko's *Almanac of the Dead* meditate on history while reenacting the continuing presence of our horrific past. Such fiction, which foregrounds history as what Joyce's Stephen Dedalus calls "a nightmare from which I am trying to awake" (Joyce 1922, p. 34), seeks how *not* to despair of making sense of human senselessness. Seeking to break with inherited destructive patterns of self and society and determine new ways of beginning, it destabilizes history's ontological status by subverting categorical boundaries.

Juxtaposing the endings of Lawrence's *The Woman Who Rode Away* (1928b) and Pynchon's *Gravity's Rainbow* (1973) illustrates the modernist/postmodernist transformation. Lawrence's final moment focuses on the sacrificial woman who, understanding now "what the men were waiting for" (p. 581), remains forever poised to receive the knife that always/ never strikes. *Gravity's Rainbow*, the great postmodernist conspiracy/ apocalypse text, reveals at its end that, with the screen "a dim page spread before us, white and silent," we have "always been at the movies (haven't we?)" (p. 887). The ending interrogates all that has gone before, rewriting its ontological status, denying it without undoing it. The final image is a rocket, "a bright angel of death," which is launched within and without the novel's film. It is poised to annihilate everyone—"Now everybody"—including the film's and the book's characters, Pynchon's readers, and the Cold War world beyond. Narrative failure in modernist texts like *Heart of Darkness*, *The Good Soldier*, *Portrait of the Artist as a Young Man*, and *The Woman Who Rode Away* results from the incompatibility between the characters' fears, memories, or desires and the fictive reality that contains them; the status of the material world beyond subjectivity remains essentially unchallenged. *Gravity's Rainbow*'s inconclusive conclusion, on the other hand, spills beyond its fictional confines and threatens not only all its represented worlds, but ours as well.

Fictionalizing the breakdown of national boundaries and wartime alliances after World War II, as well as the establishment of German zones, Pynchon (1973) juxtaposes historic and imagined events, "the new Uncertainty" of personal and political identity, without privileging either: "Ghosts used to be either likenesses of the dead or wraiths of the living. But here in the Zone categories have been blurred badly . . . some still live, some have died, but many, many have forgotten which they are . . . images of the Uncertainty" (p. 353). Seeking to reconstitute Slothrop's identity, unknown forces had sent him "into the Zone to be present at his own assembly—perhaps, heavily paranoid voices have whispered, *his time's assembly*," but the plan "went wrong. He is being broken down instead, and scattered" (pp. 860–861). *Gravity's Rainbow* identifies layers

of conspiracy (international cartels, technological forces, secret societies, alien intruders) beneath the official versions of World War II that help
to explain the paranoia of Cold War history and fiction.

Thanatology

Attempts to say the unsayable were also occurring in what came to
be called thanatology. Gorer's "The Pornography of Death" (1955, reprinted in Gorer 1965, pp. 192–199) and Feifel's "Death" (1963) show how
death had become taboo, a matter of shame, guilt, abhorrence, and
secrecy. When he first sought to work with the dying, Feifel typically
encountered hostility: "Isn't it cruel, sadistic, and traumatic to discuss
death with seriously ill and terminally ill people?" (p. 9).

Similarly, Elisabeth Kübler-Ross, a young psychiatrist at Chicago's
Billings Hospital and a recent U.S. immigrant who had worked with death
camp survivors, was discovering how little she understood the cultural
mores of a country that, having been spared the ravages of the world
wars, still sustained Forest Lawn's ethic of thanatological denial. Wanting to specialize in helping the dying, Kübler-Ross determined that, in
contrast to what was expected, greater scientific knowledge about death
had produced *decreased* understanding and acceptance. Encountering
a refusal to countenance death, Kübler-Ross (1969) wrote: "The more we
are making advancements in science, the more we seem to fear and deny
the reality of death" (pp. 6–7). To recuperate for dying patients the central role that medical personnel had usurped, she tried to create seminars in which the terminally ill would teach medical interns about their
experiences. But she, like Feifel, met only stonewalling: Chicago's largest hospital, she was told, held no dying patients.

Ariès (1981) comments that "Doctors lose their composure as they
approach the floodgates through which the chaos of nature threatens
to invade the rational city of man" (p. 405). Dedicated to healing and
trained to view death as failure, modern medical personnel seemed
unable or unwilling to acknowledge the condition of their terminally ill
patients.[7] Unsurprisingly, they often provided what their patients needed
least (technological control and encouragement in denial) during the
most traumatic transition of their lives. Disregarding those most intimately concerned, they often deployed an extraordinary apparatus to
prolong not life but the mere existence of terminal patients. For Ariès
(1981), "The ancient attitude in which death is close and familiar yet

---

[7]Enid Rhodes Peschel (1982) discusses "the defenses that people, especially paramedi-
cal—or medical—people use" (p. 80).

diminished and desensitized is too different from our own view, in which it is so terrifying that we no longer dare say its name" (p. 28).

Yet in calling this attitude "The Pornography of Death," Gorer (along with others of his generation) helped to inaugurate a second major paradigm shift. Beginning in the 1950s, thanatologists like Gorer, Feifel, Weisman, Kübler-Ross, and Shneidman persisted in naming death despite the antipathy they initially aroused—not in patients but in doctors for whom, as Feifel (1963) puts it, it was "an obscenity to be avoided." The dying themselves, Feifel found, expressed relief and gratitude to be treated as human beings "with wishes, fears, and hopes, rather than as [cases] of lung cancer or myocardial infarction" (pp. 10–11). Kübler-Ross's *On Death and Dying* recorded a cultural phenomenon in which death, once considered familial, personal, and natural, had become the prisoner of medical professionals who preached and practiced denial. And because her work and writing struck a popular chord they not only defined the condition but helped to change it. Kübler-Ross's five-stage paradigm for the affective process of death and dying—denial, anger, bargaining, despair, acceptance—provided a language for speaking about dying as natural rather than alien and mysterious. Her model has been liberating for many: family and friends, medical personnel, and especially the dying, for as she and others like her surmised and then verified many patients longed to break the conspiracy of silence surrounding them, and to speak and breathe freely and openly in the time they had left.

Kübler-Ross's model quickly gained such favor that, like van Gennep's rites of passage, it is commonly extrapolated to analogous processes like mourning. In fact, doctors and therapists who had denied that patients were dying invoked the Kübler-Ross model, although, whether perversely or having missed the point, often as a template for measuring the "success or failure" of dying patients. Thus, like most revolutions, the one Kübler-Ross helped to inspire quickly produced new forms of repression. Seeking to reclaim authority, medical personnel appropriated the means that she and others had provided for shifting the central role to the dying. And the motivation is not always benign: a way of reasserting authority, doing it to show that it can be done, the hope of seeing patients through the "appropriate" stages. Further, since more than half of a lifetime's medical expenditure is commonly incurred during the last 60 days of life, doctors and hospitals have, to their enormous advantage, tended to give priority not to preventive medicine but to sustaining lives that can, at best, be briefly (and badly) extended. Such practice has recently begun to wane: rising costs, concern for patients' rights, and a new openness and acceptance are leading to negotiated decisions that include those most affected by them.

French historical materialists like Ariès abetted the transformation that coincided with this cultural reorientation. Intending to trace pre–twentieth century attitudes toward death and contrast them with contemporary views, Ariès (1981) began by locating the boundary and transition around the turn of the century, when the present seemed to begin. Surprised, however, at the extraordinary changes occurring as he started to write (around 1965), he revised his hypothesis: "The phenomenon that I believed to be contemporary had already been at least partly outmoded before my eyes" (p. xvi). Feifel, Gorer, and Kübler-Ross had already begun to have an impact.

No longer dismissed as medical failure or just theological or philosophical speculation, death was suddenly widely discussed and debated. As throughout the nineteenth century, it was again part of medical study, the subject of sociological and legal investigation: "Shown the door by society, death is coming back in through the window, and it is returning just as quickly as it disappeared" (Ariès 1981, p. 560). Concurring, Shneidman (1976) writes that the most impressive thing about death today "is how much (and in how many different ways) various aspects of death and dying are currently undergoing dramatic changes. . . . There is a new permissiveness regarding death, almost an urgency to speak and think about it" (pp. 1, 4). Suppressed and occluded early in the modernist period, death in recent years has again became cultural currency.

Thus, Ariès encountered not death's continuing repression, as he had expected, but its sudden openness and availability. Instead of writing only about the great divide between Western attitudes before and after 1900, Ariès felt constrained to consider the later transition as well: in consequence, he wrote a very different book, less ideological and more eclectic, than he had intended. Concerning Western attitudes toward death, then, modernism began with a shift to denial from the familial, climactic death that was central to Victorian life and letters; and it ended, thanks in large part to the pioneering efforts of Feifel, Gorer, and Kübler-Ross, with death's emergence from the closet and clinic into the light of academic study, media event, social phenomenon, casual conversation. For death as cultural topos has become available and susceptible to endless interpretation, has its history being written for the first time even as attitudes toward it continue to undergo rapid alteration, and, as thanatological studies, now cuts across and subverts traditional disciplinary and ontological distinctions. These two remarkable transformations in Western attitudes toward death are fundamental to our understanding of twentieth-century literature, history, and culture.

References

Anonymous (1977). *Forest Lawn Memorial-Parks and Mortuaries*. Glendale, CA: Forest Lawn Memorial-Park Association.

Ariès, P. (1981). *The Hour of Our Death*, trans. H. Weaver. New York: Knopf.

Belkin, L. (1993). *First, Do No Harm*. New York: Simon & Schuster.

Beveridge, W. I. B. (1977). *Influenza: The Last Great Plague: An Unfinished Story of Discovery*. New York: Prodist.

Black, D., et al. (1992). *Medicine Betrayed: The Participation of Doctors in Human Rights Abuses*. London: Zed.

Bland, O. (1986). *The Royal Way of Death*. London: Constable.

Brivic, S. (1980). *Joyce Between Freud and Jung*. Port Washington, NY: Kennikat.

Buer, M. C. (1926). *Health, Wealth, and Population in the Early Days of the Industrial Revolution*. London: Routledge.

Bury, J. B. (1932). *The Idea of Progress: An Inquiry into its Origin and Growth*. New York: Dover, 1955.

Cartwright, F. F. (1972). *Disease and History*. New York: NAL, 1974.

Conrad, J. (1898–99). *Heart of Darkness*. In *Great Short Works of Joseph Conrad*, pp. 211–292. New York: Harper, 1967.

——— (1908). *A Personal Record*. London: Thomas Nelson, 1912.

Craig, D., and Egan, M. (1979). *Extreme Situations: Literature and Crisis from the Great War to the Atom Bomb*. London: Macmillan.

Darnton, R. (1990). *The Kiss of Lamourette: Reflections in Cultural History*. New York: Norton.

Drake, M., ed. (1969). *Population in Industrialization*. London: Methuen.

Eliot, T. S. (1942). Burnt Norton. In Four quartets. In *Collected Poems 1909–1962*. New York: Harcourt Brace & World, 1963.

Elliot, G. (1972). *Twentieth Century Book of the Dead*. London: Allen Lane.

Faris, W. B. (1982). 1001 Words: Fiction Against Death. *Georgia Review* 36(4):811–830.

Faulkner, W. (1930). *As I Lay Dying*. New York: Vintage, 1957.

——— (1936). *Absalom, Absalom!*. New York: Modern Library, 1951.

——— (1985). *The Portable Faulkner*, ed. M. Cowley. New York: Viking, 1946.

Feifel, H. ed. (1959). *The Meaning of Death*. New York: McGraw-Hill.

Feifel, H. (1963). Death. In *Taboo Topics*, ed. N. L. Farberow, pp. 8–21. New York: Atherton.

——— (1977). *New Meanings of Death*. New York: McGraw-Hill.

Ford, F. M. (1916). *The Good Soldier*. New York: Vintage, 1955.

Foucault, M. (1975). *Discipline and Punish: The Birth of the Prison*, trans. A. Sheridan. New York: Vintage, 1979.

——— (1976). *The History of Sexuality*, 2 vols., trans. R. Hurley. New York: Vintage, 1980.

Frazer, W. M. (1950). *A History of English Public Health, 1834–1939*. London: Baillière.

Freud, S. (1915). *Thoughts for the Times on War and Death*. Standard Edition 14:273–300.

——— (1919). *The "Uncanny."* Standard Edition 17:217–252.

——— (1920–1922). *Beyond the Pleasure Principle*. Standard Edition 18:7–64.

Freud, S., and Einstein, A. (1933). *Why War?* Standard Edition 22:197–215.

Fromm, E. (1973). *The Anatomy of Human Destructiveness*. Greenwich, CT: Fawcett, 1975.

Fussell, P. (1975). *The Great War and Modern Memory*. New York: Oxford University Press, 1977.

——— (1989). *Wartime: Understanding and Behavior in the Second World War*. New York: Oxford University Press.

Girard, R. (1972). *Violence and the Sacred*, trans. P. Gregory. Baltimore: Johns Hopkins University Press, 1981.

Gleick, J. (1987). *Chaos: Making a New Science*. New York: Viking.

Gorer, G. (1965). *Death, Grief and Mourning in Contemporary Britain*. London: Cresset.

Habermas, J. (1983). Modernity—an incomplete project. In *The Anti-Aesthetic: Essays on Postmodern Culture*, ed. H. Foster, pp. 3–15. Port Townsend, WA: Bay Press.

Haley, B. (1978). *The Healthy Body and Victorian Culture*. Cambridge, MA: Harvard University Press.

Hemingway, E. (1917–1961). *Selected Letters 1917–1961*, ed. C. Baker. New York: Scribner's, 1981.

—— (1929). *A Farewell to Arms*. New York: Scribner's, 1957.

—— (1932). *Death in the Afternoon*. New York: Scribner's, 1960.

—— (1940). *For Whom the Bell Tolls*. New York: Scribner's.

—— (1950). *Across the River and Into the Trees*. New York: Scribner's, 1978.

Holton, G. (1973). *Thematic Origins of Scientific Thought: Kepler to Einstein*, rev. ed. Cambridge, MA: Harvard University Press, 1988.

Huntington, R., and Metcalf, P. (1979). *Celebrations of Death: The Anthropology of Mortuary Ritual*. Cambridge: Cambridge University Press.

Hutcheon, L. (1988). *A Poetics of Postmodernism: History, Theory, Fiction*. New York: Routledge, 1990.

Jones, E. (1953). *The Life and Work of Sigmund Freud*. New York: Basic, 1961.

Joyce, J. (1922). *Ulysses*. New York: Vintage, 1990.

Kastenbaum, R. (1975). Do We Die in Stages? In *Understanding Death and Dying: An Interdisciplinary Approach*, ed. S. G. Wilcox and M. Sutton, 3rd ed., pp. 124–132. Palo Alto, CA: Mayfield, 1985.

Katz, S. (1968). *The Exaggerations of Peter Prince*. New York: Holt, Rinehart.

Kübler-Ross, E. (1969). *On Death and Dying*. New York: Macmillan.

Kuhn, T. S. (1962). *The Structure of Scientific Revolutions*. Chicago: University of Chicago Press.

Lang, B., ed. (1988). *Writing and the Holocaust*. New York: Holmes.

Langer, L. L. (1975). *The Holocaust and the Literary Imagination*. New Haven, CT: Yale University Press.

—— (1978). *The Age of Atrocity: Death in Modern Literature*. Boston: Beacon.

Laplace, P. S. de (1796). *A Philosophical Essay on Probabilities*, trans. F. W. Truscott, and F. L. Emory. New York: Dover, 1951.

Lawrence, D. H. (1920). *Women in Love*, ed. D. Farmer. Cambridge: Cambridge University Press, 1989.

—— (1928a). *The Man Who Died*. New York: Vintage, 1953.

—— (1928b). The woman who rode away. In *The Complete Short Stories of D. H. Lawrence*, vol. 2. New York: Viking, 1966.

Lewis, R. W. B. (1961). *The Picaresque Saint; Representative Figures in Contemporary Fiction*. Philadelphia: Keystone.

Lifton, R. J. (1986). *The Nazi Doctors: Medical Killing and the Psychology of Genocide*. New York: Basic.

McHale, B. (1987). *Postmodernist Fiction*. New York: Methuen.

Morrison, T. (1987). *Beloved*. New York: Knopf.

Nisbet, R. (1980). *History of the Idea of Progress*. New York: Basic.

Oring, E. (1986). Forest Lawn and the iconography of American death. *Southwest Folklore* 6(1):62–72.

Peschel, E. R. (1982). Callousness or caring: portraits of doctors by Somerset Maugham and Richard Selzer. *Mosaic* 15(1):77–88.

Pynchon, T. (1973). *Gravity's Rainbow*. New York: Bantam, 1974.

Ragon, M. (1981). *The Space of Death: A Study of Funerary Architecture, Decoration, and Urbanism*, trans. A. Sheridan. Charlottesville, VA: University of Virginia Press, 1983.

Rostow, W. W. (1978). *The World Economy: History and Prospect*. Austin: University of Texas Press.

Russell, B. (1954). *Human Society in Ethics and Politics*. London: Allen, 1971.

Schleifer, R. (1990). *Rhetoric and Death: The Language of Modernism and Postmodern Discourse Theory*. Champaign, IL: University of Illinois Press.

Shneidman, E. S., ed. (1976). *Death: Current Perspectives*, 3rd ed. Palo Alto, CA: Mayfield, 1984.

Silko, L. M. (1991). *Almanac of the Dead*. New York: Simon & Schuster.

Stewart, G. (1984). *Death Sentences: Styles of Dying in British Fiction*. Cambridge, MA: Harvard University Press.

Stewart, I. (1989). *Does God Play Dice? The Mathematics of Chaos*. Oxford: Blackwell.

Swift, G. (1983). *Waterland*. New York: Poseidon, 1991.

Thomas, D. M. (1981). *The White Hotel*. New York: Pocket, 1982.

Van Gennep, A. (1909). *The Rites of Passage*, trans. M. B. Vizedom and G. L. Caffee. Chicago: University of Chicago Press, 1960.

Waugh, E. (1948). *The Loved One*. Boston: Little, Brown, 1977.

Williams, T. (1947). *A Streetcar Named Desire*. New York: New Directions, 1980.

Young, J. E. (1988). *Writing and Rewriting the Holocaust: Narrative and the Consequences of Interpretation*. Bloomington, IN: Indiana University Press.

Ziolkowski, T. (1969). *Dimensions of the Modern Novel: German Texts and European Contexts*. Princeton, NJ: Princeton University Press.

PART II
Caregivers

Along with greater powers to heal, modern developments in medicine have given physicians the challenge of managing increasing numbers of patients who have illnesses that can be controlled but not cured. Balfour Mount and S. Robin Cohen (Chapter 6) treat individuals whose lives have been prolonged by medicine but who must face the prospect of dying in various states of disbility. Their work led them to consider quality of life (QOL) in this context. In developing their ideas they were impressed by how differently people interpret value in their lives. Nevertheless, they were able to distill a number of elements that apply to most patients in a new instrument designed to help practitioners and researchers measure and study QOL among terminally ill patients. In Chapter 7, Laurens White discusses a dilemma that confronts all physicians who work with the terminally ill—the request for assistance in ending life. His discussion includes social, legal, and ethical considerations concerning suicide and physician-assisted death, but his approach is ultimately a personal one. He gives poignant examples that place the reader in both the patient's and physician's shoes, and he challenges us to consider the consequences of both action and inaction. Training physicians to practice in a world that includes growing numbers of incurables is a task that Sandra Bertman (Chapter 8) takes to heart. As a Professor of Medical Humanities she has made a niche for herself teaching medical students how to use their feelings in the service of better patient care. She discusses the challenge that her students face in keeping their human responses alive from the very first "patient" (a corpse) to the last, and gives examples of how she uses art and literature to assist them in this process.

6

Quality of Life in Patients with Life-Threatening Illness

BALFOUR M. MOUNT AND S. ROBIN COHEN

What factors define our quality of life (QOL) in health and in sickness? Does QOL inevitably deteriorate as death due to fatal illness approaches? Can one accurately judge the QOL of another based on clinical assessment? When cure and prolongation of life are no longer possible, we come face to face with human transience and the recognition that our interventions are now acceptable only if they enhance QOL. Enhancing or maintaining QOL becomes the only health care goal.

"Same Disease, Different Patient, Different Illness, Pain, and Suffering" (Cassell 1991, p. 48)

In caring for the very sick, one is repeatedly confronted with the human spirit and the myriad determinants of suffering, meaning, and quality of life in the arena of death. It is not unusual to encounter two patients on the same day, both in the same physical condition, for example bed bound and within a few weeks of death. One may tell you that his/her QOL is excellent and that every day is cherished, while the other finds his/her QOL terrible and wishes to die as soon as possible. The clinical vignettes that follow illustrate the rich field of inquiry we enter in asking the above questions. These patients compel one to look beyond simplistic assumptions if their needs are to be taken seriously.

The weakness of his legs and difficulty keeping his head erect when sitting dictated the use of a walker and a special chair, both of which were a profound embarrassment for Mr. A., a 72-year-old man with prostatic cancer involving his spine. While he recognized that others cope with such dependency, and tried to do so himself, he was overwhelmed by his situation and remained miserable, observing that he could never be happy again unless he could regain his strength and mobility, goals he knew to be unrealistic. His problems escalated dramatically when he fell during a weekend visit home from the rehabilitation center, could not get up, and was admitted to the hospital.

Throughout his remaining months of life he remained in the hospital and with rare exceptions was bed bound. Initially, the anguish related to his dependency and was accompanied by a deep fear of abandonment, and by a long-standing estrangement from his siblings. He felt unliked and misunderstood by them.

To the relief of all concerned, the subsequent months of dependency became an unexpected time of transition for Mr. A. As the weeks passed, the siblings, who lived out of town, telephoned him frequently, wished to visit (but were told by Mr. A. to wait), and expressed their love and support. Years of strain and hurt were gradually washed away. At the same time, Mr. A. experienced a deepening relationship with his daughter, in whom he recognized for the first time independence and the capacity to care for her mother. He expressed great pride in the person she had become. One day Mr. A. commented that this was one of the happiest times of his life. And he smiled in satisfaction as he reflected on how far he had come in a short time.

While his physical condition had worsened, Mr. A. felt a great sense of pride and accomplishment at having successfully achieved a new plateau in relating to those he cared most about. Adversity called forth resources he had not known. And these, in turn, enabled a new perspective.

Other examples shed further light on the determinants of quality of life and its relationship to suffering. We have previously reported the cases that follow (Cohen and Mount 1992). They are repeated here because the persons involved, among our most memorable teachers, have been pivotal in shaping our understanding of the relationship between suffering, meaning, and quality of life in advanced illness.

Ms. M., a 30-year-old woman was admitted for investigation of point pain in her left groin of several months' duration. She presented a distinct contrast to her three geriatric roommates. Each morning at 7 A.M. she would make her bed, then sit perched on the pillows clad only in a transparent nightie. To the staff her behavior seemed erratic. She appeared anguished and agitated. Her affect was flat. All tests were negative. The housestaff labeled her: "Newly divorced, frustrated, and acting out." The psychiatrists were consulted. They sifted through vast piles of broken dreams and traced the blind alleys of her life. They paused to note past losses laid to rest in unmarked graves. They nodded wisely; so did the residents and interns. On the day of her planned discharge, she asked her doctors to do a pelvic examination. What, had no one done a pelvic examination? Embarrassment turned to anxiety, then guilt, with the diagnosis of locally advanced carcinoma of the cervix. Her young doctors smarted from the painful lesson learned and welcomed her transfer to the gynecology ward. Then one day they met her in the hall, wheelchair bound for radiation therapy. It was her face that stood out above all else. It was radiant. Relaxed. At peace. All anguish and distress dissolved.

Paradox! Ms. M.'s diagnosis had escalated from neurosis to mortal illness, yet her apparent QOL had improved. The explanation appeared to lie in the validation of her complaints, in the lessening, if only transiently, of uncertainty, and in the shift in perception—her own as well as that of those around her—from object to person, from irritant to focus of concern. With her personhood acknowledged, her suffering was gone.

Mrs. H., a widow, born in Eastern Europe and now in her seventies, was admitted to a palliative care ward with uncontrolled bone pain in the presence of metastatic breast cancer. Assessment suggested that the pain should have been easy to control but all efforts had failed. A daughter in her late thirties was her closest relative. Bowstring tension hummed between them. A conversation with her doctor shed light on the texture of the mother's life. "When were you last well?" "Do you mean physically?" "An interesting answer. No, I mean in yourself." "Doctor, I've never been well a day in my life." "Really! Well, if we are body, mind and spirit, where do you think the problem has been?" "I've been sick in mind and spirit every day of my life." Her "total pain" (Saunders 1967) and associated poor QOL persisted until death.

A lifetime of hurt, broken relationships, and a closing off to self and others had been characterized by unhappiness, and in her final illness significant insight into her own condition did not enable her to transcend well-established coping patterns. The experience of low QOL was assured to the end, perhaps more as a consequence of her well-established life script than as a by-product of the cancer that ended her suffering.

Mr. D. was 30 years old when he presented with a widely disseminated germinal testicular tumor. Radical surgery and chemotherapy initially resulted in his serum tumor markers reverting to negative and the hope of cure, but within months his disease progressed with ensuing profound weight loss and wasting. He died slowly over a 12-month period. Mr. D. had always stood out from his peers. He had always been a winner. Strong. Outgoing. Gracious. A world-class athlete, he was a member of the national ski team. He was successful in business and engaged to be married. A champion from a family of competitive champions, he was now melting before the raging forces of the embryonal cell. Then, just days before he died, he married his fiancee and said goodbye to those he loved, observing, "This last year has been the best year of my life."

Mr. D.'s assessment of his QOL during those months of striking physical deterioration is particularly noteworthy when considered in the light of his record of repeated physical and intellectual triumphs throughout life. The *best* year? Of *that* life? Mr. D. confided that the source of this sense of quality time was a new awareness of the spiritual dimension of human existence. Physical agony had been transcended through a journey inward that came to be characterized by grace and a sense of growth that he had not known.

> Ted Rosenthal died with leukemia in his early thirties, leaving a wife and two small children. A poet "whose only ambition was to be without any," Rosenthal (1973) recorded his feelings and experiences during chemotherapy and in facing his own mortality. "It isn't until you discover that you're going to die that you realize that whatever you have, you've already got" (p. 54). "It's that sense of already being dead that makes you feel that you don't have to be just you, or an extension of what's in your hip pocket, but the infinite potential of the whole race. Man; first man; last man; all man" (p. 55). "It cut very deeply into me, but in cutting into me, it opened me up at the same time" (p. 56). In commenting on his illness, he stated, "I'm changed; I'll always be changed. I'll always be happier for what I've gone through" (p. 69).

For Rosenthal, confrontation with death led to an experience of clarification of his understanding of human existence; of living *in* the moment rather than *for* the moment. His assertion, "I'll always be *happier* for what I've gone through" parallels the statement of Mr. D. above, and challenges the assumption that QOL invariably declines as death approaches.

What is QOL?

QOL may be defined as subjective well-being. Calman (1984) has suggested that QOL reflects the difference, the gap, between the hopes and expectations of a person and their present experience. Maslow (1954) noted that human expectations usually lie within the realm of what the individual perceives to be possible. This enables people who have difficult life circumstances (terminal illness being an extreme example) to maintain a reasonable QOL. Variables that might have been considered essential to a good QOL when in good health are now considered irrelevant. The focus lies instead on domains where achievement of a desirable state is possible. Kreitler and colleagues (1993) showed that the life satisfaction of people with head and neck cancer did not differ from that of orthopedic patients or people in good physical health. However, the people with cancer had more domains that contributed to life satisfaction, and health-related domains were less emphasized in order to maintain an acceptable level of life satisfaction. QOL is further clarified by Frankl's (1963) observation that it is tied to perception of meaning. He posited that the quest for meaning is central to the human condition and noted that we are brought in touch with a sense of meaning when we reflect on that which we have created, loved, believed in, or left as a legacy.

Why Measure QOL?

Canadian ethicist David Roy (1992) has commented, "QOL studies and measurements serve to prevent a devastating separation of a patient's body from a patient's biography during delivery of care" (p. 4). Concern for QOL acknowledges that the health care mandate must be broader than simply concern for the biology of disease. It lifts the field of reference to a larger horizon, the alleviation of suffering. People rather than diseases are treated.

Do we really need a formal measure of QOL? It appears so. Rathbone and colleagues (1994) found that when hospice inpatients were asked to identify factors impairing their QOL, 58 percent of the patients identified problems that had not been recognized by the nursing and medical staff caring for them. More than half of the unidentified problems were psychosocial in nature. Clearly the dimensions and source of patient distress frequently pass unnoticed even in settings particularly attuned to these issues. As Bruera (personal communication) has said, "To treat a diabetic without measuring the blood sugar or a person who is hypertensive without measuring the blood pressure would be deemed unethical. Can we care for the dying, confident that our ministrations are in their best interest, without ever measuring their impact?"

Qualitative studies suggest that existential well-being and positive experiences are crucial to a good QOL, which, as our case examples demonstrate, may be experienced even in the presence of advanced illness (Cohen and Mount 1992, Coward 1994, Ferrell et al. 1992a, Kagawa-

Singer 1993). Unfortunately, many of the QOL determinants elucidated by qualitative research are ignored by the quantitative instruments now in use, which tend to define QOL as the absence of health-related problems (Aaronson et al. 1993, Schag et al. 1983, Schipper et al. 1994, Selby et al. 1984).

QOL Instrument Deficiencies

General Determinants Versus Specific Contributors

Established QOL instruments have one or more of four major deficiencies. First, many attempt to measure quality of life by assessing a list of specific contributors. The impracticality of this approach is clearly seen in the experience of the oncologist (MacDonald, personal communication) who was informed by two successive patients that they felt much better than during their previous visit. When asked why, the first responded that it was because his golf handicap had returned to pre-illness levels. The second noted that his sexual prowess had returned to normal. It would be impossible to list the rich array of factors that add quality to the human experience!

There are, however, *general* determinants that are relevant to all persons. These include physical well-being, psychological well-being, and existential well-being (transcending self as a means of feeling connected to the world and an important part of it). These factors represent the needs documented by Maslow (1954) to feel physically secure, safe, and have a sense of belonging in the world; to feel both love and loved; to have self-esteem and a sense of fulfillment. To the degree that an individual feels that these needs have been satisfied, s/he will experience a good QOL.

A truly generic instrument that evaluates subjective well-being in an all-encompassing, valid way is needed. It may also be desirable, in a variety of clinical situations, to know more about a subset of QOL determinants related specifically to the disease or its treatment. However, it is important to note that while instruments that measure these disease- and treatment-specific variables may provide information about the patient's status, because they do not assess all important domains they are informing about *contributors to* QOL rather than QOL itself. Generic measures of QOL and disease- and treatment-specific measures may be used together to provide a true measure of QOL and sensitivity to important changes in specific contributors.

Two of the most widely used QOL tools, the European Organization for Research and Treatment of Cancer QOL Questionnaire (EORTC QLQ) (Aaronson et al. 1993) and Functional Assessment of Cancer Therapy

(FACT) (Cella et al. 1993), have taken this generic plus specific approach by developing a "core" questionnaire that is intended to be relevant to all types of cancer, and a set of add-on questions (modules) that measure contributors to QOL specific to the type of cancer or treatment being assessed. However, the "core" questionnaires have too many specific items to be relevant to all individuals with cancer, and are therefore not truly generic.

Domains Ignored or Underemphasized

A second problem with existing instruments is that they tend to ignore the existential domain in spite of its demonstrated significance in life-threatening illness (Belcher et al. 1989, Coward 1994, Ferrell et al. 1992a,b, Fryback 1993, Hall 1990, McCorkle and Quint-Benoliel 1983, O'Connor et al. 1990, Reed 1987) (for review see Cohen and Mount 1992, Donovan et al. 1989). The existential domain includes perception of purpose, meaning in life, and the capacity for personal growth and transcendence. Such considerations may be directly linked to QOL (Frankl 1963). Many who are seriously ill report that existential issues have increased in importance since they became ill (Belcher et al. 1989, Fryback 1993). Bone marrow transplant survivors assign existential well-being a major role when listing determinants of their QOL (Ferrell et al. 1992a). In another study, assessing current concerns following the diagnosis of lung cancer, existential concerns were more prevalent than any others (McCorkle and Quint-Benoliel 1983).

Despite this evidence, quantitative QOL measures have continued to focus on physical symptoms, performance status, psychological status, and social role functioning while ignoring the existential domain (Aaronson et al. 1993, Cella 1993, Schag et al. 1983, Schipper 1990, Spitzer et al. 1981). For example, in developing the FACT, Cella and colleagues (1993) asked people with cancer to list the major determinants of their quality of life. Existential issues (hope, spirituality) were among those listed, but were excluded by the researchers from the final version of the FACT due to inconsistency with responses in other domains. We have recently demonstrated that the existential domain is at least as important as physical symptoms, psychological distress, and support in predicting QOL throughout the disease trajectory in cancer patients and in the presence of advanced HIV disease (Cohen et al. 1996a,b).

In discussing the use of QOL instruments in the medical setting, some investigators argue that while existential issues are important to subjective well-being, we cannot expect to judge the health care system by its influence on these areas. They suggest that "health-related QOL" (HR-QOL) should be assessed rather than QOL per se (Aaronson 1990, Guyatt et al. 1993, Schipper 1990). This compromise, we suggest, reflects pre-occupation with the disease rather than the person and arises because the existential domain has been erroneously perceived as being either distal to the goals of medicine (Aaronson 1990) or too difficult to measure (Schipper 1990). People with advanced cancer, however, define *health* as a sense of personal integrity and wholeness, rather than normal physical, emotional, and social functioning (Kagawa-Singer 1993). Cassell (1982, 1991) explains the role of the existential domain in the relief of suffering:

> Our intactness as persons, our coherence and integrity, come not from intactness of the body but from the wholeness of the web of relationships with self and others. [Cassell 1991, p. 40]
>
> Suffering occurs when an impending destruction of the person is perceived; it continues until the threat of disintegration has passed or until the integrity of the person can be restored in some other manner. . . . The human body may lack the capacity to gain a new part but the person has it. . . . Recovery from suffering often involves help, as though people who have lost parts of themselves can be sustained by the personhood of others until their own recovers. This is one of the latent functions of physicians: to lend strength. . . . Meaning and transcendence offer two additional ways by which the suffering associated with destruction of a part of personhood is ameliorated. [Cassell 1982, pp. 640, 644]

The neglect of existential issues seen in QOL instrument design is frequently accompanied by an underemphasis of the psychosocial domain. Psychosocial issues are generally recognized as important to QOL (Aaronson 1990, Cella 1994a, Schipper 1990), yet are often given token consideration in its assessment. For example, the widely used EORTC QLQ-C30 (Aaronson et al. 1993) contains thirty items distributed as follows: twenty items on physical condition, two on mental status, four psychological, two social, one financial, and one global quality of life.

Some investigators have assumed that QOL declines with disease progression. Indeed they claim to demonstrate construct validity of their instrument because those with more advanced disease have lower QOL scores than those at earlier phases of the disease trajectory (Schipper et al. 1984, Spitzer et al. 1981). The assumption that *physical status* declines as the disease progresses is often reasonable, but the assumption that QOL is lower for people with advanced disease ignores the important contribution of the psychosocial and existential domains.

Similarly, the psychosocial domain has generally been ignored when testing the *responsiveness* of QOL instruments. Responsiveness has usually been tested against changes in physical status, rather than changes in global QOL (Aaronson et al. 1993, Cella et al. 1993).

Physical Domain Overemphasized

A third concern is that while assessment of physical status seems a reasonable component of QOL measurement, inclusion of long lists of symptoms, as seen in many instruments, adds to the length of the instrument and creates noise in the data. That is to say, the impact of the few symptoms that greatly affect the individual is lost among the numerous questions concerning irrelevant symptoms. The identification of relevant physical items is also a problem, if the investigator decides to list specific QOL modifiers. Cella and colleagues (1993) asked subjects with cancer to select important QOL factors from a large predetermined pool of items. On reviewing the results, the investigators commented: "It was noted that the retained items were 'lacking' in two areas (physical and sexual)" (quotes are ours, p. 572). The investigators proceeded to override the subjects' judgment and added items for these two areas. Studies we have recently completed with cancer patients suggest that while general physical well-being is an important predictor of quality of life, individual physical symptoms are unimportant (Cohen et al. 1996).

Neglect of Positive Contributors to QOL

A fourth concern is that most established instruments imply that a good QOL is determined by an absence of problems, in that they exclusively assess the impact of only negative experiences such as unpleasant symptoms and limitation in physical resources. Although there are exceptions (Cella et al. 1993, Ferrell et al. 1989), positive contributions to QOL are generally not measured (Aaronson et al. 1993, Schag et al. 1983, Schipper et al. 1984, Selby et al. 1984, Spitzer et al. 1981). Daily experience and the above clinical vignettes support the observation of Frankl (1963) suggesting that QOL is determined by the individual's perception of purpose and meaning as a result of the balance between positive and negative experiences. The absence of health problems will not result in a high QOL without positive contributions in other domains. On the other hand, as already noted, even severe illness may be associated with good QOL due to positive contributors. For example, while bone marrow transplantation is one of the most physically and emotionally challenging treatments for cancer patients, when survivors were asked how the transplant experience had influenced their QOL, four of the nine themes reported involved positive effects. These were: a second chance; an opportunity to improve QOL; enhanced spirituality (inner strength, convictions, goals, faith and trust in God, indebtedness to God); and increased appreciation of life (Ferrell et al. 1992a).

A Further Problem: Weighting the Significance of QOL Determinants

A further issue must be considered as we review the reliability and validity of current QOL instruments. The relative importance of each determinant of QOL varies tremendously from individual to individual, and over time in the same subject. Gill and Feinstein (1994) suggest that a true measure of QOL must take into account the subject's assessment of the relative importance of each determinant to their current sense of well-being. This issue is addressed in QOL instruments such as the Schedule for the Evaluation of Individual Quality of Life (SEIQoL) (McGee et al. 1991), Ferrans and Powers' Quality of Life Index (Ferrans and Powers 1985), FACT (Cella et al. 1993), and Hospice Quality of Life Index (McMillan and Mahon 1994). These instruments obtain direct ratings from each subject about the importance of each item to their QOL. However, this tends to make the measure too lengthy to be practical for people with advanced disease. FACT (Cella et al. 1993) solves this problem by measuring the importance of each domain rather than each item. At the present time the FACT items used in rating relative importance are considered experimental and are not taken into account in scoring (Cella 1994b). The Hospice Quality of Life Index (McMillan and Mahon 1994) weighs patient ratings of satisfaction by patient ratings of importance, but the method of calculation described would have the counterintuitive result of a higher (better) score for items that the patient indicates are important but where the patient is dissatisfied than for unimportant items where satisfaction is low. Streiner and Norman (1995) warn against multiplying item scores by importance ratings. They demonstrate some of the unexpected results of such multiplicative scores (p. 89).

The challenge involved in developing a method of effectively "weighting" the significance of QOL contributors remains. Indeed, the complexity, the subtleness of interrelationship and sheer number of contributors may render it impossible for a reliable measure to be devised. Two final observations: if the domains measured are selected based on areas of known importance to QOL for the population being studied, it *may* not be necessary to incorporate weighting of scores based on importance when measuring the QOL of groups. If item selection has been appropriate, the weighting of variables based on their relative importance may only be useful when the QOL of an individual is of interest, and unnecessary when measuring the differences between the QOL of groups or the changes in group QOL over time (Guyatt and Cook 1994). The weighting of scores assigned to variables contributing to QOL requires further study.

Toward a Solution

We have developed The McGill Quality of Life Questionnaire (MQOL) to measure QOL in people with life-threatening illness. MQOL content was derived from patient interviews, a review of the literature, and existing instruments, while attempting to correct the deficiencies described above. No attempt has been made thus far to weight individual items or domains based on importance to the subject.

Preliminary testing was carried out in patients cared for by a palliative care service in a tertiary care teaching hospital (Cohen et al., 1995). Practical issues considered in designing MQOL included ability to be administered verbally, the need for a self-report instrument, relevance of all questions to all subjects in relevant populations, the need for brevity and clarity, simplicity of the scoring system, and ease of interpretation of results.

MQOL measures general determinants of QOL rather than specific contributors to QOL and is designed to have subscales representing four domains: physical, psychological, existential, and support. It is intended to indicate the areas in which the respondent is doing well or poorly but is *not* designed to provide information about the specific factors contributing to that state.

Are we ignoring the holistic nature of quality of life by dividing it into domains? We believe not, if we conduct our investigations as though we are studying parts of a whole rather than discrete entities. In his studies of personality, Maslow (1954) referred to these two approaches as holistic-analytic and reductive-analytic respectively. "One essential characteristic of holistic analysis of the personality in actual practice is that there be a preliminary study or understanding of the total organism, and that we then proceed to study the role that our part of the whole plays in the organization and dynamics of the total organism" (p. 24).

QOL is subjective and therefore is best measured through self-report: "Unlike beauty, which rests in the eye of the beholder, QOL is inherently an attribute of the patient (or "beholdee")" (Gill and Feinstein 1994, p. 624). In the absence of an accepted "gold standard" or an objective way of grouping subjects according to QOL, we have used the person's QOL rating on a single-item scale (SIS) we designed, which is intended to reflect overall QOL, as the best available measure of what the person means by QOL (Figure 6–1) (Cohen et al. 1995, 1996a,b, in press).

In its present format MQOL comprises sixteen items concerning support and physical, psychological, and existential well-being (text of items in Figure 6–1). MQOL was tested for acceptability, validity, and internal consistency reliability in three populations: palliative care (n = 150) (submitted); people with cancer attending an outpatient oncology clinic

FIGURE 6–1. McGill Quality of Life Questionnaire

<u>SIS</u>

Considering all parts of my life—physical, emotional, social, spiritual, and financial—*over the past two (2) days*, the quality of my life has been:

very bad 0 1 2 3 4 5 6 7 8 9 10 excellent

MQOL (Abbreviated questions with end anchors)

The response format for all questions is a 0 to 10 scale, as for SIS above. All questions begin with "Over the past two (2) days."

1. One troublesome symptom has been..............no problem (0)/ tremendous problem (10)

2. Another troublesome symptom has been.......no problem (0)/ tremendous problem (10)

3. A third troublesome symptom has been.........no problem (0)/ tremendous problem (10)

4. I have felt.. physically terrible (0)/ physically well (10)

5. I have been depressed...................................... not at all (0)/ extremely (10)

6. I have been nervous or worried...................... not at all (0)/ extremely (10)

7. How much of the time did you feel sad?......... never (0)/ always (10)[a]

8. When I thought of the future, I was.................not afraid (0)/ constantly terrified (10)[a]

9. My life has been...utterly meaningless and without purpose (0)/ very purposeful and meaningful (10)[b]

10. When I thought about my whole life, I felt that in achieving life goals I have................. made no progress whatsoever (0)/ progressed to complete fulfillment (10)[b]

11. When I thought about my life, I felt that my life to this point has been........................... completely worthless (0)/ very worthwhile (10)[b]

12. I felt that I have...no control over my life (0)/ complete control over my life (10)[b]

13. I felt good about myself as a person...............completely disagree (0)/ completely agree (10)[c]

14. To me, the past two days were.........................a burden (0)/ a gift (10)[c]

15. The world has been..an impersonal unfeeling place (0)/ caring and responsive to my needs (10)[d]

16. I have felt supported..not at all (0)/ completely (10)

a. Based on Functional Living Index: Cancer (Schipper et al. 1984).

b. Based on Purpose in Life Questionnaire (Crumbaugh and Maholick 1968).

c. Based on Missoula-Vitas Quality of Life Index: Advanced Illness (Byock et al. 1994).

d. I. Byock, personal communication.

(n = 247) (Cohen et al. 1996a,b); and people with HIV/AIDS attending an outpatient clinic (n = 107) (Cohen et al. in press). MQOL was compared to both SIS and the self-administered version of the Spitzer Quality of Life Index (QLI) (Spitzer et al. 1981), a QOL instrument with well-established psychometric properties, in the oncology outpatient clinic study and in the palliative care study. MQOL Total score correlated more strongly with SIS (oncology rho = .73; palliative care rho = .48) than did the QLI Total score (oncology rho = .60; palliative care rho = .37), suggesting that MQOL is at least as valid as the QLI in measuring QOL. Principal components analysis from each of the three studies shows that MQOL is comprised of five submeasures. These are a single item measuring Physical Well-Being and four subscales measuring Psychological Symptoms, Existential Well-Being, and Support.

In the oncology clinic and palliative care studies, MQOL Physical Well-Being, Existential, and Psychological subscales and QLI Health and Outlook items correlate more highly with SIS than do the subscales of these instruments that reflect the major focus of HR-QOL instruments, that is, functional capacity and physical symptoms. This supports our hypothesis that the existential domain is important to the patients' concept of quality of life.

Scores on MQOL Physical Symptoms (ANOVA, $F_{1.217}$ = 9.755, p = .002) and Physical Well-Being (ANOVA, $F_{1.225}$ = 9.080, p = .0029) subscales are significantly worse for people with local or metastatic disease compared with subjects with no evidence of disease following cancer treatment. Psychological, Existential, and Support subscale scores are stable throughout the disease trajectory.

In the HIV/AIDS study, respondents with more advanced disease (indicated by lower CD4 cell counts) had significantly more problems caused by physical symptoms (ANOVA, $F_{2.85}$ = 4.163, p = .0188), but the other four MQOL submeasure scores were unrelated to CD4 cell count. These results illustrate the usefulness of obtaining separate scores for each quality of life domain, since the different domains are related but do not always vary together.

MQOL shows promise as a generic measure of QOL. We believe that in several ways it is a better measure than existing instruments, but MQOL needs to be improved. Multiple regression of MQOL subscales on the SIS showed that much of the variance in the SIS remains unexplained by MQOL. We continue to conduct studies to improve MQOL.

Conclusion

In attempting to provide optimal care for the dying, the stated aim is to improve QOL. We must continually monitor whether or not we are achieving this goal. It remains a great challenge to develop appropriate tools to accurately and reliably measure this subjective construct. Current tools do not yet meet this standard. Those who advocate holistic care of the terminally ill must participate in this endeavor to ensure that the instruments developed remain true to the holistic nature of QOL.

Feifel (1995) said it well. "Technology and competence have to be infused with compassion and benevolence. . . . life is not just a matter of length but of depth and quality as well" (p. 25).

References

Aaronson, N. K. (1990). Quality of life research in cancer clinical trials: a need for common rules and language. *Oncology* 4:59–66.

Aaronson, N. K., Ahmedzai, S., Bergman, B., et al. (1993). The European Organization for Research and Treatment of Cancer QLQ-C30: a quality of life instrument for use in international clinical trials in oncology. *Journal of the National Cancer Institute* 85:365–376.

Belcher, A. E., Dettmore, D., and Holzemer, S. P. (1989). Spirituality and sense of well-being in persons with AIDS. *Holistic Nursing Practice* 3:16–25.

Byock, I., Kinzbrunner, B., and Pratt, M. (1994). Assessing quality of life in the terminally ill: a developmental approach, at the l0th International Congress on Care of the Terminally Ill, Montreal (abstract). *Journal of Palliative Care* 10:127.

Calman, K. C. (1984). Quality of life in cancer patients: an hypothesis. *Journal of Medical Ethics* 10:124–127.

Cassell, E. J. (1982). The nature of suffering and the goals of medicine. *New England Journal of Medicine* 306:639–645.

——— (1991). *The Nature of Suffering and the Goals of Medicine.* New York: Oxford University Press.

Cella, D. F. (1994a). Quality of life: concepts and definition. *Journal of Pain and Symptom Management* 9:186–192.

——— (1994b). *F.A.C.T. Manual*, September. Chicago: Rush-Presbyterian-St. Luke's Medical Center.

Cella, D. F., Tulsky, D. S., Gray, G., et al. (1993). The Functional Assessment of Cancer Therapy Scale: development and validation of a general measure. *Journal of Clinical Oncology* 11:570–579.

Cohen, S. R., Hassan, S. A., Lapointe, B. J., and Mount, B. M. (1996a). Quality of life in HIV disease as measured by the McGill Quality of Life Questionnaire. *AIDS* 10:1421–1427.

Cohen, S. R., and Mount, B. M. (1992). Quality of life assessment in terminal illness: defining and measuring subjective well-being in the dying. *Journal of Palliative Care* 8:40–45.

Cohen, S. R., Mount, B. M., Bruera, E., et al. (in press). Validity of the McGill Quality of Life Questionnaire, in the palliative care setting. A multi-center Canadian study demonstrating the importance of the existential domain. *Palliative Medicine.*

Cohen, S. R., Mount, B. M., Strobel, M. G., and Bui, F. (1995). The McGill Quality of Life Questionnaire: a measure of quality of life appropriate for people with advanced disease. A preliminary study of validity and acceptability. *Palliative Medicine* 9:207–219.

Cohen, S. R., Mount, B. M., Tomas, J., and Mount, L. (1996b). Existential well-being is an important determinant of quality of life. *Cancer* 77:576–586.

Coward, D. D. (1994). Meaning and purpose in the lives of persons with AIDS. *Public Health Nursing* 11:331–336.

Crumbaugh, J. C., and Maholick, L. T. (1968). An experimental study in existentialism; the psychometric approach to Frankl's noogenic neurosis. *Journal of Clinical Psychology* 20:200–207.

Donovan, K., Sanson-Fisher, R. W., and Redman, S. (1989). Measuring quality of life in cancer patients. *Journal of Clinical Oncology* 7:959–968.

Feifel, H. (1995). Psychology and death: meaningful rediscovery. In *Readings in Death and Dying: The Path Ahead*, ed. L. A. DeSpelder and A. L. Strickland, pp. 19–28. Mountain View, CA: Mayfield.

Ferrans, C. E., and Powers, M. J. (1985). Quality of Life Index: development and psychometric properties. *Advances in Nursing Science* 8:15–24.

Ferrell, B., Grant, M., Schmidt, G. M., et al. (1992a). The meaning of quality of life for bone marrow transplant survivors. Part 1. The impact of bone marrow transplant on quality of life. *Cancer Nursing* 15:153–160.

———— (1992b). The meaning of quality of life for bone marrow transplant survivors. Part 2. Improving quality of life for bone marrow transplant survivors. *Cancer Nursing* 15:247–253.

Ferrell, B., Wisdom, C., and Wenzl, C. (1989). Quality of life as an outcome variable in the management of cancer pain. *Cancer* 63:2321–2327.

Frankl, V. E. (1963). *Man's Search for Meaning*. New York: Pocket Books.

Fryback, P. B. (1993). Health for people with a terminal diagnosis. *Nursing Science Quarterly* 6:147–159.

Gill, T. M., and Feinstein, A. R. (1994). A critical appraisal of the quality of quality-of-life measurements. *JAMA* 272:619–631.

Guyatt, G. H., and Cook, D. J. C. (1994). Health status, quality of life, and the individual. *JAMA* 272:630–631.

Guyatt, G. H., Feeny, D. H., and Patrick, D. L. (1993). Measuring health-related quality of life. *Basic Science Review* 118:622–629.

Hall, B. A. (1990). The struggle of the diagnosed terminally ill person to maintain hope. *Nursing Science Quarterly* 3:177–184.

Kagawa-Singer, M. (1993). Redefining health: living with cancer. *Social Science in Medicine* 37:295–304.

Kreitler, S., Chaitchik, S., Rapoport, Y., et al. (1993). Life satisfaction and health in cancer patients, orthopedic patients and healthy individuals. *Social Science in Medicine* 36:547–556.

Maslow, A. H. (1954). *Motivation and Personality*. New York: Harper and Row.

McCorkle, R., and Quint-Benoliel, J. (1983). Symptom distress current concerns and mood disturbance after diagnosis of life-threatening disease. *Social Science in Medicine* 17:431–438.

McGee, H. M., O'Boyle, C. A., Hickey, A., O'Malley, K., and Joyce, C. R. B (1991). Assessing the quality of life of the individual: the SEIQoL with a healthy and a gastroenterology unit population. *Psychological Medicine* 21:749–759.

McMillan, S. C., and Mahon, M. (1994). Measuring quality of life in hospice patients using a newly developed Hospice Quality of Life Index. *Quality of Life Research* 3:437–447.

O'Connor, A. P., Wicker, C. A., and Germino, B. B. (1990). Understanding the cancer patient's search for meaning. *Cancer Nursing* 13:167–175.

Rathbone, G. V., Horsley, S., and Goacher, J. (1994). A self-evaluated assessment suitable for seriously ill hospice patients. *Palliative Medicine* 8:29–34.

Reed, P. G. (1987). Spirituality and well-being in terminally ill hospitalized adults. *Research in Nursing and Health* 10:335–344.

Rosenthal, T. (1973). *How Could I Not Be Among You?* New York: Avon.

Roy, D. J. (1992). Measurement in the service of compassion. *Journal of Palliative Care* 8:3–4.

Saunders, C. (1967). *The Management of Terminal Illness*. London: Hospital Medicine.

Schag, C. C., Heinrich, R. L., and Ganz, P. A. (1983). Cancer Inventory of Problem Situations: an instrument for assessing cancer patients' rehabilitation needs. *Journal of Psychosocial Oncology* 1:11–24.

Schipper, H. (1990). Guidelines and caveats for quality of life measurement in clinical practice and research. *Oncology* 4:51–57.

Schipper, H., Clinch, J., McMurray, A., and Levitt, M. (1984). Measuring the quality of life of cancer patients: the Functional Living Index–Cancer: development and validation. *Journal of Clinical Oncology* 2:472–483.

Selby, P. J., Chapman, J.-A. W., Etazadi-Amoli, J., et al. (1984). The development of a method for assessing quality of life of cancer patients. *British Journal of Cancer* 50:13–22.

Spitzer, W. O., Dobson, A. J., Hall, J., et al. (1981). Measuring the quality of life of cancer patients. *Journal of Chronic Diseases* 34:585–597.

Streiner, D. L., and Norman, G. R. (1995). *Health Measurement Scales. A Practical Guide to Their Development and Use*. Second Edition. New York: Oxford University Press.

7

Helping People Die

LAURENS P. WHITE

Death seems to scare us all. Looking at death is like looking at the sun; it is painful, and we tend to avoid it. To think about suicide, one must first think about death. Seneca, my hero, said "Rehearse death." He advised that we get ready to do at a moment's notice that which we will all have to do some day. It worked for him, and when Nero, one of his more disappointing pupils, ordered him to kill himself, he did so readily. Most of us might have more hesitation than did Seneca. Most of us, however, seem bound to life less because of our passion for living than because of our fear of an unknown future after death.

The purpose of this chapter is to look not at life, with all its splendor and glory, but at death, its inevitable conclusion. Further, it is not to examine prompt and natural death, but to look at death delayed, death interminable, and death with uncontrolled pain and suffering. For most of us, death will occur without any occasion to think about, or without wanting to speed up the process. Most of us would rather delay the coming of death than to speed it up. So for most of us, the subjects of suicide or of assisted suicide will never become an issue.

Suicide

Suicide is most often a bad mistake. When successful, it ends any chance for a change in one's reality, or in one's perception of it. It sends a loud and painful, and not always well understood, message to those close to the suicide victim, the survivors. The suicide of a child is a terrible blow to any parent, creating a wound that is unlikely to heal. Suicide of a parent may well do the same to a child. A failed suicide is often an angry gesture pointed at a specific person or group, with anger and action internalized. Successful suicides may be the same, and are a one-time-only event. A failed suicide may also be a one-time-only event, not to be repeated. It is not always easy to differentiate a suicide gesture from a real attempt, and some completed suicides may have been meant to have been gestures, which went very wrong. Twenty-four of the one thousand known jumpers from the Golden Gate Bridge have survived the experience (Taylor 1995), and all can be thought of as really intending to die. Only two of these twenty-four have subsequently killed themselves, and the others appear to feel they have entered a part of life where suicide is no longer thinkable (Motto 1974). On the other hand, a fair percentage of those surviving suicide attempts will try again, and some succeed in killing themselves after many failures.

Ironically, many who fail in suicide attempts view that failure as further evidence of their many shortcomings, justifying their continued attack on their lives (Shneidman 1973). Suicide requires energy, and some suicides occur as the individual is improving after a period of depression. (This requirement may have something to do with the increasing interest in assisted suicide.) Children, and especially teenagers, have a high level of suicide attempts, with many failures. Old people, and especially old men, tend to be much more aggressive in their efforts and succeed often on the first try (Shneidman and Farberow 1961). Both groups may share a profound sense of isolation and loneliness, the real hallmark of most suicides. The loneliness may be real or imagined, and the imagination has the impact of reality. Guilt plays a role, and often a large one. Many people who kill themselves feel isolated from others, and for some the isolation is real. Many people who don't kill themselves may feel a similar sense of isolation.

Socrates chose suicide over banishment from Athens, the alternative he was offered. He had, and made, a choice, as suicide is always a choice, perhaps constricted in those who choose it. For Socrates, banishment meant not only from Athens, but from his whole life as a teacher. Suicide was, for him, a better option.

How good an option is suicide? That's a question without an answer, and always highly subjective. I believe if I had clear-cut amyotrophic lateral sclerosis (ALS), I would want to kill myself before the disease made that impossible for me and I had to rely on others to do it for me. I believe I have that option and should assume the responsibility of making that decision myself. It does mean that I would have to give up some good, or relatively good, time, time that I could still enjoy. I must accept the loss of some good time to be able to kill myself to avoid some unknown amount of helplessness and bad time. On the other hand, for the physicist Stephen Hawking, who really has ALS, an early suicide would have cost him, and all of us, twenty-five years of an extraordinary, productive life. It is a decision as fraught with error as any other decision, and I need to decide how wrong I may be in choosing suicide to avoid loss of independence.

To think of suicide as a rational solution to some problem means to have accepted death as the inevitable conclusion it is, and to have made some decisions about the relative importance of various kinds of living. I need to know that the decision may not be rational, and we have very different ways of looking at "reality." Increasing disability may be too much for some people to tolerate, although it is striking to see people adapt to losses of capacity that, in good health, they felt would have been impossible to accept. One thinks of quadriplegia, or severe burns as examples of intolerable anguish, nonetheless tolerated by many.

I have, on occasion, suggested suicide to a terminally ill patient who was mired in real pain and despair, who had gone through and failed at all therapeutic modalities, and who was in pain and unable to die. One patient seized on this suggestion with great relief. She had wanted to talk about it, but had been reluctant to bring the subject up herself, attributing the reluctance to her religion. She had extensive skin ulceration and bleeding from carcinoma of the rectum. I pointed out that if she were to take sleeping pills to kill herself, she would need help from her mother, who could not then call 911 for help. I suggested we meet to discuss these issues, which we did. She, her mother, and I talked about suicide over tea, an extraordinary tea. I left in the expectation that she would quickly end her life, but heard nothing from them for several days. I called, and the patient answered the phone and startled me by asking, "What's the matter, Laurie, getting impatient?"—and I had to admit I was impatient. She then said a really enlightening thing: "Once I knew how to kill myself and had the drugs to do it, everything changed. I was back in control, and could stand the pain better. There were some things I wanted to go over with mother, and we have done that." And that evening she died. It is worth considering whether empowerment may not be central to wanting to go on living, and helplessness, through pain, disability, weakness, or some other combination of symptoms, is the worst part of illness and slow death. Our role as physicians and health workers may therefore be to empower individuals to make their own decisions about life and death, rather than to kill them.

On another occasion, I received a call from the wife of a prominent editor. Her husband was nearly paralyzed with ALS and almost unable to speak or be understood. They wanted help in ending his life, and I met with them to discuss the issue. It was clear she would have to do the job, which she was willing to do. We talked about methods and timing, and they said they would call when they wanted specific help. Several weeks later, she called to tell me that talking about the disease, and being offered a way out of their dilemma, was all they really had needed. They wanted no more. Eight or ten weeks later, he died of ALS. My role was only to listen, and that will in many cases be the missing ingredient. Unfortunately, there is a scarcity of doctors who really listen.

Suicide is no longer against the law in the United States or in most of the world. It was a felony in most places until relatively recently. In England, when it was illegal, the penalty was confiscation of property unless the suicide was pronounced to be mentally incompetent. For several centuries, coroners' juries reported verdicts of suicide with the addendum "while the balance of his mind was disturbed." Most of the suicides I will be discussing here will be in people afflicted with slowly lethal, usually painful diseases wherein suicide is considered a solution to measureless suffering, rather than the choice of an unhappy, lonely person. The main difference in these two areas of suicide is usually in the expected lethality of the underlying medical illness. The feeling of helplessness may not be much different in the two groups.

One of the very few advantages of a fatal illness is that it will, in due course, kill you. So will living long enough. The problem for each is that it may take a very long time, and may hurt, humiliate, embarrass, or inconvenience the sick person.

Causing Death and Allowing Death

We need to differentiate between causing to die or killing, which is a real and important issue, and allowing to die, allowing a natural process to run its course. We should be able to accept the notion, as has Vatican II, that disproportionate care is not required (see Chapter 5 for a discussion of how Jewish law similarly treats this issue). The disproportion is between the extent of the care and the possible outcome of the care. For real recovery of health and independent living, a large effort would be justified. For no recovery of consciousness, no effort would be justified. There is a large gray area where recovery is uncertain, where treatment is vital until we know, or at least believe we know, that no further treatment will help. In short, we have no duty of extending the process of dying when we have passed the point of reversing the illness or curing the condition.

The last 25 years have seen a vast increase in discussion about death and about assisted suicide. The work of Herman Feifel (e.g., 1959, 1977) has pushed a reluctant public to consider these issues. Part of the concern about assisted suicide comes from a concern that physicians can keep people artificially alive for months or years, and that physicians may, for money and other reasons, do so. People are frightened of our technology and our morals.

Physician-Assisted Suicide

There have been many efforts to legalize physician-assisted suicide in the United States and elsewhere. For the past several years, the Dutch, without legalizing the practice, have declined to prosecute physicians who kill terminally ill patients if the physicians have the patient's request and certification by another physician that the patient is indeed dying and expected to die within six months of a lethal illness such as cancer. Several thousand patients have been killed in this way each year, and it is alleged that not all of these patients were in fact terminally ill (Pijoenberg 1995). Efforts to legalize physician-assisted suicide in Washington State and in California were presented to voters in those two states in the past three years. In both states, polls taken before the voting indicated strong and wide support for the legalization of the process, with nearly 70% of those polled expressing support. On election day, many of those people stayed home, for in each state the measure narrowly failed to pass (Gianelli 1995). In Oregon in 1994, a somewhat different bill passed that allows physicians to prescribe lethal doses of medication to terminally ill patients if the terminal nature of their illness has been certified by two physicians, one of whom will be the prescribing physician. The patient must take the medication himself or herself. The bill was subsequently struck down by the courts (Gianelli 1995).

Jack Kevorkian, a pathologist with little direct experience in patient care, has involved himself in more than thirty-one assisted suicides in Michigan in the last few years. Most of his victims were alleged to be suffering from end-stage cancer, although a few were not. One of these had severe multiple sclerosis and wanted to die, and one is said to have had crippling rheumatoid arthritis. Dr. Kevorkian was not a treating physician in any of these cases, and it is alleged that he made little effort to investigate the diagnoses or prognoses in any. He killed these people by intravenous administration of potassium chloride, usually after Amytal or other drugs. Some patients had plastic bags tied over their faces. In essence, he killed strangers. He is being prosecuted in five of these cases, and recently acquitted in one.

The current storm of interest in physician-assisted suicide comes from a public perception that doctors are torturing patients, keeping many mortally ill patients alive with senseless life support. There are endless heartbreaking accounts and a real fear of helplessness. Failure of adequate symptom control, especially in patients with advanced cancer, is not an illusion, and many physicians are inept and untrained in pain control. Many are afraid of producing addiction in dying patients. Narcotics, in adequate doses, will nearly always control all but the most excruciating pain, and addiction isn't an issue. There are certainly some patients in whom pain, nausea, or weakness are poorly managed, even in the most skilled hands, and they form a small group where suicide is a reasonable consideration.

The first step toward better care of patients with fatal illnesses is for physicians to talk to patients before the illness. Physicians should make sure that all patients have been urged to appoint a surrogate decision maker under the Durable Power of Attorney for Health Care Act, or have left instructions under a Natural Death Act. Either of these will minimize dilemmas in care of a patient unable to speak for himself or herself. It is largely our discomfort as physicians that prevents these discussions and instructions. We give lip service to the notion that the patient or the family should have full information to make these decisions, but we inform badly or not at all, and don't insist that these decisions be made in advance of any need. A few patients won't make these decisions under stress, but might have been willing to do so if they didn't feel the pressure of their mortality so strongly. For some patients, a stroke or accident makes obtaining their views impossible, unless obtained in advance, and this can create a dreadful dilemma when family members, not informed about the patient's wishes, differ in their own.

Much of the current interest in doctor-assisted suicide may be an outgrowth of our increasing reluctance to be responsible for ourselves. Many of us seem willing to hand off responsibility for our own decisions and our own lives to some other person. Doctors love to appear responsible, and accept these assignments. Doctors do not, however, have fewer problems about death than other groups of people. Many doctors don't want to talk about death, and handle questions about death issues badly. Some become doctors to assure that any dying will be done by the patient, not by themselves. I believe this situation is changing as more education of physicians about death increases their knowledge and comfort about the issues and their roles. People need help from others in dealing with life-and-death issues for themselves and for their loved ones. If doctors had done this job better, there would be little reason for public pressure to improve terminal care. We would be controlling pain better and listening to concerns about withdrawing life support, feeding, and fluids. We would have far fewer problems in resuscitating patients or discussing orders not to do so.

With the large majority of dying people, the issue of physician-assisted suicide will never arise. Neither the patient nor physician will feel the need to discuss it. The current furor, then, is about a small minority of patients who feel, or are, trapped in their failing or helpless bodies, and for whom their physician is the person who can help, such as patients with cancer, Huntington's disease, and Alzheimer's disease.

Others will be unable to speak, in a persistent vegetative state or in a "locked-in" state, after a thrombosis of the top of the vertebral artery. For any of these, a directive under the Durable Power of Attorney for Health Care Act would be a clear expression of their wishes.

What will physicians do with those few patients who express a desire to die or have done so in writing in advance of their need? We need to acknowledge that their pain may be great, their discomfort terrible, their ability to act for themselves severely truncated, and that their disease, while fatal, is terribly slow. I believe it should remain illegal for physicians to kill these patients. In spite of that clear conclusion, I believe that, on rare occasions, killing the patient may be the right thing to do. There may be occasions when the need of the patient is so great that the physician should consider breaking the law and ending the patient's life.

Yale Kamisar (1977), a professor of law at Boalt College of Law at the University of California, quoted Curtis in *It's Your Law*:

> If the circumstances are so compelling that the defendant ought to violate the law, then they are compelling enough for the jury to violate their oaths. The law does well to declare these homicides unlawful. It does equally well to put no more than the sanction of an oath in the way of an acquittal. [p. 408]

Kamisar and most of the medical ethicists I know believe that killing people should remain illegal, even doctor-assisted suicide. Killing should not be made easy or available. The issue may be described as "the need for voluntary euthanasia versus: 1) the incidence of mistake and abuse, and 2) the danger that the legal machinery initially designed to kill those who are a nuisance to themselves may some day engulf those who are a nuisance to others" (p. 413). The frequency of error in medicine is too high, even in cancer, to be comfortable in allowing killing on grounds of incurability and suffering.

Widely accepted in the role of the physician caring for patients with fatal illness is the act of stopping life-support treatments. When it is clear that recovery is impossible, and when the patient is brain dead or in a persistent vegetative state, I believe a physician has not only a right but a duty to terminate life support, which will include ventilation and food and fluid administration. The issue of continuing futile life support comes up most often in patients on Medicaid when the family wants everything continued at no expense to them. I believe we need to deal seriously with the issue of stopping futile care.

One other problem is that many people believe that killing patients in these situations is the responsibility of a physician. They don't trust doctors to do much without second or third opinions, yet they want doctors to kill them. They claim that doctors will know how to do it and will know whether it makes sense. They believe doctors won't make mistakes in this regard. They shouldn't count on that. We are frequently wrong.

In the current environment of "managed care," the legalization of physician-assisted suicide takes on an entirely new and perhaps sinister aspect. With HMOs trying to decrease costs and minimize the delivery of health care, it seems unwise to legalize the ultimate cost-saver— homicide. To put into the hands of the physician, who is required to cut costs, this very dangerous new power requires much study, discussion and thought. We need to increase physicians' and patients' comfort in discussing issues of dying and control of pain and suffering. Making it legal for physicians to assist in patient suicide, or legal for physicians to kill patients, may not be the most rational solution. Death is too important, and too final, to make its consideration or execution trivial or easy. Doctor-assisted suicide should remain difficult, thoughtful, illegal, and rare.

Although it will usually be a physician who is asked to play the role of helper in assisted suicide, the assistance will often be stopping artificial ventilation or feeding, rather than active killing (although there are those who regard withdrawal of life support as killing.) In practice there is a very real difference between killing and allowing to die.

Karen Ann Quinlan was the prototype case (Jonsen et al. 1992). She was a 20-year-old woman in whom a combination of drugs and alcohol produced cerebral anoxia from respiratory arrest, with a subsequent persistent vegetative state. Her family, once aware of her state, claimed she had said she wouldn't want to live in that state, but she had not signed a Living Will or Durable Power of Attorney for Health Care with instructions for such an event. Not many 20-year-olds will have done so. As usual, her doctors were a big part of the problem, refusing to remove the ventilator even after it was clear she was in a permanent coma. When the ventilator was finally turned off by order of a court, after entreaty by the family, she was able to breathe on her own. For the next seven years she was artificially fed and cared for, the care being ordered by the court. With nothing to guide them except the wishes of the family the court opted for the charade of endless, mindless care. A strange conclusion from this sad case is that everyone, even the young, should put in writing one's desires about end-of-life treatment.

People don't want to die alone, are afraid of committing suicide, and are afraid of failing at it. External assistance may be their only hope. The person who will assist must accept the responsibility. Derek Humphrey (1991), in his well-known book, failed to tell the truth about killing his first wife. He felt bad about it, and wanted me, or someone like me, to be able to kill the next wife, if the need arose.

I have two dear friends who are struggling with Alzheimer's disease: the patient hates the shame, fear, and humiliation the disease brings him with its slow and relentless pace, and his wife struggles with her sense of helplessness. Long ago he rejected help in killing himself. Now, she is planning to kill him, and then to kill herself. I am begging her not to do this. She feels she owes him a decent death and can't stand the guilt from killing him or the recrimination from her children. They have a terrible dilemma.

A somewhat different situation arose eighteen years ago, when a young woman named Elizabeth Bouvia, who suffered with extraordinarily crippling cerebral palsy and painful rheumatoid arthritis, tried to get permission to starve to death in a psychiatric ward of Riverside General Hospital in California (White 1977). Her family had long since deserted her, a brief marriage had floundered, her long-term caregiver had recently left her, and she felt physically unable to kill herself. She was admitted to the psychiatric ward as a suicide risk, and asked for their help in providing care while she refused food and fluids in an effort to die. She also asked for narcotics for her pain. Her doctors refused and sought a court order to restrain her and feed her by nasogastric tube. Her need was for physical care during the period she starved herself to death, and the doctors' need was for her to obey them. I and others suggested that a psychiatric ward, with its other suicidal patients, was a poor place for the county to house a woman who planned suicide by starvation. The final outcome was to provide her the physical support she needed in a hospital or nursing home, and she decided to start eating and drinking and remains alive all these years later. It may be that she used suicide as a threat to gain admission to a psychiatric facility since Medicaid would not provide hospitalization for cerebral palsy or for arthritis. Once the care was made available, plans of suicide ended.

Many people are trapped in useless, helpless, and often painful bodies, condemned to live for months or years dependent on others. Most, although not all, are unrecoverably ill, and no treatment will cure them. Life, under these conditions, is often frightful. Richard Lamm (1980), the former governor of Colorado, has suggested, to less than universal enthusiasm, that it is the responsibility of these people, most of them old, to die quickly and cheaply. Many pretend to be offended at his attitude that life is ever meaningless. His attitude, rather, is that some forms of painful semiconscious or unconscious living are not worth prolonging, and that these people should be allowed to die, not be killed. There are now subacute units in some hospitals in which long-term, badly damaged, often comatose patients are maintained on ventilators and artificial feeding. These have been important profit centers for hospitals, desperate for money as their real patient base declines. These units suck large amounts of money from these patients, and from the health care system, generally without any outcome useful to the patient or the family.

Summary

Suicide is usually a poor idea. It may make sense for a few people, or it may only seem to be the only solution. Self-killing should be the preferred way, rather than shifting the responsibility to some other person. Everyone should make plans, in writing, for termination of treatment and life support in the event of an accident or an illness that makes it impossible for us to kill ourselves. This will require the cooperation of others, especially doctors, but is within current law. If we delay such writing of instructions, we may wind up helpless from an accident, stroke, or other illness.

It is a better plan for us to kill ourselves than to hope someone else will be willing to do it for us. Our society seems increasingly unwilling to take responsibility. I believe the widespread push to have doctors given the right to kill patients results from the urge to let someone else be responsible for our lives. I believe it should remain illegal for physicians, even upon request, to kill a patient. It should not be easy to do or done casually. Also, doctors may be wrong about diagnosis and especially about prognosis, and are not to be considered infallible in matters of life or death.

References

Feifel, H., ed. (1959). *The Meaning of Death*. New York: McGraw-Hill.
——— (1977). *New Meanings of Death*. New York: McGraw-Hill.
Gianelli, D. (1995). *American Medical News* 38:1, August 21.
Humphrey, D. (1991). *Final Exit*. Eugene, OR: Hemlock Society.
Jonsen, A., Seigler, A. J., and Winslade, W. (1992). *Clinical Ethics*. New York: McGraw-Hill.
Kamisar, Y. (1977). Mercy killing legislation. In *Death, Dying and Euthanasia*, ed. D. Horan and D. Mall, pp. 406–479. Washington, DC: University Publishers of America.
Lamm, R. (1980). Lecture at University of California Medical School.
Motto, J. (1974). Personal communication.
Pijoenberg, L. (1995). *Euthanasia, assisted dying: the Dutch experience*. Paper presented at International Workgroup on Death, Oxford, England, June.
Seneca (1950). *Letters to Lucillius*. London: Penguin.
Shneidman, E. (1973). *Deaths of Man*. New York: Quadrangle/New York Times.
Shneidman, E., and Farberow, N. (1961). *The Cry for Help*. New York: McGraw-Hill.
Taylor, M. (1995). *San Francisco Chronicle*, July 14, p. A-1.
White, L. P. (1977). Testimony in Riverside County Superior Court.

8

From the Very First Patient to the Very Last: Soul Pain, Aesthetic Distance, and the Training of Physicians

SANDRA L. BERTMAN

In response to the medicalization and legalization of death that characterizes modern society, voices are crying out against the prolonged and needless suffering—physical, emotional, and spiritual—that has come to be synonymous with the dying process in this most technologically developed of eras. As Bruce Feldman (1994) declares, "Just as the women's movement helped to reclaim birth from the medical establishment, patients are asserting their formerly god-given right to a decent end" (p. 17).

Approaching the year 2000, it seems strange to have to argue for a natural death and the right to die decently and with dignity. Why, in this age of body consciousness and the supremacy of self, are we finding the need to fund projects that foster "gentle closure"?[1] Shouldn't we automatically be devoting our energy all along to the dying person's physical comfort, to the "naturalness of dying," and coming to terms with the life that has been led? What prompts the trend toward such "mandated" care?

Humankind has been here before. Visual testimony of our God-given right to a decent end—one characterized by communion, comfort, and closure—is exactly what the *ars moriendi* picture sermons of the fifteenth century (Figure 8–1) were all about. Death was no more the province of the medical establishment than was birth. Today, perhaps, the celestial beings pictured at the bedside might be replaced by family members,

---

[1]Project on Death in America New Program Announcement, October 25, 1994. Open Society Institute, 888 Seventh Ave., New York, New York. The project's mission is to transform the culture and experience of dying in the United States through initiatives in research, scholarship, the humanities, and the arts, and to foster innovations in the provision of care, public education, professional education, and public policy.

FIGURE 8–1. *The Goodman on his Deathbed* (1471). **Woodcut illustration, blockbook edition of** *Ars Moriendi.* **Bibliotheque des Arts Decoratifs, Paris. In Bertman 1991, p. 17.**

and the spiritual preparedness indicated by the cross and confessional, by one physican's (Eddy 1994) recollection of the way his own mother wanted to leave the world: "To be given a morphine drip that she could control, to have her family around her holding her hands, and for her to turn up the drip" (p. 180).

In fact, the physician (Eddy) was grateful that his mother died ahead of schedule. Although he knew in his heart that honoring her wishes was the right thing to do (to say nothing of her God-given right), the appropriate death (Weisman 1977)—the one his mother would have chosen for herself—is illegal in the medical establishment of the 1990s.

The enormous infusion of ethics courses and communication skills workshops into the medical curriculum has not improved the physicians' knowledge of what patients want nor resulted in diminishing their pain. The largest ever U.S. study of patients near death, an eight-year project designed to make end-of-life hospital care more humane, reports total failure on both counts (Knox 1995).

Ethicists and experts in patient rights have long believed that the care of the dying could be set right by "a few new laws and regulations, a bit more talk between doctors and patients, and a more prudent use of medical technology" (Callahan, in Knox 1995, p. 14). If they acknowledge Eddy's concerns, they would sadly concur that, "If dying patients want to retain some control over the dying process, they must get out of the hospital if they are in, and stay out of the hospital if they are out" (Annas, in Knox 1995, p. 14). Furthermore, they might even agree that what appears to be needed in our civilized society is "not just reform . . . [but] revolution" (Callahan, in Knox 1995, p. 14).

Courses in ethics, law, and communication skills are certainly part of the answer. But the language of rights and responsibilities has nothing to do with "soul" pain (Feifel 1977, Saunders 1988) and its panaceas: feelings of empathy, connectedness, caring, compassion, and, some would be so bold as to admit, love. Soul pain is difficult to define. A profound thoughtfulness, suffering, heartache, not necessarily in a negative sense, this soul pain is as real for the physician as it is for the patient. Talking about a young boy's death—even in the light of the next day— again discussing how the youngster was already dead on arrival to the hospital, and being assured she had done everything possible, an emergency resident tells of weeping until she fell asleep ("trapping [her] sorrow for years"). Despite everyone's telling her how well she managed the situation, and giving her their best support, she puts her finger on what was missing: "But no one asked [her] how [she] felt" (Kasman 1994, p. 433).

For generations physicians and others in health care have wrestled with the dichotomy between the nature of suffering and the goals of medicine (Cassell 1982). In an 1889 valedictory address to medical students at the University of Pennsylvania, William Osler (1905) delineated two virtues of the caring practitioner: an outward stance of calm and coolness even under difficult circumstances, and "aequanimitas," or equanimity, an inner calm of accepting whatever comes in life. Years later, Francis Peabody (1927) wrote that "the secret of the care of the patient is in caring for the patient" (p. 818). Others (Coles 1989, Lynn 1993) endorse the essential nobility of the medical profession characterized by altruism, social responsibility, and humility. Still others advocate a closer union of the professional and personal personae, a congruence of the many selves that reside in us all (Bertman 1991).

In their struggle with the conflicts inherent in the nature and practice of medicine, physicians often receive little support from medical textbooks and journal case studies. Consequently, they may find themselves seeking out the personal narratives of their patients, peers, and

166   DEATH AND THE QUEST FOR MEANING

family members or those recounted in the arts and literature as a source of guidance through the myriad ethical conundrums they confront. It is through these intimate "life stories" that they can grasp the nature of personal boundaries and achieve that marvelously oxymoronic quality of "detached concern."

For patients succumbing to the irreversible process of aging or to the declines inherent in terminal disease, can dying be viewed as an independent "diagnosis"? And is there a specific "treatment" for it? Addressing this issue in a special communication to the *Journal of the American Medical Association*, Jack McCue (1995) pleads for training physicians and nurses to assume "medical stewardship" of their patients and to act as advocates for the prevention of overtreatment and overtesting, so prevalent in our subspecialist, procedure-oriented medical centers. Rather than viewing death as a medical failure, McCue describes how a good death can be particularly healing: "The spiritual dimension of dying bonds persons together—family, caregivers, and strangers—and can effect dramatic changes in the lives of those touched by the death" (p. 1042).

Is there an effective way to train physicians to acknowledge this spiritual dimension, to look beyond the statistics and the lab values and achieve that elusive "aequinimitas" that Osler speaks about so eloquently? Is there a means to teach providers the value of involvement or "attached" concern when the situation warrants it? The humanities, literature, and the arts are resources relatively untapped by medical educators and clinicians. The backbone of science is logic and experiment; that of art, intuition and insight. The arts uncover realities that lie outside the quantifiable and statistically measurable. They invite us into the world of both the living and the dying in a manner every bit as penetrating as scientific analysis.

The challenge for physicians and physicians-in-training in the 1990s and beyond is to find the appropriate "aesthetic distance" that will allow them to be both effective practitioners of the science of medicine and compassionate examples of the art of medicine. Feifel and colleagues (1967) argue that physicians are particularly vulnerable to death anxiety and that they are drawn to and "utilize the medical profession . . . to help control personal concerns about death" (pp. 201–202). Feifel (1963, 1977) also submits that from a mental health viewpoint, a state of "qualified immunity" (1977, p. 69) is probably preferable to complete denial or acceptance of oncoming death. Doctors cannot be traumatized to the core by every dying patient. He was the first to articulate that for physician as well as for patient, death helps clarify and intensify life's reality and meaning and therefore, for both, is a powerful therapeutic tool. Feifel thus challenges medical educators to create an atmosphere in which the art and science of medicine can coexist, and to incorporate art into formal teaching structures.

Physicians: A Breed Apart

Medicine is and always has been a deeply spiritual profession. The earliest recorded images portray physicians as priests and priestesses. In a fourteenth century manuscript illumination *Treatise and Commentary on Medicine* (Figure 8–2), one could easily confuse the scene, which depicts a medical consultation, for a private confessional. So, too, in the contemporary painting *Mr. S. Is Told He Will Die* (Figure 8–3), Robert Pope, a fellow cancer patient, has recorded the moment during which two physicians present Mr. S. with his devastating prognosis. They are seated beside the patient on his hospital bed, literally buttressing him with their bodies as they reveal their news. Pope (1991) says of his painting, "The cross symbolizes religion, and the doctors, in their white lab coats, symbolize science. The man is grasping onto both, and neither one can save his life and he knows this" (p. 90).

I see quite a different scene: compassion incarnate. The two physicians are seated with the patient on *his* bed, *his* turf. Whatever their

FIGURE 8–2. Illumination from *Treatise and Commentary on Medicine.* Galen et al. Bibliotheque Municipale, Rheims.

FIGURE 8–3. *Mr. S. Is Told He Will Die*, **by Robert Pope (1989). Acrylic on canvas. Reprinted by permission.**

personal beliefs—or those of Mr. S.—the physicians are sharing his suffering, deliberately touching yet allowing space for their patient to absorb the import of the moment. Comfortable with the silence and heartfelt concern, willing to suspend their demanding schedules for as many moments as are necessary, they are fully present. The intimacy of the scene, the human relatedness, seems almost sacramental, an earthly embodiment of love, the essence of soul.

The physician-as-priest image is one to which physician-authors frequently allude in their own writings. Spanish physician Feliz Marti-Ibanez (1960) defines physicianhood as being "an intermediary between man and God." On a home visit to a dying patient, a Vermont physician (Loxterkamp 1993) discovers "the chausable and stole" he wears to the bedside. Medical student and author Perri Klass (1987) describes her sense of being "initiated into a priesthood" (p. 37). When the *New York*

Times essayist Anatole Broyard (1992) himself becomes a patient, he puts it more bluntly: "Every patient invites the doctor to combine the role of the priest, the philosopher, the poet, the lover. He expects the doctor to evaluate his entire life, like a biographer" (p. 54). Novelist Reynolds Price (1994) requires far less sophistication from doctors, wanting merely the "frank exchange of decent concern," the skills expected of "a teacher, a fireman, a priest." Poet Anne Sexton (1975) reminds us that physicians are human beings, "not Gods/though they would like to be . . . they are only a human/trying to fix up a human."

The rites of passage to physicianhood are like no other. In my more than twenty-year involvement with medical education, I have come to respect the innate humanity of physicians and those in training, and to empathize with their struggle to maintain compassion and authenticity in their professional lives. One of an intern's chores is pronouncing patients dead and calling their families with the news. Frequently the patient and family are barely (if at all) known to the intern, who is most likely "on call" and covering for a senior colleague. One such intern, having been called to the bedside after a death, describes a transformative moment, an unexpected yet precious sense of timelessness and peace: "I almost found comfort in those few minutes I got to spend alone with the newly dead body. I knew that there was nothing more to do than check for a pulse, listen for respirations, and spend a few minutes in silent reverence for the event that had just happened" (Peters 1990, pp. 81–82).

Even in the laboratory, practitioners are confronted daily with the struggle to remain connected and human. Pathologist F. Gonzalez-Crussi (1995), author of *Suspended Animation: Six Essays on the Preservation of Bodily Parts*, points out that "Anyone who has shed tears in a room full of formalinized specimens would readily agree . . . that the nectar of life comes dashed with flecks of death" (p. 8). Glibly, and not a little condescendingly, one reviewer of the essays responds, "Well, I'm sure anyone would—but how many of us could conceive of an occasion when we might find ourselves weeping amid shelves of jugged babies and glass tanks floating with amputated limbs? I think Dr. Gonzalez-Crussi forgets at times that his is a specialized vocation" (cited in Banville 1995, p. 8).

On the contrary, I think it is *we* who forget. A specialized vocation to be sure, perhaps a spiritual one at that. It is this dimension that makes physicians a breed apart, and this dimension too that makes them particularly vulnerable. As Alcoholics Anonymous member V. Ross put it, religion is for people afraid of going to hell and spirituality is for those who have been there. Physicians have been there from the moment they enter the profession.

The Very First Patient

> It is commonly known that medical students dissect the bodies of the dead; it is less commonly realized that these same dead do a great deal of cutting, probing, and pulling at the minds of their youthful dissectors.
>
> Gregg 1957, p. 25

Perhaps it is fortuitous that the first patient a medical student meets is a dead one. Absent in this inaugural encounter are the awkward introductions, the uncomfortable silence, and the embarrassment (for both parties) that always accompanies the first laying on of hands. Yet although a measure of comfort can be derived from knowing that neither pain can be inflicted on nor harm done to this patient, there is no getting around the fact that he or she is dead.

Medical students and practicing physicians alike make compelling arguments for early and ongoing "vaccinations" of education and training having to do with death and dying. In *A Parting Gift* pediatrician Frances Sharkey (1982) traces the development of her own "emotional detachment" as she makes her way through medical education, from her dissection experiences to the deaths of patients she has attended. She vividly recounts how frequently she dreamed about her cadaver: "He was always very much alive in the dreams. I never told this to my fellow students. We didn't talk about the effects our cadavers had on us; nor did we talk about death" (p. 16). Klass (1987) recalls being disturbed by the cautiousness about expressing feelings and the almost inhuman decorum expected of those being socialized into the medical profession. She describes how this learned self-consciousness trickles down into patient care: "It's terrifying to learn on patients how to start an I.V. You worry about making a mistake. . . . You worry about making a fool of yourself, about looking stupid on rounds" (p. 57).

The sudden death of a sister is the event that crystallizes Peters's (1990) belief in the critical importance of such training. After suffering this major personal loss, she becomes convinced that discussions with her housestaff colleagues about the feelings surrounding a death, the process of grief, and the needs of the bereaved might make them more empathetic, effective physicians. Acknowledging that dealing with death is never easy, she would hope that future generations of physicians can experience the essence of grief without having to lose someone they love.

Patients often find themselves looking to the physician for "metaphysical" expertise: "Just as he orders blood tests and bone scans of my body, I'd like my doctor to scan me, to grope for my spirit as well as my prostate" (Broyard 1992, p. 45). Physician-writer Richard Selzer (Beppu and Tavormina 1981) reminds us that when the surgeon cuts into the patient, he himself must not bleed, that he must find the appropriate, protective clinical distance or emotional armor. So how do we train physicians to know when to treat aggressively, to be action-oriented, and when (and how) to shift gears to grope for the soul instead of the prostate? How do we educate them to tolerate discomfort, ambiguity, and uncertainty when they are programmed to obtain answers and apply solutions? How do we teach them to feel comfortable sharing their own humanity with patients on the examining table or at the bedside who are grappling with the manifestations of soul pain—loneliness, hopelessness, valuelessness, meaninglessness?

To assist medical students in their first "patient" encounter—with the cadaver—many medical schools provide introductory lectures about the source of the cadavers, the history of dissection, and the parallels between dissection and patient care. Some introduce new medical students to the cadaver lab well before dissection begins (Bertman and Marks 1989, Marks and Bertman 1980, Penney 1985). Faculty advisors may be assigned at this time (Penney 1985). Some programs devise exercises or small group sessions to encourage students to reflect on what they have undertaken; others have students write narratives about their dissecting experience or what they imagine was the body donor's life and how she or he came to be a medical school cadaver (Coulehan et al. 1995, Wear 1987, 1989). Whatever the tactic, the intention is to help prepare the students not only for academic work in the anatomy laboratory but also for the emotional work that patient care—the "laying on of hands"—implies. More subtly, such careful preparation seeks to establish a lifelong foundation for introspection and the exploration of humanistic, spiritual, and existential issues in medicine.

Prior to the first dissection encounter at the University of Massachusetts Medical School, students are invited to create an image of what they expect the dissection experience will be like. These images reveal anxiety about performance, fear of becoming ill or faint, concern about body violation, inquisitiveness about the life of the body donor and his or her survivors, and reflections on the afterlife, finitude, and personal mortality.

It is astonishing how many of the images deal with the spirit or the soul of the cadaver and depict its presence both positively and negatively. Some derive solace from the spirit's presence, guidance, and approval. Others seem concerned (as some religions and cultures are) that until the body is properly buried the spirit cannot find peace. One image of a group of students praying over their cadaver before beginning their dissection recalls a fourteenth century ritual at the School of Salernum where it is said that students recited Mass each morning for the salvation of the cadaver's soul (Lewin 1946).

Many of the illustrations focus on the ghoulish: the cadaver coming to life, dismemberment, and desecration imagery—black humor to provide adaptive relief.

Some students frankly admit to self-consciousness and are concerned with how they will measure up in the eyes of their classmates and faculty. Will they appear nervous, faint, or betray caring emotions such as sympathy or sadness? Will they become nauseated and vomit? At home will they be able to eat, sleep, and make love without being haunted by the pervasive odors and images of the dissection lab? Will they be able to navigate between objectivity and empathy in the other aspects of their personal lives?

Three images epitomize the paradoxes inherent in the concepts of detached concern, the "medical gaze," and the gratification of acknowledging the silent teachings of the cadaver (Figures 8–4, 8–5, and 8–6).

Just as the students are about to start the dissection of the head and neck—a particularly difficult, often traumatic task—a montage of the class's images is presented to them in the darkness and anonymity of the amphitheater. The intention is to "lay it all out" from the students' points of view, to reveal the enormous variety yet universality of concerns, and to set the tone for exploring personal stories—deaths they

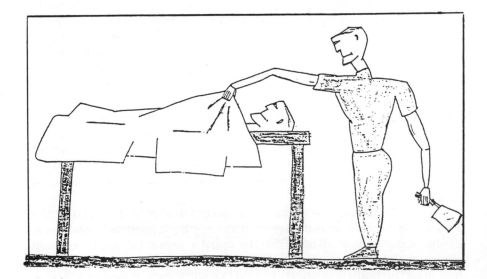

FIGURE 8–4. *The First Gaze.* Note the similarity between the face of the medical student and that of the cadaver (both colored green in the original). This illustration also raises the important issue of the mutilation of the body and the inherent feelings that the act of dissection engenders.

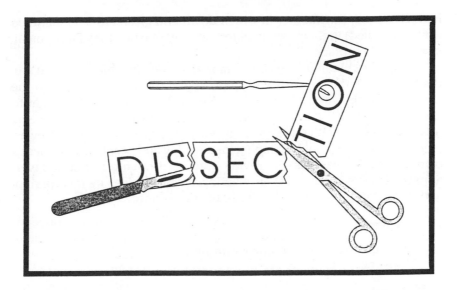

FIGURE 8–5. *Dissection as a Clinical Procedure.* Sharp, hard-edged, cold, permanent—focusing on the instruments is a means of distancing oneself from unpleasant feelings. The student's explanation: "Dissection . . . a noun. Separation of a whole into its parts for study."

FIGURE 8–6. *The Three Faces of Dissection.* Expresses nicely the medical student's transformation from repulsion through wonderment and excitement to gratitude.

had witnessed, the manner in which death and grief had been handled (or mishandled) in their own families, and the reasons they chose medicine in the first place.

The year culminates in the memorial service in which medical students through their own rituals, words, and music pay tribute to the cadavers for the gift of their bodies (Figure 8–7). Closure is brought to the dissection course and to unsettled fantasies such as the soul being unable to rest until its remains are accorded proper burial. Inside every medical student is a soul searching for meaning and peace. One student's own soul finds peace as she reviews her relationship to her cadaver, appreciates the beauty of their meeting, acknowledges its mentorship, and ultimately a new, ongoing sense of connection:

One Breath Apart

You came to take me for a walk with you.
I was afraid at first
  To meet you
  To take your hand.
I pretended you were here
  To teach me the details—
  Muscles, arteries, nerves—
And I held on tight.

Then I saw your face,
  And I knew
You came to take me for a walk with you—
  On the edge
  You on one side,
Me on the other
We are one breath apart. [Long 1995]

Michelangelo and Rembrandt: Comrades in the Most Unlikely Places

Even in this most specialized profession, the medical student is not alone. She or he has counterparts in the most unlikely places. As an apprentice, Michelangelo needed to know how the body "worked" from the inside so that he could draw, paint, and sculpt it with verisimilitude. His secret—nocturnal descents to the basement of the monastery to dissect corpses—is not unlike the medical student's "descent" to the cadaver lab. (Why is it that morgues and anatomy laboratories are always located in the nether regions, the basements of buildings?)

In *The Agony and the Ecstasy*, biographer-novelist Irving Stone (1961) chronicles Michelangelo's experience for us. The young artist's questions

FIGURE 8–7.   The culmination of the first-year module is a student organized and produced memorial service for body donors, seen here in a
courtyard at University of Massachusetts Medical School.

and concerns parallel almost exactly those of the medical student. While
medical students often wonder about the personal lives of their cadavers and how they came to be body donors, Michelangelo wonders, "What
had this unfortunate creature done that he should now, without his
knowledge and consent, be mutilated" (p. 182). Stone adds, "His first
feeling was one of pity for the dead man." While physicians are concerned
that their license permits them to maim, desecrate, and violate another
human being's body in the name of medicine, so Michelangelo questions
whether he is "obsessed" and has the right to do such things in the name
of sculpture. At one point the effect of dissecting the human face is so
ghastly that he must abandon the task. Eventually returning to it, he is
"overcome with a sense of guilt" when he cracks open the skull. And when
the medical student's self-doubt, discomfort, and horror changes to fascination, excitement, and joy in the discovery of the intricate beauty of
the human frame, so too does Michelangelo feel the thrill of his first look
at the human brain and at holding a human heart in his hands: "As quickly
as it had come, the fear departed. In its place came a sense of triumph.
. . . He felt the happiness that arises out of knowledge, for now he knew

about the most vital organ of the body, what it looked like, how it felt"
(pp. 185–186).

Other parallels can be drawn between artists and anatomists. Rembrandt's *Anatomy Lesson of Dr. Nicholaes Tulp* (Figure 8–8) introduces
the luxury of aesthetic distance and invites analysis of the concepts of
detached concern, aequanimitas, and the medical gaze. The painting is
particularly appropriate for stimulating self-reflection, discussion of personal values, and the process of professional acculturation. It is a natural for investigating the idea that the student's initiation into medicine
is a group event with its own set of rules and regulations. Mastering a
huge number of facts and information while demonstrating appropriate
decorum must be practiced in the presence of one's classmates (peers)
and instructor (authority).

The first-year curriculum at the State University of New York at
Stony Brook recognizes this important element of group accountabil-
ity in medical education. In addition to requiring students to write narratives about their own dissecting experience or their cadaver's previous
life, Stony Brook students are also expected to respond constructively
to the narratives of their peers and are given guidelines to do so. Making reasoned judgments about a peer's work and evaluating the work
of colleagues—operating and cooperating in a medical community—are
thus taken seriously from the onset of medical training (Coulehan et al.
1995).

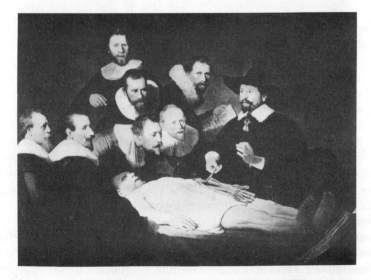

FIGURE 8–8. *The Anatomy Lesson of Dr. Nicholaes Tulp*, **by Rembrandt
van Rijn (1632). Mauritshuis, The Hague, inventory no. 146.**

Keen observation, interpretation, and critical thinking are skills basic to medicine and the arts. Challenging the specifics of *Anatomy Lesson* with medical students can serve as a useful preamble to musing over personal thoughts and recollections. For example, are the details of the dead man's body accurate? (The dissected right hand appears to be backward or upside down.) What physical aspects of the cadaver are most disturbing? Is there ever anything appealing about a dead body? Again, reminding us of Michelangelo's experience, physician-writer Selzer (1982) warns that after eleven months of dissection, the student "stands a fair risk of suffering a kind of rapture of the deep, wherein you drift, tumbling among the coils of intestine in a state of helpless enchantment" (pp. 64–65).

The aesthetic distance provided by art allows the viewer the luxury of being able to stare without feeling rude, to study a scene or situation without the need to avert the eyes. By its very nature, art invites close inspection and assumes responsibility for propriety, all the while keeping us focused on larger questions. Juxtaposing Rembrandt's *Anatomy Lesson* with Orozco's fresco *Gods of the Modern World* (Figure 8–9), Hovsepian's *The Doctors* (Figure 8–10), and a photographic "remake" of the Rembrandt (Figure 8–11) provides a more sinister portrayal of the fraternal, doctor-centered medical establishment. Orozco's physicians are depicted as skeletons in academic robes witnessing a birth. Hovsepian's

FIGURE 8–9. *The Gods of the Modern World.* **Detail from *The Epic of American Civilization*, by Jose Clemente Orozco (1932). Fresco. Commissioned by the trustees of Dartmouth College, Hanover, NH, and reprinted by permission.**

FIGURE 8–10. *The Doctors*, by Leon Hovsepian (1969). Acrylic on canvas (variation on the theme).

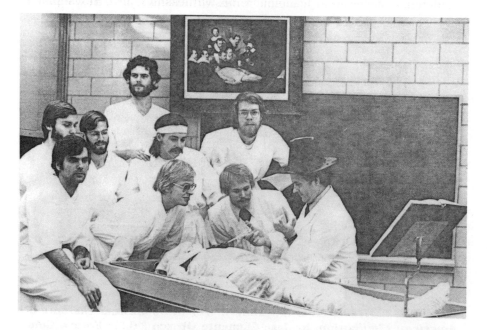

FIGURE 8–11. Re-enacting Rembrandt's *Anatomy Lesson* is a Mayo Medical School tradition founded by the first class. Reprinted with permission.

physicians might just as well join the ranks of Orozco's "gods" as they tamper with reproductive technology. The medical students' more tongue-in-cheek view (an annual "ritual" reenactment of the Rembrandt) epitomizes the need for comic relief in the anatomy lab. As viewers occupying the space in which the artist stood, we can easily become uncomfortable by a too narrowly focused medical gaze (Winkler 1993, Winkler and Bertman 1995).[2] If we step back and consider the "big picture," we may be able to appreciate the more subtle dichotomy between the quest for knowlege and the well-being of others, and the competing virtues of authority and humanity. Orozco's fresco, which occupies a wall of the library at Dartmouth Medical School, seems a fitting reminder both of the danger of such a narrow focus and the arrogance and insulation of too great a professional distance.

The Very Last Patient

> In spite of our vast knowledge and our superior technology, there are times when all of us in medicine become the treatment—when what we have most to offer is ourselves.
>
> Waller 1995

An obvious response to Feifel's challenge is that palliative medicine, which focuses on control of symptoms rather than control of disease, needs to be taught. Whether defined as a medical specialty or an approach to care, it is basic to good medicine. Specifically, palliative medicine means focusing on quality of life, along with providing psychosocial and spiritual support for dying patients and their families. These are essential to the medical management of the terminally ill patient.

Even for hospice patients there may be a place for invasive procedures, such as blood transfusions, or neural blocks to improve patient comfort. It is the physician's responsibility to ensure an environment—medically, architecturally, and attitudinally—in which a particular dying patient can flourish. Feifel (1977) sketches out this healing environment: a place where faith may be affirmed, where doubts and the meaning of impending separation may be voiced. Emily Dickinson (1865) details how little the dying need: a flower, a glass of water, a friend. This translates into "intensive care": vigilant attention to aggressive comfort measures—symptom control, privacy, an appreciation for the powerful regenerative symbols of natural beauty and art (of choice) that celebrate life—as well as to healing, salvation, grace, or whatever we call wholeness ("holiness").

---

[2]Broyard (1992) describes this gaze as just the opposite, "unfocused." Physicians view patients "panoramically," like a figure in early landscape paintings, "a figure in the distance only to give scale" (p. 50).

Admittedly, another reason for teaching palliative medicine is a practical one. How can physicians be comfortable referring patients to a hospice if they don't really understand the philosophy? They are neither abandoning their patients to their illness nor losing control of them by signing over their care. On the contrary, they are enlarging their armamentarium and expertise by bringing in collaborative partners to support patient and family and themselves. For now, much like the hospital physicians in the Pope painting (Figure 8–3) or Fildes's physician providing support, through his presence, for the family in the home of the dying child (Figure 8–12), they are free to demonstrate their "metaphysical" expertise: knowing when and how to become the medicine themselves. Very often, the most a physician has to offer turns out to be the least: simply being there.

The question should not be why teach palliative medicine but rather what to teach, when and where, and by whom (Weissman 1995).

Most curricula include lectures about death, dying, and grief throughout the first two years of medical school in connection with introductions to behavioral science, psychiatry, and the doctor–patient relationship (Mermann et al. 1991). However discouraging, the outcomes of the Robert Wood Johnson study (Knox 1995) indicate that these courses seem

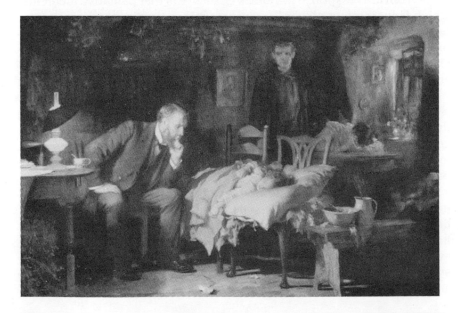

FIGURE 8–12. *Physician Watching Over a Sick Child*, by Sir Luke Fildes (1981). New York Academy of Medicine Library, NY. Reprinted in Bertman 1991, p. 183.

to do little more than provide information on how to communicate a concerning diagnosis or give bad news, how to recognize the stages of grief, and the medicolegal issues surrounding living wills and the termination of care. Several medical schools offer a problem-based curriculum that emphasizes the case study approach, which theoretically stimulates more comprehensive thinking. Some schools provide electives in chronic illness, suffering, loss and death, or address psychosocial issues through standardized patient programs. A few even require rotations through palliative care units.

The Center for Palliative Studies (CPS) at San Diego Hospice offers both formal and informal training in pain management, ethics, and the psychosocial aspects of terminal illnesses and bereavement (Herbst 1995). Like first-year students at Stony Brook and University of Massachusetts medical schools who commit to paper their visual and verbal images regarding dissection, those at the CPS are expected to record their experiences in journal or essay form. The comments are then used to address troublesome thoughts and to stimulate discussion. One student apologetically described the two main issues that kept surfacing for him:

> I wish that I could say that they were more medically oriented, e.g., pain management in cancer patients or the ethics of assisted suicide, but instead they are more personal and selfish. The first one is about handling grief, both from a personal perspective and from the perspective of someone who will someday take care of grieving people. The other issue is how working with patients who are dying changes the way I view the world. [Laurenson 1995, p. 21]

Others cited statistics from 1991 that 80 percent of patients with advanced cancer experience inadequate pain management (Walsh 1991). One participant wrote, "This statistic is a shameful indictment of modern medicine's straying from its roots of relieving suffering" (Waikar 1995). Another admitted her own ignorance of misinformation about drugs and how much damage physicians can do by not taking patients' pain seriously enough:

> I thought of powerful pain medications as somehow mind-altering drugs that take away a patient's reality (and dignity) as well as suffering. Now I appreciate them as a tool to help a patient's dignity, to help her or him focus on something other than pain. [Dodge 1995, p. 15]

Another student used Christian imagery to describe his experience with an AIDS patient who was suffering from neuropathic pain. A Christian neither by faith nor temperament, the student felt himself at one with Christ:

> The spiritual meaning of Christ's passion impressed itself forcibly upon me. He did not die once on a cross two millennia ago. He is here among us every day and our pain is His. Wherever we serve a suffering person, we are, in effect, serving the Lord. I walked out of that room with a deeper appreciation for Christianity, as well as for the ultimate goals of medicine—or at least of how I want to practice medicine. [Moviac 1995, p. 26]

This same student beautifully refutes detachment in the way he admits to carrying hospice home with him. He believes he has become more appreciative and loving as a result of his experience:

> Especially I've noticed that I've started to grieve their deaths in advance, as it were, in moments here and there (most frequently as I drive home from Hospice). As I image the deaths of my wife and son, their absence in life, the reality and inevitability of loss sinks home a little deeper and I become grateful for all the love and blessings I currently have. It occurs to me, too, that our loved ones are in a sense always dying to us. [Moviac 1995, p. 24]

The Remedy of Aesthetic Distance: The Case Study as an Educational Tool

Is there an educational method or technique that can, finally, accomplish the goal of preparing doctors in training for both the professional and the personal challenges that lie ahead of them, particularly for facing the death of a patient? Perhaps the increasingly popular case-study method of analysis, applied to the arts, can be a useful tool for teachers and students alike.

It has been said that poetry is what evaporates in translation. In a like way, the art or poetry of medicine—not the science of healing but the human response to profound suffering—is what evaporates, perhaps deliberately, in the case-study method of analysis. In case studies (indeed, as in the day-to-day practice of medicine) treatment plans are reviewed vis-à-vis the medical, ethical, and humanistic concerns of the patient, family members, and the caregiving team. The values, wishes, and emotions of everyone involved hold equal weight in the decision-making equation with the test results, chemotherapy protocol requirements, and hospital regulations.

Using a Poem as a Case Study

As with the Rembrandt painting, the intention in using a poem as a case study is neither to conduct a traditional morbidity and mortality conference, and certainly not to analyze the work as if in an English class, which itself could distance any student too comfortably and self-complacently by stressing theory, technique, or style. Rather, using the poem, juxtaposed against a fictitious medical "case," sets the stage for the exploration of personal stories—the deaths one has witnessed, the struggles of family members often not in agreement, the intertwining nuances of pain, grief, and love that at once are heartbreaking yet remind the observer of her or his essential humanness. The case study becomes an exercise in "physician heal thyself"; the major benefit is the acknowledgment of the remedial value that aesthetic distance can provide.

The Case

This is a fictional case study constructed by the author. Details of the case are unimportant. The discussion facilitator should create a scenario consonant with the piece of poetry, prose, or painting chosen.

A 76-year-old Caucasian male with end-stage cancer. Family members—his wife, two daughters, and a son—are called to the bedside as the moment of death approaches.

The Poem

Accomplishment

What not to do for him
was hardest, for the life left in us
argued against his going
like a moon banished in fullness, yet
lingering far into morning, pale
with new light, gradually a view of
mountains, a sea emerging—its prickly
channels and dark shelves
breeding in the violet morning. Ships too,
after a while. Some anchored, others
moving by degree, as if to leave without affront
this harbor, a thin shoal curved like an arm—
ever embracing, ever releasing.

He too was shaped to agreement, the hands
no longer able to hold, at rest
on the handmade coverlet. His tongue
arched forward in the open mouth where breath
on breath he labored, the task beyond all strength
so the body shuddered like a chill
on the hinge of his effort, then rose again.

After a time, we saw the eyes gaze upward
without appeal—eyes without knowing or need
of knowing. Some in the room began to
plead, as if he meant to take them with him,
and they were afraid. A daughter bent near,
calling his name, then gave her own,
firmly, like a dock he might swim or cling to.
The breath eased, then drifted momentarily,
considering or choosing, we did not know.

"At some point we have to let him go."
"I know," she said. "I know."

In the last moments the eyes widened and,
with the little strength left, he
strained upward and toward. "He had to be
looking *at* something. You don't look
at nothing that way." Not
pain, but some sharpening beyond
the visible. Not eagerness or surprise, but
as though he would die in time to intercept
an onrushing world, for which
he had prepared himself
with that dead face. [Gallagher 1984, pp. 39–40]

After reading the poem aloud, the agenda is to use it to stimulate reminiscence and responses to the following questions: (1) Have you seen deaths in which the person seemed to be accomplishing something? (2) Who was the first dying person you attended? What was that death like? (3) Who was the first intimate family member or friend to whose dying you were a close witness? Who was the most recent? What were those deaths like? (4) What personal experiences prompted you to choose medicine as a career?

As with the Rembrandt painting, it might make sense to begin with the objective, the "what" rather than the "why" or the "how." Discussing the specifics of the case provides the safety of "technology," which, according to Max Frisch (1959) "is the knack of so arranging the world that we do not experience it" (p. 178).

Probe: Are the details of the dying man's body (the labored breathing, the arching tongue, the upward gaze) accurate and telling? (Compare with Rembrandt's hand, apparently anatomically incorrect.)

Follow-up: What physical aspects of dying are most disturbing to you? Is the act of dying always repulsive? Is there ever something appealing about certain dying bodies?

Probe: Is the family behaving as you have seen families behave when they witness the last moments of life? What about the ambivalence of the family to "let him go"? Or their fear "as if he meant to take them with him"? What about the daughter who calls his name, then gives her own, "firmly, like a dock he might swim or cling to"—offering herself to her "drifting" father so that he can feel safe and not go out to sea? Initially, the family wants to keep even this pale reminder of the full person the father was. They want simultaneously to embrace him but also to release him. How does this compare with scenarios you have witnessed?

Follow-up: Who is the person in the poem who says, "At some point we have to let him go"? Physician? Nurse? Hospice worker? Clergyperson? Other family member? How do you as a clinician handle the process of encouraging the patient and family to "let go"? Is there a point at which this becomes your goal? How do you as the patient's physician let go?

Probe: We can probably recognize the poet's description of the dying man's eyes as "without knowing." But what does it mean when she adds "[without] need of knowing"? Does this suggest something about her opinion of the hereafter? Does the information provided in stanza five—"the eyes widened. . . . 'He had to be looking *at* something. You don't look at nothing that way'" add or detract from this issue?

Follow-up: What about the survivors' faiths and/or beliefs about the afterlife? What about our own? Is there a role for discussion of these deeply personal issues at the time of death? After the death has occurred?

Probe: Poems often depict a crisis or a turning point. What do you think of the idea that dying is not a passive phenomenon but, as the title suggests, an active "accomplishment"? Contrast the passive act of being born with the action of dying.

Follow-up: Have you witnessed deaths in which the person seemed to be accomplishing something? What about family members? What can they accomplish by letting go? How does the physician facilitate the process?

How might the accomplishment be interpreted as the physician's? How does providing an appropriate physical and emotional environment—in which family members can be present, say their good-byes, grieve, and offer acts of love—constitute an accomplishment? Could this scenario serve somehow as a metaphor for physician-assisted death?

In what ways is the poem itself an accomplishment? Has the poet, in the act of recording this piece of personal history, translated reality into memory and thus given it meaning? In what ways might "writing it down" reduce the pain of her loss as she participates in the ritual of recording and preserving the evidence?

We used a variation of this exercise recently as one of three case studies for analysis at an annual meeting of the Academy of Palliative Care

Physicians. The poem was also used as one of three case studies at the second annual meeting of Hospice Physicians at the International Hospice Institute Symposium in Vancounver, July 14, 1995. If our experience holds true, these questions will provide more than enough stimulation for discussion on several levels. The issues that the poem generates and its usefulness notwithstanding, we must remember that it is, first and foremost, a work of art. As such, and to assure that it has truly not "evaporated" in translation, it is appropriate to preserve some time at the end of discussion to reread the poem aloud. The impact that such a rereading creates is often surprising and may even provide that wonderful "Aha!" that individual students may have struggled to achieve while grappling with their own deeply personal recollections.

Conclusion

> We shall not cease from exploration
> And the end of all our exploring
> Will be to arrive where we started
> And know the place for the first time.
> [Eliot 1942]

The arts, as we have seen, can serve as a useful ally to physicians and physicians-in-training as they brave the universal experiences of life and death. Literature and painting (and, Herman Feifel would hasten to add, music) have an amazing aptitude for moving us from complacency and self-absorption toward a more purposeful involvement with others. For physicians in particular—this breed apart—the arts can provide the comfort of aesthetic distance as they navigate the emotional tightrope between detached and involved concern.

Whatever their value for provoking controlled, enlightened introspection, the methods I have outlined for employing the arts in the medical school curriculum can serve still another purpose—that of helping to restore a measure of humanity to today's frighteningly impersonal health care system. By focusing attention on the individual—by seeking to establish or reestablish connections between the personal and professional personae—medical educators can help smooth the rough terrain of intention and desire that often lies between patient and provider, patient and family, and individual and psyche. With unwavering attention to the universality of experience and the simple truth expressed by art through the ages, physicians can learn to bolster their humanity from the strength and consolation they derive from being party to a good death.

Acknowledgments

None of our work at the University of Massachusetts Medical School with "The Very First Patient" would have been possible without two decades worth of commitment, guidance, and support from Sandy Marks, Jr., who believes as firmly as Herman Feifel that medicine should help us live better with our mortality.

My colleagues Joanne Trautmann Banks and David Barnard, Chairman of the Humanities Advisory Committee to the Academy of Hospice Physicians, contributed to the preparation of the physician facilitators. I must also acknowledge Barbara Sourkes for introducing me to the poetry of Tess Gallagher.

References

Adson, M. A. (1995). An endangered ethic—the capacity for caring. *Mayo Clinic Proceedings* 70(5):495–500.

Beppu, K., and Tavormina, M. T. (1981). The healer's art: an interview with Richard Selzer. *Centennial Review* 25:20–40.

Bertman, S. L. (1991). *Facing Death Images, Insights, and Interventions.* New York: Taylor & Francis/Hemisphere.

Bertman, S. L., and Marks, S. C., Jr. (1989). The dissection experience as a laboratory for self-discovery about death and dying—another side of clinical anatomy. *Clinical Anatomy* 2:103–113.

Broyard, A. (1992). The patient examines the doctor. *Hippocrates*, April, pp. 75–78. Reprinted in *Intoxicated by My Illness*, by A. Broyard, pp. 31–58. New York: Fawcett Columbine.

Cassell, E. J. (1982). The nature of suffering and the goals of medicine. *New England Journal of Medicine* 305:639–645.

Coles, R. (1989). *The Call of Stories. Teaching and the Moral Imagination.* Boston: Houghton Mifflin.

Coulehan, J., Williams, P., Kandis, D., and Naser, C. (1995). The first patient: reflections and stories about the anatomy cadaver. *Teaching and Learning in Medicine* 7:61–66.

Dickinson, E. (1865). The dying need but little, dear. In *The Complete Poems of Emily Dickinson*, ed. T. Johnson. Boston: Little, Brown, 1960.

Dodge, J. (1995). In *Medical Student Experiences in Hospice Care, San Diego Hospital.* Paper presented at Palliative Medicine Curriculum Development for Physicians-in-Training Conference sponsored by the Center of Palliative Studies San Diego Hospice and University of California San Diego School of Medicine, September 28–30, San Diego, CA.

Eddy, D. M. (1994). A conversation with my mother. *JAMA* 272(3):179–181.

Eliot, T. S. (1942). Little Gidding. In Four quartets. In *Collected Poems 1909–1962*. New York: Harcourt Brace & World, 1963.

Feifel, H. (1963). Death. In *Taboo Topics*, ed. N. Farberow, pp. 8–21. New York: Atherton.

——— (1977). The function of attitudes towards death. *Death and Grief: Selected Readings for the Medical Student.* New York: Health Sciences Publishing.

Feifel, H., Hanson, S., Jones, R., and Edwards, L. (1967). Physicians consider death. *Proceedings, 75th Annual Convention*, APA, pp. 201–202.

Feldman, B. (1994). Dimensions of dying. *Yale Alumni Magazine*, October, pp. 54–57.

Frisch, M. (1959). *Homo Faber*, trans. M. Bullock. New York: Harcourt Brace Jovanovich.

Gallagher, T. (1984). Accomplishment. *Willingly*. Port Townsend, WA: Graywolf.

Gonzalez-Crussi, F. (1995). *Suspended Animation: Six Essays on the Preservation of Bodily Parts*. New York: Harcourt Brace. Cited in Rest in pieces, by J. Banville. *New York Times Book Review*, November 12, 1995, p. 8.

Gregg, A. (1957). *For Future Doctors*. Chicago: University of Chicago Press.

Herbst, L. (1995). *Medical student experiences in hospice care, San Diego Hospital*, presented at Palliative Medicine Curriculum Development for Physicians-in-Training Conference, sponsored by the Center of Palliative Studies San Diego Hospice and University of California San Diego School of Medicine, September 28–30, San Diego, CA.

Kasman, D. (1994). When a heart stops. *Annals of Internal Medicine* 120:432–433.

Klass, P. (1987). *A Not Entirely Benign Procedure: Four Years as a Medical Student*. New York: Putnam.

Knox, R. (1995). Project to diminish pain for dying called a failure. *Boston Globe*, November 22, pp. 1, 14.

Kromhout, A. (1995). Thoughts on hospice care. In *Medical Student Experiences in Hospice Care*, ed. L. Herbst, p. 17. San Diego, CA: San Diego Hospice.

Laurenson, K. (1995). Patient care in palliative care settings. In *Medical Student Experiences in Hospice Care, San Diego Hospital*. Paper presented at Palliative Medicine Curriculum Development for Physicians-In-Training Conference sponsored by the Center of Palliative Studies San Diego Hospice and University of California San Diego School of Medicine, September 28–30, San Diego, CA.

Lewin, B. D. (1946). Psychosomatic medicine. *Psychoanalytic Quarterly* 3(8):195–199.

Long, N. (1995). One breath apart. Poem read at University of Massachusetts Medical School Memorial Service, May 24.

Loxterkamp, D. (1993). "A good death is hard to find." *Journal of the American Board of Family Practice* 6:415–417.

Lynn, J. (1993). *Travels in the Valley of the Shadow*. Unpublished manuscript.

Marks, S. C., Jr., and Bertman, S. L. (1980). Experiences in learning about death and dying in the undergraduate anatomy curriculum. *Journal of Medical Education* 55: 48–52.

Marti-Ibanez, F. (1960). To be a doctor. *MD* Medical Newsmagazine. Reprinted in *On Doctoring*, ed. R. Reynolds and J. Stone. NY: Simon & Schuster, 1991.

McCue, J. (1995). The naturalness of dying. *Journal of the American Medical Association* 273(13):1039–1043.

Mermann, A. C., Gunn, D. B., and Dickinson, G. E. (1991). Learning to care for the dying: a survey of medical schools and a model course. *Academic Medicine* 66:35–38.

Moviac, M. (1995). My experience at San Diego Hospice. In *Medical Student Experiences in Hospice Care, San Diego Hospital*. Paper presented at Palliative Medicine Curriculum Development for Physicians-in-Training Conference sponsored by the Center of Palliative Studies San Diego Hospice and University of California San Diego School of Medicine, September 28–30, San Diego, CA.

Osler, W. (1905). *Aequanimitas with Other Addresses to Medical Students, Nurses and Practitioners of Medicine*, 3rd ed. London: HK Lewis, 1948.

Peabody, F. W. (1927, 1984). The care of the patient. *Journal of the American Medical Association* 88:877–882, 252:813–818.

Penney, J. C. (1985). Reactions of medical students to dissection. *Journal of Medical Education* 60:58–60.

Peters, A. (1990). Death and medicine: a personal account. *American Journal of Medicine* 89:81–82.

Pope, R. (1991). *Illness and Healing: Images of Cancer*. Nova Scotia, Canada: Lancelot.

Price, R. (1994). *A Whole New Life*. New York: Atheneum.

Saunders, C. (1988). Spiritual pain. *Journal of Palliative Care* 4(3):29–32.

Selzer, R. (1982). Toenails. In *Letters to a Young Doctor*, pp. 64–69. New York: Simon & Schuster.

Sexton, A. (1975). Doctors. In *The Awful Rowing Toward God*. Boston: Houghton Mifflin.

Sharkey, F. (1982). *A Parting Gift*. New York: St. Martin's Press.

Stone, I. (1961). *The Agony and the Ecstacy*. New York: Doubleday.

SUPPORT Investigators (1955). Care for seriously ill hospitalized patients. *Journal of the American Medical Association* 274(20):1591–1598.

Waikar, M. (1995). My experience at San Diego Hospice. In *Medical Student Experiences in Hospice Care, San Diego Hospital*. Paper presented at Palliative Medicine Curriculum Development for Physicians-in-Training Conference sponsored by the Center of Palliative Studies San Diego Hospice and UCSD School of Medicine, September 28–30, San Diego, CA.

Waller, D. (1995). Quoted by Lewis, C. R. (1995). Teaching palliative medicine at the bedside. Paper presented at Palliative Medicine Curriculum Development for Physicians-in-Training Conference sponsored by the Center of Palliative Studies San Diego Hospice and UCSD School of Medicine, September 28–30, San Diego, CA.

Walsh, T. (1991). An overview of palliative care in cancer and AIDS. *Oncology* 5(9): supplement.

Wear, D. (1987). Medical students' encounters with the cadaver: a poetic response. *Death Studies* 11:123–130.

——— (1989). Cadaver talk: medical students' accounts of their year-long experience. *Death Studies* 13:379–391.

Weisman, A. (1977). Psychosocial considerations in terminal care. In *Death and Grief: Selected Readings for the Medical Student*, ed. D. Peretz et al. New York: Health Sciences Publishing.

Weissman, D. (1995). Why teach palliative care? Presented at Palliative Medicine Curriculum Development for Physicians in Training Conference. Center for Palliative Studies, San Diego Hospice, September 30.

Winkler, M. G. (1993). Visual arts and medical ethics. *Second Opinion* 18:60–69.

Winkler, M. G., and Bertman, S. L. (1995). Medicine and the arts. *Academic Medicine* 70(9):822–823.

PART III
Children and Adolescents

Young people die and experience the deaths of others. There is also an undeniable link between young people's attitudes toward death and those of the adults they become. These realities make it vitally important for all of us to understand the meaning of death, dying, and bereavement in the world of children and adolescents. In her survey of the literature, Hannelore Wass (Chapter 9) takes a critical look at the progress that has been made during the last forty years. She finds that considerable knowledge has been gained in comprehending the needs of dying and bereaved children and their families, but that studies of death attitudes and beliefs among healthy children are sparse. She surmises that the taboo on death that Herman Feifel broke in the area of adult study is still apparent in the realm of young persons. Charles Corr (Chapter 10) takes the reader into the world of children as they think about death and its meaning. Using Maria Nagy's classic study as a starting point, he surveys the literature on children's questions about death and gives a developmental account of how their ideas change. Like Wass, Corr finds that there is a need for considerably more research than has been done up to now.

PART IV

Children and Adolescents

9

Children, Adolescents, and Death

HANNELORE WASS

As we honor Herman Feifel, the person who has played a pivotal role in the emergence and expansion of the modern death movement, it may be appropriate to cast a somewhat critical eye on the movement's accomplishments, perhaps to appreciate the intransigence of the fundamental questions concerning the meanings of death, but also to derive some guidance for future study. Although research alone cannot solve social problems, it can contribute to the knowledge base from which effective social action can spring.

This century has often been called the "century of the child," and in fact, great strides have been made in such fields as child development, psychology, psychiatry, health care, and education. It is reasonable to raise the question about how children have fared in thanatology. (In this chapter the words *children* and *childhood* will be inclusive, denoting also *adolescents* and *adolescence* unless specified otherwise.) One looks in vain for discussions of death—or even mere mention of the subject—in the major texts and professional books in the fields concerning children. Yet even a cursory review of the literature on death and dying shows the remarkable scope and range of this area of study, with contributions from psychology, medicine, nursing, social work, and education, adding up to a considerable amount since the outset of the death movement. Such omission of thanatological content from professional texts may simply reflect a paucity of knowledge. On the other hand, it may be part of a general pattern, a lack of integration of the basic findings, concepts, and wisdom into the mainstream of the relevant professional disciplines and fields (Wass 1992). For example, although numerous studies have pointed to the importance of psychosocial care for dying persons and offered hospices as a model for integrating such care into the medical component, and although hospice programs have operated for more than two decades, such knowledge seldom appears in medical curricula or textbooks. Similarly, despite a voluminous literature on bereavement and grief that has accumulated, such research rarely receives mention in standard course work in clinical or counseling psychology. Three related questions, then, may be asked: (1) How much attention have children received as the field of death and dying evolved? (2) What findings have emerged that may constitute a knowledge base? (3) What gaps exist and challenges lie ahead for researchers, practitioners, and society? In this chapter I will attempt to answer these questions in terms of the issues of dying, bereavement, orientations toward death, and education.

Dying

Although early studies on dying children tended to concentrate more on issues confronting adults (e.g., strains on parents' marriage, anticipatory grief, needs for emotional support, and communications with children), groundbreaking studies gave important insights into children's attitudes toward their illness. In particular, they showed that dying children experience fears and anxieties (Natterson and Knutson 1960, Vernick and Karon 1965), are aware of their condition (Waechter 1971), and, in fact, develop considerable knowledge about it (Bluebond-Langner 1978). Although the implications of these findings for open communications and psychological support seem obvious, hospitals were slow in responding. Meanwhile the hospice movement, a grass-roots effort to provide alternative care for the terminally ill, began in the United States with the first program in New Haven, Connecticut in 1974, and expanded to more than 2,000 organizations. As programs of person-centered care that address social, psychological, and spiritual as well as medical needs, hospices may be the most visible barometer of success in the death movement. Yet for more than a decade children were conspicuously absent from the hospice population. Surely this reflects the difficulties adults have, caregivers included, in accepting that children die. Child advocates among health professionals, in particular the organization Children's Hospice International, have urged the inclusion of children in hospice care. As a result of these efforts, today more than a fourth of the hospice organizations in the United States do admit children (Miller-Thiel et al. 1993). This is all the more remarkable in view of the advances in medical research and technologies concerning childhood malignancies, bringing with them new hope for cure and added press to continuing aggressive treatment even if chances of successful outcome are extremely slim.

Effective and compassionate care for dying children need not be confined to hospices. As Children's Hospice International and others suggest, principles and procedures of hospice care can be applied in traditional health care settings (Armstrong-Dailey 1991). Health professionals agree, provided there are structural flexibility, resources, and adequate education (Wheeler et al. 1986).

New studies on the psychological impact of terminal illness, especially childhood cancer, confirm pioneering findings. Young children know about their illness even when no information is given (Claflin and Barbarin 1991); hospitalized young children often refuse to play with the toys of diseased peers and avoid mentioning their names (Bluebond-Langner 1989). And a close inverse relationship between knowledge and anxiety, found in recent investigations, suggests that knowledge of illness and treatments can significantly reduce children's anxiety while at the same time meeting a strong need for information (Katz et al. 1980, Susman et al. 1987). Although some children need denial as a way of coping with their emotions, to protect family members or to maintain privacy, it is agreed today that open communication among child, family, and the caregiving team is an essential aspect of care. A number of clinical studies have added to the understanding of the agonies and suffering, the hopes and frustrations, as well as the courage and inner strength in children as they confront the central issue in their lives, the issue of loss—loss of life, of control, of self, and of relationships—and have underscored the associated needs for love and security, support, sense of belonging, and self-respect (e.g., Adams 1984, Papadatou 1989, Sourkes 1982, Waechter 1984, Zeltzer 1988). Research on stress among professionals who care for terminally ill children has provided further insights into the dynamics of stress and pointed to ways some of this stress can be alleviated (Vachon and Pakes 1984). Increasingly, hospitals are responding to the child's needs and those of the family with an array of social-psychological services, both inpatient and outpatient, such as counseling, social work, expressive therapies, hospital/home-bound teaching, group support, and cancer camps.

Living with Life-Threatening Illness

In many cases questions about whether to offer hospital, hospice, or home care have become irrelevant. Because of dramatic advances in the treatment of childhood malignancies, with increasingly higher survival rates and long periods of remission following initial diagnosis and treatment, cancer has, in effect, become a chronic illness. This has created a new set of issues for child, family, and health care professionals. Correspondingly, newer studies have focused on description and analysis of these issues and on ways child and family can be supported (Dowell et al. 1988). Emerging from this work is the identification of perhaps the greatest problem for these children, namely, to navigate and reconcile the two different worlds in which they live—one medical, in which there is the threat of relapse and death, and often painful treatment with uncomfortable side effects, and the other the social world of home, school, and community in which the child has to reestablish relationships and learn to function successfully. To achieve such integration the child is confronted with at least four major tasks. First, the child has to learn to create a normal life despite the uncertainty of the illness. Second, the child needs to develop skills for coping with the illness-related stresses and pain. Third, the child has to maintain positive self-esteem and personal identity. Fourth, the child has to maintain positive relationships with parents, caregivers, peers, and teachers (Zeltzer 1988). Each of these tasks involves smaller tasks and challenges. For instance, illness-related stress may involve pain caused by treatment, and may call for specific coping skills such as mental rehearsal and relaxation exercises. None of the tasks may be more challenging than the first. Creating a normal life under these circumstances may require major restructuring of the child's life and involves the child's reconstruction of the meaning and purpose of life. Similarly, in light of medical procedures often leading to disfigurement and other negative physical consequences, the child may need to learn to look far beyond the physical to mental and spiritual aspects of personhood, a formidable task for young people in whom personal identity is closely linked with the one concrete aspect of the self—the body. The need for a coordinated network of support from family, the medical team, and the community to help the child with these tasks is emphasized (Chesler and Barbarin 1987).

Bereavement in Childhood

Although there is an extensive research literature on bereavement, comparatively far fewer studies have focused on children than on adults. Pioneering explorations such as Bowlby's (1960) on infants' reactions to loss and separation, and Furman's (1974) observations of bereaved young children in therapy, largely stood alone in the early years of death studies. Fortunately, there has been considerable interest in the study of childhood bereavement since the mid-1980s. From the research and clinical literature a number of findings have emerged.

Healthy Grieving

Many acute reactions to loss in children resemble those of adults, with children exhibiting similar somatic symptoms (e.g., sleep and digestive disturbances and uncontrolled sobbing), and similar responses in the cognitive-affective domain (e.g., shock, confusion, distress, losses in self-esteem). Behaviorally children respond by acting out or withdrawing, by lack of concentration, and by lowered academic achievement (Kranzler et al. 1990, Wessel 1984). However, in normal circumstances and supportive environments, children tend to show resilience and hardiness and the ability to go forward with their lives and developmental tasks and generally to cope successfully with their loss without the need for special professional intervention.

New results from an extensive longitudinal study of nonpsychiatric children contribute substantially to the definition of healthy and normal responses to bereavement in childhood, at the same time identifying a new dimension of grieving in children (Silverman et al. 1992, Silverman and Worden 1992). They show that most children maintain active connections with their dead parents, dreaming about them, feeling close to them, talking to them, and perceiving them to be their guides. In the psychoanalytic literature, hallucination about dead parents' presence is understood to be a coping mechanism of denial and considered maladaptive. In contrast, the new data suggest that mental constructions of dead parents are normal and apparently function to facilitate coping (such continuing bonds are also reported for bereaved adults). Similarly, "anniversary reactions," cyclic reactivation of intense grief on birthdays, anniversaries of the funeral, and so on, observed in children as in adults, are considered a normal part of long-term adjustment to loss (Johnson and Rosenblatt 1981).

This is not to suggest absence of problems and complications with grief in childhood and later, as shown in studies of adult psychopathology and effects of traumatic deaths such as in war and in the Holocaust, and other horrendous deaths (Krell 1985, Leviton 1991), and in ongoing studies indicating the presence of posttraumatic stress disorders in children surviving violent deaths (Frederick 1987, Saigh 1985).

Developmental factors seem to be related to the experience of grief, although the strength of this relationship is unclear. While the early belief that children are incapable of grieving has proven incorrect, it is less clear when they are capable. Bowlby's (1960) observations of infants' and young children's responses to maternal separation, in which he identified a sequential pattern of behavior he labeled "protest," "despair," and "detachment," may be one of the earliest to lead to the suggestion that grief and mourning are present at early ages. Similar responses found in monkeys may point to a biological basis for grief (Laudenslager et al. 1993). While some new studies report children as young as 3 years of age as able to express grief (Kranzler et al. 1990), others indicate that young children are often uncertain about what they feel (or perhaps what they think they ought to feel), or are unable to articulate their feelings

(Silverman and Worden 1992). Whether this inconsistency is a reflection of individual differences or differences in the sampling and other methodological procedures remains open. Still, the level of cognitive development appears to contribute substantially to the ability to grieve. Children with an immature understanding of death are often bewildered and frightened, believe that the parent deliberately left, perhaps in anger, and are fearful that the surviving parent will also leave. Although following the death of a parent the sense of basic security may be threatened in *all* children, cognitive immaturity may cause the young child to be *more* bewildered and *more* threatened. Psychologists and educators have stressed that, along with providing love, reassurance, and support, the child will be helped when adults communicate openly and give correct, specific, and patient explanations, over a period of time if needed (Furman 1984, Grollman 1990, Wass and Corr 1984).

Studies focusing on bereavement in the adolescent years, especially following the death of a sibling (Balk 1983, Hogan and DeSantis 1992, Martinson et al. 1987), suggest that adolescents' grief may not differ significantly in kind or quality from that of younger children (or adults), but rather that grief issues superimposed on critical developmental issues in this phase, those of identity and interpersonal relationships in particular, may be a compounding factor as surviving adolescent siblings attempt to cope with their loss. Future studies may lead to improved understanding of these dynamics. An important step in this direction is the development of a theory of adolescent grief that posits the trajectories of grief and personal growth as well as continuing attachments and relationships among them (Hogan and DeSantis 1996). Surprisingly few new studies have examined the impact of a parent's death in adolescence, considering the important role of parents in helping children to resolve issues of identity and autonomy in this period of transition, and also considering the critical role of parents in coping with death identified in the literature. Although there is evidence suggesting that the death of a parent complicates the resolution of these issues (Krupnick 1984), further studies are needed to provide better insights into the dynamics of grief following a parent's death in this developmental period.

Family and Community Support

The literature is clear on the critical importance of a supportive family for successful grief resolution in childhood. Early studies in adult psychiatry retrospectively implicated the loss of a parent in childhood as a cause of later maladaptations such as depression and schizophrenia (Beck et al. 1963), and ground-breaking observations of parentally bereaved young children in psychoanalytic treatment by Furman (1974) and her associates, pointed to persistent problems in adjustment beginning early in life. Supporting early observations, recent studies have identified emotional health of surviving parents, family stability, and the quality of family life as critical factors for successful coping in children (Fristad et al. 1993, Kranzler et al. 1990). Attention to the family as a system has opened new avenues for exploration such as the effects on the child of the often serious unbalancing of status and shifts in relationships following the death of a family member (Hare-Mustin 1979). Similarly, the effects of familial communication patterns and unspoken codes may affect the child. In some families, for example, parents respond to a death by keeping distant and covering up feelings, in others the topic of death is taboo, while in still others pain, anger, sadness, and other emotions are shared in open communication (Raphael 1983). Recognition of such patterns and codes and identification of different, potentially conflicting coping strategies by adults in the family may assist in planning support for the bereaved child.

Combining these factors with the effects of the high levels of stress experienced in many families, it becomes apparent that bereaved families, children and adults alike, can benefit from social and emotional support and counseling offered by community agencies and other groups. When a child has lost a parent through death the surviving parent has lost a spouse, and when a child's sibling dies parents lose a child. It is understandable, therefore, that the adult family members may exhaust their own inner resources, leaving none to tend to the needs of their child. Thus, support for adults can be a valuable resource that indirectly benefits children as well. Mutual support groups and services for adults became popular in the 1970s and 1980s, the time when a large volume of data on adult bereavement was produced. The Compassionate Friends, an international organization for bereaved parents, established more than 400 chapters throughout the United States and Canada. Support is also increasingly available through hospices, community-based crisis intervention, and long-term family counseling programs following disasters. Since the mid-1980s, the value of *direct* social and emotional support for bereaved children has been recognized. Consequently, in addition to adult services, communities have begun to develop programs specifically designed for children, typically provided by hospices, hospitals, or by community-based volunteer groups. Even public schools have become more sensitive to grief-related issues, as illustrated by teachers' responses to the explosion of the U.S. space shuttle Challenger 10 that killed seven astronauts, including a teacher, which millions of schoolchildren watched on television (Blume et al. 1986). Schools have also begun to offer suicide intervention and grief support programs (Leenaars and Wenckstern 1991, Wass et al. 1990), albeit not at a desirable level of quality (Sandoval et al. 1994).

Attitudes Toward Death

The study of attitudes is one of the most complex subjects that has emerged in psychology, generating dozens of theories, several hundred operational definitions, and numerous variables thought to be involved in attitude change (Durlak 1994). In this discussion the word *attitudes* is defined in the broadest terms, including both the cognitive and the affective dimensions. It would be presumptuous to claim such complexity can be adequately represented in the context of a single chapter. Still, a survey of the literature focusing on children and death-related attitudes may be instructive. The understanding of death-related orientations in children was very much a concern among pioneers as evidenced in Feifel's ground-breaking work *The Meaning of Death* (1959) in which two chapters are devoted to this subject. In Feifel's *New Meanings of Death* (1977) a third chapter is added and numerous references to children are found throughout the book. But a striking finding from a survey of the entire literature is that researchers have concentrated on the development of the understanding of death in children, neglecting other cognitive aspects, such as beliefs and concerns, and have largely ignored the affective dimensions.

Understanding Death

From early investigations of European children (Anthony 1940, Nagy 1948) to studies in the United States four decades later, findings indicate that the comprehension of death progresses from an immature understanding in early childhood to a more mature understanding in older childhood. This process is consistent with general principles of development and by many psychologists considered essentially compatible with Piaget's model of cognitive development, which suggests that the child acquires concepts not in random fashion but in a general sequence as the child's reasoning abilities develop (Jenkins and Cavanaugh 1985, Koocher 1973, Reilly et al. 1983, Wass 1995, White et al. 1978). Thus, pronounced qualitative differences between younger and older children's understanding of death are closely linked to the differences in their reasoning abilities. Very young children with an immature reasoning capacity tend to understand death as a reversible event, a temporary restriction, externally caused, with life restorable by various means, as compared with older children at more mature levels. At least three aspects of a mature understanding of death—the concepts of universality (the understanding that all living things die); irreversibility (the understanding that after a living thing has died, its physical body cannot be made alive again); and nonfunctionality (the understanding that all life-giving functions cease at death)—are more or less sequentially acquired in a four-year period in the early school and preadolescent years (Speece and Brent 1992). As in any developmental process, transitions from one phase to another are uneven and children differ in the rates at which they progress. But even greater differences may be caused by other factors.

Developmental Patterns and Meanings

A number of problems are inherent in the study of developmental processes, death-related concepts and attitudes included. One problem is the neglect of social, cultural, and situational factors that may influence this development. Assessing these factors is particularly challenging to the social scientist. Most of the studies reported in this literature were conducted with middle-class white children—a population that is accessible to researchers. Consequently, the findings may not be universally valid. They do not necessarily apply to the substantial numbers of children in the United States who live and grow up in environments radically different from middle-class children and whose experiences with death often are also radically different. To date there are no empirical data that might provide an understanding of how social conditions such as poverty, prejudice, and family violence influence children's concepts, beliefs, or concerns about death.

Determining when a child has the cognitive capacity to understand death in the ways Western cultures have determined are "mature" is not the same as discovering what death *means* to a child, and what his or her beliefs, concerns, preoccupations, and fears about death are. Ultimately, such meanings may be unique, based on particular constellations and interactions among developmental factors and forces in a child's life. Nonetheless, empirical studies attempt to discover what the critical factors and forces are and what patterns and configurations children have in common. Thus while there are wide variations among children in all aspects of attitude development—understanding, beliefs, and concerns— relationships do exist between cognitive capacity and content.

There is evidence of a developmental pattern in the preoccupation with violent death, showing young children concerned about being devoured by monsters or wild animals, shot or stabbed by people, or killed in accidents, and older children concerned about war and destruction of the environment (Koocher 1973, Nagy 1948, Schilder and Wechsler 1934, Wenestam and Wass 1987). Not surprisingly, violent death themes are more prominent in boys than in girls throughout the childhood years (Tamm and Granqvist 1995).

There is less clarity about the concerns in adolescents, those young persons in the state of transition between childhood and adulthood. Professionals in developmental psychology and mental health disagree on the definition of adolescence and on its predominant features. Some suggest that this period is one of emotional upheavals, of "storm and stress," while others believe it is one in which young persons are relatively carefree, enjoying life, and regarding themselves highly. Many studies do suggest that these transitional years are often problematic, especially in this culture (Csikszentmihalyi and Larson 1984, Kazdin 1993). Most professionals also agree that the central issues in adolescence concern the achievement of personal identity, autonomy, and mature social relationships. But their association to death and dying are not clear. Those few who have considered such relationships suggest that while perhaps not consumed with existential angst, adolescents nevertheless are confronted with issues of being, not being, and becoming, and are at least vulnerable to such anxiety (Kastenbaum 1986). From existing studies it appears that the preoccupation is primarily with life and future. While adolescents continue to be concerned with violent death, there seems to be a shift in focus from concerns about the forms of dying to concerns about the state of death. Studies in nuclearism in the 1980s focusing specifically on the nuclear threat, suggest that adolescents worry less about the possibility of nuclear war than do children at younger ages (Goldberg et al. 1985, Solantaus et al. 1984). It has also been theorized that linked with the ability for abstract reasoning characteristic of the later childhood/adolescent years is a personal egocentrism, which entails the twin feelings of personal uniqueness and indestructibility. This would explain why adolescents engage in risky, life-endangering behaviors. But new evidence shows adolescents to feel no more invulnerable than adults (Quadrel et al. 1993). More parsimonious explanations might be that adolescents are impulsive and often give in to peer pressure. Other variables may underlie risk-taking behaviors, such as frustration, a sense of alienation, a lack of purpose in life, and a pessimistic worldview. The dramatic increase in the rate of suicide among adolescents also points at issues accentuated in this period of life. The problem is that there are a number of speculations but few empirical data. There is a great need for further studies in which the dynamic interactions between the intellectual and emotional components of death-related attitudes are examined more closely.

Developmental status also influences children's religious beliefs. What children understand about concepts such as Heaven and God reflects the thinking and reasoning modes at their developmental level.

While the volume of work on children's religious beliefs is slim, past studies indicate a positive relationship between cognitive capacity and belief. According to these observations, for example, children developmentally at the level of concrete reasoning ability tend to hold concepts of Heaven and God that are based on their experiences. Many younger children view God concretely as a father figure, except that He is much stronger, taller, older, and wields more authority than their earthly fathers. He provides food and gives permission for dead people to become angels; he imposes certain restrictions, for example one can't play noisy games in Heaven; and there is no ladder to get back down to earth (Gartley and Bernasconi 1967, Heller 1986). Other children use their scientific knowledge as a basis for disbelief or skepticism about the existence of Heaven (Nagy 1948). Adolescents, by contrast, having reached the level of formal operations or abstract reasoning, tend to formulate abstract ideas about death and afterlife as a state of darkness, eternal light, transition, spiritual existence at another level, a state of fulfillment, peace, beauty, or as a void, nothingness (Tamm and Granqvist 1995, Wenestam and Wass 1987).

Fears and Anxieties

There is a dearth of empirical knowledge about death-related fears, anxieties, and concerns in healthy children. What little information there is relies heavily on clinical case reports and anecdotal material or data that emerged as a by-product of cognition-oriented studies. There may be many reasons for this gap in the literature, such as professional concerns about research with vulnerable subjects and lack of accessibility. But other reasons for this neglect may reside in the major theoretical orientations in psychology in this century. After all, in Freud's psychoanalytic thinking, death anxiety is not part of normal psychological development but derived from other anxieties (Wass and Cason 1984), and when it occurs it is a symptom of neurosis. Cognitive theories tend to neglect affective dimensions of personality development and functioning or translate them to fit into their models. And behaviorism generally bypasses internal phenomena such as fear, anxiety, and other emotions. Even a casual perusal of the literature on the effects of filmed and televised aggression shows the critical outcome variable commonly studied has been behavior (and the theoretical basis, in the main, social learning and modeling theory). But even in the enormous literature on death anxiety that is largely atheoretical—nearly 1,000 studies in all (Neimeyer and Van Brunt 1995)—practically no studies exist on children. Nor have any of the numerous instruments for measuring death fears or anxieties been adapted for use with children.

Thoughts and conclusions of early studies may be of historical interest, as the suggestion that two types of death anxiety are present, chronic and critical; the first is the child's reaction to his or her own aggressive impulses and does not depend on a clear understanding of death, while the second appears when the child recognizes that he or she is an independent being and therefore can die (Anthony 1940). Or one may note, in contrast, the conclusion based on galvanic skin responses to death-related and neutral words that children experience death anxiety, regardless of age or developmental status (Alexander and Adlerstein 1958). However, studies are needed in today's cultural and social context in order to understand death-related attitudes and behaviors and their etiology in the contemporary generation of children.

Themes of Violence and Children

However much we abhor violence as individuals and even though the subject has become a favorite in political campaigns, as a society we encourage, accept, or tolerate it in many forms, real and symbolic. How children can escape its effects and how violence can be prevented in the first place surely are among the most pressing questions of our time.

Symbolic violence seems rampant. From the heroes of the Wild West to the modern day Rambos and Schwarzeneggers, the settling of interpersonal conflicts and dispensing of "justice" with a gun are the stuff that heros are made of. Television violence may have reached an all-time high. Its significance with respect to children is underscored in view of at least three factors. One such factor is *exposure*. According to one conservative estimate, children watch an average of twenty-five hours of television each week, more than any other out-of-school activity (Timmer et al. 1985). Even with the availability of numerous independent channels, there are relatively few programs designed for children. This may be one reason why the majority of young viewers watch prime-time programs. Not only does prime-time drama contain a great deal of violence, but aggressive acts are committed by heroes, not only by villains, and by secondary characters as well, and are commonly rewarded. The repetitiveness of such portrayals may lead to the perception that violence is normal (Comstock and Paik 1991). More children watch news than previously, at a time when images of starvation, war, and genocide, in horror and magnitude almost beyond imagining, are transmitted to the television screen. Adding the access to a largely unrated home video market, it becomes clear that children are flooded with images of violence in their daily lives.

Perceptions of reality is a second factor. The influence of television on adult opinions, views, and perceptions of reality has been documented and evidence suggests such influence on children as well (Comstock and Paik 1991). In fact, the impact on children may be more profound because distinctions between fantasy and reality are less clear in childhood. The trend to merge news and entertainment (e.g., in the "docudrama"), and improved technologies for visual reconstruction of events, may further contribute to distorted perceptions.

Parental attitudes are a third factor. Parents are surprisingly tolerant of media violence. Studies show them to be only slightly concerned that their children may seek out obscene and savagely violent material (Lin and Atkin 1989). Film rating systems are based more on sexual than on violent content. Adults commonly take young children to see movies that are extremely violent. With multiple television sets, channel capabilities, and (in three-fourths of households) VCRs, parental monitoring and mediation have become less and less feasible.

Yet negative effects of filmed and televised aggression on children have been demonstrated extensively in the literature. One of the most significant services by a professional organization in connection with media violence is the work of the American Psychological Association's Commission on Violence and Youth (APACVY). As part of a two-year study, the commission heard expert testimony and reviewed and summarized the findings of four decades of research on the effects of filmed aggression on child viewers. (The most recent prior summary of research was published by the National Institute of Mental Health in 1982.) The commission concluded that televised violence has at least these four effects on children: frequent viewing is associated with increased acceptance of aggressive attitudes and behavior; television violence increases the fear in children of becoming a victim; it desensitizes children to violence; and it increases apathic behavior (APACVY 1993).

Children's toys and games further indicate the enculturation of violence in children, especially boys. Toy stores display large numbers of toys and games manufactured for the imitation of war and interpersonal aggression. Between 1984 and 1990 alone, the sale of war toys rose 500 percent, and for a number of years the best-selling single toy during Christmas season has been a war toy (Carlsson-Paige and Levin 1990). Some of the many types of toy guns with which children play are so closely imitated that they are increasingly mistaken for real guns even by police officers; conversely, several thousand young children shoot themselves and other children by playing with real guns they find in their homes. The popularity of video games and video arcades that have sprung up across the country gives an idea of the extent of playful violence in older children.

Given the increasing frequency of children's viewing of televised news and the frequency of reports of disasters, wars, and horrendous deaths, it is important to examine the effects of such viewing on children's fears and concerns, thereby extending the data that already exist on the influence of violent themes in drama on attitudes. Further investigations into the effect of television violence, in both fictional and factual programs, on children's perceptions of the physical and social world may improve our understanding of their sense of safety and security, their outlook, and their sense of their role in the world.

Many other questions remain about the nature, characteristics, and dynamics of death-related fears in children. How are such fears manifested? To what extent may they be masked or absent? Is an apparent absence of fear a sign of apathy and psychological numbness or of callousness in the face of too many destructive messages? Why do many children, although frightened by televised violence, nevertheless seem to seek out and apparently enjoy such fare? What are the relationships between fears and destructive behaviors? These are just a few of the questions. Answers to these and others may lead to better insights into risk-taking behaviors and assist in the development of more effective drug and AIDS education, and efforts to prevent violent behavior.

The most jarring data on fears and violent behavior in children in this country come not from empirical study but from simple statistics compiled by federal agencies. Children may or may not fear death or dying as thanatologists define these concepts, but they certainly and for good reasons fear for their lives. Statistics on homicidal behavior are at least one dramatic indicator of effects of violence on *some* children.

Actual violence, although not as extensive as people's perception of it, is nonetheless a stunning fact of life in our society. Nearly half of all American households have firearms, approximately 200 million, many of them handguns, and among them sophisticated semiautomatic and automatic assault weapons. Although according to FBI statistics individual homicides in the United States have consistently been around 25,000 per year, the rate is one of the highest in developed countries (Stark 1991). The number of injuries caused by violence is 100 times higher than the death rates. Many children witness violence. A study of eighth grade students in Chicago revealed that three-fourths had seen someone robbed, stabbed, shot, or killed (APACVY 1993). Not surprisingly, children arm themselves at an ever-increasing rate. One in five students carries a weapon to school, one in twenty admits he or she carries a gun according to a recent survey (Centers for Disease Control 1991), causing schools to install metal detectors and hire security guards to protect their students.

Despite the consistency of the overall homicide rate, homicidal behavior in young people has been rising at an alarming rate in the United

States. Murder arrests among 17-year-olds increased by 121% from 1985 to 1990, and was double this figure for 13- to 16-year-olds (Ewing 1990). In 1991, according to FBI statistics, the total number was 1,500—the highest ever reported (despite a decrease in youthful populations). There are believed to be close relationships between the drug business, drug abuse, and the increase in the number and criminal activity of youth gangs. Three-fourths of adolescent killings, either as victims or perpetrators, involve guns (APACVY 1993), yet the enactment of federal gun control seems unlikely in the near future.

The United States not only has the highest rate of individual homicide among developed countries, but also it is the only country among them with capital punishment. Thirty-seven states have death penalty laws; since 1976 close to 200 prisoners have been executed by electrocution, hanging, firing squad, gas chamber, or lethal injection. There is increasing pressure by the media to record executions "live" on television. According to polls, three-fourths of the population favor the death penalty.

Toward Solutions

A number of social forces, such as prejudice, economic inequity, domestic violence, and violence in the popular culture, contribute to the development of antisocial attitudes and behaviors. Consequently, prevention is an enormous task in which, ideally, scientists, practitioners, policy makers, and the public all participate. Two recent efforts merit attention, one focusing on media violence, the other dealing with the more general and complex issue of violent behavior.

The Television Violence Act, passed by the U.S. Congress in 1990, is a significant achievement considering the basic conflict that exists between public interest and the television industry, illustrated in the history of public policy-making regarding children's programming (Huston et al. 1992). The result of years of efforts by professional and citizen's advocacy groups (e.g., American Academy of Pediatrics, National Coalition on Television Violence), the Television Violence Act requires the industry voluntarily to reduce the violence level of material offered during prime time by threatening legislative action. Of course, political realignments can significantly alter various courses of actions, including follow-through and enforcement of enactments, thus the future of the television industry's self regulation with respect to the level of violence, remains open.

The second effort is the initiative taken by the American Psychological Association, first in appointing a commission to address the issue,

then in the extensive work of the Commission on Violence and Youth
outlining the problem in terms of developmental, social, and cultural
factors affecting violent behaviors in young people, and offering recommendations for the development of programs of intervention and long-
term prevention (APACVY 1993). This initiative is particularly remarkable considering that the major disciplines concerned with people, the
health, behavioral, and social sciences, have largely neglected the problem of violence, especially lethal violence. While the official federal and
organizational response to homicidal behavior has been the compilation
of ever-more discouraging data and statistics, relatively few serious studies have focused on the psychosocial causes and dynamics of homicidal
behavior, in effect relegating the entire issue to a criminal justice system that is ill-equipped to handle it. Of course, cultural and subcultural
factors raise particular problems for research because they resist the
usual methods of analysis. More fundamentally, traditional models for
homicidal behavior relying on such concepts as "passion" or "killer
instinct" may be dated, and alternative theoretical formulations such as
Becker's (1975) or Stark's (1991) needed to lead to more adequate explanations of the complex problem of homicide in our era. But at the most
fundamental level, the lack of attention to individual homicide and, with
few exceptions (e.g., Leviton 1991), to war and the phenomenon of "horrendous" deaths, may have its basis in a pessimistic view about human
nature. Although most social scientists the world over reject the theory
of genetic or evolutionary determination of human aggression, instead
viewing human aggression as preventable, the debate on this issue continues (Scott and Ginsburg 1994). Meanwhile children continue to grow
up surrounded with violence in various forms and continue to be affected,
some more profoundly than others. With its work on violence and youth,
the American Psychological Association is challenging professionals in
the social and behavioral sciences, policy makers, and others to be optimistic about the efficacy of social prevention, and to work to resolve a
problem that is in need of urgent solution.

Within the multidisciplinary approaches necessary for the understanding and prevention of violence, psychologists in particular are challenged to examine more closely those factors that contribute to violent
behavior in young people. They may profit from reexamination of variables already implicated, such as low self-esteem and lack of personal
identity, parental neglect or rejection, and lack of personal and social
skills. Further understanding may be gained by studying variables that
have not been explored in this context, such as attitudes toward life,
outlook, optimism, death fears and anxiety, perception of social reality,
empathy, caring, and altruism.

Death Education

Education represents a relatively neglected area in thanatology, despite its critical importance for making the results of basic research and scholarship available to the public. The public, of course, includes children, even though they may not come to mind immediately. The idea of death education for children was advanced early in the death movement (Leviton 1969). Death education has been promoted since then as demonstrated by numerous books and articles published to assist teachers with instructional goals, methodological approaches, and activities for different educational levels, and other resources (Crase and Crase 1984). The kind of death education for children proposed through the years essentially is concerned with giving basic knowledge about natural death, funeral and memorial customs, reactions to the loss of a loved one, and ways people can cope effectively with death and help others to cope—fairly straightforward goals in the minds of death educators. Nevertheless, death education has not been generally accepted or instituted. Less than a fourth of the public high schools in this country offer a unit or module on death in health education (promoted by leaders a quarter of a century ago), and in only a fraction is thanatological content integrated into other subjects in the regular school curricula (Wass et al. 1990). This lack may be a barometer of the general public's attitude toward death.

Schools are conservative institutions reflecting the values and orientations of the mainstream culture. If death were acknowledged as a significant part of the human experience, then basic knowledge of it would be a part of the cultural heritage passed on to the next generation. But this has not happened to an appreciable extent. This is not to disregard the valuable contributions that have been made. But special programs, separate and unincorporated into relevant subjects (e.g., biology, psychology, social events, and family life), usually rely on commitments of individual educators rather than the larger systems. And while the schools are becoming more open to crisis intervention efforts, developmental/preparatory death education does not appear to be on the horizon. Hostility from religious and political conservatives, resistance by school officials, apparent discomfort on the part of teachers, and even criticism by some professionals may conspire to keep death the controversial subject that it is in the schools. Yet the goals for preparatory death education, articulated by the pioneers and other leaders, remain valid today.

Death education for children is more complex. It is difficult always to distinguish clearly between the scientific aspects and those in the arena of values and beliefs or to keep emotionally neutral in intellectual discussion of the subject. This inherent problem makes the concern about professional standards and the quality of death education efforts, to which critics have pointed, all the more significant. But important steps toward the establishment of such standards have been taken by two major professional associations, the Association for Death Education and Counseling (ADEC) and the International Work Group on Death, Dying and Bereavement (IWG). ADEC has established a code of ethics and standards for death educators and counselors, which it distributes to its membership. Over a period of several years IWG has worked to articulate the basic assumptions and principles for education concerning death, dying, and bereavement (IWG 1994). Setting standards for death education is particularly important in programs for young people. Researchers have already shown that methodology influences teacher effectiveness (Durlak and Reisenberg 1991), have identified qualities of effective teachers (Durlak 1994), and admonished teachers to be mindful of different experiences with death that individual students bring to their classes. While these findings are based primarily on meta-analytic studies involving programs for college age and adult students, they may be extended to children as well. Classroom teachers and coordinators of crisis intervention efforts need to establish defensible and clear instructional goals and coordinated activities for achieving them. Similarly, qualities of effective teachers of college students, including knowledge of the subject matter, responsiveness to students, an understanding of group dynamics, skills in interpersonal communication, and the ability to counsel students in distress, should also be qualities in teachers and crisis team members working with children.

Long-term preparatory death education may, to a large degree, reduce the emotional intensity present in crisis situations, instead taking low-key approaches in which the subject of death is embedded in larger contexts. For both teaching and crisis intervention, the challenge will be to continue work toward establishing professional standards and to provide adequate professional preparation.

Death education for children may now be more important than ever. First, it may constitute a powerful antidote to the distorted perceptions resulting from the portrayal of death in the popular culture. By discussing causes of death, empathic human responses to death, and the experience of grief, the distortions created by the glorification of violent death can be counterbalanced. New content designed to develop media literacy (e.g., relationships between commercial sponsors and programming, types of programs, and rating systems) may assist children with a critical appraisal of media violence. Presentation of national statistics may lead to more realistic perceptions of lethal violence. Together, such information has the potential for reducing fears. It may be time to weigh concerns about arousing anxieties through death education in terms of its potential for reducing those already strong. Second, education can contribute to the prevention of violent behavior through the development of prosocial skills (e.g., cooperation, negotiation, interpersonal communication, tolerance, and empathy) as well as personal skills (e.g., management of anger and frustration).

Concluding Comment

Despite an uneven pattern of attention to the study of personal experiences with death in childhood, a considerable amount of knowledge has been generated. As a result we are communicating more openly with dying and bereaved children, have gained a better understanding of their needs, and have begun to provide improved care and support. In contrast, there has been far less interest in the vast majority of healthy, nonbereaved children and far less inclination to consider their needs or engage in helpful mediation. Scant attention has been given to determining their basic orientation toward death in the context of both cultural diversity and the homogenizing influence of the mass media. Ironically, the problem of death-related fears has been largely ignored, as have their implications for children's mental health. And even though homicidal behavior in children has been rising steadily, little is known about its dynamics. Death still (or once again) seems to be the scandal—to use Herman Feifel's term—that it was in the 1950s. Apparently scientists have not been interested in studies that associate healthy children with death and too many people find the connection morbid and inappropriate. There is little room for the topic in the curricula of the public schools, even as violent death is a favorite theme in the entertainment industry, and as statistics and reports are pointing to its negative impact on the minds, psyches, and actions of children. Death studies in the twenty-first century can ill afford to ignore the complex psychosocial problems that shape the meanings of death and quality of life in children and adults.

References

Adams, D. W. (1984). Helping the dying child. In *Childhood and Death*, ed. H. Wass and C. A. Corr, pp. 95–112. New York: Hemisphere.

Alexander, I. E., and Adlerstein, A. M. (1958). Affective responses to the concept of death in a population of children and early adolescents. *Journal of Genetic Psychology* 93:167–177.

American Psychological Association Commission on Violence and Youth (1993). *Violence and Youth: Psychology's Response*, vol. I. Washington, DC: American Psychological Association.

Anthony, S. (1940). *The Discovery of Death in Childhood and After*. London: Kegan Paul.
Armstrong-Dailey, A. (1991). Hospice care for children, their families and health care providers. In *Children and Death*, ed. D. Papadatou and C. Papadatos, pp. 225–229. New York: Hemisphere.
Balk, D. E. (1983). Adolescents' grief reactions and self concept perceptions following sibling death: a study of 33 teenagers. *Journal of Youth and Adolescence* 12:137–159.
Beck, A. T., Sethi, B. B., and Tuthill, R. (1963). Childhood bereavement and adult depression. *Archives of General Psychiatry* 9:129–136.
Becker, E. (1975). *Escape from Evil*. New York: Collier Macmillan.
Bluebond-Langner, M. (1978). *The Private Worlds of Dying Children*. Princeton, NJ: Princeton University Press.
——— (1989). Dying children. In *Encyclopedia of Death*, ed. R. Kastenbaum and B. Kastenbaum, pp. 46–50. Phoenix: Oryx.
Blume, D., Whitley, E., Stevenson, R. G., et al. (1986). Challenger 10 and our school children: reflections on the catastrophe. *Death Studies* 10:95–118.
Bowlby, J. (1960). Grief and mourning in infancy and early childhood. *Psychoanalytic Study of the Child* 15:9–52. New York: International Universities Press.
Carlsson-Paige, N., and Levin, D. E. (1990). *Who's Calling the Shots? How to Respond Effectively to Children's Fascination with War Play and War Toys*. Philadelphia: New Society.
Centers for Disease Control (1991). Weapon-carrying among high school students. *Journal of the American Medical Association* 266:23–42.
Chesler, M., and Barbarin, O. (1987). *Childhood Cancer in the Family*. New York: Brunner/Mazel.
Claflin, C. J., and Barbarin, O. A. (1991). Does "telling" less protect more? Relationships among age, information disclosure, and what children with cancer see and feel. *Journal of Pediatric Psychology* 16:169–191.
Comstock, G., and Paik, H. (1991). *Television and the American Child*. New York: Academic Press.
Crase, D. R., and Crase, D. (1984). Death education for older children. In *Childhood and Death*, ed. H. Wass and C.A. Corr, pp. 345–363. New York: Hemisphere.
Csikszentmihalyi, M., and Larson, R. (1984). *Being Adolescent: Conflict and Growth in the Teenage Years*. New York: Basic Books.
Dowell, R. E., Copeland, D. R., and van Eys, J., eds. (1988). *The Child with Cancer in the Community*. Springfield, IL: Charles C Thomas.
Durlak, J. A. (1994). Changing death attitudes through death education. In *Death Anxiety Handbook: Research, Instrumentation, and Application*, ed. R. A. Neimeyer, pp. 243–260. New York: Taylor & Francis.
Durlak, J. A., and Reisenberg, L. A. (1991). The impact of death education. *Death Studies* 15:39–58.
Ewing, C. P. (1990). *Kids Who Kill*. Lexington, MA: Lexington Press.
Feifel, H. (1959). *The Meaning of Death*. New York: McGraw-Hill.
——— (1977). *New Meanings of Death*. New York: McGraw-Hill.
Frederick, C. J. (1987). Psychic trauma in victims of crime and terrorism. In *Cataclysms, Crises and Catastrophes*, ed. G. R. Vandenbose and B.K. Bryant. Washington, DC: American Psychological Association.
Fristad, M., Jedel, R., Weller, R. A., and Weller, E. B. (1993). Psychosocial functioning in children after the death of a parent. *American Journal of Psychiatry* 150:511–513.
Furman, E. (1974). *A Child's Parent Dies*. New Haven, CT: Yale University Press.
——— (1984). Children's patterns in mourning the death of a loved one. In *Childhood and Death*, ed. H. Wass and C. A. Corr, pp. 185–203. New York: Hemisphere.
Gartley, W., and Bernasconi, M. (1967). The concept of death in children. *Journal of Genetic Psychology* 110:71–85.

Goldberg, S., Lacombe, S., Levinson, D., et al. (1985). Thinking about the threat of nuclear war: relevance to mental health. *American Journal of Orthopsychiatry* 55:503–512.

Grollman, E. A. (1990). *Talking About Death: A Dialogue Between Parent and Child*, 3rd ed. Boston: Beacon Press.

Hare-Mustin, R. T. (1979). Family therapy following the death of a child. *Journal of Marital and Family Therapy* 5:51–59.

Heller, D. (1986). *The Children's God.* Chicago: University of Chicago Press.

Hogan, N. S., and DeSantis, L. (1992). Adolescent sibling bereavement: an ongoing attachment. *Qualitative Health Research* 2:159–177.

———— (1996). Basic constructs of a theory of adolescent sibling bereavement. In *Continuing Bonds: New Understandings of Grief*, ed. D. Klass, P. R. Silverman, and S. L. Nickman, pp. 235–254. Washington, DC: Taylor & Francis.

Huston, A. C., et al. (1992). *Big World, Small Screen: The Role of Television in American Society*. Lincoln, NB: University of Nebraska Press.

International Work Group for Death, Dying, and Bereavement (1994). *Statements on Death, Dying, and Bereavement*. IWG Secretariat. London, Ontario: King's College.

Jenkins, R. A., and Cavanaugh, J. C. (1985). Examining the relationship between the development of the concept of death and overall cognitive development. *Omega* 16: 193–199.

Johnson, P., and Rosenblatt, P. (1981). Grief following childhood loss of a parent. *American Journal of Psychotherapy* 35:419–425.

Kastenbaum, R. (1986). Death in the world of adolescence. In *Adolescence and Death*, ed. C. A. Corr and J. N. McNeil, pp. 4–15. New York: Springer.

Katz, E. R., Kellerman, J., and Siegel, S. E. (1980). Behavioral distress in children with cancer undergoing medical procedures: developmental considerations. *Journal of Counseling and Clinical Psychology* 48:356–365.

Kazdin, A.E. (1993). Adolescent mental health. *American Psychologist* 48:127–141.

Koocher, G. P. (1973). Childhood, death, cognitive development. *Developmental Psychology* 9:369–375.

Kranzler, E. M., Shaffer, D., Wasserman, G., and Davies, M. (1990). Early childhood bereavement. *Journal of the American Academy of Child and Adolescent Psychiatry* 29:514–520.

Krell, R. (1985). Child survivors of the holocaust—40 years later. *Journal of the American Academy of Child Psychiatry* 24(4):378–380.

Krupnick, J. L. (1984). Bereavement during childhood and adolescence. In *Bereavement: Reactions, Consequences and Care*, ed. M. Osterweis, F. Solomon, and M. Green, pp. 99–141. Washington, DC: National Academy Press.

Laudenslager, M. L., Boccia, M. L., and Reite, M. L. (1993). Biobehavioral consequences of loss in nonhuman primates: individual differences. In *Handbook of Bereavement*, ed. M. S. Stroebe, W. Stroebe, and R. O. Hansson, pp. 129–142. New York: Press Syndicate of the University of Cambridge.

Leenaars, A. A., and Wenckstern, S., eds. (1991). *Suicide Prevention in Schools*. New York: Hemisphere.

————, ed. (1991). *Horrendous Death, Health, and Well-Being*. New York: Hemisphere.

Leviton, D. (1969). The need for education on death and suicide. *Journal of School Health* 39:270–274.

Lin, C. A., and Atkin, D. J. (1989). Parental mediation and rule making for adolescent use of television and VCR. *Journal of Broadcasting and Electronic Media* 33:53–67.

Martinson, I. M., Davies, E., and McClowry, S. G. (1987). The long-term effect of sibling death on self-concept. *Journal of Pediatric Nursing* 2:227–235.

Miller-Thiel, J., Glover, J. J., and Beliveau, B. (1993). Caring for the dying child. *Hospice Journal* 9:55–72.

Nagy, M. (1948). The child's theories concerning death. *Journal of Genetic Psychology* 73:3–27.

National Institute of Mental Health (1982). *Television and Behavior: Ten years of Scientific Research and Implications for the Eighties*, vols. I and II. Washington, DC: U.S. Government Printing Office.

Natterson, J. M., and Knudson, A. G. (1960). Observations concerning fear of death in fatally ill children and their mothers. *Psychosomatic Medicine* 22:456–465.

Neimeyer, R. A., and Van Brunt, D. (1995). Death anxiety. In *Dying: Facing the Facts*, ed. H. Wass and R. A. Neimeyer. 3rd ed. New York: Taylor & Francis.

Papadatou, D. (1989). Working with dying children: a professional's personal journey. In *Children and Death*, ed. D. Papadatou and C. Papadatou, pp. 285–292. New York: Hemisphere.

Quadrel, M. J., Fischhoff, B., and Davis, W. (1993). Adolescent (in) vulnerability. *American Psychologist* 48:102–116.

Rando, T. A. (1993). *Treatment of Complicated Mourning*. Champaign, IL: Research Press.

Raphael, B. (1983). *The Anatomy of Bereavement*. New York: Basic Books.

Reilly, T. P., Hasazi, J. E., and Bond, L. A. (1983). Children's conceptions of death and personal mortality. *Journal of Pediatric Psychology* 8:21–31.

Saigh, P. A. (1985). An experimental analysis of chronic post-traumatic stress among adolescents. *Journal of Genetic Psychology* 146(1):125–131.

Sandoval, J., London, M. D., and Rey, T. (1994). Status of suicide prevention in California schools. *Death Studies* 18:595–608.

Schilder, P., and Wechsler, D. (1934). The attitudes of children toward death. *Journal of Genetic Psychology* 45:406–451.

Scott, J. P., and Ginsburg, B. E. (1994). The Seville statement on violence revisited. *American Psychologist* 49:849–850.

Silverman, P. R., Nickman, S., and Worden, J. W. (1992). Detachment revisited: the child's reconstruction of a dead parent. *American Journal of Orthopsychiatry* 62:494–503.

Silverman, P. R., and Worden, J. W. (1992). Children's reactions in the early months after the death of a parent. *American Journal of Orthopsychiatry* 62:93–104.

Solantaus, T., Rimpela, M., and Taipale, V. (1984). The threat of war in the minds of 12–18 year olds in Finland. *Lancet* 1:784–785.

Sourkes, B. M. (1982). *The Deepening Shade: Psychological Aspects of Life-Threatening Illness*. Pittsburgh, PA: University of Pittsburgh Press.

Speece, M. W., and Brent, S. B. (1992). The acquisition of a mature understanding of three components of the concept of death. *Death Studies* 16(2):211–229.

Stark, E. (1991). Preventing primary homicide: a reconceptualization. In *Horrendous Death, Health and Well-Being*, ed. D. Leviton, pp. 109–136. New York: Hemisphere.

Susman, E. J., Dorn, L. D., and Fletcher, J. (1987). Reasoning about illness in ill and healthy children and adolescents: cognitive and emotional developmental aspects. *Journal of Developmental and Behavioral Pediatrics* 8:226–273.

Tamm, M. E., and Granqvist, R. N. (1995). The meaning of death for children and adolescents. A phenomenographic study of drawing. *Death Studies* 19:203–222.

Timmer, S. G., Eccles, J., and O'Brien, K. (1985). How children use time. In *Time, Goods, and Well-Being*, ed. F. T. Juster and F. P. Stafford. Ann Arbor: Institute for Social Research, University of Michigan.

Vachon, M. L. S., and Pakes, E. (1984). Staff stress in the care of the critically ill and dying child. In *Childhood and Death*, ed. H. Wass and C.A. Corr, pp. 151–182. New York: Hemisphere.

Vernick, J., and Karon, M. (1965). Who's afraid of death in the leukemia ward. *American Journal of Disease of Children* 109:393–397.

Waechter, E. H. (1971). Children's awareness of fatal illness. *American Journal of Nursing* 71:1168–1172.

—— (1984). Dying children: patterns of coping. In *Childhood and Death*, ed. H. Wass and C. A. Corr, pp. 51–68. New York: Hemisphere.

—— (1992). Disseminating our thanatology knowledge. In *The Thanatology Community and the Needs of the Movement*, ed. E. J. Clark and A. H. Kutscher, pp. 37–49. New York: Haworth.

—— (1995). Death in the lives of children and adolescents. In *Dying: Facing the Facts*, ed. H. Wass and R. A. Neimeyer, pp. 269–301. Washington, DC: Taylor & Francis.

Wass, H., and Cason L. (1984). Fears and anxieties about death. In *Childhood and Death*, 3rd ed., ed. H. Wass and C.A. Corr, pp. 37–38. New York: Hemisphere.

Wass, H., and Corr, C. A. (1984). *Helping Children Cope with Death: Guidelines and Resources*, 2nd ed. New York: Hemisphere.

Wass, H., Miller, M. D., and Thorton, G. (1990). Death education and grief/suicide intervention in the public schools. *Death Studies* 14:253–268.

Wenestam, C. G., and Wass, H. (1987). Swedish and U.S. children's thinking about death: a qualitative study and cross-cultural comparison. *Death Studies* 11:99–121.

Wessel, M. A. (1984). Helping families: thoughts of a pediatrician. In *Childhood and Death*, ed. H. Wass and C. A. Corr, pp. 205–217. New York: Hemisphere.

Wheeler, P. R., Lange, N. F., and Bertolone, S. J. (1986). Improving care for hospitalized terminally ill children: a practicable model. In *Hospice Approaches to Pediatric Care*, ed. C. A. Corr and D. M. Corr, pp. 43–60. New York: Springer.

White, E., Elsom, B., and Pravat, R. (1978). Children's conceptions of death. *Child Development* 49:307–320.

Zeltzer, L. K. (1988). Self-perceptions of the child with cancer. In *The Child with Cancer in the Community*, ed. R. E. Dowell, D. R. Copeland, and J. van Eys, pp. 5–20. Springfield, IL: Charles C Thomas.

10

Children and Questions about Death

CHARLES A. CORR

In his pioneering book, *The Meaning of Death*, Herman Feifel (1959) reprinted and brought to widespread attention an edited version of an article by a Hungarian researcher (Nagy 1948) on children's understandings of death. In so doing, Feifel directed attention to one of the central subjects in the field of death, dying, and bereavement: What do children think about death?

This question and the underlying subject that it represents are related to several other important issues. Some of those issues and the additional questions that they generate focus on death-related concepts—in childhood and in other eras in the human life span. For example: What are children capable of thinking about death? Why do children think as they do about death? What do adolescents and adults think about death? What are the differences (and the reasons behind those differences) between ways in which children, adolescents, and adults think about death?

Other important issues and their related questions maintain the connection to childhood but go beyond subjects that are confined to conceptual issues. For example: How do children's thoughts about death relate to their attitudes concerning death? How do children's concepts of death influence ways in which they cope with loss, grief, and bereavement? How do children's concepts of death influence ways in which they cope with life-threatening illness and dying? And how can adults help children in their understandings of death and in their interactions with death-related issues?

This is a tantalizing menu of questions and issues, many of which have not yet been addressed by empirical research and theory in the field. Issues related to children's understandings of death have received most attention from researchers—work that has been reviewed by

Speece and Brent (1984, 1996), Stambrook and Parker (1987), and Wass (1984). In addition, a number of theorists have spoken to issues related to death-related fears and anxieties in childhood (Wass and Cason 1984).

Nevertheless, there is a long way to go before one can claim that satisfactory answers are available for many of the questions noted above. For example, much of the research on children's understandings of death has focused on cognitive capacities, not on factors that would explain why children think about death as they do. And we are only beginning to hear suggestions about distinctive aspects of adolescent understandings of death (e.g., Noppe and Noppe 1991, 1996).

For these reasons, the focus of this chapter is limited to two central issues involving children and questions about death: (1) a review of some questions that have been put to children in order to determine what they are capable of understanding about death; and (2) a preliminary exploration of questions raised by children that may help to develop further insights into what children are seeking to understand about death and how they are going about that quest. The first of these issues is represented here by the work of Maria Nagy; the second by the author's observations of children's questions about death (Corr 1995), a survey of questions posed by British children attending camps for bereaved youngsters (Tegg 1994), and a review by Speece and Brent (1996) of over 100 reports on research concerning children's understandings of death. The goal of this chapter is to help readers become more sensitive to death-related understandings and concerns among children, and to suggest some ways in which they can help children in these matters.

Maria Nagy: The Child's Theories Concerning Death

Interest in death-related attitudes and concepts among children is not new. Formal research in this area extends at least as far back as the 1930s. Such research is evident in the work of Schilder and Wechsler (1934), Anthony (1939, 1940), and Nagy (1948). It should be noted that although Nagy's research was conducted in the 1930s, it was not published until after World War II. Nevertheless, Nagy's 1948 article remains perhaps the single, best-known piece of literature in this field (for surveys of the literature, see Speece and Brent 1996, Stambrook and Parker 1987, Wass 1984). Nagy's work is considered here as both a classic text and a model of its type.

The Study, Its Methodology, and General Results

In her 1948 article, Maria Nagy, a member of the Department of Psychology at Pazmany University in Budapest, focused her attention on a single question: "What does the child think death to be, what theory does he construct of the nature of death?" (p. 3). To answer this question, Nagy studied 378 children who were 3 to 10 years of age and who lived in or near Budapest just prior to World War II. The children were almost equally divided by gender (51 percent boys, 49 percent girls) and came from different religions, schools, and social backgrounds. In the 1959 reprinting of her article, we are told that Nagy's subjects ranged from dull normal to superior in intelligence level, although most were said to fall in the normal range.

In undertaking this research, Nagy commented in the 1959 version of her article that she had been surprised by "the slim, almost neglected, attention given to the child's conception of death" (1959, p. 79) within the extensive research in child psychology during the fifty years prior to her own efforts. She noted that "it is in childhood that the adult's outlook concerning death begins to take on basic form" (p. 79) and that previous studies of children and death (with two exceptions) had dealt with children's feelings about death. As a result, she had undertaken and was reporting "an investigation, from the genetic standpoint, of the ideas of children, aged 3 to 10 years, concerning the meaning of death" (p. 79).

Nagy's methodology was as follows: (1) children in the 7- to 10-year-old range were instructed to "write down everything that comes to your mind about death" and were given one hour to carry out this assignment; (2) as a result of an initiative on the part of some children who began on their own accord to make drawings about death once they had finished their compositions, children in the 6- to 10-year-old range were asked to make independent drawings about death (and many of the older children also wrote explanations of their creations); and (3) discussions were held with all of the children.

The discussions served slightly different purposes depending on the children involved. For the older children, open-ended individual discussions were intended to avoid arbitrary interpretations of their compositions and drawings, and to provide those children with opportunities to amplify and clarify their views. This last goal was pursued by questions such as: "Tell me all you can think of about death"; "What is death?"; "Why do people die?"; "How can one recognize death?"; "Do you usually dream? Tell me a dream about death." In the case of 3- to 6-year-old children (who had usually not provided a composition or a drawing), the discussions were designed to establish meaningful rapport with the children, confirm that they understood what was being asked, and get them to talk about their ideas and feelings about such words as *table*, *death*, *life*, *birth*, and *brother*.

This approach produced a total of 484 "protocols"[1]: 294 compositions, 40 drawings, and 151 discussions.

---

[1]Nagy (1948) gives the figure of 484 in both her table and text, but there is clearly an error in either the total number or in one of the component numbers, which add up to 485.

According to Nagy (1948), replies given by the children to the question "What is death?" "can be ranged in three groups" (p. 7). Further, "as the different sorts of answers can be found only at certain ages, one can speak of stages of development" (p. 7). These three stages of conceptual development were described by Nagy as follows: "The child of less than five years does not recognize death as an irreversible fact. In death it sees life. Between the ages of five and nine death is the [*sic*] most often personified and thought of as a contingency. And in general only after the age of nine is it recognized that death is a process happening in us according to certain laws" (p. 7). In the 1959 version of her article, Nagy cautioned that "it should be kept in mind that neither the stages nor the above-mentioned ages at which they occur are watertight compartments as it were. Overlapping does exist" (p. 81). Nevertheless, she believed that her results did "reflect definite modal developments in the child's thinking about death" (p. 81). All of the major segments of Nagy's research are worth close attention here.

Stage One. The characteristic feature of what Nagy called the first stage in the development of children's concepts of death is, in her language, that *there is no definitive death*. Many other commentators have interpreted this to mean that death is not seen as final. In Nagy's language, this means that "the child does not know death as such" (1948, p. 7; 1959, p. 81). Both life and consciousness are attributed to the dead. This is accomplished in one of two ways: (1) either death is understood as a departure or as sleep; or (2) the fact of physical death is recognized, but death is not separated from life and thus is conceived as gradual or temporary.

In the first alternative, death is interpreted either as sleep (a continued life form) or in terms of continued life elsewhere. In the version of this view that emphasizes departure or travel, Nagy suggested that it is as if the dead individual had been transported to a different world and was now living in that other world. In both of these versions, death involves a kind of living on under changed circumstances. In each of these versions, no essential change is recognized within the dead person, although his or her new circumstances (e.g., being confined in a coffin) may constrain various activities. Note also that where death is understood as a kind of departure, a child may invert the relationship and understand departure as death.

Nagy reminded her readers that it would be a mistake to conclude that children who interpret death as sleep or departure/travel are unaffected by or uncurious about the implications of that understanding of death. Clearly, the lives of those who are left behind by the departure of the dead person are significantly altered. They no longer live with that

person and cannot interact with the deceased in ways that had characterized most of their previous relationships. The implications of separation that characterize this understanding of death can be painful for
children.

Further, it will not be surprising that "most children . . . are not satisfied, when someone dies, that he should merely disappear, but want
to know where and how he continues to live" (Nagy 1948, p. 12). Connections were frequently made between the absence of the dead, their
funerals, and the disposition of their bodies. Accordingly, the children
in Nagy's study often expressed views that the dead person continued
to be active (perhaps in limited ways) in the coffin or in the cemetery.
Some interpreted this diminished life form as a kind of sleep in the grave.
Children's speculations or inquiries about the nature of life in the grave
may appear quite fanciful or unusual to many adults, as is evident in the
question one child posed to Lonetto (1980): "Do dead people eat choco-
late cake?"

The essential point for Nagy in this first way of thinking about death
is that it denies death entirely, because it does not recognize the finality
or complete cessation of bodily activities that is characteristic of death.
She offered the view that "its desires guide the child even at the price of
modifying the reality. Opposition to death is so strong that the child
denies death, as emotionally it cannot accept it" (Nagy 1948, pp. 12–13).

Nagy identified a variation on this first stage in children's conceptualizations of death in the recognition among some 5- and 6-year-olds that
death does exist but is not accepted as a definitive fact. Children who
hold this view "acknowledge that death exists but think of it as a gradual
or temporary thing" (Nagy 1948, p. 13). Nagy maintained that these children offered realistic descriptions of the physical changes that take place
in death (e.g., the dead cannot move or breathe), but coupled that with
an incomplete distinction or separation of death from life. Hence, in this
view death is seen as a gradual process that is intertwined with life and
that may involve different degrees of death or be seen as a temporary
situation in which links with life have not yet been completely severed.
In other words, life and death are either held in simultaneous relation or
they are interpreted as being able to change places with one another
repeatedly. Nagy insisted that this "gradualness in death is not merely a
matter of insufficiency of expression" (p. 14).

Nagy summarized her account of this variation on the first stage of
children's understanding of death in the following way: "The children of
the second group already accept death to a certain extent. The distinction between life and death is, however, not complete. If they think of
death as gradual, life and death are in simultaneous relation; if it is temporary, life and death can change with one another repeatedly" (p. 15).

In other words, this is a "higher order" conception since it does not entirely deny death. Children who adopt this view do so because their appreciation of reality has led them to begin to respect a distinction between life and death. As that distinction is not yet fully developed, they settle for a compromise position: death exists but is not definitive. Such a view may be associated with an egocentric and animistic point of view in young children whereby no absolute distinctions are made between the children themselves, other living things, lifeless or nonliving things, and the dead. The point is that *death exists, but it is not absolutely final or in complete opposition to life.*

Many adults who read or hear summaries of research such as Nagy's appear to have concluded that children in this first stage of cognitive development do not understand or have a concept of death. That is wrong: such children have *a* concept of death—for example, one related to travel, sleep, gradual diminution of life functions, or interwoven activities of life and death. The distinctive point is that such children do not appear to possess what is commonly thought of as *the* "mature" or "scientific" concept of death. As Nagy wrote, "living and lifeless are not yet distinguished" (1948, p. 26), and this animistic point of view is extended to death—which is then interpreted as a kind of living state. It seems clear that the concepts that these young children hold are naturally drawn from experiences that are most familiar to them, such as cycles of departing and returning or sleeping and waking.

Stage Two. Nagy described the second stage in the development of children's concepts of death as the view that *Death = a Man.* In other words, this stage represents the personification of death. Nagy found this conception in all age groups among the children that she studied, although she judged it to be most characteristic of children between the ages of 5 and 9. According to Nagy, "the personification of death takes place in two ways. Death is imagined as a separate person, or else death is identified with the dead" (p. 16). In the first of these versions of personification (representing about two-thirds of the children in this group), death was thought of as some kind of a (grim) reaper or as depicted in some other individual picture—a skeleton figure, king of the dead, a ghost, a death man, a death angel, or some other type of distinct personality (usually said to be secretive and of ill will) who can carry off living persons.

In the second version of personification (representing about one-third of the children in this group), death was still seen as some type of outside force, but in this case one identified with the dead themselves or individuals who have already died. Nagy noted that in many languages, terms for the abstract state or general concept (*death, der Tot, la mort*) and for those who have died (*the dead, tot, mort*) are cognates that might easily be confounded. But she expressed surprise that the children in her study should substitute the Hungarian word for death (*halal*) for the quite different term for the dead person (*halott*). It seemed extraordinary to Nagy that this linguistic exchange occurred so consistently in her subjects.

For Nagy, the essential point about this second stage in the development of children's concepts of death was that the existence and definitiveness of death have been accepted. Nevertheless, she contended that children have a strong aversion to the thought of death. That is, these children are said to display an increased sense of reality, but one that is contrary to their desires. As a result, they interpreted death not as an internal process, but as a reality outside or remote from themselves. Death was a kind of distant "other." For that reason, death was understood as avoidable or not inevitable and not universal. Those whom the external force catches do die; those who escape or get away from the clutches of that force do not die. There is again a kind of egocentric or anthropocentric dimension to this outlook—sometimes referred to as "artificialism"—whereby all events or changes in the world are thought to derive from the activity of persons. If that is true, then there must be a death person who brings about the changes associated with death.

In contrast to Nagy's interpretation, many later researchers have emphasized the theme of death's avoidability in this stage, rather than its personification (Gartley and Bernasconi 1967, Kane 1979, Koocher 1973, 1974; but compare Lonetto 1980). That is, depicting death as an external force or person may simply be a way in which some children express the possibility of outwitting or avoiding death. A similar view appears in Ingmar Bergman's film *The Seventh Seal* (1956), when one character (Antonius Block, the knight) plays chess with death (a hooded figure in a black robe who carries a scythe) with the knight's life as the prize. In Woody Allen's film *Love and Death* (1975), a comparable, but more plebeian, competition is offered in the form of a game of cards.

Stage Three. Nagy described the third stage in children's development of the concept of death as a recognition of the *cessation of corporal life*. That is, death is recognized as a process operating within us. If this is true, then as a part of our very lives death applies to all of us. As Nagy wrote, "When he [the child] reaches the point where death is a process operating within us he recognizes its universal nature" (1948, p. 25). In other words, this understanding conceives of death as final and universal, an aspect of life which is inevitable and not avoidable. Nagy concluded that this understanding of death reflected a realistic view of both death and the world, one that was generally achieved only after the age of 9.

Some Interim Comments

One could criticize some aspects of the methodology that is reflected in Nagy's work. For example, Nagy employed different techniques with different children among those whom she studied (Table 10–1). She gave no direct attention to methodological limitations or special features of her subjects, and it has already been noted that later research with other populations of children has not confirmed the emphasis that Nagy placed upon personification in her second stage.

The limitations inherent in Nagy's research would not be so significant if work such as hers had not been popularly understood to support much stronger conclusions than it warrants. For example, this type of account has been generalized in claims that apply to all children throughout the world. The data provided in Tables 10–2 and 10–3 support Nagy's report (although they do not necessarily support all of her interpretations) about the Hungarian children whom she studied. But it is not clear, on this ground alone, that similar data would be obtained from, or that Nagy's account of children's understandings of death would apply to, other populations of children.

In addition, researchers in this field have not always been sufficiently careful to maintain clear distinctions between two quite different matters: developmental stages and chronological age. Nagy was sensitive to the import of this distinction. Accordingly, she confined her comments to the children whom she studied and tried to justify the connections that she drew about developmental stages and chronological age within those children. Nevertheless, insufficient attention to this fundamental distinction has all too often led to broad and unsubstantiated claims that children under some specific age—9 or 10 years of age?—are unable to understand the concept of death.

Moreover, work like Nagy's subtly encourages a tendency in many adults to focus too exclusively on cognitive aspects of children's development and of their death-related concerns. After all, when Tolstoy's

TABLE 10–1. Distribution of material according to age

	Age								
	3	4	5	6	7	8	9	10	Total
Composition	—	—	—	—	63	81	93	57	294
Drawing	—	—	—	8	9	9	12	2	40
Discussion	7	13	16	26	32	23	29	5	151
Total	7	13	16	34	104	113	134	64	484

Source: Nagy (1948).

TABLE 10–2. What is death? (Composition)

	Age								
	7		8		9		10		Total	
	N	%	N	%	N	%	N	%	N	%
2nd stage	12	92.3	21	91.3	27	71	4	16.7	65	65.3
3rd stage	1	7.7	2	8.7	11	29	20	83.3	34	34.7
Total	13	100	23	100	38	100	24	100	98	100

Source: Nagy (1948).

(1886) Ivan Ilych thought back to his logic course in college, he remembered that he had learned and understood the validity of the syllogism, "Caius is a man"; "All men are mortal"; therefore, "Caius is mortal" (p. 131). What Ivan had not realized until much later in his life when he was dying was the personal significance of what he had learned many years earlier.

Freud (1915, p. 305) said that "at bottom no one believes in his own death, or to put the same thing in another way, in the unconscious every one of us is convinced of his own immortality." However, a study by Feifel and Branscomb (1973) offered a more complex interpretation, that "the dominant conscious response to fear of death is one of repudiation; that of the fantasy or imagery level, one of ambivalence; and at the nonconscious level, one of outright negativity" (p. 286). Feifel and Branscomb concluded that "this apparent counterbalance of coexisting avoidance-acceptance of personal death most likely serves powerful adaptational needs, allowing one to maintain communal associations and yet organize one's resources to contend with oncoming death" (p. 286). If that is so, then these researchers suggested that such a conclusion "asks for reconsideration of Freud's . . . dictum that there is no representation of one's own individual death in the unconscious" (p. 287).

Other researchers have drawn attention to the role of life experiences in relationship to death-related understandings and attitudes among children with a life-threatening illness. For example, Waechter (1971) conducted the first direct, systematic, and controlled study in this area, one that employed four groups of children between the ages of 6 and 10 matched as to sex, age, race, social class, and family background: nonhospitalized, well children; children with brief illness; children with chronic disease with a good prognosis; and children with chronic disease for whom death was predicted. Waechter employed a set of eight pictures and a general anxiety scale to elicit individual responses from the children, and a tape-recorded, semistructured interview with their

TABLE 10–3. What is death? (Discussion)

		Age																
		3		4		5		6		7		8		9		10		Total
		N	%	N	%	N	%	N	%	N	%	N	%	N	%	N	%	N	%
1st stage		6	85.7	7	50	6	33.3	2	7.8	—	—	—	—	—	—	—	—	21	12.9
2nd stage		1	14.3	7	50	12	66.7	21	80.7	19	57.6	14	53.8	16	53.3	2	22.8	92	56.4
3rd stage		—	—	—	—	—	—	3	11.5	14	42.4	12	46.2	14	46.7	7	77.8	50	30.7
Total		7	100	14	100	18	100	26	100	33	100	26	100	30	100	9	100	163	100

Source: Nagy (1948).

parents. Results demonstrated that anxiety levels in the fatally ill children were nearly twice that of their ill counterparts and three times the score of the healthy children. This was true even though most of the fatally ill children had been given no information or largely unrealistic information about their condition and its prognosis.

.   Heightened anxiety in the children studied by Waechter poses challenges for adults who might wish to think that lack of knowledge or limited conceptual development means that significant concerns are not to be found in children with life experiences associated with illness and death. Other researchers subsequently supported Waechter's conclusions (Spinetta and Maloney 1975, Spinetta et al. 1973). Moreover, when Waechter (1984) replicated her initial study at a later date, concerns of this sort persisted under many changed circumstances and an awareness of the seriousness of their illness was identified in children as young as 4 years of age.

Similarly, Bluebond-Langner (1977, 1978) employed the techniques of cultural anthropology with hospitalized, terminally ill, leukemic children to show a correlation between children's processes of acquiring information and shifts in their self-concepts. That is, as children obtained information about their illnesses and their experiences, they drew from it changing understandings of themselves. Bluebond-Langner concluded that important life experiences can lead children to understand both the content of aspects of the concept of death and the personal significance of that information. This parallels the conclusion of a seminal article by Alexander and Adlerstein (1958) that the central point for consideration may not be just a matter of a child's conceptual capacity and what he or she may be able to understand about death, but the situation of the child in question and how he or she relates understandings to his or her own life.

Nagy's Conclusions

The immediate conclusions in Nagy's research have been outlined above. But they are not the last word in her study. The final two sentences of Nagy's report offer the following advice: "To conceal death from the child is not possible and is also not permissible. Natural behaviour in the child's surroundings can greatly diminish the shock of its acquaintance with death" (1948, p. 27).

Adults often seek to conceal death from children in the mistaken belief that if a child is not told about death and not introduced to death-related experiences, then he or she will be innocent of that subject and will not need to deal with its implications. That is not a reliable belief. Children learn about death from the many (often conflicting and confusing) messages they receive on that subject from the societal death system within which they live, from their parents and others around them, and from their own life experiences. One really cannot effectively isolate children from death and its implications.

More to the point, misguided protectionism or efforts at quarantine are counterproductive. Segregating children from this aspect of reality would not constitute an effective preparation for living out their lives. Hothouse flowers are not well suited to flourish in the real world. On the contrary, effective preparation for living requires adults to draw useful lessons from their experiences, offer caring support, communicate productive insights, and implement practical guidelines in ways that children can grasp and incorporate into their own lives.

When it is read carefully and seen in larger contexts, the work of Maria Nagy and other researchers can constitute an important springboard from which adults can learn to understand and assist children on the concepts of death, dying, and bereavement. Nagy alerts us to, and thus cautions against reinforcing, inadequate concepts of death in childhood. Also, Nagy suggests constructive ways in which adults and children can come together in their efforts to understand and cope with death. Some of this can be organized around the questions that children ask about death.

Children's Questions About Death

Children ask many questions about death. One example of such questions appears in an audiovisual about life, death, and bereavement in childhood. The question (which is also used as the title of the audiovisual) is: "Where is dead?" (Encyclopedia Britannica Films 1975). This is not a question that an adult would be likely to ask since the question does not pose the issue in ways that seem appropriate or familiar to adults. Most adults realize that *dead* is an adjective describing a state or condition (*death*), not a place. Clearly, the young girl who posed this question in the audiovisual was struggling to understand death and what it means to be dead, as well as to find ways to articulate what it is that she wanted to know. The odd or puzzling qualities of the question only dramatize the force of the child's query.

In the case at hand, the child went on to ask, "Where do you go when you're dead?" Immediately, some main directions in the child's thinking become more readily apparent. Now we realize that the initial question assumes that there is a *you* following death, that there is a *where* involved in death or being dead, and that the *you* engages in a process of transfer or transformation to that (*some*)*where*.

It might be tempting for an adult to answer these questions by say-ing, "Nowhere." If the child were to remain consistent with her initial point of view, she might only reply, "But where is that?" Once again, the impli-cation is that everything—including "nowhere"—must be located in some place. Little progress will be made if we do not enter more fully into children's questions, learn how to respond more effectively, and assist children to articulate questions in ways that will help them to understand both the central elements embraced by the concept of death and their meaning.

Examples of questions posed by British children and bearing on the implications of death-related experiences have been gathered together by Tegg (1994). The children were bereaved youngsters, survivors of the death of a parent, sibling, or other significant person. These child survi-vors attended residential weekend camps conducted by Winston's Wish, a grief support program for children in Gloucestershire, England. During 1992 to 1994, four camps were held with a total of ninety-two chil-dren in attendance. At each camp, the children were invited to formu-late "Questions for the Doctor." The 114 questions that resulted covered a wide range of topics:

Medical information giving: "What is cancer?"; "What is a coma?"; "What does chemotherapy mean?"; "Why can't doctors make people with chest problems better?"

Emotions and fears: "Can you catch cancer?"; "If lots of people I know have a heart attack, will I have one too?"; "If you have AIDS and you pass it on, does it mean you don't have it anymore?"; "Why did I feel guilty when my mum died and when I visit the grave?"

Searching for an explanation: "Why can't doctors make everyone better?"; "My brother died in a car crash, some of the other people in the car didn't die. Why did my brother have to die?"; "Do you think I should blame the hospital because my Mummy died there?"

Suicide: "Why do people want to commit suicide?"; "If people are depressed, why can't they ask for help from family and friends instead of killing themselves?"; "What could make someone feel that they want to kill themselves?"

Spiritual questions: "Where do people go when they die?"; "If people go to heaven, can they see you all the time?"; "Will people ever come back?"; "What do you eat in heaven?"

Other questions: "How old is the oldest person?"; "Have you helped lots and lots of people?"; "What time does a doctor go home?"

The diversity of these questions indicates that queries from chil-dren can take many forms and have many different foci. It would be

desirable to develop a comprehensive schema or typology of all possible questions concerning death. Such a framework does not currently
exist. Its development may be challenging given the broad ramifications
of death and its close interweaving with so many facets of life. For our
purposes, it will be useful to narrow the scope to those questions that
center on the content of the concept of death and some of its immediate implications.

One helpful strategy is to organize children's questions about the
concept of death around an analysis of five subconcepts that are, or
appear to be, immediately implicated in that concept. Such an analysis
has recently been offered by Speece and Brent (1996) in a report on more
than 100 research studies conducted between 1934 and the early 1990s
by investigators who were attempting to examine children's understandings of death.

Speece and Brent's review of the literature demonstrated the not-
unsurprising conclusion that the concept of death is not a simple, uncom-
plicated notion. It embraces a number of distinguishable subconcepts
or components, each of which is a central element in what children reveal
about their master concepts of death. Some of these subconcepts have
their own subordinate components or elements (Speece and Brent 1984).

In particular, Speece and Brent (1996) proposed that there are five
principal subconcepts involved in children's concepts of death:

1. universality
2. irreversibility
3. nonfunctionality
4. causality
5. some type of continued life form ("noncorporeal continuation"
   in the language of Speece and Brent)

We will consider each of these in turn, along with children's questions
that are related to each subconcept (Table 10–4) (Corr 1995).

Universality

From the questions that follow it can be seen that children who seek
to grasp the subconcept of *universality* in their understandings of death
are challenged to comprehend what is involved in recognizing that all
living things must eventually die. This involves bringing into their thinking three closely related notions:

1. all-inclusiveness
2. inevitability
3. unpredictability.

TABLE 10-4. Subconcepts embraced by the concept of death

Universality
All-inclusiveness
Inevitability
Unpredictability
Irreversibility
Nonfunctionality
Causality
Some type of continued life form

Adapted from Speece and Brent (1996).

All-Inclusiveness.   One group of death-related questions posed by children is the following:

Does *everyone* die?
Do children or animals die, too?
Can some people (animals or other living things) *escape* death?
Could I or the people that I know and love *avoid* coming to be dead?

In these questions it is evident that children are inquiring about whether the concept of death applies to some, many, most, or absolutely all living things. In other words, these questions reveal children's efforts to grasp the notion of *all-inclusiveness* in terms of the extent of the group of living things to which the concept of death applies.

Inevitability.   A second group of death-related questions posed by children is the following:

Does everyone *have* to die?
Do *you* have to die?
Do *I* have to die?
Is death something that *must happen* to living things?

In these questions it is evident that children are inquiring about whether the force of the concept of death, which includes all living things, is so compelling or powerful as to make it inevitable. In other words, these questions reveal children's efforts to grasp the notion of *inevitability* in terms of the necessity with which death applies to living things.

These last queries lead some children to further questions about the possibility that death might not be inevitable:

Could some living things *avoid* death?
If so, for which things is death not inevitable?

Can we prevent living things from dying?
What can I do so that I will never have to die?

From these questions it appears that many children are aware that particular individuals can and do sometimes avoid particular causes of death. For example, in children's cartoons on television and in real life, familiar persons may evade or be resuscitated from a specific threat of death. If so, the challenge in grasping the inevitability of death as an aspect of its universality is to understand that, despite one's awareness that death has been or can be avoided in specific cases, no living individual can ultimately avoid death indefinitely.

Unpredictability.   A third group of death-related questions posed by children is the following:

When do people or other living things die?
When will *you* die?
When will *I* die?

In these questions it is evident that children are inquiring about whether the all-inclusiveness and inevitability of the concept of death mean that the timing of death would also be certain and predictable. In other words, these questions reveal children's efforts to grasp the notion of the *unpredictability* of death—a third and apparently paradoxical element associated with the universality of death. What children learn from this third group of questions is that death is not predictable. Therefore, as they strive to achieve an understanding of the universality of death children must bring into that concept a grasp of the notion that death is an inevitable but not a predictable outcome in the lives of living things.

In response to children's questions about the predictability or exact timing of death, adults may be tempted to say, "Death will not occur for a very long time." In many cases, perhaps even in most cases, that may be true. But if death is truly unpredictable, how can we be sure? How can an unpredictable event be known in advance—except in its all-inclusive universality and inevitability? How can death be both absolutely necessary and yet uncertain or unpredictable?

A child who pursues reflections on the theme of unpredictability in the subconcept of death's universality is likely to encounter even harder questions with a powerful personal impact:

How can it be that we know that death *must* come to all living things without *also* knowing *when* death will or must occur?
If it is generally true that we do not know in advance precisely when an individual will die, does that mean that *any* living person or thing might die at *any* time?

Could *you* die at any time?
Could *I* die at any time?

Irreversibility

A fourth group of death-related questions posed by children is the following:

How long do you stay dead after you die?
Once you have been "deaded" are you *always* dead?
Can dead persons *become alive again* after they are dead?
If I did some special thing, like called 911 or gave a pill to someone who was dead, could he or she be alive again?
Can you or I come back to life after you or I die?

In these questions it is evident that children are inquiring about the *irreversibility* of death or what is involved in recognizing that once the physical body of a living thing is dead, it can never be alive again. Irreversibility is one aspect of what is meant by the finality of death. But finality can indicate both irreversibility and nonfunctionality (see below). So perhaps it is better to think of irreversibility in terms of irrevocability or permanence.

Speece and Brent (1996) have explained that irreversibility involves both the processes that distinguish the transition from being alive to being dead and the state that results from them. Thus, the unconditional irreversibility of death means that the physical body can no longer be restored to its former life.

Note that everything asserted here about understanding the concept of death and its various subconcepts excludes two considerations that might occur to children, but which are really outside the scope of this concept. First, we are discussing natural processes or states. Miraculous or magical events and explanations are excluded from this account by definition. As supernatural possibilities, they would (if they really did or could occur) go beyond ordinary human understanding and are not considered here.

Second, in recent times medical resuscitation has complicated the subconcept of irreversibility. But that only means that there is a kind of boundary region between being alive and being dead, a region of ambiguity within which a person may be incapable of autonomous cardiopulmonary functioning but from which resuscitation may be possible (Brent and Speece 1993). If so, the person has not crossed the final boundary to death, a state from which life in the physical body is irreversibly absent.

Nonfunctionality

A fifth group of death-related questions posed by children is the following:

> *What do you do* all the time when you're dead?
> Can you see anything, hear noises, or feel the heat and the cold when you're dead?
> Do dead people continue to eat, play, or go to the bathroom?
> Do dead people get angry or sad?

In these questions it is evident that children are inquiring about the subconcept of *nonfunctionality* in their understandings of death. Grasping this subconcept involves gaining an understanding that once a living thing is dead, all of the life-defining capabilities or functional capacities that are typically attributed to a living physical body cease. This is the second aspect of the finality of death. *Irreversibility* refers to the inability to reverse the processes and the state involved in death; *nonfunctionality* refers to the complete and final cessation of bodily functions.

Life-defining functions that children typically attribute to a living human being are of two types:

1. external or observable functions, such as breathing, eating, walking, or playing; and
2. internal functions, which are not directly observed but are inferred from what is observed or expected of a living thing, such as feeling, thinking, or dreaming.

Nonfunctionality includes the cessation of both external and internal functions.

There is widespread agreement among researchers about these first three subconcepts as aspects of the master concept of death. But two other subconcepts also warrant attention here.

Causality

A sixth group of death-related questions posed by children is the following:

> *Why* do people die?
> What *caused* the death of my pet cat?
> What is it that *makes* living things die?
> Do people die because they are bad?
> Can people die because someone wished that they would die?
> When Mommy was mad at me and said, "You'll be the death of me some day," and then was in the accident, did that mean that I made her die?

In these questions it is evident that children are inquiring about the sub-concept of "causality" in their understandings of death. Grasping this subconcept involves comprehending what it is that really does or can bring about the death of a living thing. For example, children frequently suggest magical causes, such as bad behavior or wishing that someone would die, and specific or individual causes, such as an unusual event that caused a particular death and is restricted to that individual situation, for example, being killed by a television character.

Some researchers (e.g., Speece and Brent 1996) believe that a mature understanding of the subconcept of causality involves an abstract (or generalizable) and realistic understanding of both external and internal events that might bring about death. This view suggests that to comprehend the causality of death, one must understand that death can result from external causes, but that even when such outside factors are not present it will ultimately result from internal causes (or at least from a combination of external and internal causes). Furthermore, this view might claim that merely citing old age does not indicate an adequate grasp of the causality of death since old age on its own is not a specific cause of death. Note that adults in our society and in other cultures do not always agree on what is involved in a fully developed understanding of the causality of death.

Some Type of Continued Life Form

A seventh group of death-related questions posed by children is the following:

What happens *after* death?
Where does your *soul* go when you die?
Even though my body dies, will my *spirit* go on to a better life?
Will *I* ever come back to life again?
Will I be alive again *in this body* or *in some different form*?

In these questions it is evident that children are striving to grasp or to articulate their understanding of some type of continued life form as a part of their overall concept of death. Research by Brent and Speece (1993) has shown that both children and adults commonly report as a part of their concept of death an understanding that some type of continued life form—often a mode of personal continuation—exists after the death of the physical body. This has been described as beliefs in an afterlife, but it may take many forms, such as those involving the soul's ongoing life in heaven without the body or the reincarnation of a soul in a new and different body. Speece and Brent (1996) have called this notion "noncorporeal continuation," but that phrase might be challenged by those who believe in a nonpersonal continuation or in a resurrection of the body. Researchers have not agreed about some type of continued life form as a subconcept in the master concept of death, even though many children and adults include this element in their understandings of death.

Conclusion

Questions that have been put to children about death, and children's questions about death, reveal a rich and intriguing field of interaction between adults and children. There are many difficulties that hamper research on children's understandings of death. Not the least of these are disagreements among researchers on the key concepts or subconcepts to be studied and appropriate ways in which to articulate such concepts or subconcepts. For this, the attempt by Speece and Brent (1996) to offer a comprehensive outline of the central subconcepts associated with the concept of death and to define those subconcepts with some precision is a most useful contribution to the field.

In the future, effective research in the field of children's understandings of death will depend on more rigorous conceptual and methodological precision than has hitherto been typical. Only then will it be possible to speak with authority about the nature and acquisition of a mature understanding of the central components of the concept of death (Speece and Brent 1992). At present, it is not difficult to agree with Stambrook and Parker (1987) that "the methodological limitations and inadequacies of measurement instruments in most of the research preclude the ready acceptance of definitive statements on the development of children's concepts of death" (p. 135).

Research into children's questions about death is of a different sort and should be undertaken promptly with different groups of children in diverse situations. The examples given in this chapter were offered by bereaved children. But we need not wait until children have been affected by the death of a significant person or other living things in their lives to inquire into the questions that they may have about death. Surveying such questions and organizing them into a helpful conceptual typology can be undertaken at any time. More reliable systematic studies of children's attitudes toward death would also be desirable.

Until better and broader research is available on death-related understandings and concerns in childhood, the challenge for adults is to help children grasp the personal significance of death in ways that still provide some sense of the safety and security that all humans need in order to live productive and satisfying lives. This must be accomplished in the context of a lesson about death-related questions and their limitations that is offered by an adult to a child in *A Taste of Blackberries* (Smith 1973, p. 43): "'Honey, one of the hardest things we have to learn is that some questions do not have answers.'" In response, the child thinks to himself: "This made more sense than if she tried to tell me some junk about God needing angels."

References

Alexander, I. E., and Adlerstein, A. M. (1958). Affective responses to the concept of death in a population of children and early adolescents. *Journal of Genetic Psychology* 93:167–177.

Anthony, S. (1939). A study of the development of the concept of death [abstract]. *British Journal of Educational Psychology* 9:276–277.

—— (1940). *The Child's Discovery of Death*. New York: Harcourt, Brace and Company. [Second edition: *The Discovery of Death in Childhood and After*. New York: Basic Books, 1972.]

Bluebond-Langner, M. (1977). Meanings of death to children. In *New Meanings of Death*, ed. H. Feifel, pp. 47–66. New York: McGraw-Hill.

—— (1978). *The Private Worlds of Dying Children*. Princeton, NJ: Princeton University Press.

Brent, S. B., and Speece, M. W. (1993). "Adult" conceptualization of irreversibility: implications for the development of the concept of death. *Death Studies* 17:203–224.

Corr, C. A. (1995). Children's understandings of death: striving to understand death. In *Children Mourning, Mourning Children*, ed. K. J. Doka, pp. 3–16. Washington, DC: Hospice Foundation of America.

Encyclopedia Britannica Films (1975). *When Is Dead?* 16 mm film, Chicago.

Feifel, H., ed. (1959). *The Meaning of Death*. New York: McGraw-Hill.

Feifel, J., and Branscomb, A. B. (1973). Who's afraid of death? *Journal of Abnormal Psychology* 81:282–288.

Freud, S. (1915). Thoughts for the times on war and death. In *Collected Papers*, vol. 4, pp. 288–317. New York: Basic Books, 1959.

Gartley, W., and Bernasconi, M. (1967). The concept of death in children. *Journal of Genetic Psychology* 110:71–85.

Kane, B. (1979). Children's concepts of death. *Journal of Genetic Psychology* 134:141–153.

Koocher, G. P. (1973). Childhood, death, and cognitive development. *Developmental Psychology* 9:369–375.

—— (1974). Talking with children about death. *American Journal of Orthopsychiatry* 44:405–411.

Lonetto, R. (1980). *Children's Conceptions of Death*. New York: Springer.

Nagy, M. (1948). The child's theories concerning death. *Journal of Genetic Psychology* 73:3–27. [Reprinted with some editorial changes in H. Feifel, *The Meaning of Death*, pp. 79–98. New York: McGraw-Hill, 1959.]

Noppe, L. D., and Noppe, I. C. (1991). Dialectical themes in adolescent conceptions of death. *Journal of Adolescent Research* 6:28–42.

—— (1996). Ambiguity in adolescent understandings of death. In *Handbook of Adolescent Death and Bereavement*, ed. C. A. Corr and D. E. Balk, pp. 25–41. New York: Springer.

Schilder, P., and Wechsler, D. (1934). The attitude of children towards death. *Journal of Genetic Psychology* 45:406–451.

Smith, D. B. (1973). *A Taste of Blackberries*. New York: Thomas Y. Crowell.

Speece, M. W., and Brent, S. B. (1984). Children's understanding of death: a review of three components of a death concept. *Child Development* 55:1671–1686.

—— (1992). The acquisition of a mature understanding of three components of the concept of death. *Death Studies* 16:211–229.

—— (1996). The development of children's understanding of death. In *Handbook of Childhood Death and Bereavement*, ed. C. A. Corr and D. M. Corr, pp. 29–50. New York: Springer.

Spinetta, J. J., and Maloney, L. J. (1975). Death anxiety in the out-patient leukemic child. *Pediatrics* 56:1034–1037.

Spinetta, J. J., Rigler, D., and Karon, M. (1973). Anxiety in the dying child. *Pediatrics* 52:841–849.

Stambrook, M., and Parker, K. C. H. (1987). The development of the concept of death in childhood: a review of the literature. *Merrill-Palmer Quarterly* 33:133–157.

Tegg, S. (1994). *Questions for the Doctor*. Gloucester, England: Winston's Wish, unpublished manuscript.

Tolstoy, L. (1886). *The Death of Ivan Ilych and Other Stories*. New York: New American Library, 1960.

Waechter, E. H. (1971). Children's awareness of fatal illness. *American Journal of Nursing* 71:1168–1172.

—— (1984). Dying children: Patterns of coping. In *Childhood and Death*, ed. H. Wass and C. A. Corr, pp. 51–68. Washington, DC: McGraw-Hill/Hemisphere.

Wass, H. (1984). Concepts of death: A developmental perspective. In *Childhood and Death*, ed. H. Wass and C. A. Corr, pp. 3–24. New York: McGraw-Hill/Hemisphere.

Wass, H., and Cason, L. (1984). Fears and anxieties about death. In *Childhood and Death*, ed. H. Wass and C. A. Corr, pp. 25–45. New York: McGraw-Hill/Hemisphere.

PART IV
Grief and Bereavement

As noted elsewhere in this volume, medical advances have created a growing population of individuals who struggle with lengthy illnesses that end in death. In this context, the process of coping and grieving has changed for the person with the illness and his or her family. Building on the work of Kübler-Ross, Pattison, and Weisman, Kenneth Doka (Chapter 11) offers a stage-based model of how individuals grapple with life-threatening illness from the moment they begin to perceive that they are sick. In his model, the coping process is a complex one involving major changes in one's self-concept and relationships with significant others. The goal is to maintain dignity and the integrity of one's personal experience. Just as Feifel might envision it, the coping process outlined by Doka is ultimately steered by the individual's philosophical and religious beliefs about the meaning of life and death. In Chapter 12, Therese Rando offers an insightful look at a recent development in the Western experience of grief—vicarious bereavement stimulated by mass media coverage of violence and tragic death. After placing vicarious bereavement in historical context, she describes two types of vicarious grief responses and observes that complicated vicarious bereavement may be increasing as the media spends more and more time covering wars, natural disasters, and man-made deaths. She challenges us to consider the consequences of this development as well as its necessity.

11

The Quest for Meaning in Illness, Dying, Death, and Bereavement

KENNETH J. DOKA

In truth, most dying patients do not expect miracles. . . . The summons is to help the person recreate a sense of significant being, to be an individual even though dying. The paradox in much of our current treatment is that at the very moment we enhance attention to the patient's physiological needs, we isolate the patient psychologically and socially.

Feifel 1977, p. 7

Herman Feifel's *The Meaning of Death* (1959) was pivotal for a number of reasons. The book challenged academicians and clinicians to explore the ways that humans cope with dying and loss. In many ways, the consequent death studies movement, the development of hospice, and the expansion of bereavement counseling are influenced by his ground-breaking work.

Even more significantly, Feifel challenged us to explore the meanings that dying and death have for contemporary man and woman. But in a sense, that work needs to be explored even further. One of the most significant changes, at least in Western medicine, is that the process of dying has become both extended and less certain. Many illnesses that once were fatal are now life threatening but not necessarily fatal. This represents more than a simple change in terminology. It is a reminder that people live with life-threatening illness for a considerable period of time, usually out of hospital care.

In some ways, this makes the quest for meaning far more complex. For at different points in the illness, even if one recovers from the disease, distinct existential questions are raised. This chapter explores the nature of these questions at different points in the illness experience. But to do so, it is first critical to provide a model of the process of life-threatening illness. Once that is offered, the key existential questions at each phase of the illness can be discussed and developed.

A Model of Life-Threatening Illness

One of the earliest models of coping with fatal illness was Kübler-Ross's (1969) stage theory of dying. Kübler-Ross's work had a significant impact on the death studies movement. It was a clear and simple conceptualization of the dying process that outlined six major coping mechanisms (i.e., denial, anger, bargaining, depression, acceptance, and hope). In addition, Kübler-Ross was a charismatic advocate for her work, which offered a nostalgic and romantic perspective of death that fit in well with the values of the era (Klass 1982, Lofland 1978).

In recent years, there has been increasing criticism of her stage theory (Corr 1993, Doka 1993, Kastenbaum 1991). Some criticisms are primarily methodological. Kübler-Ross presented little information about her sample, measurements, data collection, or findings. Other criticisms are theoretical. Her theory of stages is ambiguous as a linear model (e.g., individuals skip stages and move between them). In addition, although Kübler-Ross disclaims it, acceptance is clearly seen as a preferred manner of coping. There are other criticisms as well. Individuals may cope in many ways other than those mentioned. Denial can be a very effective coping pattern. And denial and acceptance are far more complex than the model acknowledges (in that dying is affected by a person's life processes and environment). Finally, the model has little empirical support (Schultz and Aderman 1974).

In addition to the Kübler-Ross stage model, others have suggested ways of understanding how individuals cope with life-threatening illness. Some theorists preferred paradigms that recognized life-threatening illness as a process that has distinct phases. For example, Pattison (1969, 1978) describes the "living-dying" interval as the time between diagnosis and death. It has three phases: an acute phase centering around the crisis of diagnosis; a chronic phase stressing living with disease; and a terminal phase, in which impending death is both certain and paramount.

Weisman (1980), too, recognized this temporal element in the study of the dying, and placed death into four phases. The first phase, existential plight, begins with the initial shock of diagnosis as an individual confronts his or her own vulnerability and mortality. In the second phase, mitigation and accommodation, the sense of crisis recedes as the individual begins treatment. During this period, the ill individual must accommodate the illness and threat of death with his or her prior coping skills, roles, and identities. This struggle mitigates the earlier acute crisis of diagnosis. A person's energies are focused on maintaining earlier levels of well-being. As an individual further declines, remission becomes shorter and relapses more common. Then a third phase of decline and deterioration is reached. Persons may still struggle to maintain prior roles, but the limitation of disease and the threats of impending death are clear. Finally, there is the last phase of preterminality and terminality. Here the treatment becomes palliative and the individual prepares for the arrival of death.

Both Pattison (1969, 1978) and Weisman (1980) offer clear advances in conceptualizing the dying process. Each emphasizes that, at different points in the illness experience, persons with life-threatening medical conditions encounter distinct issues and problems. However, neither extensively identifies these particular problems. In addition, both Pattison and Weisman clearly identify three periods of life-threatening illness:

1. An acute phase centering around the crisis of diagnosis that confronts an individual with the threat of possible death.
2. A chronic phase, in which an individual must live with disease and maintain a quality of life as well as roles and relationships as he or she copes with the problems posed by the illness and treatment.
3. A terminal phase, in which an individual is now actively dying and must cope with impending death.

However, there seem to be two other phases that are also part of the illness experience. In my own work, I have added two amplifying phases (Doka 1993):

4. A rediagnostic phase, in which an individual begins to suspect illness and or take actions to cope with the possibility of disease.
5. A recovery phase: not every individual dies from life-threatening illness, but even with limited or partial recovery, individuals must cope with the residues of life-threatening illness.

These phases should not be viewed as stages that every individual must experience. The phases may simply represent different points in the ways in which many individuals experience illness. Depending on the trajectory of the illness, individuals may experience one or more of these phases. For example, some may receive diagnosis of a life-threatening illness but quickly recover. Others may recover after a long chronic period. Still others with a short trajectory may face death soon after diagnosis. However, the use of phases emphasizes that individuals have to cope with distinct challenges and issues at different points in life-threatening illness.

In addition to phases, a new model that encompasses a task approach to coping with each phase has distinct value. In recent years, task-based models have been proposed for understanding the experience of bereavement (Corr 1992, Doka 1993, Moos 1977, Rando 1984). Task-based approaches are advantageous for a number of reasons. First, they adopt an active perspective, focusing on coping activities or work. Unlike models that view the person as passively, toward, responding to, or defending against a crisis, a task model emphasizes that the individual has to develop ways to cope with the problems now posed by the occurring crisis.

Second, task-based approaches allow for a more individualized approach, stressing that each person copes with tasks in a unique and idiosyncratic way. Third, the concept of tasks allows a self-determinative perspective. Individuals retain the freedom to decide what tasks they choose to cope with at any given time. Fourth, task-based approaches provide a framework for individuals and caregivers to understand and cope more effectively with the challenges posed by life-threatening illness. These challenges are multifaceted. Individuals must respond to life-threatening illness on cognitive, affective, and behavioral levels. They must cope with the physical, psychological, social, and spiritual implications of disease. In these models, the tasks generally may be described as:

1. Responding to the physical fact of disease;
2. Taking steps to cope with the reality of disease;
3. Preserving self-concept and relationships with others in the face of disease;
4. Dealing with affective, existential, and spiritual issues created or reactivated by the disease.

While these represent the general tasks that individuals must cope with in life-threatening disease, each phase of such an illness creates its own special issues. Accordingly, tasks may be differentiated in each phase, as noted in Table 11–1.

In addition, as one reviews the way that individuals responded to the threat of possible illness in the prediagnostic phase, one retrospectively recognizes that such individuals completed three tasks:

1. Recognizing possible danger or risk;
2. Coping with anxiety and uncertainty;
3. Developing and following through on a health-seeking strategy.

Understanding the ways individuals responded to these tasks may provide useful clues to the coping strategies that they will employ as they continue to face illness.

Even in a recovery, individuals still have to cope with the aftermath of an encounter with life-threatening illness. These tasks then can be expressed as:

TABLE 11-1. Tasks in life-threatening illness

General	Prediagnostic	Acute phase	Chronic phase	Recovery	Terminal phase
Responding to the physical fact of disease.	Recognizing possible danger or risk.	Understanding the disease.	Managing symptoms and side effects.		Dealing with symptoms, discomfort, pain, and incapacitation.
Taking steps to cope with the reality of disease.	Developing and following through on a health-seeking strategy.	Maximizing health and lifestyle. Maximizing one's coping strengths and limiting weaknesses. Developing strategies to deal with the issues created by the disease.	Carrying out health regimens. Preventing and managing health crisis. Managing stress and examining coping. Maximizing social support and minimizing isolation. Normalizing life in the face of disease. Dealing with financial concerns.	Dealing with psychological, social, physical, spiritual, and financial aftereffects of illness. Examining life and lifestyle issues and reconstructing one's life.	Managing health procedures and institutional stress. Managing stress and examining coping. Dealing effectively with caregivers. Preparing for death and saying good-bye.
Preserving self-concept and relationships with others in the face of disease.		Exploring the effect of the diagnosis on a sense of self and others.	Preserving self-concept. Redefining relationships with others throughout the course of the disease.	Redefining relationships with caregivers.	Preserving self-concept. Preserving appropriate relationships with family and friends.
Dealing with affective and existential spiritual issues created or reactivated by the disease.	Coping with anxiety and uncertainty.	Ventilating feelings and fears. Incorporating the present reality of diagnosis into one's sense of past and future.	Ventilating feelings and fears. Finding meaning in suffering, chronicity, uncertainty, and decline.	Coping with fears and anxieties about recurrence.	Ventilating feelings and fears. Finding meaning in life and death.

1. Dealing with psychological, social, physical, spiritual, and financial aftereffects of illness;
2. Coping with fears and anxieties about recurrence;
3. Examining life and lifestyle issues and reconstructing one's life;
4. Redefining relationships with caregivers.

It is important to remember that while this or any model can be useful, it is, at best, a general description of a complicated and highly individual process. Not every individual will experience the situations and reactions that are described here. Nor will every life-threatening illness proceed methodically or precisely through these phases.

These phases are a critical limitation to this model. Life-threatening illness is only part of life. Throughout the time of the illness, at whatever phase, individuals continue to meet many needs and to cope with all the issues, including existential ones, and problems that they had prior to the diagnosis. The experience of illness may affect the perception of these needs and issues, however, and may continue throughout the illness. While this model emphasizes the experience of the illness, living with life-threatening illness recognizes that all the previous challenges of life—dealing with family and friends, coping with work and finances, keeping up with the demands of a home or apartment, finding purpose and meaning in life—remain ongoing parts of the larger struggle of life and living.

Nevertheless, models have value in organizing information that is already available and in providing an agenda for research and education. The model proposed here reminds researchers of the need to examine the many different responses and reactions that individuals, as well as families and caregivers, may have at different phases of illness, as well as the specific problem caused by each disease and the variety of psychological, social, cultural, spiritual, and other variables that influence adaptation.

The Quest for Meaning in Life-Threatening Illness

In *The Meaning of Death*, Feifel (1959) reaffirmed that one of the unique aspects of human experience is that we attempt to find meaning even in incomprehensible events such as life-threatening illness and death. Ernest Becker (1973), in his classic *The Denial of Death*, further developed the paradox suggested in Feifel. There is an aspect of human experience that is transcendental. To Becker, humans have always sought immortality, for there seems a part of us that even death cannot touch. Yet Becker concedes that humans also have the mind to recognize their own mortality. To Becker then, the human paradox is that while we believe there is a part of us that can never die, we can also acknowledge and understand our own mortality. We can contemplate the unfairness of our death. To the existentialist this becomes then a central human question. How can we live fully in the face of death?

Becker (1973) explored the various ways that humans deny death and thus escape that central existential question. Yet that question can become more compelling when one is forced into an encounter with life-threatening illness. For here the urgency of the illness creates an "existential plight" (Weisman 1980) that can force a confrontation with the question of meaning.

These questions can differ at distinct phases of the illness. For example, in the prediagnostic phase, the individual is struggling with the possibility of disease. In this phase, which occurs between the recognition of some symptom and the decision to seek medical help, the individual often has his or her own fears, often with the question: Am I the type of person who gets this disease?

This evaluation includes, then, a strong sense of personal biography. For example, a sexually active homosexual may respond to panic when experiencing a night sweat, an early indicator of HIV, while someone else might consider such an isolated episode an event of little significance. Similarly, someone with a family history of heart disease may interpret chest pain differently from one who has no such history. A person who has recovered from cancer may be far more sensitive to symptoms that suggest a possible relapse.

The point is that even at the very onset of an illness, people try to make sense of the experience. Symptoms always are interpreted within the context of who one is, what one does, as well as the nature and context of the times. Thus, the first touch of illness can create an issue for meaning. What can this pain mean for me? Am I the type of person who could or should have such disease?

This struggle with meaning continues in the diagnostic phase. Here the individual is confronted with the confirmation of fears. Like Tolstoy's (1886) Ivan Ilyich, an encounter always brings the question, "But tell me, in general, is this complaint dangerous, or not?" (p. 122). And like Ilyich the answer that death is possible is, in fact, the dangerous one. The symptoms are not minor. The illness is serious. One can die.

Frequently, this encounter with life-threatening illness forces a review of both one's sense of past as well as one's future. The nature of life-threatening illness frequently reintroduces previously unresolved issues such as the way one copes with illness and of the expectations one can have for support. Earlier issues such as dependency may be reactivated by the illness. In summary, one often explores the meaning of one's past for help in coping with the present crisis.

But future meanings are also explored. All facets of one's prior lifestyle, such as personal priorities and relationships, are open to review. To many, this can be a positive aspect of an unwelcome experience. After recovery, some individuals will claim the experience allowed them to review and reorder their lives in a far more meaningful way. Even others, who do not recover, may experience a desire to reprioritize their remaining time.

While the illness may cause individuals to grapple with questions of the meaning of past and future lives, they may struggle with the critical existential questions of Why me? and Why now? This is often the key question of meaning in the diagnostic phase, the period that Weisman (1980) referred to as existential plight.

This question is the heart of the human struggle. "Why do I deserve possibly to die?" To some, the focal point of their defense will be one of lifestyles: "I watched my weight, I exercised, I practiced a careful diet." To others, the center of struggle may be timeliness. "I just received a promotion. My children are young." Still, others may pose more spiritual concerns. "I am a good person. There is still much I can contribute. I do not deserve to die."

Generally, these questions are not fully confronted at this phase. For many, the existential panic at the point of diagnosis recedes as the individual begins treatment. The initial fears are replaced by a cautious optimism. "I can, and will, get through this. Or at least, I can try. I have a chance."

But in the chronic phase of the disease other questions about the meaning of life and death emerge. As mentioned earlier, the chronic phase is characterized by the ongoing treatment of the disease. In many cases, this is an intense period of struggle. The disease itself can be painful and progressive. The treatments can also be painful and difficult, as well as have delirious side effects. Unlike the diagnostic and terminal phases in which friends and family are likely to be present and supportive, the person may feel more alone in the chronic phase.

Often in this phase the individual struggles with two related issues. First, the individual may confront the issue of suffering. Second, the individual may wonder whether the suffering is worth it. Might one ask if death is preferable to the suffering imposed by uncertain treatment?

Suffering can be defined as a subjective interpretation of physical pain. According to this definition, suffering is a psychological state rather than a physical fact.

Suffering has always been part of the condition. To existentialists, this is the heart of human absurdity. Ivan Ilyich in the midst of struggle asked that very question, "Why this suffering?" And Tolstoy reminds that "the voice answered, 'For no reason—they just are so'" (p. 149). One seeks answers to questions that have no answer. Yet this question is even more problematic in an age where suffering is devalued. Ariès (1987) pointed out that in the Medieval period, suffering made sense. Time spent suffering now atoned for one's sins. It prepared one for death and bought time from purgatory. The feared death was not the death where one suffered but sudden death that caught one unawares.

Suffering raises anew the question, "Why can this be happening to me?" The challenge of contemporary caregiving is to be able to respond to that question. It means being able to acknowledge that the answer to suffering is not found alone in the technical response to pain. It is found in facilitating the sufferer as he or she struggles to find purpose in pain.

For if that person is unable to do so, it may raise an additional question as to whether the living itself is worth the price of suffering and struggle. Throughout the chronic period, this question may be repeatedly asked. Some, at one point or another in this period, may make the decision that in fact there is no reason to continue. They decide to suspend treatment. Still others may seem to will themselves to die, giving up and rapidly declining even in the face of continuous treatment. Yet, many will continue to struggle, providing a testament to power of human hope and perseverance.

And some will recover. But even the very nature of recovery requires existential tasks to redefine one's self after the illness and to give meaning to the very experience of surviving a life-threatening illness. "Who am I now? What do I believe in after this experience?"

Compared with the mass of material attentive to the needs and psychology of the dying, comparatively little has been written about the issues of those who survive a life-threatening illness (e.g., Doka 1993, Koocher and O'Malley 1981). However, it does seem evident that there are often significant aftereffects to a life-threatening illness. These can include both the physical scars and the residual disabilities that result from the illness and treatment. For example, these residual disabilities may inhibit or prevent participation in prior activities or challenge one's self-concept.

There may be emotional and social effects, too. One may still experience many emotional responses to the illness including ongoing anxieties, anger, and perhaps guilt. There may be a sense that others were not as supportive as one hoped. Some may find it difficult to plan for the future or establish intimate relationships. Jobs, careers, families, and finances may all be affected.

All of these experiences and reactions may need to be processed. Often in recovery there may be a deep desire to go back to the life experienced prior to the illness. But this is not possible nor even in some cases desirable, since poor health or lifestyle practices may have contributed to illness. In addition, a person may experience a sense that one's own priorities have changed.

In summary, even in recovery, persons still need to struggle with the meaning of the illness. In some cases this may involve working through the negative residual effects of the illness. But in other cases it means acknowledging the lessons that have been learned from the illness. In the face of death, the value of friends and family may have been enhanced. There may be new personal insights about self or life. There may be a renewed appreciation of personal strengths or a renewed sense of faith. In all of these cases, a brush with the potentiality of death gives life new meaning.

But some will die. In the process of dying, questions of meaning, perhaps raised in the acute phase but set aside as one struggles with treatment, may now again loom large. Often in the terminal phase, there are three spiritual needs that delineate struggles to find meaning.

The first need is to die an appropriate death. As Weisman (1972) reminds us, this is a death appropriate to one's own sense of self. Not everyone needs to die accepting death or in some other state of psychoanalytic grace. To some, an appropriate death may be one where one fights death until the end. To another, an appropriate death means avoiding the mention or recognition of impending loss.

One's sense of appropriate death may be more than how one approaches death. It may mean that the dying individual wishes to put his or her affairs in order as one nears death. The meanings of this, too, can differ. To some, it may mean making sure papers are in order or that final decisions are carried out. To others, it may mean reconciling or visiting with family members or providing necessary acts of closure.

The issue of the appropriateness of death is also complicated by technology. For in the terminal phase, there may be decisions about when it is appropriate to cease medical intervention. These decisions are often encased in ambiguity. Western technological society has lacked consensus both on when life begins and when it ends. The former issue underlies debates over abortion while the latter structures debates on the termination of treatment. Even advance directives may not readily resolve these issues since there may not be consensus on what constitutes extraordinary care or limited chances of recovery. But these debates may well impinge on individual meanings of the appropriateness of death.

In addition to dying appropriately, individuals in the terminal phase may also struggle with the very meaning of their lives. For not only do dying persons want to die in a way that seems acceptable, they want to find meaning in their lives. Developmental psychologists and sociologists (Butler 1963, Erikson 1950, Marshall 1980) have recognized that an awareness of one's own finitude can generate an intense search to find meaning in one's life. Erikson expressed this as an ability to integrate life's goals and values, that is, to find a sense of significance in one's life. The individual who achieves that, according to Erikson, reaches a state of "ego integrity." The alternative is to believe that one's life was useless and wasted, giving rise to a sense of "ego despair." To Erikson this is primarily a function of age. As one becomes older, one realizes that one's life is nearing completion. Others (Doka 1993, Marshall 1980) suggest that this is less a process of age than a recognition of impending death. Even dying children and their families may ask similar questions (Bluebond-Langner 1978, Doka 1993).

Reminiscence and life review are often part of this process to construct meaning. Some may find meaning in their accomplishments or legacies. Others may discover significance in being a witness of great historical events. This life-review process can be a time-consuming, individually directed, interactive period. Individuals may have to reminisce and struggle with many conflicting emotions. It can also be an extremely painful period. The life-review process can uncover many feelings, emotions, and memories of events that were submerged and avoided for long periods of time. Unresolved conflicts can create considerable tension and struggle for the dying person. But this should not imply that every individual will experience an intense and painful struggle as he or she tries to construct meaning and purpose and find significance in one's life. Some individuals may have had a sense throughout their lives that they achieved and accomplished what they had wanted or that whatever they achieved had made their life and their living worthwhile.

Dying individuals may also struggle with another spiritual need—to find hope beyond the grave. This struggle is the heart of Becker's (1973) paradox that humans recognize both their transcendence and their mortality. It is also interwoven in the earlier struggle of finding meaning in one's life. Frequently, the meaning that is found is in the legacy that lives on even when one has died.

In their work with survivors of Hiroshima, Lifton and Olsen (1974) delineated five modes of immortality by which individuals have often found hope. One mode was a religious one. Here hope was found in the religious belief of a personal afterlife. In one real sense, whether in heaven or in a reincarnated state, one would live another life. Two other modes were also inherently spiritual. In the transcendental mode, one saw hope in some form of union with a higher being. A third mode, which Lifton and Olsen labeled "eternal nature," described those who found comfort in continuing the cycle of nature.

Lifton and Olsen (1974) discussed two other modes that emphasize more material accomplishments. In their "creative" mode, one lived on by virtue of one's works, accomplishments, and legacies. The "biological" mode emphasized that one continued in one's biological progeny. I noted two other modes of immortality that could be added to Lifton and Olsen's categories (Doka and Morgan 1993). Some may find comfort in a "medical immortality" where one lives on in the contributions made to medical knowledge from participating in medical protocols or contributing organs or tissues. In a "communal mode" of immortality, one continues as long as one's community survives.

It is evident then that this struggle for meaning in the terminal phase may deeply affect the dying person's decisions or behavior. Decisions, for example, that seem medically or personally dubious may, in fact, be an attempt to achieve or leave a lasting legacy that can be a critical task for the dying. For example, an individual may choose to be part of a medical experiment even though the decisions may seem to do little to enhance one's quantity or quality of remaining life. It may, however, allow a person to feel that he or she has left a lasting legacy that validates his or her life death.

In summary, one of the critical tasks in coping with life-threatening illness is dealing with the affective and existential/spiritual issues created or reactivated by the disease. In different phases, this task is expressed in distinct ways. For example, in the acute or diagnostic phase, one has to incorporate the present reality of the illness into one's sense of past and future. Persons in the chronic phase will need to find meaning in suffering while dying persons must find that meaning in life and death. Even in recovery, individuals will still need to reexamine and to reconstruct their life. At each phase, then, there is a struggle for meaning. Each individual will respond to the struggle differently. For some, interpretive frameworks, however simple or complex, will be readily found. For others, the struggle will be arduous.

Task models have become valued ways to conceptualize not only the dying but also the grieving process (Corr and Doka 1993). For example, Worden's (1991) four tasks have been seen as a useful way to understand the process of grieving:

1. To accept the reality of the loss;
2. To work through the pain of grief;
3. To adjust to an environment in which the deceased is missing;
4. To emotionally relocate the deceased and move on with life.

Yet Worden's tasks, while highly useful clinically and well accepted within the field, do not give adequate attention to the struggle to find meaning in loss that is the heart of the spiritual crisis in grief. Like the dying person, the bereaved needs to interpret death, validate the deceased's life and their role in that life, and maintain a perspective that allows them a sense of continuance of the deceased. It seems critical to add a fifth task:

5. To rebuild philosophical or faith systems challenged by loss.

In some cases, their systems of meaning, their religious-philosophical perspectives, can provide the necessary support for that quest. But in other cases, the very nature or condition of the loss can create an intense crisis of meaning. One's philosophical and/or religious beliefs simply do not seem to allow one to find meaning in the loss. In such cases, there may be a crisis of faith. C. S. Lewis (1961), in *A Grief Observed*, captured this crisis well:

> Meanwhile, where is God? . . . But go to Him when your help is desperate, when all other help is vain, and what do you find? A door slammed in your face. . . .
>
> Not that I am (I think) in much danger of ceasing to believe in God. The real danger is coming to believe such dreadful things about him. [p. 9–10]

The bereaved person, then, is struggling simultaneously with two losses—the loss of the deceased and the loss of the efficacy of his or her own belief system. This, then, is that fifth task in bereavement—to rebuild faith and philosophical systems that are challenged by the loss. For the loss may cause one to question prior beliefs about the nature and fairness of life, the existence of a higher power, or even the very nature of God.

This struggle to find meaning in loss can have a variety of outcomes. In some cases the bereaved may, after intense introspection, simply reaffirm one's earlier beliefs, understanding the loss within one's prior framework. In other cases, the struggle may allow the bereaved person to deepen or modify one's existing beliefs. C. S. Lewis, responding to the loss of his beloved wife, found that he could no longer reconcile the notion that God was both merciful and omnipotent. Yet he rejected any solution to this paradox by acknowledging the mystery of God. *A Grief Observed*, then, chronicled C. S. Lewis's deepening faith. Not all cases are so readily resolved. In other situations, the bereaved may reject one's existing philosophical or religious beliefs and adopt a new or different system. Or in other cases, the bereaved may simply feel that one's own belief system is not adequate and then find a suitable replacement. The loss of belief, not meaning, becomes one of the most enduring and perhaps painful aspects of the bereavement experience.

Conclusion

The crisis of life-threatening illness and loss is found on a variety of levels. There are medical and physical crises as well as psychological and social ones. But there are also spiritual crises as an individual struggles to find the meaning in the midst of disease, death, and loss. At each phase of the illness or subsequent loss, the ill person, as well as his or her family, may confront different issues. But in each case the question is essentially the same: "What can this possibly mean?"

As implied throughout this chapter, our spiritual and philosophical systems of beliefs and thought provide the building blocks for this quest. For these are essential beliefs that provide tentative explanations that are tested against the crisis at hand. It is this underlying spirituality that allows persons with illness, and their family and friends, explanations or understandings of crisis as well as concepts such as forgiveness, value, altruism, love, and sacrifice that can help surmount the crisis.

In the end, the quest for meaning in life-threatening illness and subsequent loss is a critical crucible. To some their concerns will be strengthened and reaffirmed. To others, the inability to find meaning leads, as mentioned earlier, to an enduring sense of despair. Such a result reminds us that an underdeveloped sense of spirituality can be crippling as we struggle with life-threatening illness. Not to have pondered life's mysteries, at least on some level, leaves one ill-prepared to confront death. But still, to others it is a transformative event that offers individuals new meanings for understanding life, illness, and death. These rediscovered or reconstituted meanings can allow individuals, even in the midst of a devastating crisis and an alarming awareness of personal mortality, to experience new insights, to find renewed strengths, and to achieve personal growth.

References

Ariès, P. (1987). *The Hour of Our Death*. New York: Knopf.

Becker, E. (1973). *The Denial of Death*. New York: Free Press.

Bluebond-Langner, M. (1978). *The Private Worlds of Dying Children*. Princeton, NJ: Princeton University Press.

Butler, R. (1963). The life review: an interpretation of reminiscence in the aged. *Psychiatry* 26:65–76.

Corr, C. (1992). A task-based approach to coping with dying. *Omega* 24:81–94.

—— (1993). Coping with dying: lessons we should and should not learn from the work of Kübler-Ross. *Death Studies* 17:69–83.

Corr, C., and Doka, K. J. (1993). Current models of death, dying, and bereavement. *Critical Care Nursing Clinics of North America* 6:545–552.

Doka, K. J. (1993). *Living With Life-Threatening Illness*. New York: Lexington.

Doka, K. J., and Morgan, J. (1993). *Death and Spirituality*. Amityville, NY: Baywood.

Erikson, E. (1950). *Childhood and Society*. New York: Norton.

Feifel, H. (1959). *The Meaning of Death*. New York: McGraw-Hill.

———— (1977). Death in contemporary America. In *New Meanings of Death*, ed. H. Feifel, pp. 4–12. New York: McGraw-Hill.

Kastenbaum, R. (1991). *Death, Society and Human Experience*, 4th ed. Columbus, OH: C. Merrill.

Klass, D. (1982). Elisabeth Kübler-Ross and the tradition of the private sphere: an analysis of symbols. *Omega* 2:241–267.

Koocher, G., and O'Malley, J. E. (1981). *The Damocles Syndrome: Psychological Consequences of Surviving Childhood Cancer*. New York: McGraw-Hill.

Kübler-Ross, E. (1969). *On Death and Dying*. New York: Macmillan.

Lewis, C. S. (1961). *A Grief Observed*. Toronto: Bantam.

Lifton, R., and Olsen, G. (1974). *Living and Dying*. New York: Bantam.

Lofland, L. (1978). *The Craft of Dying*. Beverly Hills, CA: Sage.

Marshall, V. (1980). *Last Chapters: A Sociology of Aging and Dying*. Monterey, CA: Brooks/Cole.

Moos, R. (1977). *Coping with Physical Illness*. New York: Plenum.

Pattison, G. M. (1969). Help in the dying process. *Voices* 5:6–14.

———— (1978). The living-dying process. In *Psychological Care of the Dying Patient*, ed. G. Garfield, pp. 163–168. New York: McGraw-Hill.

Rando, T. A. (1984). *Grief, Dying and Death: Clinical Interventions for Caregivers*. Champaign, IL: Research Press.

Schultz, R., and Aderman, D. (1974). Clinical research and the styles of the dying. *Omega* 5:137–143.

Tolstoy, L. (1886). *The Death of Ivan Ilyich*. New York: Signet, 1960.

Weisman, A. (1972). *On Dying and Denying: A Psychiatric Study of Terminality*. New York: Behavioral Publications.

———— (1980). Thanatology. In *Comprehensive Textbook of Psychiatry*, ed. O. Kaplan. Baltimore, MD: Williams & Wilkins.

Worden, J. W. (1991). *Grief Counseling and Grief Therapy*. New York: Springer.

12

Vicarious Bereavement

THERESE A. RANDO

When I first laid eyes on him in the summer of 1976, my initial impression was that he looked like a sweet elf. He was wiry and animated, light of coloring, with brilliantly twinkling eyes surrounded by a few warm wrinkles. He beamed the most charmingly disarming smile. However, once the man opened his mouth the images were most un-elfin. He had the energy of a dozen men and the razor-sharp intellect of an academy of scholars. His wit was piercingly keen and accompanied the most self-assured attitude. The intensity he generated was almost palpable. When he boomed, "[The fear of] Death is all the time . . . and in our bowels," we knew that it was, and our temporarily nudged defenses briefly permitted a relatively more acute awareness of it. I had gotten my first personal glimpse of Herman Feifel and would never forget it.

In the years that have passed, through many more experiences of personal and bibliographical exposure to Herman and his work, I had come to the point where I sometimes had difficulty differentiating whether a particular notion about personal or societal meanings of death derived from myself or had been yet again another adaptation of Herman's work. In contemplating my contribution to this book, I have concluded that his influence upon me personally, and as a psychologist and a thanatologist, has been so profound and so productive of fundamental conceptualizations that such discrimination is nearly impossible. For the past forty years, Herman Feifel has provided not only to thanatologists but also to psychologists, psychotherapists, gerontologists, health care personnel, sociologists, philosophers, historians, and students of religion the concepts, philosophy, and language necessary both to comprehend and to intervene in the meanings of death to the human being and society. Consequently, there are few, if any, thanatologists today who have not incorporated into their own work some aspect of his, whether consciously or unconsciously.

There is a direct relationship between my topic in this chapter and Herman Feifel as the subject of this *Festschrift*. Upon being asked to contribute to this work, I immediately determined that I wanted to be Feifelesque in approach. In attempting to be so, like Herman in his classic volume, *The Meaning of Death* (1959), I have decided to direct scrutiny to a relatively unexamined phenomenon and to question its impact upon human beings and its relationship to contemporary society. The experience of vicarious bereavement is the focus of my observation. It is my hope that I can draw attention to this experience in a way that will be useful to those encountering it through identifying two types and generating hypotheses about its nature, some of the psychosocial factors that stimulate it, and the consequences that may derive from it.

Previous Observations on Vicarious Bereavement

While related concepts of empathy, sympathy, and identification repeatedly have been the focus of psychological attention throughout the history of the profession, it is only relatively recently that vicarious bereavement has been addressed in the literature. Robert Kastenbaum (1987) reported how he had unexpectedly observed what he termed "vicarious grief" during a time-perspective interview study conducted with elderly residents of the Sun Cities area of Arizona. Discussing it as the sorrow one feels for a loss suffered by another person, Kastenbaum noted comparable expressions to "direct grief" (e.g., weeping, sighing, chill, a sense of emptiness and constriction, difficulties in sleeping, loss of appetite, and obsessional review), along with hypothesizing important differences as well (e.g., duration of response). The vicarious grief phenomenon spontaneously was expressed by eleven of the seventy-nine adults interviewed. Women expressed vicarious grief more frequently than men (ten women to one man). In the cases of the women—on whom Kastenbaum's report focused—the vicarious grief was attributed to a relatively recent death. All occurred within the previous four months, with eight out of ten having taken place in the previous six weeks.

Looking at the intergenerational dynamics found in his data, wherein he found older women to be particularly sensitive to the problems faced by younger people, especially females, Kastenbaum observed the capacity to feel pain for a person who has not yet felt the pain herself. Speculating that the experience gained over a long life may lead an older person to recognize hazards and implications more fully than the younger person who is primarily involved in the loss, Kastenbaum also noted that the capacity to feel vicarious bereavement may not be unrelated to the often expressed parental wish to absorb the pain from their children who are suffering or endangered.

Kastenbaum's article raised a number of questions about vicarious grief that still remain unanswered. For instance, further explanation is warranted to determine whether women would still express vicarious grief and with greater frequency if a more varied population were to be studied; whether vicarious grief could also arise from non-death losses; whether its direction is limited to a shorter time period, as suggested by the present results; what might be the personality and life experience characteristics of individuals who are especially susceptible to vicarious grief; and whether the key to vicarious grief is to be found in past experiences of loss that are somehow rekindled by a loss suffered by somebody else or found in a differential capacity for empathy.

With the exception of Kastenbaum's work, the notion of vicariously experiencing loss or trauma always has been addressed in thanatology within a context wherein the vicarious mourner-to-be has a personal relationship with and/or direct contact with the individual experiencing actual loss or trauma, and then identifies and empathizes with that person to such an extent that subjective feelings of loss or traumatization ensue. This is not an uncommon occurrence for caregivers, counselors, therapists, or rescue workers, among others, who, in the course of their professional work, develop powerfully strong or long-term relationships, or encounter high-intensity experiences, with individuals contending with loss or trauma. This experience is often inherent among those who, for instance, do hospice work, provide acute emergency medical treatment or rescue disaster victims, or engage in psychotherapy with acutely grieving or traumatized individuals. Notable works, among many dealing with this phenomenon in these populations, would include Vachon's (1987) work analyzing occupational stress in the care of the critically ill, the dying, and the bereaved, Raphael's (1986) discussion of victim-helper relationships after catastrophes, Larson's (1993) description of the helper's journey in working with individuals facing grief, loss, and life-threatening illness, and McCann and Pearlman's (1990) delineation of the phenomenon of vicarious traumatization as a framework for understanding the psychological effects of working with victims.

A New Conceptualization of Vicarious Bereavement

As defined in Webster's Tenth New Collegiate Dictionary, the term *vicarious* refers to that which is "experienced or realized through imaginative or sympathetic participation in the experience of another." As will be conceptualized here, vicarious bereavement refers to the experience of loss and consequent grief and mourning that occurs following the deaths of others *not* personally known by the mourner. Thus, the initial experience of bereavement is stimulated by a specific loss sustained by someone other than the vicarious mourner, this person herein termed the *actual mourner*. The vicarious experience of the loss is the central dynamic that differentiates this mourner's bereavement from a personally experienced one, herein termed *conventional personal bereavement*.

It is often the case that a vicarious bereavement experience can potentiate within the mourner actual personal losses in reaction. There are, therefore, actually two types of vicarious bereavement. In type I, the losses are exclusively vicarious, and are those that are mild to moderately identified with as being experienced by the actual mourner (e.g., the vicarious mourner feels that this is what it must be like to be in the actual mourner's position). In type II, in addition to the vicarious losses being identified with, there are personally experienced losses. These are stimulated by and develop as a consequence of (a) relatively intense reactions to the actual mourner's loss (e.g., the vicarious mourner feels quite personally shocked, shaken, and adversely impacted in response to the actual mourner's experiencing a sudden death loss), and/or (b) any assumptive world violations sustained by the vicarious mourner. One's assumptive world, or worldview, is an organized schema containing everything the individual assumes to be true about the world and the self, based on previous experience. It consists of all the assumptions, expectations, and beliefs the individual sustains, which in large part determine the individual's needs, emotions, and behavior, and give rise to hopes, wishes, fantasies, and dreams. It is the internal model against which the person constantly matches incoming sensory data in order to orient self, recognize what is happening, and plan behavior (Parkes 1988). Assumptive world violations can be caused by heightened identification with the actual mourner (e.g., the vicarious mourner so identifies with the actual mourner that he/she experiences a shattering of his/her own sense of parental control when the actual mourner's child dies) and/or traumatization of the vicarious mourner secondary to the circumstances of the death under which the actual mourner lost the loved one (e.g., the vicarious mourner becomes traumatized by the violent and mutilating death of the actual mourner's loved one and consequently experiences personal assumptive world violations, such as a loss of a feeling of security). Table 12–1 identifies the elements and causal agents associated with each type of vicarious bereavement.

Since vicarious bereavement actually can stimulate personal bereavement, the term may seem a little bit of a misnomer in some instances. However, it is still quite useful since it focuses attention on the fact that bereavement initially can be stimulated by losses not personally experienced by the mourner. As hypothesized here, the vicarious mourner must experience the vicarious bereavement either sufficiently intensely and/or actually experience personal assumptive world viola-

TABLE 12–1. Elements and causal agents for each of the two types of vicarious bereavement

Type I

   Loss(es) exclusively experienced through mild to moderate identification with actual mourner

Type II

   Type I + personal losses experienced consequent to:

      intense reactions to actual mourner's loss

      assumptive world violations secondary to:

         heightened identification with actual mourner

         traumatization of the vicarious mourner

tions related to the death of the actual mourner's loved one in order to activate his/her own second set of personal losses (i.e., type II vicarious bereavement). Lacking these, vicarious bereavement still occurs, but the focus remains solely on the actual mourner, with no personal losses incurred for the vicarious mourner (i.e., type I). The empathy, sympathy, and identification the vicarious mourner directs toward the actual mourner are very real, even if they do not lead to, or are not associated with, the experience of personal loss.

Contemporary Catalysts of Vicarious Bereavement

Three recent incidents have called my attention to the phenomenon of vicarious bereavement. Each of these events generated worldwide attention and elicited significant reactions from the public—reactions I have come to view in large part as indicative of vicarious bereavement. Certainly, these are not the only examples of initiators of vicarious bereavement. Nor are my hypothesized factors giving rise to it the only ones. I have not, for instance, addressed the psychological makeup of the vicarious mourner, which may lend that mourner to be particularly susceptible to vicarious bereavement. Rather, I have used these three incidents to help define several factors that I believe to be particularly conducive to stimulating vicarious bereavement in our society today, although in no way exclusively so.

I believe that upon analysis it will be possible to see how this phenomenon of vicarious bereavement has been manifested before, although not to the current extent due to the prevailing sociocultural factors identified below that escalate the probability that it will occur. It is my contention that, taken together, these three specific tragedies provide us unparalleled, contemporary, and vivid portraits from which we can derive information about what stimulates vicarious bereavement—particularly type II—and about its nature and its similarities to and differences from conventional personal bereavement.

The first of these circumstances transpired in England on February 12, 1993, when a 2-year-old boy, James Bulger, was lured away from his mother in a Liverpool shopping center by two 10–year-old boys. The boys then bludgeoned him to death with rocks and threw his lifeless body on the train tracks to be cut in half by an oncoming train.

The second occurrence took place in the fall of 1994 and involved a young mother, Susan Smith, 23, who initially reported that her children had been abducted when an African-American stranger carjacked her vehicle. Smith ultimately recanted that story and admitted to rolling her car into a lake with her two small sons, ages 3 years and 14 months, strapped in their car seats in the backseat.

The third event was the bombing of the Alfred P. Murrah Federal Building in Oklahoma City on April 19, 1995, wherein 168 people lost their lives and an estimated 600 were injured in the building and its surrounds. Most notably among the victims, there were nineteen children who perished in the America's Kids daycare center on the building's second floor, with the major consensus being that the random assault on the children was central in defining to the rest of the country the significance of the event. While clearly the loss of 149 adult lives in Oklahoma City must never be overlooked, it appears that there were special reactions stimulated by the deaths of the children. Without any disrespect for or demeaning of the significance of the loss of adult lives, it is the death of the children that this chapter will focus on.

Along with rage and a strong sense of injustice, all three of these incidents involving the sudden, violent deaths of children provoked a profound outpouring of grief, nationally as well as internationally. In the case of all three, media images and interviews attested to the fact that countless people were experiencing strong emotional and physical reactions to the deaths and the manners in which they took place, and that many were compelled to undertake symbolic or ritualistic action to express their deep emotions. For instance, flowers, ribbons, photographs, written messages, toys, stuffed animals, and so forth were left as memorials to the young victims from individuals who had never known them personally in life, but who had been poignantly touched by them in their deaths. Comments from the public as reported in the media illustrated the great sense of personal loss that many people felt.

What became clear to me through media coverage, listening to my patients, discussions with friends and colleagues, and observing my own responses, was that very real grief reactions were being experienced. Despite the fact that we did not know these children, we felt bereaved by their deaths and sustained all manner of typical acute grief reactions in consequence.

As I have reported elsewhere, grief is experienced in four major ways: psychologically (as manifested through affects, cognitions, perceptions, and defenses and/or attempts at coping); behaviorally; socially; and physically (through symptoms indicative of biological signs of depression, anxiety and hyperarousal, and other physiological responses to distress) (Rando 1993). In reaction to these three tragedies, along with the aforementioned rage and sense of injustice, I observed that people reported a great many of the common psychological responses to loss in terms of affect (e.g., sadness, frustration, vulnerability); cognition (e.g., disbelief, bewilderment, preoccupation with the deceased, spiritual confusion); perception (e.g., feelings of unreality); and defenses and attempts at coping (e.g., shock and numbness, protest, search for meaning, identification with the deceased, dreams of the deceased). In contrast, I perceived fewer of the common behavioral, social, or physical responses to loss insofar as they were independent of manifestations of anxiety and sadness (e.g., crying and tearfulness, depressed mood, feelings of emptiness and/or heaviness, tightness in the throat, trembling).

What Stimulates Vicarious Bereavement?

Extrapolating from the three recent incidents that I contend gave rise to vicarious bereavement, it appears that a complex interplay between three sets of variables can predispose a person in today's society to be particularly vulnerable to experiencing vicarious bereavement: (1) the psychological processes of empathy, sympathy, and identification; (2) selected high-risk factors of the deaths; and (3) a level of media coverage resulting in traumatization of the vicarious mourner. The more these variables are present, the greater the potential for activating type II as opposed to type I vicarious bereavement.

Three Psychological Processes

Inherently, vicarious bereavement demands some amount of awareness about and sensitivity to another's loss, and necessarily involves the psychological processes of empathy, sympathy, and identification associated with that individual and his/her loss of the loved one. It appears that the experience is stimulated only when the vicarious mourner-to-be is particularly touched in some fashion by the plight of the individual sustaining the loss and/or the circumstances of the death. No matter what the other associated issues or influencing variables, these psychological processes must be activated for vicarious bereavement to occur.

Selected High-Risk Factors of the Death

In previous work (Rando 1993) I have delineated the seven high-risk factors for complicated mourning. Four of them pertain to the specifics of the death event: (1) sudden and unanticipated death, especially when it is traumatic, violent, or mutilating; (2) loss of a child; (3) death from an overly lengthy illness; and (4) death that the mourner perceives as preventable. Analysis of the three recent incidents that I believe gave rise to substantial vicarious bereavement reveals that out of the four high-risk factors associated with a death circumstance known to complicate any individual's grief and mourning, three were present in each of these cases, i.e., the deaths were sudden, traumatic, violent, and mutilating; they involved the losses of children; and they were preventable. While the second factor, loss of a child, usually refers to parental loss of one's own child, I believe that, as observed below, healthy adults have sufficient feelings about children as a generic group that would warrant the factor legitimately applying here to some extent.

While it goes beyond the scope of this chapter to delineate specifically how each of these high-risk factors complicate mourning the death of a loved one (the reader is referred to the original source), the main element they have in common is the monumental assault each wreaks upon the mourner and the devastating traumatization and consequent vulnerability that ensue from it. It appears that deaths under these circumstances heighten the possibility of engendering vicarious bereavement secondary to the imposition of these vulnerable feelings and the visitation of a type of trauma upon the vicarious mourner-to-be.

Certainly, from Beverley Raphael's (1980) work we know that in terms of caregivers, mutual empathy and identification develop in crisis situations. This occurs because the loss experience is so universal that we all have experienced its impact and inability to be controlled, making it difficult not to overidentify and causing caregiver vulnerability to countertransference phenomena. I contend that similar dynamics play out with regard to the vicarious mourner being in the position of Raphael's caregiver, and experiencing heightened empathy toward and identification with the actual mourner. This leaves the vicarious mourner in a position of feeling dimensions of the traumatization and vulnerability experienced by the actual mourner.

In this scenario, it is the trauma that heightens the identification with the actual mourner, which in turn prompts vicarious bereavement and, in some instances, personally experienced losses in the vicarious mourner's assumptive world. It can work in the reverse order as well: the vicarious mourner so identifies with the actual mourner that some measure of trauma is personally experienced, which then heightens further empathy and identification. In either case—whether the vicarious mourner experiences identification leading to trauma or experiences trauma leading to identification—the two elements are pivotal in the creation and maintenance of vicarious bereavement. Without a doubt, these vicarious and personally experienced feelings of trauma and vulnerability would not be as intense or debilitating to vicarious mourners as to those more personally involved with the victims. However, the potential exists to experience them to some extent in reaction to situations that share the aforementioned characteristics of suddenness and trauma, loss of a child, and preventability, and that are brought home to the individual's awareness in particularly forceful ways by the media. (See Traumatization Secondary to Media Coverage, below.)

Impacts of the Deaths of Children. While all three of the incidents I have cited share characteristics of suddenness, trauma, violence, mutilation, and preventability—and these heighten the potential for vicarious bereavement—it is perhaps the common denominator of their victimization of children that pulls from the public the most profound reactions necessary to create vicarious bereavement. Indeed, probably few, if any, would argue that the greatest tragedy that can befall a parent is the loss of one's child. It has been demonstrated repeatedly that the worst death to encounter is that of one's child (Rando 1986), and that for rescue workers the worst personal reactions are stimulated by those incidents involving the deaths or injury of children (Dyregrov and Mitchell 1992).

The conclusion is very clear: When it comes to children being hurt or killed, the general adult response is first to be shocked, then to deny, then to be pained and sickened, then outraged, and then frightened for the welfare of one's own offspring. Along the way, deep empathy, sympathy, and identification with the bereaved parents take place. When randomness is a factor, when it could have been one's own child just as easily as someone else's, additional trauma is added, and those three reactions are even more heightened. We imagine what the parents must have felt; certainly projecting our own feelings and fears, but also in large part correctly assuming and identifying their thoughts and emotions as we think how we would respond in a similar circumstance.

As support for my contention that the deaths of children is a crucial factor in the stimulation of vicarious bereavement, one only has to reflect upon the bombing of the World Trade Center in New York City on February 26, 1993. The toll in human life involved six people killed and approximately 1,000 wounded. While that incident certainly evoked outrage among the citizens of the nation, it paled in comparison to what was sparked following the Oklahoma City bombing. I believe the critical difference lies in the fact that a daycare center was involved in the latter, and innocent children were murdered and maimed.

One of the main issues in the deaths and injuries of children is the inherent and massive violations in one's assumptive world that come along with these events. The assumptive world of the healthy adult in Western society contains a number of beliefs, expectations, and assumptions pertinent to valuing, taking care of, and protecting children. There is the expectation that, as in the plant and animal kingdoms, the young will survive to grow up and replace the old. Children are not supposed to predecease their elders. It violates the very laws of orderliness and predictability in nature. All of these things being held by the adult to be true, the injury and deaths of children beget a terrible assault upon that adult's assumptive world, as elements thereof are viciously violated. While certainly in the three scenarios of child death above there are other elements in the assumptive world that are violated by the suddenness and lack of anticipation, violence, mutilation, and preventability of the deaths (e.g., violation of one's perception of the world as meaningful or of one's sense of personal invulnerability), it is the violation of those assumptions, expectations, and/or beliefs associated with children that appear to be particularly traumatizing. In essence, the trauma of what had happened to those children assaulted the assumptive worlds of the adults who witnessed these events, and the assaulted assumptive worlds of these adults then brought home to them their own traumas, which in turn facilitate and are facilitated by vicarious bereavement.

Traumatization Secondary to Media Coverage

Current sociocultural trends in Western society essentially are helping create—and, as noted below, will continue to help create—increasing numbers of vicarious mourners. This is due to the particularly forceful manner of media coverage of deaths that are sudden and traumatic, preventable, and involve the loss of children. One hundred years ago, to hear that nineteen unknown children died in a blast would bring some distress and sadness to anyone with a heart. However, it is doubtful that as many individuals would be as vicariously affected in the same types of ways, or to the same extents, for instance, as were persons vicariously affected by the deaths of the children in the Oklahoma City bombing.

What contributes to the differential impact on potential vicarious mourners-to-be in these two scenarios? I believe that it accrues to the impact of today's media in confronting the public with graphic images of and horrifying information about not only the high-risk deaths that embody the aforementioned critical characteristics, along with the carnage and destruction that surrounded them, but also with the traumatized reactions of those whose loved ones died those deaths. Such personal confrontation with gruesomely explicit images and accounts of violence perpetrated upon helpless children, and with the intense reactions expressed by those who have lost them, can arouse great anxiety, an internal sense of terror and helplessness, frightening perceptions, and traumatic sequelae in the audience. In essence, witnessing the trauma of others can in some sense traumatize the witnesses. That this happens has been very clearly observed, for instance, among therapists who treat victimized individuals (McCann and Pearlman 1990).

This traumatization created by media exposure to sudden, traumatic, preventable deaths of children is not to be unexpected given recent changes in the diagnostic criteria for posttraumatic stress disorder in the *Diagnostic and Statistical Manual for Mental Disorders–IV* (1994). These modifications now permit recognition that posttraumatic stress disorder develops following exposure to a traumatic event in which (a) the person experienced, witnessed, or was confronted with an event or events that involved actual or threatened death or serious injury, or a threat to the physical integrity of self or others, and (b) the person's response involved intense fear, helplessness, or horror. For instance, these criteria clearly were met for many of those who watched events unfold in Oklahoma City or saw some of the startling photographs, such as the Pulitzer Prize–winning photograph of the firefighter carrying out the lifeless body of the bloody and debris-covered toddler.

Further, the audience to the aftermath of that particular catastrophe contended with stimuli well known to produce tormenting reactions in most observers. For example, Raphael (1986) observed that a witness's distressing encounter with the deaths of others—the sights, smells, sounds, and especially bodily mutilation and deaths of children—produce reactive phenomena that require psychological integration in order to deal with the intrusive memories, images, and nightmares that can develop, and with the possible retriggering of memories and the original experience's emotional intensity, which can alternate with defensive avoidance, repression, and general numbing. While these responses typically describe reactions of many survivors and rescue workers in catastrophes, I submit that the current realities of media exposure, coupled with the violent, mutilating, and preventable deaths of innocent children, can give rise to this type of stress response reaction in those individuals not directly involved as survivors or rescue workers.

The experience of merely being witness to these types of deaths can create dimensions of posttraumatic stress and stimulate a measure of grief, in this case type II vicarious bereavement. The witness's own responses of terror and helplessness pierce through normal defensive barriers and potentiate escalated propensities for the psychological processes of empathy, sympathy, and identification, which initially create the vicarious bereavement and now further intensify it. The shock and increased senses of vulnerability, helplessness, violation, and death anxiety over self and loved ones—which are stimulated in general by witnessing violence, mutilation, and destruction—all add fuel to the fire of any personal experience of bereavement that has been prompted in the vicarious mourner. In essence, a vicious cycle is established wherein the situation of witnessing these types of deaths traumatizes the mourner, who then is more susceptible to vicarious bereavement, which then further traumatizes the mourner, making him/her more vulnerable to additional vicarious bereavement, and so on. Whenever the mourner is traumatized in such a fashion, by definition type II vicarious bereavement is present.

Personal Sequelae and Societal Issues Associated with Vicarious Bereavement

Thanatologists and other students of human behavior necessarily have to appreciate the impacts wrought by vicarious bereavement, and how it interfaces both with the individuals experiencing it and the society within which it takes place. In this section, I briefly raise a number of psychosocial sequelae that appear to be associated with vicarious bereavement and delineate the larger social concerns that derive from them.

Individual Mourner

In terms of the impacts on the individual experiencing vicarious bereavement, it seems that there may be detrimental sequelae as well as positive benefits. The more type II vicarious bereavement is present, the greater will be the impact upon the individual mourner—whether positive or negative.

With regard to potential negative consequences of vicarious bereavement, several issues of concern are immediately apparent. The most obvious is that the vicarious mourner is at greater risk for suffering all of the ill effects of being a disenfranchised mourner (Doka 1989). These effects tend to leave the mourner with complicated mourning and any of a number of its attendant symptoms and problems (Rando 1993). Lacking social recognition for and validation of his/her losses, whether exclusively experienced in relation to the actual mourner (type I) or personally sustained as well (type II), the disenfranchised vicarious mourner experiences grief that is not openly acknowledged, publicly mourned, or socially supported. Not unrelated to this, the vicarious mourner may have within him/herself stirred up emotions (e.g., anxiety), with nowhere to put them and no chance to work them through. Both of these situations are quite nontherapeutic for the vicarious mourner and can breed substantial problems.

As addressed above, the vicarious mourner also can become vicariously traumatized. This in itself can interfere with the requisite processing of the loss(es) and the unaddressed issues can cause unresolved grief or complicated mourning and any of its numerous associated problems.

Being in the position of a vicarious mourner can place an individual in a role wherein he/she experiences bereavement overload (Kastenbaum 1969). This may transpire because of the number of losses that accumulate that are associated solely with the vicarious bereavement, the resurrection of earlier losses or traumas, or the additional demands placed upon the individual who already is mourning other losses and then experiences new ones related to the vicarious bereavement. The person is then in a multiple-loss situation, which can complicate mourning for all the losses. The consequences of bereavement overload may include, among other reactions, helplessness, desensitization, anxiety, depression, and/or psychic numbing. Very simply, the individual can become traumatized when experiencing too many or too intense losses at one time. Obviously, any of these consequences can cause their own difficulties in turn, for example, desensitization and psychic numbing can interfere with appropriate emotional connections or responses in life in general.

Finally, because vicarious bereavement involves imaginative or sympathetic participation in the experience of another, the vicarious mourner can create additional problems for him/herself when the imaginings of the deceased's death are worse than the actuality, and perhaps even worse than the imaginings of the actual mourner. Not unlike other survivors of loved ones who die in sudden and violent ways, vicarious mourners may imagine what the deceased's last moments were like and suffer additionally when they construe the death to have been worse than in fact it was.

Notwithstanding these potential problematic sequelae, there are within vicarious bereavement the seeds of potential for positive benefits. Vicarious bereavement may give one the opportunity to experience—with a little useful distance—what a given loss may be like and to work through some of the anxiety associated with it. It can be a rehearsal of sorts for a personal loss that the vicarious mourner ultimately may encounter, and may offer him/her the chance to worry about it in advance. This may in essence provide some measure of the therapeutic experience of the "work of worrying" (Janis 1958) well known in appropriate amounts to facilitate adaptation to upcoming stressful events. Additionally, vicarious bereavement can provide the forum in which strongly held beliefs, expectations, and assumptions can be challenged, tested and reexamined, with the lack of such opportunity having been identified as leaving individuals at high risk for personal devastation and adjustment problems if future victimization occurs (Janoff-Bulman 1985). Also, vicarious bereavement can be therapeutic in prompting the grief work necessary to address the unfinished business that remains with old losses. Finally, the experience of vicarious bereavement has the distinct possibility of being instrumental in bringing about the kind of awareness following healthy confrontation with death that potentially can lead to significant survival consequent to that awareness stimulating accentuated values and goals of life (Weisman 1972).

Despite our knowledge of the problems and benefits that can be occasioned by vicarious bereavement, there are numerous questions that remain to be answered. What determines if a vicarious bereavement experience has an impact of note upon the vicarious mourner? What determines if the impact is detrimental or beneficial? Under what other conditions does a vicarious mourner go beyond empathizing, sympathizing, and identifying with an actual mourner and sustain personal losses him/herself? Is it better or worse to experience the two sets of losses in type II vicarious bereavement? Does vicarious bereavement influence subsequent grief and mourning for those the individual loses? If it does influence it, how so? Is it in quantity, that is, does the experience of vicarious bereavement cause someone to have more or less grief when that person later suffers the loss of someone loved? Is it in character, that is, does vicarious bereavement affect our capacity to feel or work on grief and mourning? What are the similarities and differences between the experience of vicarious bereavement and conventional personal bereavement? Are there other realms in addition to subsequent personal losses in which vicarious bereavement may have an impact? What types of assumptive world revisions can vicarious bereavement stimulate? What conditions are necessary for it? Is there a struggle in which the vicarious mourner must engage, or in which actions must be undertaken, to ensure that any impact from vicarious bereavement is positive as opposed to negative? Are there other circumstances beyond those identified herein that predispose individuals to experiencing vicarious bereavement? Are there certain factors associated with individuals that make them more susceptible to experiencing vicarious bereavement? What are the similarities or differences, if any, in how vicarious bereavement needs to be supported or treated as compared with conventional personal bereavement? These are only some of the myriad questions that arise regarding vicarious bereavement and its impact on the vicarious mourner.

Society

Vicarious bereavement has a powerful and direct relationship with contemporary society. I believe that in many instances society creates and helps perpetuate the existence of vicarious bereavement. Two major causes of vicarious bereavement have been identified in this chapter, specifically, sudden and traumatic deaths of children and the manner in which they are brought home to the viewing public through distressing media coverage. These types of death specifically are on the rise in Western society due to the increasing number of unnatural deaths (i.e., sudden, traumatic, violent, mutilating, and preventable deaths) and the corresponding relative decline of natural deaths. This relative change stems primarily from today's (a) prevalence of accidents, (b) impact of technological advances, (c) increasing rates of homicide and escalating violence and pathology of perpetrators, and (d) higher suicide rates (Rando 1992–93).

As a result of many of the same sociocultural trends that have fostered these four agents of change in the ratio of unnatural to natural deaths, the media in our society have become increasingly obsessed with and focused on unnatural deaths and the reactions of the victims' survivors. This means that one potent trend—violence—becomes both the object of media scrutiny as well as the precipitant of the acts being scrutinized. Certainly, contemporary society not only condones, but escalates, violence. Books, television, movies, music videos, and songs perpetuate the belief that violence is not merely acceptable, but exciting and very newsworthy. A look at the proliferation of tabloid television shows reveals just how far the media will go to exploit violence and its traumatization of survivors. It is not only because of the dramatically changed capacity of the news industry to bring us the sights and sounds of violence, tragedy, and suffering almost from the moment of occurrence that our society is inundated with the forceful stimuli that help create vicarious bereavement, but also because of the industry's active search for such events and stimuli. This leaves the audience inundated with powerful, graphic images and information about sudden and traumatic death, and the searing agony and grief that comes in its wake.

One has to question the impact of this on the prevalence, intensity, and character of vicarious bereavement. While in some ways it can desensitize individuals, in others it appears to have the opposite effect and can escalate the potential for vicarious bereavement. Certainly, television reporting of tragic death is nothing new—we experienced having the war in Vietnam vividly brought home into our living rooms; however, today's experiences with news reporting far exceed the bounds of what previously was considered appropriate, respectful, or in good taste. Consequently, microphones are pushed into the faces of trauma survivors; notifications of death are publicly witnessed; and images of violence, mutilation, destruction, and death bombard the society in incessant ways that are increasingly difficult to avoid. With escalating frequency, as a nation we see more of trauma survivors, hear more details of their horrifying stories, and feel more intensely their pain. All of this not only heightens our potential for creating or maintaining vicarious bereavement through intensifying our identification with the actual mourners, but can traumatize us individually as well, increasing the probability of our experiencing our own type II personal losses secondary to our intensified reactions and/or our assumptive world violations.

My point here is not to indict the media for contemporary news coverage, but rather to indicate how and why vicarious bereavement can be expected to be increasing in prevalence. The sensationalism and exploitation of tragic death and suffering can have a number of unhealthy effects psychologically, of which vicarious bereavement is only one. Sometimes denial of dying and death is stimulated. At other times, the consequences include an increase in annihilation anxiety and in feelings of personal vulnerability. These can serve to initiate any of several reactions: one can become overloaded and overwhelmed; one can overcompensate by become aggressive or, conversely, becoming detached from others and from active involvement in life; one can depersonalize, desensitize, and/or demean the situation in order to minimize its impact; or one can close off one's awareness and heighten defenses by repressing and denying the grim realities of dying and death (Rando 1987).

I assert that the current degree of "in-your-face" presentation of traumatizing sudden, violent, mutilating, and preventable death prompts the anxiety and personal vulnerability that today frequently precipitate the individual's becoming overloaded and overwhelmed. The public often becomes traumatized to some degree. That experience—especially when associated with the deaths of innocent children—prompts among other responses the psychological processes of empathy, sympathy, and identification with the actual mourner. Hence are sown the seeds of vicarious bereavement, which may remain exclusively vicarious and associated solely with identification with the actual mourner (type I), or may go on to include as well losses personally experienced by the vicarious mourner consequent to intense reactions to the actual mourner's plight and/or personally experienced assumptive world violations (type II).

Conclusion

As the nature of deaths becomes more traumatizing because of suddenness, violence, mutilation, and preventability, as more children die these deaths, and as the graphic images of and gripping information about the agonizing suffering wrought over the deaths of these innocent victims bombard and traumatize a somewhat captive audience, the potential is escalated for the creation of vicarious bereavement and, quite frequently, vicarious bereavement of the sort that engenders personal losses as well in the vicarious mourner.

For the better or worse, our contemporary society essentially is begetting vicarious mourners through spawning the very conditions precipitating vicarious bereavement. It will be important for thanatologists to further investigate this interesting phenomenon and ultimately to offer treatment recommendations for those experiencing vicarious bereavement, along with pointing out its relevant societal implications. It is my hope that this discussion helps stimulate this process.

References

American Psychiatric Association (1994). *Diagnostic and Statistical Manual of Mental Disorders*, 4th ed. Washington, DC: American Psychiatric Association.

Doka, K., ed. (1989). *Disenfranchised Grief: Recognizing Hidden Sorrow*. Lexington, MA: Lexington.

Dyregrov, A., and Mitchell, J. (1992). Work with traumatized children—psychological effects and coping strategies. *Journal of Traumatic Stress* 5:5–17.

Feifel, H. (1959). *The Meaning of Death*. New York: McGraw-Hill.

Janis, I. (1958). *Psychological Stress: Psychoanalytic and Behavioral Studies of Surgical Patients*. New York: Wiley.

Janoff-Bulman, R. (1985). The aftermath of victimization: rebuilding shattered assumptions. In *Trauma and Its Wake: The Study and Treatment of Post-Traumatic Stress Disorder*, ed. C. Figley, pp. 15–35. New York: Brunner/Mazel.

Kastenbaum, R. (1969). Death and bereavement in later life. In *Death and Bereavement*, ed. A. Kutscher, pp. 28–54. Springfield, IL: Charles C Thomas.

——— (1987). Vicarious grief: An intergenerational phenomenon? *Death Studies* 11:447–453.

Larson, D. (1993). *The Helper's Journey: Working With People Facing Grief, Loss, and Life-Threatening Illness*. Champaign, IL: Research.

McCann, I., and Pearlman, L. (1990). Vicarious traumatization: a framework for understanding the psychological effects of working with victims. *Journal of Traumatic Stress* 3:131–149.

Parkes, C. (1988). Bereavement as a psychosocial transition: processes of adaptation to change. *Journal of Social Issues* 44(3):53–56.

Rando, T. (1987). Death and dying are not and should not be taboo topics. In *Principles of Thanatology*, ed. A. Kutscher, A. Carr, and L. Kutscher, pp. 31–65. New York: Columbia University Press.

———— (1992–93). The increasing prevalence of complicated mourning: the onslaught is just beginning. *Omega* 26:43–59.

———— (1993). *Treatment of Complicated Mourning*. Champaign, IL: Research.

————, ed. (1986). *Parental Loss of a Child*. Champaign, IL: Research.

Raphael, B. (1980). A psychiatric model for bereavement counseling. In *Bereavement Counseling: A Multidisciplinary Handbook*, ed. B. Schoenberg, pp. 147–172. Westport, CT: Greenwood Press.

———— (1986). *When Disaster Strikes: How Individuals and Communities Cope With Catastrophe*. New York: Basic Books.

Vachon, M. (1987). *Occupational Stress in the Care of the Critically Ill, the Dying, and the Bereaved*. Washington, DC: Hemisphere.

Weisman, A. (1972). *On Dying and Denying: A Psychiatric Study of Terminality*. New York: Behavioral Publications.

PART V
Current Topics on Death

The contributors to this section honor Herman Feifel's pioneering spirit by tackling novel subjects in creative ways. Currently retired from a long and distinguished career in psychiatry, Avery Weisman (Chapter 13) takes us into his world as an aging but still vital member of society. He finds that he must create meaning in the context of ill-fitting norms and values. His sensitive wanderings provide much food for thought, but he avoids trivializing the circumstances of old age and giving pat responses to questions that we ultimately must answer for ourselves. Daniel Leviton (Chapter 14) is concerned with society's capacity for creating death and its responsibility for ending death and misery whenever possible. He demonstrates an important role for thanatologists in arguing for social policies that will help eliminate unnecessary death and suffering. In describing global health as a function of death minimization, Leviton hopes to enlighten citizens and policy makers about the important role of death, dying, and bereavement in the well-being of all people. Robert Fulton (Chapter 15) acknowledges American society's move away from guiding philosophical and religious creeds, but he believes that our persistent wish for immortality keeps us from fully shaking the influence of our Judeo-Christian heritage. Fulton makes a convincing argument that everyday funeral practices, spending habits, Mardi Gras, and even the tradition of saying gesundheit to someone who sneezes, represent derivatives of our underlying belief that we can control death and ultimately be returned to a state of immortality. For John Morgan (Chapter 16), death can be a muse. Here he develops a historical context for understanding how the knowledge of death and finitude can serve a creative function, and provides intriguing examples to demonstrate his thesis. The position of honor of finishing this toast to Herman Feifel goes to Robert Kastenbaum (Chapter 17), who asks, What is the future of death? In a delightful trip through a number of thanatological domains, he challenges us to think freshly and reconsider basic assumptions. For example, how should life and death be counted—are these categories or end points on a continuum? How long can life be stretched out and death forestalled? What about cloning? Perhaps some day our genetic material (if not us) will be re-created in the form of another human being. Will this be the immortality we thirst for?

13

Ambiguity in Aging

AVERY D. WEISMAN

Somewhere a hermit sits on a mountaintop, or maybe in a cave, deliberately cut off from the world. He seeks enlightenment, and so spends a large portion of his time contemplating death. Perhaps he has already found what he was searching for. I wish him well, but his way of life is not for me. I would probably profit from his wisdom and from learning what he became enlightened about, but if his goal is to embrace death with total equanimity, his life is not a model to emulate. I am all for contemplation, and certainly could use more wisdom and enlightenment. At the same time, while I strongly advocate the so-called appropriate and acceptable death I believe that contemplation need not be an end in itself, but rather a means to understand and cope more effectively with this world, not the next.

If I reject the hermit's values and way of life I am obligated to recommend something better, especially during old age. Are there distinct and unique values limited to old age? If not, then the values inherent to old age are simply carryovers from middle age and even younger phases of life. This does not seem right, because if values for young people depend on work, family life, accumulation of wealth, fame, and fortune, and so on, then old people will have a problem. Based on an ambiguity that centers on work and achievement, old people are shunted to a siding where opportunities for appropriate action based on these guidelines are absent. How, then, can old age justify itself, or find a relevant purpose, while living according to standards for another time?

What is acceptable behavior for an old person? What should be the guiding directives and prohibitions in old age? Is the onus strictly on the old person or is bias against the aged also to be held responsible for discrimination? There is no doubt that changes of all sort occur in a lifetime. But what changes and what remains the same? An adolescent might live by a standard that puts value on, say, popularity, having many friends, and being busy on weekends. Conformity becomes a cause for some adolescents even if it takes nonconformity to pull it off. After adolescence becomes just another equivocal memory, its values may persist in different forms. Popularity turns into reputation and success. Old grads like to be looked up to, so alumni notes regularly report triumphs and those of their children. Almost anything that draws a favorable opinion is central to middle-age values.

Nevertheless, the best age to be is strictly opinion or, more exactly, how one happens to feel at the moment when this tedious question is asked. The best age to be is the age when you feel at your best, whatever and whenever that is. Old people are not exempt from feeling that old age is not such a bad time. Some may be complacent about a number of things, including past achievements, and many old people, regretfully, are in despair, far from feeling self-satisfied, and doubt their own reason or purpose in continuing to survive when suicide offers quiescence. Extremes are usually dangerous, like radical beliefs that prompt ill-thought-out actions. Polarities are not the best position for figuring out what means what. Even virtue creates problems; an excess of virtue may lead to an arrogant dogmatism that feeds on controlling others. However, modulation, moderation, and composure are traits worth cultivating, just as learning is valuable and courage helps to confront ambiguous predicaments.

It is customary to assign certain descriptive phrases to different ages simply to sensationalize and polarize and minimize complex situations. Old age is no more a special age of anxiety or anomie than any other age. It does seem to be an age of prostheses and prescriptions, however, which is a product of devices and drugs designed to bolster diminished capacity as well as physical, mental, and social disability. I maintain that whatever helps to sustain and support normality and autonomy is to be praised, not scorned, at any age. If old age is supposed to have a corner on wisdom, it is a dubious achievement since much so-called wisdom is untested. In any case, who pays attention to the bromides, passing as wisdom, that circulate?

Normalizing old age means trying to live well and cope effectively without cruel and dogmatic imposition of standards that no one ever chose.

> You are old, Father William, the young man said,
> and your hair has become very white;
> and yet you incessantly stand on your head—
> Do you think, at your age, it is right?
>   [Lewis Carroll 1865, p. 67]

Not every oldster wants to play golf or read *The Decline of the West* (Spengler 1926–1928), a long-forgotten classic. When society stops pigeonholing the elderly, then perhaps those considered old will respect themselves enough to seek out individual ways of recognizing and rectifying the mixed messages and ambiguities that carry over decade after decade. What is old age from the inside? There is as much proscription as prescription as old age comes upon us.

Several months ago I unearthed an ancient portable typewriter that I used many years ago. I had replaced it with an up-to-date electric typewriter which, in turn, became obsolete, and another electric typewriter with new functions took *its* place. Now, friends urge me, the current electric typewriter should be discarded for a word processor. I have thus far refused.

Thirty or forty years have gone by since I last used the old portable. I changed much more than the typewriter during this time, which, kept in its case, was scarcely dusty. Other than finding that the printing is now exceedingly small, even tiny, and hard to read, there is not much wrong with this apparatus except that it is old. The same is true for me. We are both capable of doing a job such as writing a letter or a manuscript, but not much more. Neither of us is a word processor nor, I must insist, an obsolete relic like so many bottles on a rubbish heap. I hold no great value in acquiring a word processor, whatever its putative advantages. I need to generate and process clear ideas more than I need to shift paragraphs around and write quickly.

I cannot fault my old portable (or my present electric typewriter, which is also superannuated) for not being a modern computer. Neither of us is flashy or spectacular. My old-style typewriter, now electric in its present incarnation, does its job. And so do I, with an old-style endurance and pragmatism suitable to what I am capable of doing. I must confess, however, that my very old portable now has been honorably restored to the attic where it awaits another incarnation in some collector's study.

In my old age there are inconsistencies, rigidities, and irritabilities that, together, are not very admirable, and bother me more than such shortcomings might have several decades ago. In part this irritation is due to my own preformed biases, fears, and stereotypes about what happens to old people. I am reluctant to become a cranky, opinionated old man, instead of the serene sage I'd prefer to be. While I would also like to be at least conversant with the very latest in medicine and modern technology, I am not driven to do this. Doing what I do well, even with a glimmer of excellence, has greater priority than struggling to be a full-fledged contemporary of those I am not. I manage, for example, to keep track of telephone numbers and dwindling appointments in a little notebook, and do not need to keep a handy-dandy, pocket-sized machine to print out the last known address of a distant cousin I seldom communicate with.

Nevertheless, there is an agelessness about being aged in that, from the inside, I find a continuity belied by what the mirror reflects. All of us, without exception, are droplets in an ancient genetic stream that Heraclitus never imagined. Although seemingly fixed at any given moment, and firmly in place so far as its importance is concerned, the affairs of mankind that seem so pressing and discouraging are still in transition and flux. History is always being revised, and evolution goes on. I am as sure of this as that the sun comes around whether or not there are clouds obscuring it. Few could live in utter chaos, going backward and forward, side to side, without imposing an order, sequence, and even rationality that appeals to a sense of security. We all need guidelines, even if they do not predict very reliably. Just for simple clarity, maybe with a little absolutism, the most useful basis for order in the personal universe is a beginning, middle, and end. Then we can loop back and talk about cause and effect, reason and consequence. Whether such order helps mitigate ambiguity and uncertainty I do not know, but it is surely relevant to old age where the beginning, middle, and end can be viewed all at once, as if agelessness were palpable and genuine.

Order in the personal universe is hard to come by, so we turn to manmade explanations of how the world is or might be. However, whatever we happen to believe depends on many unspoken conditions that are themselves uncertain. Ambiguity is built right in to the way we live and where we live. Unspoken versions of "usually . . . but . . . in my opinion . . . it seems to me . . ." keep me honest whenever I find myself spouting dogmatically. A bell-shaped curve is aesthetically pleasing, and for some purposes very useful. But from the inside—the personal standpoint— there are important things that do not lend themselves to coverage by a statistical canopy. For example, as a matter of objective information old age has a beginning, middle, and end, although when these transitions occur is fairly ambiguous. When old age is considered strictly as an inner experience, however, statistics fail and anecdotes take over our dotage. But the subjective is not that reliable, and defies generalizations, while objective, outside-in observations may be too abstract (and therefore irrelevant) for human experience in the here and now.

I appreciate contemporaries who wistfully claim, "But I don't *feel* like 80!"—as if specific feelings could be matched with birthdays and years spent being alive. I suppose they mean that 80 is old, and people of that age are inevitably weary as well as ancient. People tend to brag or bemoan their advanced age, depending on whether they are looking for compliments or commiseration.

In her recent book, Betty Friedan (1993) went to great lengths exploring the idea that old age is a fountain of opportunity, which I am always glad to hear about. She found a large number of older people who were successful earlier in life and continued to thrive after retirement. This was a gratifying discovery, refuting the notion that old age necessarily implies progressive dilapidation.

Nevertheless, older people are generally supposed to be too old to work at a regular job, so they must find their own gratifying niche. I cannot wholly separate myself from the dictum that work and worth go together, and that worthwhile work implies a contribution of some sort, or at least to be somewhat productive in old age. Perhaps this is particularly prevalent among those who devoted considerable time to working at a business or profession that required a certain dedication.

Consequently, after retirement, when work is taken away, the old person, including me, needs to look hard for a sense of purpose. Without it self-regard is shaky, and it is difficult to feel effective when there is nothing to be effective about. From the inside out, however, I have not relinquished the self-expectation of a contribution that might last longer than I do. Nor can I be satisfied with a wan reassurance that few people make contributions at any time. But my wish is not, or cannot be, a monumental contribution, although that would be nice. It is just unlikely. The ambiguity here is between a personal value of a lasting contribution and an objective realization of my own limitations. Nevertheless, there is little consolation about confronting personal limitations because retirement should mean more than retrenchment and recreation. A very successful former business executive told me about his life in a high-rise luxury commune. "Every day I do something interesting, or at least that's what I am told. Monday is my day of rest: I don't have to play golf." For him work means worth, and worth needs work. Being out to pasture, sentenced to graze, is punishment without pain.

The question of what to do with retirement is highly practical and goes beyond such vague recommendations as the life review, which is like cultivating righteousness. What to do is also a different question than how to make the best of it. Here are a few samples drawn from Cicero's account of Cato the Elder (Cicero 44 B.C.).

> If a man controls himself and avoids bad temper and churlishness, then he can endure being old.
> Old age has its own appropriate weapons: namely, the study and practice of decent, enlightened living. [p. 216]
> Four reasons why old age is an unhappy time:
> (1) It takes us away from active work,
> (2) It weakens the body,
> (3) It deprives us of practically all physical pleasures,

(4) It is not far from death. [p. 219]

I would rather stay old for a shorter time than become old prematurely.

Age has to be fought against. Its faults need vigilant resistance ... follow a fixed regimen, exercise in moderation, food and drink to strengthen, not overburden. ... the mind and spirit need even more attention than the body, for old age extinguishes them. [p. 225]

Age will only be respected if it fights for itself, maintains its rights, avoids dependence, and asserts control over its own sphere as long as life lasts. [p. 227]

It would be hard for me to improve on Cato the Elder's directions. I cannot but wonder if Cicero achieved these noble goals, because I think such sentiments are practical enough and quite attainable. The wisest people, it seems, die with the greatest equanimity.

While I believe as strongly as Cicero in the validity of these comments (indeed, who could refute them?), my own initial response to actual retirement, the fact itself, seemed to follow a commonly reported pattern: rue and relief, clutching at half-truths, self-doubt, an ample degree of denial, and considerable uncertainty about the entire project of post-work activity. Retirement is a kind of relief, combined with freedom from keeping schedules, but it also suddenly lifts responsibility. I already knew that planning for retirement is a wise maneuver, although plans are not synonymous with tactics and strategies for carrying them out. Given good health, retirement can last almost as long as middle years. Nevertheless, new opportunities for the newly retired and the aged, to use that cumbersome, heavy term, are not very rich. Consequently, newly retired people I spoke with often volunteered that they were "busier than ever." I questioned them further, and finally concluded that they were busier than ever doing things that in the past required far less time. The situation was a clear example of one of Parkinson's laws that work tends to fill the time available to do it.

Retired people often joke about themselves. A friend told people who asked that he was "quasi-retired." Then, by the time they figured out what "quasi-" meant, they lost interest in the question, and he didn't have to answer. For myself, I did the usual things at first: enrolling in various courses, reading books I hadn't had time for, and so forth. I volunteered at a humane society, and set up a pet-loss bereavement program. But this did not last. Then I registered for extension courses as a regular student, seeking credit, as if to prove that I was still able to do assignments and submit work respectable enough to be graded. While glad that my work in psychiatry was behind me, I was frankly envious of colleagues still engaged in research. I observed Cato's recommendations because they corresponded with what I had advocated for a long time. But I was more churlish than I liked, and during much of the early retirement years had to recognize and restrain the traditional irascibility said to be typical of old age.

Every day I read about opportunities for volunteers, which turned out to be well intended, but unlikely. Those who praise and recommend volunteerism should know better. At best, it can be a semi-therapeutic endeavor, helpful to volunteers coming to terms with certain problems from the past. It is a very mixed opportunity, in my opinion, to make a slight contribution for a dimly worthwhile purpose. But perhaps this is true for many people, even those doing paid work: slight contribution, faintly worthwhile purpose. In old age, however, volunteering takes up much more time than it does for younger people who are working at paid occupations. There is little recognition; the basic compensation is self-reward. The volunteer happens to be doing for free what no one is willing to pay for, or that no one who is paid is willing to do. Worst of all, should the volunteer actually be doing something of genuine value, paid workers may feel that the volunteer is depriving a real worker of a livelihood. Except for very brief periods, volunteering is short on esteem, and much shorter on any kind of compensation.

Respect and Regard

Woe to the old person who seeks to earn more than very meager hourly pay for a job of any kind. Self-esteem is bound to be a problem in old age, as, indeed, it is at any age, except that now it stands out boldly. If retirement is free of worries about health and finances, then the next goal or value is retaining respect and regard. I am inclined to believe that if a person does not go into old age with self-respect and reasonable regard by others, he or she is unlikely to find them in retirement without special effort. Most of us are middlemen of sorts, regardless of what we do for a living. Something or someone enters our sphere, is worked on, and sent forth again. A psychiatrist, say, is consulted by a patient with complaints and symptoms. The work of therapy is carried out, and, with luck, the patient goes away feeling and behaving much better. The same could be said for any physician, or for a merchant who deals with a product that someone wants. In his old age Picasso painted ashtrays, dishes, flower pots, which immediately became valuable because of his signature. How rewarding this was to Picasso I have no idea, but it is hardly a feasible plan for the rest of us. Some people, after retirement, continue as consultants to the business they had run before. But in using the skill and knowledge of earlier work, they gradually find themselves obsolete. Gaining respect and regard starts in the past, but to be sustained must come from somewhere else. Even being a legendary figure is no bed of roses, and most of us are far from that. Many older people settle for being a self-appointed expert on old age.

Respect (meaning self-respect) and regard (meaning esteem from others) cannot be demanded. Veneration of the aged is not indigenous. The sense of being wholly defunct is a strange emotion, especially in a setting of desolation. What was once taken for granted is now ambiguous, replaced by regrets about what cannot be rectified. Rumination about the "path not taken" dulls appreciation of the good things already found on the path taken. No one can know if another path would have made any difference, or if it is just an imaginary supposition without consequences.

Goals in Old Age

Ambiguity means no longer being sure what familiar things mean. This not only includes choices and consequences, but one's relationships with people. Unfortunately, old people who experience loss or uncertainty about what-means-what are deemed pathological. "Uncle Joe is not himself. He is so mean, he never seems to remember, and he shows no interest in what we do." While this scenario is commonly true, the reverse is also true just as often. Uncle Joe may be suffering from deep ambiguity about himself and those he depends on.

We know that life is not fair, evil is seldom punished, mistakes cannot often be corrected, and other people are changelings. Middle-age standards are generally inappropriate for old age, since there is a wider gap between expectation and opportunity. This is not surprising to parents of grown children, or to former executives well equipped for honorific inactivity. Clearly, it is insufficient merely to continue being a law-abiding citizen; we are all defined, designed, and designated by the surrounding, prevalent culture and circumstances. Old people, operating with a double sense of half-truth, often declare something to the effect, "I've earned my rest, recreation, and leisure. I've worked for them," as if old age were simply a time of recompense, or balancing accounts. Ambiguity of meaning is still there. For example: It was bad to be unemployed back then, but good not to need work now. Good not to need work now, but bad, back then, to loaf or fritter away time, a precious commodity.

Once in a while some well-meaning person, usually a younger person, advises another to live each day as it comes, as if it were the last, or next to last. What this advice is supposed to mean, or do, is unclear to me. For old people it is sure to be offensive. Old people are very aware that time fleets, and that there is no guarantee about tomorrow. Furthermore, even when an older person is blessed with material and physical health, it is sometimes hard to justify or find purpose in being alive. With or without confidence in sharing a worthwhile purpose or goal, in old age the cautionary phrase, "subject to change without notice," is all too pertinent.

Although it is an obvious fact that time may run out at any time, most people are able to understand and ignore its relevance. I hope gerontologists come up with a better occupation than conducting the "life review," which, I surmise, old people tend to do anyway, in a desultory fashion. I find no particular pleasure in rehashing the past, even including the positive as well as the negative. I do on occasion have poignant flashbacks, which help me understand the past a little better, and to cope with the present, which triggered the flashback. There are times when I am regretfully reminded of something I can do nothing about. I would like a second, third, or even fourth chance. Since any chances are out of the question, why not imagine many chances to do again what should have been done, or not to do what was done? Maybe it is just as well that second chances are impossible; we might make the same mistakes all over again.

I admit no nostalgia for the past, only an occasional regret that I was as I was, and could not do otherwise. Regardless, the past must be relinquished unless it has a practical application to the present. And if there is no significant present, there is hardly a past worth mulling over.

> When I was one and twenty,
> I thought that life
> would be a horn of plenty.
>
> But now that I am eighty-one
> I wonder what became of
> all that fun?

I recall that jingle without a scrap of recognition. The up-close facts are that I had no such expectations—if other young people did, and had all that fun, I was certainly not a part of it. In retrospect, however, 21 is a key metaphor for transition to adulthood from youth. For me, candidly, time can be a menace, not just a metaphor with a thousand meanings. We can use it, kill it, waste it, exhaust it, make the most if it, and so on. At the presumably luminous age of 21 time can be a promise, although for some, time is vastly empty. For the middle-aged, time's passage is still remote enough from the twilight of old age. But temporal demarcation of inner, immediate experience that overlaps past and future is simply a marker. It is what we measure in order to keep a schedule.

For me, as I grow older, time means something more than keeping a schedule, which I need less and less. It reminds me of those who are no longer present, except that their absence is not marked by chronology, but by commemoration. I cannot go to the telephone and ring them back into existence. Rather than relegating their memory to the past, however, they have a right-now recollection reminiscent of a flashback, almost exempt from the sequence known as time. This is a limbo of consciousness, graveyards notwithstanding, in which they remain alive, and their influence remains even as their absence is recalled. When we stop reminiscing, they are dead for sure. Terminability is not yet termination. I do not plan to bundle up, however, preparing for the winter of life. Nevertheless, if there is ever a more appropriate time to examine the ramifications of longevity, I am sure that it is in old age, or better, just in that brief moment after death, the "just-dead-enough" to evaluate your own game plan and its consequences, good or bad. According to some myths, the souls of the just-dead hover around the vacant body, reluctant to leave. Survivors are in awe of these disembodied souls, so recently released. But what are the survivors, next-of-kin, friends, significant others, fearful of? What conversations might the newly dead have with the still living? Are there secrets known only to those who have died?

Resolving Ambiguity About Old Age

Whether modern gerontologists actually know more and have an advantage over ancient sages who grappled with similar issues is a question that does no discredit to either. I am sure that even the wisest ancient, say, Socrates, would be bewildered by contemporary society, with both its technology and its travails. However, genuine wisdom should know no obsolescence; only the problems take different forms. Wisdom always struggles against history; cultural disparity tends to confound. But what is "wisdom" anyway? Classical and contemporary sages will, I trust, be referred to generations from now. They will be studied, even be topics of future dissertations, and come back to earth as old examination questions. The ambiguity here is that while we draw upon the past, every generation starts anew. Merely to be modern is no security about being wrong or irrelevant. Montaigne (Frame 1958), that skeptical humanist with a flair for wisdom, repeatedly quoted the ancients more than he did contemporaries, and might have done them both an injustice. Our society, diverse in almost every respect, also has different standards for old people. Old people, consequently, are caught up in cultural symbols and find themselves expected to be hale and independent on the one hand, but expected to need more money for health care on the other. The spread between vigorous old age and decrepit, demented, old age could scarcely be wider, so it is often a bitter enterprise for anyone trying to avoid stereotyping.

It requires very little research to decide that old age can be a rewarding and reasonable time, given enough assets to survive successfully (Kastenbaum 1992). Or it can be enormously frustrating. My purpose in this discussion is to show that much dissatisfaction in old age is aggravated by its ambiguities. Instead of citing numbers of clients or individuals living in old age settlements, I shall vary from this customary approach and be more personal, if not actually autobiographical. I assume that every old person has his or her characteristic sentiments that pertain to existential issues, which, while not readily generalized, have advantages over more abstract discourse.

Old age and death are not at all equivalent. Death can arrive at any time that the Fates decree. Old age has its own life to lead, despite sometimes drastic changes in physical capacity, competence, and status. I call the point of "just dead" the postscript period, which, as in some letters, often comes to express what the main text was all about, only more succinctly. I hope that it will erase some of the ambiguities that pose problems for old people, who are held up to different standards and expectations than are young and middle-aged people. For example, old people are expected to be healthy and independent, with enough self-esteem not to mind the axiom that work and worth go together. How can being old justify itself? Old people are urged to live long and well, but they are resented if they live too long and exert an unseemly amount of influence. They are prodded to make their final years significant and exemplary, but no one really cares. That patronizing phrase, "the golden years," has properly been laughed to death, especially by old people who realize that almost everything valuable is geared to youth, who have so little appreciation of it. Hypocrisy notwithstanding, old people are often regarded as semi-parasites, unless, of course, they contribute something that profits those who are younger. Our numbers are increasing, yet old age remains a time for being quietly obsolete and supernumerary.

The future is where most of us will spend considerable time. The here and now applies to everyone, except that it has no meaning when taken out of the context of customs, values, and practices long established by past generations. The past is left behind, but cannot be altogether banished or ignored as if it never existed. Many young people do ignore the likelihood of growing old, and not even old people can be indifferent to the future. Whatever anyone does has consequences, and the future is highly unpredictable, however rigorously the present is analyzed. Therefore, old age is a prime time for self-examination and even self-discovery, including such questions as how I came from nothing into something and back again. The future remains tenuous, but we already know that old age is not yet nothing at all, and that old people do not exist in stationary suspension before being launched into the nearest graveyard. Since death has no discernible schedule, the cord of life can be severed at any time, or allowed to run to a frayed termination. While old age deserves no special merit for outliving younger cohorts, being shorn of respect is unjustifiably harsh.

Vulnerability at any age takes two forms: actual distress that occurs when potential for suffering is punctured, and the propensity toward distress when dealing with problems that challenge our fallibility. Ambiguity is part of the distress because unless the immediate problems are understood, especially the parts that are feared, coping is more difficult.

Old people have their own share of vulnerability and ambiguity to deal with, not always a function of age, but of uncertainty itself, a first cousin to anxiety and fear. I contend that death as a prospect is less distressing than dread of disability, helplessness, dependence, and dementia, about which prevention is notoriously uncertain and often inadequate. The personal predicament about being old is not helped by glib guides and reassurances. Gerontologists sometimes give the impression that they, personally, are exempt from old age, and what they write about is shielded by the patina of academia from that of individuals struggling with ambiguity.

From now on, I shall try to confront a couple of ways in which I deal with ambiguity in my life. How I contend with waning physical strength is the topic of this section. A later section contains an imaginary dialogue between the "just dead" and a representative of unrealized potential. So far, mental waning has not been a problem, and the topic won't be addressed here.

Another morning has arrived and I find myself striding solemnly and purposefully, even grimly, with utmost boredom and impatience, on a health club treadmill. It is practically a daily routine. Alongside a half-dozen other sweating men and women, I note their pace and stamina. And as I walk far faster than I would ordinarily, I dismiss with difficulty the thought that I am older than the others. I take no special pride in being older, but occasionally I wonder what they, my companions, will be like at my age. I am very aware of my vulnerability, venerability, and ambiguity in being here in the first place.

I do know why I am here: to foster and promote an elusive ideal called *physical fitness*. While no one questions for whom and what, regular exercise is generally recommended. Not only are you supposed to feel better, but exercise is said to help prevent a number of debilitating and undesirable diseases. The morning mirror has already exposed the steady incursion of physical slackness, despite my having exercised vigorously (more or less) for many years. I compare myself to my ambulatory companions and feel somewhat chagrined by my own bodily changes. Although I accept the potential benefits of regular exercise, even its prophylactic value, I also realize an existential dread of an enfeebled old age. I do what I can to prevent it, although in some respects exercise expresses only a pious wish.

The exercise routine is not a game played casually; it is a form of deadly serious solitaire. I am not competing with anyone, except, of course, my contemporaries, and other people, because deep down we are all racing against senescence and disability, including death. The race is not an unusual struggle in which survival is a prize. It is a habit, a value, not unlike keeping clean, eating well, sleeping enough, and enjoying leisure. Nevertheless, boredom notwithstanding, exercise sustains hope for an extended survival with good health in abundance.

There is also a parallel with the habit practiced by so many (with the same degree of hope) of attending some religious institution regularly for routine observances. Sweat, of course, knows no denomination, but regular routines of both religious practice and exercise are both expected to be good for you, although proof of their efficacy is lacking. Nevertheless, the devoted swear by their value and feel remiss when they skip.

In both physical fitness and religious practice, rules are observed faithfully. Infractions and absence are penalized by a haunting guilt, not unlike that stemming from indolence, sloth, gluttony, and other vices. Value comes from regularity, and regularity depends on faith. Both are hopeful pilgrimages. Years of second helpings, junk food, accumulated cholesterol, and unexpended calories nettle the sluggard into exercise, much as a repentant sinner is driven to reaffirm faith and return to regular religious practices. Actually, however, devotees of exercise or faithful adherents of religious routines have usually done so, well, religiously, for many years and need little prodding. New converts are few. Both have another parallel among those who habitually practice self-analysis. Self-scrutiny of personal motives, search for vindication, study of memories, generous cultivation of introspection, and so forth, need not be limited to intellectuals. Being vulnerable is a frightening realization, and self-examination just may contribute to a heightened measure of self-reliance and confidence in being able to cope well. Just as blubber is self-indulgence incarnate, the unexamined life has its own preventative canon. Cato would not have approved striving for absolute virtue, but rather the directive of accepting vulnerability and erasing ambiguity whenever discovered. Give us this day our daily dread, and allow us our transgressions.

Longevity by itself has no intrinsic value, nor much satisfaction. Mere succession of years is not a special accomplishment, except, perhaps, to boast about genes. Getting and being old may be only an indulgence of time, rather like an unpaid debt owed to nothing in particular. Evanescence is inevitable, anyway. How we came from nothing into something, then nothing once more, is miracle enough to meditate upon. Only astrologers find a connection between humans and the heavens.

Theories about old age and purpose in life testify only to the mystery of being here in the first place. Generations yet unborn will live and die. We are only left with a gambler's chance of being a ghost, surviving for no special purpose in another realm. If old age does bring wisdom, what are we wiser about? One possibility is that dedication, devotion, and compassion may have enduring value that far exceeds nebulous prospects of death, rebirth, and renewal in a hypothetical next world.

Being old is a private matter, but certain young people today are showing a curious interest in preserving the recollections of elderly friends and family who are unlikely to be interviewed by anyone else. For the old person, this is a variant of the "life review." It may do both young and old some good, but it cannot be just amiable, self-indulgent rambling about olden times, or worse, grumbling about lost opportunities. Fate may have deprived older people of what they claim to deserve. But it is more beneficial to understand what actually happened along with candid self-examination, which they may not choose to share. Fiction and fantasy about the past tend to weave themselves into a fabrication called memory. Usually, these are pleasant, even to the point of having overcome obstacles. Fear of dying, which seems practically universal, may come from the dying of the dream, from the unrealized life never led, desire never fulfilled, ambitions wasted away by procrastination. Maybe the wisdom imputed to old age arrives when we realize that not every unfulfilled dream should or could have been consummated, and that by not becoming true or real, much evil may have been prevented.

Resolving remaining ambiguity through regular examination of the past as it survives in the present is a difficult but ennobling task that demands fully as much dedication as regular exercise and prayer. It can be painful; the only reward for regret is that it is largely over and done with. The could have, should have, and finally did, along with their negatives, need to be differentiated. This helps separate one meaning from another, and therefore contributes to clarifying ambiguity. Mere speculation about what is past and what was worth the effort is unending, and has no Disneyland ending. But the impromptu dialogue between what is and what might have been should be edifying, as I trust the next section will demonstrate.

The NX Factor: What Is and Might Have Been

It is easy to recognize what never could have happened. It is some-what more difficult to accept it. For example, I did not have the basic competence or capacity to become, say, a truly world-class scientist, perhaps not even a first-rate anything except what I am. While I regret this, I hope it was not my fault, and that I did not betray myself through avoidable mistakes. Unrealized potential is a nagging enigma, which is often mistaken for real possibility just beyond reach. For an old person, this plight might be very painful and frustrating, when time and capac-ity dwindle.

There is a theory, more like a fascinating speculation, that everyone has a double somewhere who is physically identical, but leads an entirely different kind of life. In the case of actual doubles, such as identical twins, the emphasis is on uncanny mental resemblances rather than differences. Novelists have sometimes used this fantasy; *The Prince and the Pauper* is a well-known example. Rank's *Myth of the Birth of the Hero* (1952) is a familiar story in which the son of noble birth is abandoned and raised by humble people, and then somehow is restored to his rightful, lofty status. Here the double is condensed into two antithetical fortunes for the same person. Further discussion about doubles, twins, and secret nobility is beyond my purpose. I am using the theme of unbeknownst doubles to follow the question, which is relevant in old age, about unre-alized potential among the ambiguities, "What might have been?"

Now, just for speculative fun, let us grant the possibility of a double out there. There is no reason why such fantasies cannot be multiplied, so that many doubles might exist. Or, not unlike multiple personalities inhabiting one person, there might be other personalities inside of any-one, representing "what might have been" but didn't happen. Unrealized potential might exist, but only as that, not elaborated into a distinct personality. You and I might be someone else's possibility actualized. In short, this hypothesis is like ambiguity itself. One meaning implies its own contradictory as well as other relevant meanings that have differ-ent consequences. I am used to the principle that in order to have a dis-tinct meaning, something's antithesis or contradictory must exist and have a meaning. If you are what you are, what would your unrealized or contradictory endowments be like?

I summon these ghostly imagined existences in order to understand myself better. The "never was" might have been realized through its in-fluence on the me that did exist. Therefore, let me indulge my imagina-tion a little further as I report a fragmentary conversation between *Me*, the actual *I*, that possesses a personal history, a record of mixed meanings and ambiguities, a variety of complaints, documented identification in the world at large, and a skeptical disposition, with an entirely hypothetical other *I* who is not an actuality except in my mind and by the reader's indulgence. For simplicity's sake, although there might be other doubles out there or in me, this non-actual *I* is the only one I speak with. To make it clear, the actual me is labeled W_I. My imagined partner is labeled W_{nx}. The subscript n stands for a number of unspecified qualities, while unknown and unrealized potential goes by the familiar symbol x. W_I and W_{nx} are talking about that ambiguous concept called unrealized potential.

I must emphasize that the second *I* is an imaginary, spectral somebody who might have been me, but as it is, only represents a number (n) of qualities, virtues, and traits not shared by me. The most appropriate scene should offer an excellent perspective for retrospective reflection: the immediate period just after my death, "just dead enough." This is the postscript period previously referred to. If you happen to believe in life after death, everything up to now is preface. If you do not hold this belief, then life up to now is it and ends at the grave, main text, without a postscript. In case anyone wonders, I belong to neither group.

W_I Well, here I am at last, just beyond the margin. It's hard to believe I'm here and still have a measure of consciousness, and have someone to talk with. Frankly, I expected not to wake up. This is like an afterglow that I imagine will soon fade away. Meanwhile, the best I can say is that I must be barely dead.

W_{nx} Here I am, too, the spokesman for your colony of unrealized possibilities. But I have always been there, never truly existing as you did, but having more influence than you ever imagined.

W_I I had no idea. Do you really hover around recently dead bodies just like the old superstitions imagined?

W_{nx} I have nothing against old superstitions, but people are frightened of their unrealized possibilities.

W_I Now that you're here, or, I mean, now that I'm here, wherever that is, or in whatever shape I'm in, I want to ask you a couple of questions that have always bothered me. You may know them.

W_{nx} If you think I know the answers to those ultimate questions you seem so fond of (Weisman 1993), spare me! Not even those of us who account to no one have answers to those twisters. Being dead doesn't entitle you to any more wisdom that you had before, but I can tell you that wisdom here is just as untested. You can suspend judgment indefinitely, which may be a good thing.

W$_I$ Please, just one question that you, my unrealized potential, might have some information about: Here I am, but what of it? Could I have turned out better than I did? Now that it doesn't matter anymore, I'm not getting older, and certainly no wiser. Would anything have made a difference?

W$_{nx}$ Don't forget that about all you can be sure of right now is that you're not going to get older, just as you're now immune to those troubles, including sicknesses, that the living are at risk for. I don't have to care about grammar, either!

W$_I$ I wondered right up to the last what being old meant.

W$_{nx}$ One thing it doesn't mean is what the calendar says. From the inside you were yourself at any age, all at once, yet you were old by any measure, that's what the ambiguity was all about. And, by the way, why are you writing this chapter for Herman Feifel?

W$_I$ Is that all it means, that old is old, and dead is dead? That's pretty discouraging.

W$_{nx}$ Just because you couldn't find a convincing purpose in being alive as you were, would you rather have been one of us, your brothers in limbo who never really existed?

W$_I$ No thanks. I'm glad I did live, even with the suffering that happened from time to time. I put up with consequences, instead of just being someone's ghost—unrealized potential, that is. I'm beginning to sound pretty pompous.

W$_{nx}$ Not really. You are—were—far from being pompous. Among your faults, that was not one of them. Being a ghost is a joke, perhaps, but no laughing matter. We—meaning the rest of us here—never existed on our own. We were more like understudies who were never called upon except when the star was indisposed. We knew the script, of course, and had our say in more things than you know, different from understudies who just stand by patiently and never get their call.

W$_I$ What is this about the understudy? Maybe the understudy would be better than the star, which is what my question is about. By the way, did you really know the script—that is, how things were going to turn out?

W$_{nx}$ The script is just about your question: What would you have been, if you hadn't become what you are, I mean, were? Remember that we limbo people hitchhike on you.

W$_I$ Well, given another chance, I'd be younger, since it seems that we are always too old or too young. I found very few benefits in being old, except that I was glad I wasn't an adolescent. Maybe there were some compensations in old age that I forgot.

W$_{nx}$ What compensations, what benefits? What made you expect any reward for being old? Did you expect anything for being young or middle-aged? Was being old so bad that you looked for a benefit or two?

W$_I$ I . . . uh . . . uh.

W$_{nx}$ I thought so. You were more afraid of old age than of dying and wanted to take the sting away. But I'll bet your answer is no. I'm already aware that you thought death might overlook you.

W$_I$ I think that being young might make a difference, although in what I'm not sure. By the time I found out if I had other choices, I'd be old again, without choices!

W$_{nx}$ You always had choices, even if they weren't great choices. That is what really is the difference between there, where you were, and here. Unrealized potential is only for those who die young, not for old folks. It's only a bedtime story for old people who remember.

W$_I$ But I did try to make good choices, when I could, or is that just a bedtime story, too?

W$_{nx}$ My friend, or at least you were occasionally a friend, I cannot balance the books for you. You made some pretty bad decisions in your time, a few others weren't so bad. As for the other decisions . . . well, ambiguity is very uncertain, as you know. I'll tell you this: in your case, saint and sinner don't have to be reconciled like bad neighbors who ought to get along. You are your own ambiguity.

W$_I$ You seem very sure of yourself, even arrogant. I suppose that happens when you only live in limbo, by courtesy of my imagination, and don't have to suffer consequences.

W$_{nx}$ Please don't patronize me. Living in *your* imagination was no bed of roses. You gave us all a hard time. For instance, during those years of psychoanalysis when you kept trying to be someone else, except you didn't know who. I knew at the time that you were just trying to please your analyst.

W$_I$ Oh, I do remember, and I apologize. You were bugging me, and I wanted to get rid of you. In my heart, I knew you wouldn't desert me.

W_{nx} It's not a question of who deserts or bugs the other. Just realize that whatever decision you thought about making whether you did or did not, we were all in on it. You weren't in full control. I think you knew it at the time, and wanted to tone us down.

W_l Frankly, I thought you were the enemy. I see now that I didn't show you enough respect.

W_{nx} I wonder if you do now. Some of us didn't do you much good, but none of us were your enemy. There were even a few friends among us.

W_l I've blamed you, or something I know was you, now. I didn't pay you enough respect or attention.

W_{nx} Blame and praise are not important, just foolish. What worried me then and now is that even at the age you just were, you were still trying for perfection, calling it unrealized potential. Up the good, down the bad, although you weren't sure which way was up— please don't interrupt me, as I see you're about to do. Perfection is not only impossible to know and attain, it isn't worth it, either. No one would notice or care if you *were* perfect, even you. Guilt would get in the way. Certainly, no one is pleased by having a paragon in their midst. Others prefer imperfections, it makes them feel much better. You've turned your distaste for your own imperfections into fretting about unrealized potential. It's a crazy notion, if you stop to think about it.

W_l The longer I listen to you, the more I think you would have done a better job of being me than myself. Maybe you would have done something really important, with enough courage and opportunity. But that's magical talk.

W_{nx} Spare me. You keep wanting me to be someone else, and forget that I'm you—the you that never was, even in old age. You are courageous and compassionate with enough opportunity. More than most people, less than some others. Just between us, I have it on very good, in fact impeccable authority, that you couldn't have been what you wanted to be anyway. You enjoy regrets, I am sorry to say, but that only makes you feel virtuous about having high standards.

W_l Hearing you talk, I still think you should have been the psychoanalyst, not me. You don't answer my questions, either.

W_{nx} My job is not to make you feel better, or worse for that matter. I have no job whatsoever, unless it is to tweak your soul (don't ask me to explain that). Without nettling and nudging, you wouldn't have amounted to much or had much reality, and then, none of us could have lived, even in limbo.

W_I I think I'm beginning to get it. Don't lose contact with the lives you never led, which, I suppose, are all part of you.

W_{nx} The conversation has gone on long enough. We're going to have plenty of time, providing that I don't get impatient and annoyed with you in your "just now dead" state. Let us agree that we are the fiddlers, playing second fiddle to you, Jack Horner, sitting in a corner, hating cherry pie, but collecting pits.

W_I I am sorry not to be alive any more. I must remind myself that being old is still being alive. There's a lot of ambiguity I still have to deal with, and that's unrealized potential. But coming to a conclusion isn't all bad.

W_{nx} You are not ageless, of course, except now. Maybe you made a difference. What you seem to want now is a huge sign saying, "Man without a Country, Come Home! All is forgiven, even your virtues."

Postscript

Unless you believe that this, right now, is the one and only main text, then what's past is prologue. But if it is true that just about everything that happens has consequences, and therefore is a preface to something else, coping with the main text includes conjectures and contacts about a future.

A postscript is more than an addendum; it may summarize succinctly and even put another slant on the principal message, or main text. From the viewpoint of the just dead, the postscript is an excellent retrospective platform to review a familiar quandary: the unrealized potential for being something more and better. Is it a reality or an illusion that life might have been significantly different?

The postscript period compels anyone to assess the difference between right-now reality and what is past and beyond passive recollection. At least if the postscript is possible then I imagine that the past is worth examining. Otherwise, how do we make the most of being a ghost?

Not that I have ever seen or heard a ghost, or even sensed a ghostly presence. Truly sensitive people are supposed to be able to tell when significant events occur from afar, even when they doubt extrasensory perception. But old people know a great many other people who are forerunners in death. Occasionally, these individuals are recalled vividly, so vividly that they shunt out ordinary notions about reality. The phrase "dead but not forgotten" on gravestones acquires an emotional patina not customary for clichés. Memories vary in sharpness, from a passive and passing recollection, such as, "This reminds me of that," to a more active and singular experience, almost like Banquo's ghost who manifested himself only to Macbeth. I intend nothing supraterrestrial. Nor do I draw lofty conclusions from this everyday fact: absent people will on occasion make their presence felt in unexpected ways. Their presence is by no means like a hallucination, although I have heard that bereaved people will have just such experiences, months or years after an important death. A woman once told me about seeing her dead daughter ride by on a bicycle just as she was debating about addressing a group on bereavement and its aftermath. A modern shaman, shuttling between this world and the next, would understand what I just stated, because this is what he does for a living.

A skeptical disposition prevents me from giving any further credence to the banal tales of near death and dubious platitudes emanating from the beyond. Preambles to life everlasting are understandable sentiments. In my view, doctrines of rebirth and immortality are generalized doctrines about the theme of unrealized potential; they are pious hopes for a better life than the one folks are familiar with.

Nevertheless, I imagined a postscript in which a recently demised W_l engages in conversation with an aspect of himself, W_{nx}, that never was. This is actually no more outlandish a proposition than hearing old people boast about their eternal youth or youthfulness (the latter being a more acceptable notion). Their denial of old age amounts to belief in agelessness, itself an age-old dream. "Old age? Why, that's only for really old people. And I do not consider myself old. This aging business is just a matter of attitude. You don't have to let it happen. Young people consider me one of them, and don't treat me any different! Old age is not a serious problem at all." What young people would say about this matter, I leave open. Such speeches are not uncommon, usually unsolicited, and betray a contempt for aging and old people who can and do remain vigorous while conceding that years exact a toll rather than conferring a reward.

What prompts antipathy toward old age? Obviously, as in youth and middle age, not every old person deals with the same issues, or copes with problems in an identical fashion. Some are vigorous and alert, others are demented and decrepit, and a wide gap is filled with those in between. Old people with intact intellect are not oblivious to history and tradition, and are therefore capable of evaluating the past without excessive bias. Take this notion one step further and when that old person is "just dead," he or she belongs to the postscript period. It is a "life review" from the viewpoint of death, fun as well as educational, sharpening the mind and making no demands on the body.

Hope for positive change, even after death, is a sign only of good morale. It does not require denial, nor belief in an afterlife. The postscript does not have to take place anywhere, and if it did, I would be surprised to find a celestial community center where all sorts of pleasant diversions are available. I can imagine an unending struggle between good and evil, because I am sure it does not come close to resolution here.

I sympathize with those who imagine a concept of necessary evil that mitigates conviction about an absolute good. I also sympathize with doctrines of necessary good amidst absolute evil. Even in a most congenial afterlife I doubt that there is universal agreement, or that people get along all the time. I have only a very cursory understanding of the major religions, but they share a universal promise, here and elsewhere, that bad things will get better somehow. But about the "just-dead" status: in order to be there you are required to be dead. This is a simple corollary to the longer we live, the older we get. A skeptical pilgrim is satisfied that the postscript has no surprises, fanciful or otherwise. The psychological watch stops. I am disappointed that there are no absolute truths, and that even generous and humane intentions have stern underlying conditions. Old age is a time neither to dull expectations nor to accept limitations and uncertainties too readily. To look both ways before crossing the street is excellent advice, but hardly enough to qualify as an infallible guide. Much else is needed to clear up more pressing ambiguities. Old age is its own anachronism, but forever is far longer than anyone needs. After all, who wins—good or evil? Is there a beatitude for brutes, or forgiveness for sins unrequited?

I hold Herman Feifel responsible for his part in compelling us to contemplate old age and death, and to put our ideas to a practical test without getting bogged down in sentimental and sententious clichés. His humor, scholarship, friendship, and contributions have combined over his lifetime to set a goal of excellence worth emulating if only it were possible. Let us then put aside forlorn brooding and take up a challenge. Herman's quest makes us ponder our place in the scheme of things, provided, of course, that there is a scheme in which we have a legitimate place.

References

Carroll, L. (1865). *Alice's Adventures in Wonderland*. Berkeley, CA: University of California Press, 1982.

Cicero, M. T. (44 B.C.). Cato the Elder (on old age). In *Cicero. Selected Works*, trans. M. Grant, pp. 211–247. London: Penguin, 1971.

Frame, D. (1958). *The Complete Works of Montaigne*. Stanford, CA: Stanford University Press.

Friedan, B. (1993). *The Fountain of Age*. New York: Simon & Schuster.

Kastenbaum, R. (1992). *The Psychology of Death*, 2nd ed. New York: Springer.

Rank, O. (1952). *Myth of the Birth of the Hero: Psychological Interpretation of Mythology*, tr. E. Robbins and S. E. Jellife. New York: Robert Brunner.

Spengler, O. (1926–1928). *The Decline of the West*. New York: Knopf.

Weisman, A. D. (1993). *The Vulnerable Self: Confronting the Ultimate Questions*. New York: Insight Books/Plenum.

14

Horrendous Death

DANIEL LEVITON

This book is a testimonial to the affection and respect the contributors have for Herman Feifel. Count me a member of that band since 1965. When I was a doctoral student my mentor, Dr. Warren R. Johnson, encouraged me to integrate the study of death with health and well-being. A few months later, while visiting with Dr. Bert Boothe at the National Institute of Mental Health, the conversation turned to my interest in death and its relationship to health and well-being. As I turned to leave, he said, "You might find this volume of interest," and he handed me Feifel's classic, *The Meaning of Death* (1959). After reading it (in one night), I was elated. Why? Because Herman legitimized my thoughts concerning thanatology and behavior.

In 1965 I included three lectures on death in a required health education class at the University of Maryland. In the summer of 1970 I taught my first class solely devoted to death education. It was a class of thirty students. That fall, and every semester after that, 150 to 350 students registered for the course. Death is generally second to sex (education) in popularity at the University of Maryland, which is probably the way it ought to be.

A few articles were published resulting in an invitation to speak at the first conference on death education convened by Betty Green and Don Irish at Hamline University in February 1970 (Green and Irish 1971). Herman was the first keynote speaker, followed by John Brantner (a unique person in his own right) and myself.

I had never met Herman. After arriving I was shown to my room, and given time to freshen up before going to a reception, and subsequently Herman's kickoff address. At around 5:30 my hosts knocked on my door, and allowed that we would go down the hall to get Herman, and then on to the reception. Our host, Don Irish, tapped unobtrusively at his door with that slight hesitancy reserved for those of great reputation. There was no answer. He knocked louder. Still no answer. On the third effort, the door swung open. There was Herman in his undershirt with a hand towel wrapped around his index finger. "I cut myself shaving," he exclaimed. He was obviously concerned. I thought to myself, My God, the father of the thanatological movement thinks he is going to die because of a cut finger? Herman recovered magnificently to enthrall his audience with a speech that was pure Herman—brilliant, erudite, and insightful.

Like Faust, he enjoyed his earthy pleasures as well. At the first research symposium devoted to thanatology held in Berkeley, we adjourned to an epicurean dinner at a renowned Chinese restaurant. Herman was seated next to Phyllis Silverman. I was two seats removed, busily "pigging out" when Phyllis asked Herman, "How do you like this grand meal, Herman?" I remember his reply. "It isn't so hot—do you want to get some ice cream?" Phyllis, always a fine researcher and writer, is the stereotypical Jewish mother. She looked at Herman for a moment, and replied, "Eat, my friend, eat." Nonetheless, after the feast we went for ice cream. If I recall correctly Herman's favorite is coffee.

For me, Herman's love of ice cream is symbolic of his love of life. Over the years, our conversations ranged from sports to thanatology to religion. Actually, I talked about sports, and listened while Herman discoursed about everything else.

He must be a great mentor for he is always encouraging and complimentary. When we talked about the death education movement he would say that I was responsible for starting the whole thing when others probably taught the topic before I did. "Yes, Dan . . . but you were the one who . . ." did this or that. So I would walk away feeling rather good. His concern and interest in others was part of his character. In our conversations over the years Herman would ask about mutual friends: "How is Father Wendt? Has he cut down his cigarettes? Ah, that Bill—he is a real mensch. Give him my regards."

There are several of the old guard in the thanatological movement who are truly well read, articulate, and passionate in their beliefs. Herman is one. Edwin Shneidman is another. It was fun listening to them go head to head in verbal riposte. Both are eloquent, and broadly knowledgeable. They are masters with the written word or in oratory.

There was a time when I thought they would come to blows. At an American Psychological Association meeting in Honolulu they were debating a point. It was like a dueling match between Robin Hood and Cyrano De Bergerac, and appeared to me to be deadly. The thought of these pillars of thanatology being at odds was unsettling to say the least. After the session I called Herman's room to see if there was a chance of rapprochement. Herman laughed, and educated me to the fact they were good friends and enjoyed the verbal give and take. Relieved, I thought to myself that I would be eaten alive if I ever got into a debate with either. Knowing Herman he would have taken it easy on me.

Introduction to the Horrendous Death (HD) Concept

As will be shown below, Herman was concerned with our increasing capability to destroy one another. He felt that the study of death might reduce the probability of people-caused destruction. I think it is the public health problem of our time. The horrendous death (HD) concept is about preventable death and the process of prevention. It is about addressing causes as well as symptoms. People can generally face up to the fact of death. It is the how, when, where, type, and style of dying or death that pose the problem. To die prematurely, unnecessarily, and torturously is an abomination.

This chapter defines HD, discusses its cost in human lives and dollars, and suggests a process for addressing the problem. Three levels of action are discussed. Action is the bottom line. It is time to implement existing research and analyses of the problem. What has been lacking is the means to the end.

What is Horrendous Death?

HD, type I, is characterized by being

1. man-made (the sexist terminology is intentional);
2. motivated by the desire to kill, maim, injure, torture, or otherwise destroy another;
3. torturous in quality;
4. premature;
5. deadly to large numbers of people.

Examples are thermonuclear and conventional war, assassination, terrorism, homicide, death resulting indirectly or directly from racism and ethnic hatred, and man-made starvation. HD, type I, is the focus of this chapter.

In another type of HD, type II, the motivation to kill another is lacking. Examples are death because of unintentioned starvation; indirectly as a result of racism or poverty, motor vehicle, environmental, and other accidents; and drug and tobacco abuse. But by *HD* I am referring to HD type I.

The crucial question is how to motivate people and institutions to act in their best health interests by preventing HD. It is well known that having suffered the HD, or threat of HD to loved ones, is often a stimulus to action. What about the general, impersonal threat of HD? Paradoxically the threat, by itself, is not enough for most people. Although the headlines and television scream nightly of the toll of HD, few act. Here are some typical headlines:

- Teenager's Slaying Stuns Peaceful Gaithersburg—Hye Ja Yi (age 18) had been sexually assaulted and then stomped to death, Montgomery County police said (*Washington Post*, April 30, 1985).
- Decapitated Body of Boy Found (*Washington Post*, January 13, 1986).
- Loaded Gun Taken From Fifth Grader's Desk (*Washington Post*, February 4, 1986).
- Nearly 220 teenagers and children have been shot or stabbed in Washington during the first eight months of the year (1988), an average of about one young victim a day (*Washington Post*, October 12, 1988).
- Gunplay Blights Childhood in D.C. Hundreds become victims in epidemic of shootings (*Washington Post*, September 14, 1992).
- Dozens of U.S. Items Used in Iraq Arms (*Washington Post*, July 22, 1992).
- Selling [Arms and Munitions] to Scoundrels: Why We Won't Stop (*Washington Post*, November 15, 1992).
- 30 Million Hungry in U.S., Report Says (*Washington Post*, September 7, 1992).
- Childhood Poverty Rate Rose During Prosperous '80s (*Washington Post*, July 8, 14, 1992).

We read this and shudder, but only momentarily, as the mind shifts its focus to other matters. But what if one's child, grandchild, beloved other, or oneself is substituted for the victims in the headlines? What is the effect? This sort of contemplation of futurity, with its threats to everyone's health, everyone's life and limb, and everyone's future should be maddening. Ernest Becker (1973) elaborated on Pascal's observation:

> Men are so necessarily mad that not to be mad would amount to another form of madness. . . . If we had to offer the briefest explanation of all the evil that men have wrecked upon themselves and upon their world since the beginning of time right up until tomorrow . . . it would be simply in the toll that his pretense of sanity takes, as he tries to deny his true condition. [p. 29]

That condition is where we know we and our loved ones are mortal and vulnerable to HD, and at the same time think that we are immortal.

Herman saw potential good in removing that denial to which Becker referred. In my own work on HD I wrote (Leviton 1991b, p. 14),

As Freud saw repressed sexuality as a powerful factor in explaining human behavior, so Feifel saw death. Feifel felt that the meaning given death influenced our fear of old age, for old age and decrepitude were stark reminders of death and decay. Fear of death, too, might well be a powerful etiological factor in our denial of reality. He wrote, "*If we accept death as a necessity . . . this might possibly mute some of the violence of our times, for energies now bound up in continuing attempts to shelve and repress the concept of death would be available to us for the more constructive aspects of living, perhaps even fortifying man's gift for creative splendor against his genius for destruction*" (my emphasis) (Feifel 1959, p. 12).

He repeated the same theme at the Hamline conference: "Unfortunately, the idea of death is not an easy one for mid-twentieth century man. In the Middle Ages man had his eschatology and the sacred time of eternity. More recently, temporal man lived with the prospect of personal immortality transformed into concern for historical immortality and for the welfare of posterity. Today we are vouchsafed neither. Physical science has presently made it possible for all of us to share a common epitaph. Social immortality and descendants are now menaced along with the individuality of death" (Feifel 1971, pp. 3–4).

In 1992, at the Association for Death Educators and Counselors' annual conference, Herman was asked how he thought the association and thanatology might best make a contribution. He instantly replied, "By influencing social policy."

Thus, there is no doubt that Herman saw the linkage between the study of thanatology and violence. However, as a psychologist he did not use the language of public health. As a professional health educator I was struck by Feifel's message. My variation of Feifel's insight was that the meaning given death very much affected individual and group health and well-being.

When Herman wrote his words cited above in 1959 and 1971, his metaphor for HD was the Bomb. Today, more than the Bomb threatens us. Like Medusa's head, HD is a mass of killer vipers. It is death caused by people: homicide, terrorism, assassination, racism, undernutrition, unemployment and poverty, accidents, and assaults upon the environment. The hope is that since HD is caused by people, it could be prevented and eliminated if we would but act. Carrying out the process that results in the reduction or elimination of HD is the ultimate task.

HD, as threat or experience, is seen as a motivator that can reduce the probability of HD in the future. Others have used terms similar to HD such as *omnicide* (Goodman and Hoff 1990, Schuetz 1991), and *democide* (Rummel 1990, 1991a,b). All see HD and its variations as a preventable public health problem. Yet, little is written about the process that would motivate national and global policy makers and the public at large to act in their own and their children's best health interests to eliminate these preventable deaths. Any systematic approach to eliminating HD requires participation and cooperation of representatives of domains of influence and power (described later) at local, national, and global levels. Complex issues within and between nation-states in the areas of economics, politics, business and industry (with special reference to multinational and international corporations), ecology, religion, population control, harmony between diverse cultures, and education need to be systematically addressed.

The 10-second sound bite suitable for politician, corporate executive, media personality, pope, or you and me is this: If we wish ourselves and our children to live long and well, then we must act in our best interests. Action is the only way. The remainder of this chapter responds to the question of how to elicit action. First, there is a need to understand the scope of the problem.

The Health (Mortality) Cost of HD

There is little mention of HD in the international and national health establishment's official publications and statistics. The only HD-related data included in the *World Health Statistics Manual* are motor vehicle traffic accidents, and suicide and self-inflicted injury (World Health Organization 1993).

In the United States, deaths resulting from accidents and adverse effects, suicide, and homicide and legal intervention are the types of HD listed in the government's public health literature (National Center for Health Statistics 1993). Blueprints for improving the nation's health such as *Health United States 1986 and Prevention Profile* (National Center for Health Statistics 1986) and *Healthy People 2000: National Health Promotion and Disease Prevention Objectives* (U.S. Department of Health and Human Services 1992) say little of the variations of HD and their deleterious effect on the health of people.

It is in works such as *The State of the World Atlas* (Kidron and Segal 1981), *World Military and Social Expenditures* (Sivard 1991), *State of the World* (Brown et al. 1991), and other publications of the World Watch Institute, the valuable materials published by the Stockholm International Peace Research Institute (SIPRI), and computer networks such as The Association for Progressive Communications (APC)/Institute for Global Communications (Young 1994) that the human, economic, and health costs of HD can be assessed.

Estimates of mortality due to three causes of HD, type I—genocide, homicide, and war—give some idea of the deadly cost of HD, that is, the number of preventable deaths. However, the true mortality picture is obscured because the disease, physical and mental illness, and suffering associated with HD are not included.

Genocide. Rummel (1990, 1991a,b), in his painstaking investigation of genocide, estimates that since 1900, over 120,000,000 people have been murdered by their governments.

Homicide. Among the industrialized countries, the United States by far leads the world in homicide rates (Reiss and Roth 1993). The United States is also higher in childhood mortality due to homicide than eight other developed countries (Germany, France, The Netherlands, England and Wales, Sweden, Canada, Japan, and Australia) (Vobejda 1994). Homicide is the third leading cause of death for elementary and middle school children (Vobejda 1994). In the United States in 1991, 26,513 people were killed due to homicide and legal intervention. They are the leading cause of death for the African-American population aged 15 to 24 (National Center for Health Statistics 1993).

War. William Eckhardt, Research Director of the Lentz Peace Research Laboratory, calculated the war and war-related deaths (including interventions and invasions) by region and country, from 1500 to 1990 (Sivard 1991). Absolute numbers of civilian and military deaths were reported. The total number of deaths for civilians was 75,649,000, and for the military was 63,709,000, for a total of 139,358,000 men, women, and children killed in war.

Quality of Global Health

With an understanding of the idea of HD, quality of global health (QGH) is defined as

$$QGH = LF_{max}/HD_{min} \text{ or }_{elim}$$

where HD is minimized or eliminated and lifegenic factors (LF) are maximized. Lifegenic factors increase the probability of living long and well. Examples are:

1. Meaningful education
2. Meaningful employment
3. Meaningful love and friendship relationships
4. Financial security
5. Quality health care
6. Opportunity for self-actualization
7. Opportunity for enjoyable leisure, recreation, and play

8. Purpose and meaning in life
9. Opportunity to achieve spirituality needs
10. Opportunity to maximize health
11. Opportunity for artistic and creative expression.

Thus, a high value would show a high QGH index.

A goal for a highly civilized global society is the elimination of HD and maximum LF.

The Process

Theorists and researchers in the area of health behavior have yet to come up with a valid and reliable intervention to reduce the probability of HD (Glanz et al. 1990a,b, Jaccard et al. 1990, Janis 1982a,b, Lewis 1990, Perry et al. 1990, Rosenstock 1990). The HD concept suggests that health behavior models need to factor in the individual's perception and meaning given to the future. Even the World Health Organization's definition of health should be modified to read, Health is the *process* toward, and *perception* of *acceptable* physical, mental, and social *well-being* and not merely the absence of disease and infirmity *here and now, and as expected in the future*.

The HD → Fear of Death → Removal of Denial → Anticipatory Grieving → Action → Health and Well-Being Outcome Linkage

It is suggested that the perception of the quality, circumstances, and type of death is related to the level of denial (or awareness) of dying and death. For example, facing the death in old old age of a friend due to a heart attack, evokes a fear of the friend's death. That fear increases when the death is due to murder by gun or knife, napalming in war, gassing in a concentration camp, or torture of one's child or grandchild. Thus, fear of dying and death is affected by the quality of the attachment, type and circumstances of dying and death, the appropriateness of the death in terms of age and expectations of death, and the meaning given to the future of oneself and the dead person (e.g., themes of afterlife, symbolic immortality) (Lifton 1979).

The HD concept focuses on the beloved child due to the powerful, protective love that normally exists between parent and child. Also, the death of a child is untimely, unexpected, and otherwise inappropriate. Denial of the death of a loved one or oneself is high. It is this denial that oneself or loved ones can die in such brutal ways that prevents action to reduce the probability of HD. The denier rationalizes that if a child is murdered it will be the amorphous other. It will not be and cannot be his or hers.

It is hypothesized that the more horrible the type or style of dying and/or death is perceived, the greater the fear; the greater the fear, the greater the denial; and the greater the denial, the less chance of action to eliminate the very causes of such torturous deaths. Low and high fear of HD are associated with low probability of action. There is a *middle knowledge* (Weisman 1974) that wafts and wanes between denial and awareness of HD that is probably associated with action.

The Removal of Denial

Removal of the denial of HD of oneself and others is prolegomenon to action (Beck 1991, French 1991a,b, Leviton 1991b,c,d). Why is it that people act to prevent HD after a child or spouse has died because of, say, drunk driving, or homicide? The founders of Mothers Against Drunk Driving (MADD) and Parents of Murdered Children acted after the HD of their beloved children. HD had become a reality. Must people suffer the death of a beloved or escape HD, say, surviving terrorism, the Holocaust, and the like?

Perhaps one way to avoid the cost of direct experience is to make the unthought of circumstance and the unbelievable real. Nathan McCall (1994a), a former penitentiary inmate, now a newspaper reporter and author of the autobiographical account *Makes Me Want to Holler*, tells of being in prison, and visited by his girlfriend, and his revered grandmother, Bampoose.

> "Why did y'all bring Bampoose? I didn't want her to see me in here like this?" . . . My stepfather helped Bampoose to the seat. I'd only been locked up a few months, but it seemed Bampoose had aged a lot since I had seen her. She looked frail and brittle. She put the phone to her face, smiled weakly and said, "Hey, boy. How you doin?"
>
> "I'm fine, Bampoose. How about you?" . . . As I spoke, I felt myself choking inside. In all the other previous weekly visits from family and friends, I'd been able to put on a strong face, but the sight of Bampoose weakened me. I was ashamed for her to see me in jail. For all our lives, Bampoose had quietly set an example of hard work and sacrifice in our family. In her dignified way, she'd always been there to lend support to everybody and done what she could to help. Everyone wanted Bampoose to think well of them, and I was no exception. [McCall 1994a, p. 10]

Facing the reality of embarrassment before his crime through, say, role playing might have given McCall time to reflect upon the cost of living the street life. Also, he had not considered that his son would grow up fatherless. Again, the question is how to make the threat of HD and its ramifications salient, resulting in health-protective action before their actual occurrence.

Perhaps denial might be removed by simulating as closely as possible the HD of oneself, child, or other beloved. One method is to visualize the death of the child or beloved by means of napalm, murder, and so on. It must be strong imagery but not to the extent that it would cause avoidance and/or result in anger as the only response rather than action.

Another variation is to show pictures of children who have died or are dying an HD (burned to death, starved, murdered, etc.) and to superimpose the face of the viewer's child. Strong stuff to be sure but the alternative, the continuation of the HD status quo, is worth the price.

Another approach suggests promise—testimonials. There is a group of young people who were shot by police while engaged in criminal activity, and subsequently paralyzed from the waist down, that visits neighborhood schools. The group's peers see the risk of paralysis, pain, and suffering. The group emphasizes to its audience that the risk of death or paralysis was never contemplated.

Another variation is the Shock Mentor Program in Prince Georges County, Maryland, which has high school students visit a local shock trauma unit to literally see the suffering of young victims of crack cocaine and various forms of violence (Hill 1994).

Sometimes viewing a video or film, or even reading a poignant book, story, or article will result in empathy and pave the way to action. An example from my local newspaper:

> Jessica Bradford knows five people who have been killed. It could happen to her, she says, so she has told her family that if she should get shot before her sixth grade prom, she wants to be buried in her prom dress.
>
> Jessica is 11 years old. She has known since she was in the fifth grade what she wanted to wear at her funeral. "I think my prom dress is going to be the prettiest dress of all," Jessica said. "When I die, I want to be dressy for my family." [Brown 1993, p. A1]

If this child can be so threatened then so can anyone's child. She is anticipatorily grieving her own death. In the HD process, anticipatory grieving is prolegomenon to action. Participants would internalize the HD by grieving the figuratively dead child. They would observe whatever mourning ritual is appropriate, for example, Mass for the Catholic, Shiva for the Jew.

The weakness in all of the above examples is that the confrontation with the reality of HD was not followed by (1) grieving, and (2) subsequent, immediate involvement in concrete forms of action. Also, the leaders of domains of influence and power should be subjected to the same denial-removing exercises as the potential young victims.

Domains of Influence and Power

From whom is denial of the possibility of HD to be removed? Two groups come to mind. One group is made up of potential victims, his or her survivors, and those who work with potential victims and their survivors in a rehabilitative way. This group might be labeled average citizen. In working with average citizen the goal might be to avoid HD, say, by staying away from geographic areas where homicide rates are high. Or it may be to have more police officers posted in a certain area. If the availability of surrogate parents reduces the probability of the young becoming violent offenders, then the awareness of HD might serve to develop such a neighborhood program where all members of the community participate.

The second group targeted for removal of denial are the thirteen representatives of the domains of influence and power. They are influential and powerful enough to implement national and global policy. Government, politics, and law is one domain. Others include finance, corporations, labor, the military, medicine and public health, religion, the media, education, science, philanthropy, non-governmental organizations, and the community. Some are as powerful as government and politics. For example, it would be nice to have the support of President Clinton and Newt Gingrich. However, the project would have a greater chance of success if influential people like Paul Volcker and Alan Greenspan (finance), Bill Gates (industry), Ted Turner (media), George Soros (finance), Morton Abramowitz (philanthropy), and Ralph Nader, Kweisi Mfume, and Hugh Price (community) were also involved.

Their motivation to participate in the HD concept? Their loved ones and themselves are as vulnerable to HD as anyone else. Presidents, popes, and CEOs of multinational corporations have been murdered, killed by terrorists, and are being poisoned by contaminated drinking water and air. It is in the best interest of all domains, including the military, to have a healthy and peaceful physical, psychological, and social environment.

Regardless of the individual or group, the process in removing denial is the same—visualization, superimposed photos of the target person's children, role-playing, and the like—followed by anticipatory grieving. Often plain, straight talk will do. The question, repeated *ad nauseam*: do our loved ones have to die or do we have to be directly threatened before acting?

Toward Action: Happiness and Well-Being
as Social Policy

All institutions have the ultimate goal of improving the quality of
health and well-being for its constituency. This concept was central to
the sanguine philosophy of Francis Hutcheson during the prerevolu-
tionary war period. His *Essay on the Nature and Conduct of the Passions
and Affections* articulated a philosophy that was the opposite of the
Hobbesian view that people were selfish and aggressive (Burns 1991).
Hutcheson felt that kind and generous affections were potent sources of
human bonding and the good society. Jefferson, influenced by Hutcheson,
intentionally included happiness rather than property in the profound
trinity of the pursuit of life, liberty, and happiness in the Declaration of
Independence. In a similar vein the Preamble to the Constitution provides
for the common defense and promoting the general welfare. Both happiness and general welfare are operationally similar to our definition of
quality of global health and well-being, that is, the absence of HD and
maximum of lifegenic factors.

Motivation

Any plan of action must consider motivation. One personality type
or motivation that escapes the HD concept is that which Fromm called
the death or war lover (Fromm 1973). But the HD concept should appeal
to the motivation of nearly all others. For example, if one is motivated
by altruism, that is, wishes to improve the world for future generations,
the HD concept should make sense. At the other extreme, the individual
motivated by greed and the acquisition of possessions is usually motivated to leave a legacy to his or her children and grandchildren. And if
they are not alive? What, then, is the benefit of wealth and power? One
has to be alive to use either. Similarly, if hedonism is the predominant
drive, the individual must be alive and well to enjoy pleasure. Suppose
fear of death or annihilation is the motivation? Then removal of one set
of premature, torturous deaths should offer some relief.

Even the individual who profits in HD—a trader in weapons—needs
to be alive and to have a future to enjoy the fruits of his murderous labor.
Arms dealers, too, have children for whom they wish health and longevity. The arms supplier needs to recognize that the weapons that he mer-
chandises may destroy his own children in the end. That scenario is real
for it is established that exported weapons, made in the United States,
eventually kill U.S. soldiers (Saul 1994).

In the past the privileged could escape HD. Today, no one can escape. Assassination and assassination attempts on presidents, the
Pope, multinational corporation executives, and others holding power

are not unusual. Terrorism is part of the world scene. The probability of escape by influential gatekeepers of power decreases as people become more sophisticated in the sociology, psychology, and technology of power and death. One expects targets of HD to increasingly include children of the powerful, political dissidents, and the opposition, however defined.

The Manhattan Project Model

How might the HD Concept be actualized? A Manhattan-type project similar to that which produced the atomic bomb during World War II is one model that might serve as a catalyst to coordinate initiatives to get at the root causes of HD (Leviton 1996). At that time, the finest scientific minds were mobilized for the task. Cost was no object. The HD variation would not produce a bomb. Instead the product would be national, and ultimately international policy to improve the quality of global health and well-being. Certainly, the threat to the country and globe is just as great as it was during World War II. Getting at root causes, dealing with symptoms, prevention, intervention, and postvention would need to be considered.

Former U.S. Secretary of Defense Robert McNamara had a similar idea. When he was offered the presidency of the Ford Foundation he thought:

> "The job was clearly a plum: The Ford Foundation was the largest foundation in the country and was spending approximately $200 million a year to advance human welfare around the world." Then he adds, "One can think of that as mobilizing 2,000 of the world's most capable scholars and policy analysts (at $100,000 each in compensation, expenses, and overhead) to focus on the most critical economic, political, social, and security problems facing humankind. As I later observed after serving as a Ford Foundation trustee for 17 years, the foundation did just that under Mac's [McGeorge Bundy] leadership. When I became World Bank president, I borrowed or 'stole' many of their ideas concerning population planning, poverty reduction, agricultural research, and environmental preservation—ideas enormously helpful, to the World Bank and me, in dealing with problems in developing nations. [McNamara 1995, p. 235]

The participants in the new Manhattan Project, that is, the representatives of the domains of influence and power described earlier, would be motivated and focused on their task by a process involving the removal of denial that would result in awareness of the threat of HD to themselves and their most beloved. Thus, the specter of HD would serve as a stimulus to their staying on the agenda.

Anne Platt's (1995) view concerning public health efforts to stop biological epidemics suggests one outcome of the new Manhattan Project:

> Stopping the world's growing epidemic of epidemics may not be possible, in fact, until considerations of human health are integrated into all major human activities. Since infections [substitute HD] do not stop at the borders of communities and countries, neither should control efforts. Individual nations need to coordinate with WHO and with each other to establish a reliable global surveillance system which would provide early warning, monitor incidence, and coordinate the response. [p. 32]

The United Nations Environmental Programme

One model exists that has integrated a *domains of influence and power to reduce people-caused deaths* concept. It is the United Nations Environmental Programme (UNEP) Executive Director's Advisory Group on Banking and the Environment (see on the Internet/WWW, http://www.unep.ch/finance/bankl.html) (Hertsgaard 1996). Global banking and insurance have found that they have a vested interest in reducing global warming as industry continues to pump 6 billion tons of carbon dioxide and other heat-trapping greenhouse gases into the atmosphere every year (Hertsgaard 1996). UNEP has helped the banking-corporations-business domain to see that their economic interest is served by improving the quality of the environment. Certainly, their health and well-being interest is served as well. One wonders whether the UNEP model can be applied to other forms of HD, and to other domains.

Paul Hawken, in his constructive book *The Ecology of Commerce* (1993), discusses ways to achieve an enduring society, ". . . where each and every act is inherently sustainable and restorative. Business will need to integrate economic, biologic, and human systems to create a sustainable method of commerce. . . . We must design a system of where . . . doing good is like falling off a log, where the natural, everyday acts of work and life accumulate into a better world as a matter of course, not a matter of conscious altruism (Hawken 1993, p. xiv). His book elaborately presents an action plan.

Underlying Root Causes

Governments tend to deal with symptoms of HD rather than root causes. For example, in the United States the governmental response to increasing violence is to build more jails. However, the priority should be given to improving economic status and education. Both are well-documented as causative factors of nearly all forms of HD (e.g., for discussion of causes of *violence* see Anonymous 1995, Centerwall 1995, Developmental Research and Programs 1993, Pappas 1994, Reiss and Roth 1993, 1994a,b, and of *poverty* see Danziger et al. 1995, Durning 1989, Gorlick 1991, Sivard 1993, Swinton 1991, Tidwell 1992). What can be said is that it is time to *apply* existing research and programs to prevent HD by addressing causes as well as symptoms. A word about two root causes: economic and educational issues.

The Economic Factor. There are two major areas in need of reform if HD is to be prevented, reduced, or eliminated: economics and education. However, the causative factors are not independent of one another. Resolving the economic or educational causes of any of the forms of HD will not lessen it. All causes need to be addressed, and all of the domains of influence need to be involved.

In October 1994 I posted this question to an Internet discussion group concerned with health promotion: "Why wasn't the prevention of the forms of horrendous death a burning (or even tepid) issue for those of us in the health field and its related disciplines?" One astute response focused on the issue of economics:

> You are asking questions so dangerous that they cannot be asked in this system. As Deep Throat told Woodward and Bernstein, "Follow the money." EVERY ONE of the preventable causes of disease and death you mention—homicide, war, pollution—generates profits to powerful groups, be they drug companies, hospitals, arms merchants, polluting corporations, or simply economic elites that benefit from a self-destructive, self-controlling underclass. In a world of capitalism triumphant, your commonsense concerns cannot and will not be addressed.

Until we begin to question and change the economic structures of our society, and the values they inculcate and promulgate worldwide, we will proceed down the spiral of violence we so rightly abhor. There's a lot of work to do, and the first step is to accurately identify the nature and scope of the problem. I would start here (communication via Internet, October 17, 1994).

Economic issues that affect HD involve priority and values (for example, social vs. military-industrial expenditures, unnecessary federal subsidies, and waste), distribution of wealth, job training, and reconversion. A caveat: no one person has the answers to the complex problems associated with eliminating HD. I don't. What I do have is something to say about goals, motivation, and the process involved. The new Manhattan Project, by definition, requires the coming together of highly motivated people to address the issue of the elimination of HD.

That profits are made from HD has been well established. Over the years Sivard (1993) has documented the costs of war and its effect on social indices of health and well-being. Also, the U.S. Arms Control and Disarmament Agency reported that the U.S. doubled its share of arms exports between 1981 and 1991 and moved ahead of the then Soviet Union as the world's number one arms supplier. The report showed that the U.S. exported $59 billion in arms between 1987 and 1991, with $35 billion, or 59 percent, going to developing countries. In that period, Saudi Arabia purchased $5.1 billion in arms, Israel $5 billion, and Taiwan $3 billion. U.S. arms exports declined by almost 34 percent between 1989 and 1991, but world arms sales were dropping even more, by 53 percent.

The result was that the U.S. share doubled—from 19.3 to 37.8 percent—while the Soviet Union's share declined from 43 percent in 1986 to 26 percent in 1991.

The leading exporters were, in order, the U.S., the Soviet Union, the United Kingdom, West Germany, France, China, Canada, Israel, Czechoslovakia, North Korea, the Netherlands, Italy, Poland, Brazil, and Bulgaria (Associated Press 1994).

Cohen and colleagues (1994) described a framework for calculating the costs of violent behavior in the U.S. such as homicide, rape, robbery, and assault. They grouped costs in the categories of direct property losses, medical and mental health care, victim services, lost workdays, lost school days, lost housework, death, legal costs associated with tort claims, and long-term consequences of victimization. The aggregate cost of violent behavior was calculated as follows: rape, $8 billion; robbery, $20.5 billion; and assault, $81.3 billion.

Society's response to an intentional injury incurs costs associated with fear of crime, precautionary expenditures/effort, the criminal justice system, victim services, other noncriminal programs (such as hotlines and public service announcements), incarcerated offender costs, "overdeterrence costs" (such as innocent individuals accused of offense and restriction of legitimate activity), and "justice" costs (such as constitutional protections to avoid false accusations and cost of increasing detection rate to avoid differential punishment). The aggregate cost of society's response to murder, rape, robbery, and aggravated assault was calculated at $18.8 billion. All calculations were based on 1987 dollars and should be increased by 25 to 30 percent (Cohen et al. 1994).

The position that one person's cost is another person's profit, or that there would be a tremendous savings if HD could be eliminated, are two sides of the same coin. In war and the sales of the accoutrements of war the profit motive is obvious. "Violent behavior" also provides monetary benefits to hospitals, mental health workers, law enforcement agencies, the funeral industry, weapons manufacturers, etc. Thus, if HD were significantly reduced or eliminated funds could be channeled to meet social needs locally and globally.

Another economic issue has to do with the distribution of wealth. In the United States the 20 percent of the poorest households share 4 percent of the wealth while the richest 20 percent own 46 percent of the wealth. Worldwide, the poorest 20 percent own 4 percent of the wealth, and the richest own 58 percent of the wealth. The variation between nation-states is high with China (its cities), the former Soviet Union, and Japan having the least inequity between poor and rich, and Turkey, Mexico, and Brazil having the greatest (Durning 1989).

I mention other countries because any attempt at reducing the probability of HD must ultimately be global in scope. It is axiomatic that if HD can occur in any country it can occur anywhere else. Globally the picture is mixed. There have been dramatic improvements over the past fifty years in several areas of human life, wrote Ed Ayres (1994) in *World Watch*. Citing the United Nations Development Programme's (UNDP) *Human Development Report 1994*, gains included greatly improved nutrition, higher life expectancies, and higher levels of literacy. The world is safer today from the threat of nuclear holocaust. More countries have established democratic forms of government. And while 70 percent of the world's people lived in what UNDP defines as "abysmal" conditions as recently as 1960, only 32 percent did in 1992.

On the other hand, noted Ayres, there were grave setbacks: The gap between the world's rich and poor widened. In 1960 the poorest fifth of the global population had incomes 1/30th those of the richest fifth. In 1990 the share of the poorest fifth (approximately one billion people) had fallen to 1/61st that of the richest fifth.

While the superpower arms race has ended, arms trade remains rampant. In 1992 world military spending was equal to the income of 49 percent of the world's people—$815 billion. Even a small portion of that amount, if it had been spent on social needs instead, could have provided primary education, health care, family planning services, and adequate nutrition for virtually everyone in the world who lacked them.

While the industrial countries sent $60 billion in official development assistance (ODA) to poor countries in 1992, the recipients had to pay $160 billion in debt service charges in the same year. Both the World Bank and IMF received more money from impoverished countries in the past two years than they loaned out. Despite humanitarian efforts, cash continues to flow from the poor to the rich.

Of the $60 billion that went to developing countries in 1992, little was invested in the places where it was most needed. While ten countries accounted for 66 percent of the world's poorest people, they got only 32 percent of the development assistance. India, with its 27 percent of the absolute poor, received only 5 percent in aid.

The report concludes that the greatest threat to human security in the post–Cold War era lay not in military conflicts between nations but in conflicts within nations, often originating in "socioeconomic deprivation and disparities." In such a milieu, conclude the authors, "security . . . lies in development, not arms" (Ayres 1994).

This scenario of social chaos and implosion is becoming increasingly probable. In a powerful article in the *Atlantic Monthly*, Robert D. Kaplan (1994) wrote of the relationship between economic deprivation and social disintegration:

> To understand the events of the next fifty years, one must understand environmental scarcity, cultural and racial clash, geographic destiny, and the transformation of war. The order in which I have named these is not accidental. Each concept, except the first, relies partly on the one or ones before it, meaning that the last two—new approaches to map making and to warfare—are the most important.
>
> It is time to understand "the environment" for what it is: *the national-security issue of the early twenty-first century.* The political and strategic impact of surging populations, spreading disease, deforestation and soil erosion, water depletion, air pollution, and possibly rising sea levels in critical, overcrowded regions like the Nile Delta and Bangladesh—*developments that will prompt mass migrations and, in turn, incite group conflicts—will be the core foreign policy challenge from which most others will ultimately emanate, arousing the public and uniting assorted interests left over from the Cold War.* [p. 44, my emphasis]

By "map making" is meant that the social cohesiveness once ascribed to nation-states is being replaced by ethnic, racial, and special interest tribalism. The greater allegiance may be ascribed to one's group or cause. Warfare, Kaplan (1994) predicts, will increasingly take the form of violent crime using guerrilla and terrorist strategies and tactics where it will be difficult to distinguish the "enemy" from the ally. In such a scenario geographic borders within and of nation-states become meaningless.

Chaos theorists feel that the price of government breakdown is social disintegration. Chaos theory suggests that "famines, civil wars, overpopulation, 'ethnic cleansing,' terrorism, and environmental stress will generate a tidal anarchy" (Rosenfeld 1994). Supporters of the theory like Jonathan Moore, a former U.N., state department, and Kennedy School official, call for a focused response very much akin to the new Manhattan Project.

On the other hand, Rosenfeld (1994) reports that Jeremy Rosner, a former Clinton national Security Council aide, sees "a misplaced tendency to credit environmental determinism, rather than malice, bad governance, or lack of democracy for social collapse. He faults the implication of some chaos theorists that the nation-state is withering away and that only world government will save us" (p. A31). From the HD perspective, it makes little difference who is right. The conditions that foster HD exist and must be acted upon.

Other economic issues such as job training and reconversion need to be addressed as part of the effort to reduce the probability of HD. Economic reconversion implies a reallocation of budgets to make funds available for nonviolent purposes such as improving the quality of health and well-being. "It is more than a bookkeeping exercise," writes Michael Renner (1990). "Conversion encompasses an adaptation of research, production, and management practices in arms-producing factories to civilian needs and criteria. This requires a retraining of employees as much as a refashioning of production equipment. It means finding civilian uses for military bases and personnel" (p. 8). Again, a mountain of research is available for application.

The Education Factor. Formal and informal education must be considered as one means to prevent HD. A volume could be written on the reforms in education suggested by the HD concept. Education toward knowledge and wisdom was always considered the cornerstone of a successful representative democracy. During the beginning of the seventeenth century citizens were involved in government. Newspapers and journals of the day were voraciously read, and issues debated, thanks to the influence of the Protestant ethic that commanded that every person should be able to read God's word in the Bible independent of a pastor or anyone else (Beard et al. 1960). Education provided the basis for quality government during the early history of the United States.

I don't think that is the case today. Reading books, journals, and newspapers is no longer the primary means of gathering news for a large proportion of the population. Television and, increasingly, radio talk shows provide the "news" for a large segment of the population. The formal education provided in the high schools and colleges is centered on the acquisition of technical and "marketable" skills and less on gaining insight and wisdom from a global health and well-being perspective. Also much of education is simply boring as it deals with abstractions and less with action (which would cause John Dewey much concern).

What is suggested is an integration of classical, health, and death education where the end results are knowledge, understanding, wisdom, and action. Classical education focuses on great literature, drama, and visual arts. The value of the classics is their emphasis on wisdom more than the acquisition of facts or technical skills, wisdom that underscores the responsibility we have to one another.

If the classics utilize the wisdom of the past to resolving the problems of today, health and death education are concerned about the problems relating to living long and well today and tomorrow. What should be the subject matter of health education? If health and well-being are the Yin, thanatology is the Yang. Each is a side of the same coin. Health education should enhance the value of life and living by describing the fragility and interdependence of all life. I would include the causes, and emotional, economic, physical, and social effects of HD, and educate students to enable them to become agents of change and to act in global society's best interests.

It has been said that any damn fool can be a parent or politician without benefit of education or training. We constantly see evidence of both. There is a great need for parent education. That children are physically beaten under the guise of "discipline" or for other reasons is routinely reported in the media. It is also well established that childhood brutality is related to later violence (Developmental Research and Programs 1993, Reiss and Roth 1993, 1994a). Parent education would teach parents and parents-to-be fundamentals of human development (including the need for love, reinforcement of self-concept and esteem, and security), ways of shaping the child's behavior without physical or psychological abuse, the need for physical activities, parental responsibilities, providing children with challenges, conflict-resolution techniques, and barriers and gateways to responsible parenting.

Children tend to learn by reinforcement and modeling. They need to study and emulate those who have acted to improve the lot of humankind even at risk to their personal reputation and safety, such as Socrates, Einstein, Gandhi, Jesus, Martin Luther King, Ralph Nader, Paul Robeson, and Rachel Carson.

That which promotes affection, tolerance, and understanding between cultures and people is to be encouraged. Thus education should encourage student exchanges, overseas study programs, and programs such as the Peace Corps and ACTION. There is another gain. Such programs involve the application of abstractions and theory to practice. Children in kindergarten through college are activity oriented. They need to be doing more than sitting and listening. A continuous complaint of students in practically all grades is boredom. Yet they are not bored in so-called extracurricular activities such as sports, band and orchestra, or the projects mentioned above.

For example, former president Jimmy Carter has participated in Habitat for Humanity, a program to build affordable housing. What a wonderful way for children, adolescents, and the rest of us to apply mathematical and cooperative skills. Other programs have students and others learn to repair houses or cars for those in need.

When my son Matt was younger, he had a problem learning math. "I can't do it," he said. I asked him to figure out his batting average if he got four hits in ten times at bat. His immediate response was .400. "How about two for three," I asked? "That's easy—.666," he shot back. He had applied division to figuring out a percentage. The application to baseball provided the motivation and insight. Sometime later he was having difficulty understanding the Pythagorean theorem. I asked if he knew the distance from home plate to first base, and home to third? He did: 90 feet. "Then what is the distance from first to third," I asked? It took some time but he got it (127 feet).

Matt was not interested in physics or biomechanics until he realized that they were crucial to understanding and executing proper baseball pitching mechanics. Now, at 18 years of age, and a freshman pitcher at a major university, he talks of levers, torque, linear force, and rotation like an engineer or physicist.

As mentioned earlier, education by itself cannot prevent or eliminate any form of HD. Other factors such as economics, population growth and trends, culture, the environment, and social stresses must be considered as well. That is the task of the new Manhattan Project.

The University as Catalyst? The academy, with its diverse expertise, might serve as the catalyst to carry out a new Manhattan Project. Some of the disciplines necessary in carrying out the project include education and health education, economics, psychology, sociology, cultural anthropology, medicine, law, and ecology. One gain for any university is that the endeavor would unite the campus in a common purpose. Similarly, the traditional mission of education, research, and service would be focused. Finally, by integrating education, service, and research to improving the health and well-being of the citizenry, the utility of the academy would become clarified and meaningful in the eyes of the public.

An Example of Local Action: The Adult Health and Development Program and the National Network for Intergenerational Health

One often hears the expression, "Think globally, act locally." One cannot wait for the new Manhattan Project to come to fruition. There are thousands of examples of people, individually and in groups, acting in their own way to eliminate HD. One day they will organize under an umbrella—and that will be a force to reckon with.

Much of my energy is devoted to the Adult Health and Development Program at the University of Maryland at College Park (AHDP/UMCP) and the National Network for Intergenerational Health (NNIH) (Leviton 1989, 1990, 1991a,d, 1992, Leviton and Santa Maria 1979, Leviton and Wendt 1983). How do they reduce the probability of HD? Both use physical and social activities, and health education as a process to reduce labels and stereotypes. Labeling and stereotyping are risk factors for hostility and aggression. Playful activities and health education are nonthreatening and usually fun. No one is trying to exploit another; quite to the contrary—they are mutually supportive of one another. Thus, people, despite age and socioeconomic and health status, come to see one another as individuals.

The NNIH is the proliferation of the AHDP to six to ten other colleges and universities. These are intergenerational health promotion and rehabilitation programs where university and high school students and people from the community (called "staffers") are trained to work on a one-to-one basis with institutionalized and noninstitutionalized older adults (called "members"). That is the key—the one-to-one match up.

The primary goal is to positively affect the health and well-being of the member while allowing the staffer the opportunity to apply his or her creativity, insight, and knowledge. The staffer serves as a "friendly coach" helping his or her member get into a health and well-being groove. In turn, the member can be helpful to the staffer. He or she is a repository of living history. Members have lived through the Great Depression and World War II. Many have experienced McCarthyism, Jim Crowism, the Holocaust, and seen Babe Ruth hit home runs. They have also experienced the vicissitudes of life. Since physical and social activities and health education are nonthreatening, the member-staffer will usually become friends despite differences. And there are differences! They vary in age, socioeconomic status, ethnic and racial heritage, and health status.

Members can be categorized in four groups: community members, a subgroup of the "foreign-born," Veterans Administration (VA) nursing home residents, and members with developmental disabilities. Staffers, too, are a diverse group. Many members and staffers return year after year. Some have been involved for over ten years.

AHDP/UMCP members are tolerant of individual and group differences. One question that members are asked on the first and last day of the AHDP/UMCP taps acceptance or rejection of the diversity of members and staffers. The question is, "I find the *diversity* of the members and staffers in terms of ethnic and racial background, age, and health and well-being status to be . . ." Members respond on a five-point Likert-type scale with 1 equal to the very highest, positive rating, and 5 the lowest, most negative rating. Using the spring 1994 members' responses as an example, the mean response on the first day was 1.7, and on the last day was 1.5. In both cases the variance was small.

One VA nursing home patient who came to the AHDP for years illustrates how the AHDP/NNIH contributes to the tightening of the social fabric. Mr. X was a self-educated African-American man who served in World War II, had minimal function of his lower extremities, and was clearly a favorite with the staffers. During the spring 1989 semester he gave me an audiotape that was a combination oral history and legacy. He noted, without any bitterness, that he had fought the "white man's war" only to return to his country with its racism, hatred, and bigotry. As objective as any scientist, he noted the changes for good that had occurred over time, such as improvements in civil rights, African-Americans winning elective office, and so on. Better, he saw a change in attitude as the races became integrated often in the spirit as well as the letter of the law. Still, he recognized the fact that to be an African-American was a health, economic, and mortality risk. The first to die in war and homicide, and the last to be employed in a decent job and to receive an education. He laughed when I suggested that if a male wished to live long he should choose white parents and go through a sex-change procedure.

He went on to say, shortly before his death, that unless we come together, worldwide, as we do in the AHDP, we will destroy one another. He did not wish that for "his kids," the AHDP staffers, or others. Over the years, he taught us much. Prior to his last semester in the AHDP/UMCP, he was told that he did not have much longer to live. Initially, his physicians wished him to cease coming to the program. He convinced his adult children and the VA physicians to allow him to continue to attend his beloved program. He came until the very end.

Conclusion

The HD → Global Health and Well-Being concept links the study of death with improving the quality of life that Feifel spoke and wrote about so frequently. Carrying out the idea is an ongoing and difficult process; however, there is a strategy. It involves sensitizing people from the various domains of power toward action. Like Paladin (Have Gun Will Travel), I talk to all groups, and find that the churches are particularly receptive. Networking and collaborating with those individuals and groups (such as MADD [Mothers Against Drunk Driving], COPS [Concerns of Police Survivors], and Parents of Murdered Children) who have suffered an HD are an obvious priority. Above all, I hope to make the HD → Global Health and Well-Being concept a political-societal issue. The goal is to establish a new Manhattan Project as a start toward eliminating HD.

The price of failure to eliminate or reduce the causes of HD is that HD will increase and spread to populations formerly untouched. For example, in the U.S. the possession of handguns and drug use has spread from the inner city to suburban schools. So have its victims. It is white as well as black young people who die prematurely. In the future it will increasingly include the children of the representatives of the domains of influence and power. Does that have to occur before the "leaders" realize we are all in this together?

Thus, I worry about the anarchy and implosion here and abroad of which Kaplan (1994) and the chaos theorists write (see Rosenfeld 1994). I worry as well about the always present danger of nuclear war, terrorism, and the like. Still, one perseveres. Like-minded people exist. It is a matter of leadership, time, and organization.

Now, Herman—all things in their time and place—let's get some ice cream.

References

Anonymous (1995). Professor Alfred Blumstein of Carnegie Mellon University. *Law Enforcement News*, April 30, pp. 1–10.

Associated Press (1994). U.S. Doubled Arms Export Share in '80s. *Washington Post*, April 1, p. A4.

Ayres, E. (1994). A 50-year report card for the human condition. *World Watch*, September/October, p. 7.

Beard, C., Beard, M., and Beard, W. (1960). *The Beard's History of the United States*. Garden City, NY: Doubleday.

Beck, K. H. (1991). Human response to threat. In *Horrendous Death, Health, and Well-being*, ed. D. Leviton, pp. 31–47. Washington: Hemisphere.

Becker, E. (1973). *The Denial of Death*. New York: Free Press.

Brown, D. (1993). Getting ready to die young. *Washington Post*, November 1, pp. A1–A8.

Brown, L. R., Durning, A. T., Flavin, C., et al. (1991). *State of the World: 1991*. New York: Norton.

Burns, J. M. (1991). *A People's Charter*. New York: Vintage.

Centerwall, B. S. (1995). Race, socioeconomic status, and domestic homicide. *Journal of the American Medical Association* 273(22):1755–1758.

Cohen, M. A., Prothow-Stith, D., Guyer, B., and Spivak, H. (1994). The costs and consequences of violent behavior in the United States. In *Understanding and Preventing Violence, Volume 4: Consequences and Control*, ed. A. J. Reiss, Jr., and J. A. Roth, pp. 67–166. Washington, DC: National Academy Press.

Danziger, S. H., Sandefur, G. D., and Weinberg, D. H., eds. (1995). *Confronting Poverty: Prescriptions for Change*. Boston: Harvard University Press.

Developmental Research and Programs (1993). *Communities That Care*. Seattle: Developmental Research and Programs.

Durning, A. B. (1989). *Poverty and the Environment: Reversing the Downward Spiral*. Worldwatch paper No. 92. Washington, DC: Worldwatch Institute.

Feifel, H. (1959). *The Meaning of Death*. New York: McGraw-Hill.

——— (1971). The meaning of death in American society. In *Death Education: Preparation for Living*, ed. B. R. Green and D. P. Irish, pp. 3–12. Cambridge, MA: Schenkman.

French, P. (1991a). The psychology of survival-directed action: Part I: The national pathway to survival. In *Horrendous Death and Health: Toward Action*, ed. D. Leviton, pp. 51–71. New York: Hemisphere.

——— (1991b). The psychology of survival-directed action: Part II: The citizens' pathway to survival. In *Horrendous Death and Health: Toward Action*, ed. D. Leviton, pp. 73–161. New York: Hemisphere.

Fromm, E. (1973). *The Anatomy of Human Destructiveness*. New York: Holt, Rinehart, & Winston.

Glanz, K., Lewis, F. M., and Rimer, B. (1990a). *Health Behavior and Health Education: Theory, Research, and Practice*. San Francisco: Jossey-Bass.

——— (1990b). Moving forward: research and evaluation methods for health behavior and health education. In *Health Behavior and Health Education: Theory, Research, and Practice*, ed. K. Glanz, F. M. Lewis, and B. Rimer, pp. 428–435. San Francisco: Jossey-Bass.

Goodman, L. M., and Hoff, L. A. (1990). *Omnicide: The Nuclear Dilemma*. New York: Praeger.

Gorlick, C. (1991). Unemployment and poverty: correlates of morbidity/mortality. In *Horrendous Death, Health, and Well-being*, ed. D. Leviton, pp. 191–204. Washington, DC: Hemisphere.

Green, B. R., and Irish, D. P., eds. (1971). *Death Education: Preparation for Living*. Cambridge, MA: Schenkman.

Hawken, P. (1993). *The Ecology of Commerce: A Declaration of Sustainability*. New York: HarperCollins.

Hertsgaard, M. (1996). Who's afraid of global warming? Washington, DC: *Washington Post*, January 21, p. C1.

Hill, R. (1994). Maryland students get a gut-wrenching view of violence. Washington, DC: *Washington Post*, December 9, p. B1.

Jaccard, J., Turrisi, R., and Wan, C. K. (1990). Implications of behavioral decision theory and social marketing for designing social action programs. In *Health Behavior and Health Education: Theory, Research, and Practice*, ed. K. Glanz, F. M. Lewis, and B. Rimer, pp. 103–142. San Francisco: Jossey-Bass.

Janis, I. (1982a). Psychological and social ambivalence: an analysis of nonadherence to courses of action prescribed by health-care professionals. In *Stress, Attitudes, and Decisions*, ed. I. Janis, pp. 193–216. New York: Praeger.

——— (1982b). *Stress, Attitudes, and Decisions*. New York: Praeger.

Kaplan, R. D. (1994). The coming anarchy. *Atlantic Monthly*, February, pp. 44–76.

Kidron, M., and Segal, R. (1981). *The State of the World Atlas*. New York: Simon & Schuster.

Leviton, D. (1989). Intergenerational health education: The Adult Health and Development program. *Hygie* 8(2):26–29.

——— (1990). Horrendous death as a stimulus to intergenerational health protective action and global well being. In *Proceedings of the 32nd ICHPER Anniversary World Congress*, ed. S. Haberlein and H. Cordts, pp. 15–21. Frostburg, MD: Frostburg State University.

——— (1991a). From theory to practice: the Adult Health and Development Program and theories of children's love and peace behaviors. In *Horrendous Death and Health: Toward Action*, ed. D. Leviton, pp. 245–260. New York: Hemisphere.

——— (1991d). Toward rapid and significant action. In *Horrendous Death and Health: Toward Action*, ed. D. Leviton, pp. 261–283. New York: Hemisphere.

——— (1992). The Adult Health and Developmental Program: more than just fitness. In *Physical Activity, Aging and Sports: Volume II: Practice, Program and Policy*, ed. S. Harris, R. Harris, and W. S. Harris, pp. 232–250. Albany: Center for the Study of Aging.

——— (1996). Preventing "people-caused deaths" must be a priority. *The Nation's Health* 26(1):2.

————, ed. (1991b). *Horrendous Death, Health, and Well-being.* New York: Hemisphere.·
————, ed. (1991c). *Horrendous Death and Health: Toward·Action.* New York: Hemisphere.
Leviton, D., and Santa Maria, L. (1979). The Adult Health and Developmental Program: descriptive and evaluative data. *Gerontologist* 19:534–543.
Leviton, D., and Wendt, W. A. (1983). Health education, the denial of death, and global well-being. *Health Education* 14(3):3–7.
Lewis, F. M. (1990). Perspectives on models of interpersonal health behavior. In *Health Behavior and Health Education: Theory, Research, and Practice,* ed. K. Glanz, F. M. Lewis, and B. Rimer, pp. 242–251. San Francisco: Jossey-Bass.
Lifton, R. J. (1979). *The Broken Connection.* New York: Simon & Schuster.
McCall, N. (1994a). It's me against the world. Washington, DC: *Washington Post Magazine,* January 30, pp. 7–27.
———— (1994b). *Makes Me Want to Holler: A Young Black Man in America.* New York: Random House.
McNamara, R. S. (1995). *In Retrospect: The Tragedy and Lessons of Vietnam.* New York: New York Times Books.
National Center for Health Statistics (1986). *Health United States, 1986.* DHHS Publication No. PHS-87-1232. Washington, DC: US Government Printing Office.
———— (1993). *Advance Report of Final Mortality Statistics, 1991.* Monthly vital statistics report vol. 42, no. 2, suppl. Hyattsville, MD: Public Health Service.
Pappas, G. (1994). Elucidating the relationships between race, socioeconomic status, and health. *American Journal of Public Health* 84(6):892–893.
Perry, C. L., Baranowski, T., and Parcel, G. S. (1990). How individuals, environments, and health behaviors interact: Social Learning Theory. In *Health Behavior and Health Education: Theory, Research, and Practice,* ed. K. Glanz, F. Lewis, and B. Rimer, pp. 161–186. San Francisco: Jossey-Bass.
Platt, A. (1995). The resurgence of infectious diseases. *World Watch* 8(4):26–32.·
Reiss, A. J. Jr., Miczek, K. A., and Roth, J. A., eds. (1994). *Understanding and Preventing Violence, Volume 2: Biobehavioral Influences.* Washington, DC: National Academy Press.
Reiss, A. J., Jr., and Roth, J. A., eds. (1993). *Understanding and Preventing Violence.* Washington, DC: National Academy Press.
———— (1994a). *Understanding and Preventing Violence, Volume 3: Social Influences.* Washington, DC: National Academy Press.
———— (1994b). *Understanding and Preventing Violence, Volume 4: Consequences and Control.* Washington, DC: National Academy Press.
Renner, M. G. (1990). *Swords Into Plowshares: Coverting to a Peace Economy.* Worldwatch Paper No. 96. Washington, DC: Worldwatch Institute.
Rosenfeld, S. S. (1994). Concerning chaos. *Washington Post,* November 11, p. A31.
Rosenstock, I. (1990). The Health Belief Model: explaining health behavior through expectancies. In *Health Behavior and Health Education: Theory, Research, and Practice,* ed. K. Glanz, F. Lewis, and B. Rimer, pp. 42–43. San Francisco: Jossey-Bass.
Rummel, R. J. (1990). *Lethal Politics: Soviet Genocide and Mass Murder Since 1917.* New Brunswick, NJ: Transaction.
———— (1991a). *China's Bloody Century: Genocide and Mass Murder Since 1900.* New Brunswick, NJ: Transaction.
———— (1991b). *Democide: Nazi Genocide and Mass Murder.* New Brunswick, NJ: Transaction.
Saul, J. R. (1994). Arms addiction: how the west got hooked on exporting weapons. *Washington Post,* February 6, p. C3.
Schuetz, A. (1991). Casualties in future wars. In *Horrendous Death, Health, and Well-being,* ed. D. Leviton, pp. 83–107. New York: Hemisphere.

Sivard, R. (1991). *World Military and Social Expenditures, 1991*, 14th ed. Washington, DC: World Priorities.

—— (1993). *World Military and Social Expenditures, 1993*, 15th ed. Washington, DC: World Priorities.

Swinton, D. H. (1991). The economic status of African-Americans: permanent poverty and inequality. In *The State of Black America 1991*, ed. J. Dewart, pp. 25–75. New York: National Urban League.

Tidwell, B. J., ed. (1992). *The State of Black America 1992*. New York: National Urban League.

U.S. Department of Health and Human Services (1992). *Healthy People 2000: National Health Promotion and Disease Prevention Objectives*. Boston: Jones and Bartlett.

Vobejda, B. (1994). Children's defense fund cites gun violence. Washington, DC: *Washington Post*, January 21, p. A3.

Weisman, A. D. (1974). *The Realization of Death: A Guide of the Psychological Autopsy*. New York: Jason Aronson.

World Health Organization (1993). *1992 World Health Statistics Annual*. New York: World Health Organization.

Young, J. E. (1994). Greenspeed: accelerating eco-communications. *World Watch* 7(1):20–26.

15

Death, Society, and the Quest for Immortality

ROBERT FULTON

Herman Feifel (1982) once remarked that death is "lodged in our bowels." Such colorful imagery serves to remind us that we are born to die and that all human relationships end in separation. Herman spent the greater part of his career as a psychologist examining the implications of these two fundamental facts of life. Since 1956, when he chaired a symposium on death and dying for the American Psychological Association, which led, subsequently, to his path-breaking compendium, *The Meaning of Death* (Feifel 1959), Herman has addressed this question: How do we, as human beings, comprehend the prospect of our deaths?

American psychologists have long been concerned with the different issues surrounding mortality. In 1915 the distinguished psychologist G. Stanley Hall addressed the issue of death in his classic essay, "Thanatophobia and Immortality," and later in his book, *Senescence* (1922). Throughout the succeeding decades, psychologists such as W. Bromberg and P. Schilder (1936), F. Deutsch (1936), W. C. Middleton (1936), M. H. Means (1936), S. Anthony (1940), M. Nagy (1948), and R. May (1950) explored such issues as death symbols; attitudes toward death among children, college students, and psychoneurotics; the relationship between religious beliefs and death; death anxiety; and euthanasia. For the most part, however, these studies and observations were restricted to a limited academic audience. It was Herman, who, in 1959, brought the discussion of death out of the halls of academe and into the public forum. The process by which he accomplished this, however, was, as he has wryly observed, "not an easy birth" (Feifel 1963).

The Denial of Death

From the end of the First World War until the late 1950s, death in America, it could be said, took a holiday. Paradoxically, the public discussion of death—despite its ubiquitous and oftentimes dramatic appearance—was, for the most part, meager or muted and almost always euphemistic. Death was considered such an omnipotent omnipresence, something beyond all human understanding or control, that it was not generally discussed. Indeed, it was considered impolite to talk about death, as though to utter the word would be to evoke its presence.

A striking example of the taboo that surrounded death, even within the academic community during this period, can be found in the four volume social science survey entitled *The American Soldier* (Stouffer et al. 1949). This prodigious project examined the attitudes and reactions of more than two million soldiers concerning their Second World War experiences, and helped to establish the basis for the Point Program that determined which military personnel, and in what order, would be returned home from active duty following the war's cessation. The social science researchers asked a comprehensive series of questions on a diverse range of relevant topics but, markedly, failed to ask a single question about a soldier's experiences with, or fear of, death.

The Second World War, a cataclysmic event of unprecedented magnitude that eclipsed even the devastation of the First World War, claimed more than 52 million lives worldwide. It resulted in the destruction or damage to thousands of cities, towns, and villages across the world, left millions of men, women, and children without food or shelter, and millions more as refugees. A kaleidoscope of images from that time readily comes to mind: London in flames; the devastation of Pearl Harbor; the gaunt and exhausted face of a young soldier; the bleak landscape of Hiroshima; the horror of Auschwitz. The American public recoiled from such apocalyptic visions and, psychologically, turned away.

In addition to the trauma of the two world wars, the lacuna in the American public's interest in death, and in the issues surrounding mortality that Feifel identified, were due to many different historical trends and social developments that had slowly emerged over the preceding decades. Among the many different developments that were instrumental in this shift in attitude were improved health and medical services; a rise in the birth rate coupled with a significant decline in infant mortality; increased longevity; a rise in the geographic mobility of the population; and, especially, the emergence of segregated retirement communities for the elderly.

Concomitantly, these and other changes led to a pivotal change in American funeral customs and practices. In a strikingly short period of time, funeral accoutrements and apparel that traditionally served to signify a death, such as the funeral wreath, widow's weeds, and the black hat, arm band, and tie, virtually disappeared from the American scene.

On the other hand, private funerals, cremation, and the number of memorial parks increased.

Since the "rediscovery" of death by Feifel the discussion surrounding human mortality, particularly in the United States, has been focused primarily on the individual, and understandably so. It is, after all, the individual who takes ill, sickens, and dies, or who is killed, or who ends his or her own life, or dies by misadventure. The significance of mortality, however, for the collective public—that is, society—has generally received less attention. As a consequence, our understanding of the social and psychological issues surrounding individual grief and bereavement has been greatly enhanced over the past few decades, while the significance of death and its sequelae for society has generally not been addressed. What I propose to do in this chapter, in honor of my dear friend Herman, is to make a modest overture in amending this omission.

The Judeo-Christian Worldview

I propose that the fact of human mortality (death) and the belief in immortality (life after death), have served as the nucleus of an elaborate system of beliefs, customs, laws, and social practices that constitute social life in Western societies. These two interrelated foci, I would argue, are integral to the foundation of the Judeo-Christian worldview. This worldview is explicated in the sacred text, the *Holy Bible*, which has inspired religious thought, and provided a paradigm of social reality for the past two millennia. In the Bible, the existence of a Supreme Creator (God) is announced; the origin of life—including human life—is chronicled; the purpose of human existence revealed; human death is explained and immortality proffered.

Permit me to detail, briefly, the biblical account of creation. To do so establishes the groundwork for the discussion that follows.

In Genesis, the first book of the Bible, it is stated that "In the beginning" heaven and earth were created by God; that He created man (Adam) in His image and created woman (Eve) so that man would not be alone, commanding them to "be fruitful and multiply"; He caused them to live in a garden in Eden, where grew the tree of life and the tree of the knowledge of good and evil; He commanded that they eat freely of every tree in the garden except the tree of the knowledge of good and evil, "for in the day that you eat of it you shall die"; tempted by the serpent (Satan), Eve took of its fruit and also gave some to Adam and he ate; upon learning of this transgression, God cursed the serpent and said to the woman, "In pain you shall bring forth children"; and to Adam He said, "Cursed is the ground because of you, in toil you shall eat of it all the days of your life. . . . In the sweat of your face you shall eat bread till you return to the ground, for out of it you were taken, you are dust, and to dust you shall return"; God sent Adam and Eve from the garden of Eden in order to prevent Adam from eating also from the tree of life, and "live forever" (Genesis 1:3).

From this biblical account we learn that death is an imposition, a punishment, inflicted upon humankind for the transgression of eating fruit from the tree of knowledge. The account implies that death is not natural to humankind—indeed, the tree of life (immortality) is also present in the Garden of Eden and its fruit was not forbidden to Adam and Eve before their sin. It is only after their banishment that a cherub and a flaming sword were placed in the garden to prevent their partaking of its fruit, and thus live forever.

The concept of immortality, that we have the prospect to live like God, that is, eternally, is thus implicit in the chronicle. As a consequence, it offers the profound hope that at some time and in some way God will relent, that He will lift the punishment of eternal banishment, and humanity will once more be reconciled with Him and live with Him in eternity.

While the concept of immortality raises our hopes that we as individual human beings might live forever, it also compels the question of what it is that we must do to overcome the chastisement of mortal death, and with it the prospect of spiritual separation from God. The Judeo-Christian text instructs us as to the nature of the tasks that must be undertaken before we can hope to achieve the longed-for reconciliation with the Creator.

The Bible informs us that God must be worshiped and honored above all other gods; His praises must be sung and sacrifices offered in His honor; His laws, as enumerated in the Mosaic Code (Ten Commandments), as well as the law to "love one another," must be obeyed; and the imperative "be fruitful and multiply" must be heeded. Meanwhile, punishment of the flesh is to be endured—men by their labor and women through the agony of birth—and ultimately, by corporal death.

Death in Contemporary Society

The question of human mortality, or the belief in life after death in a modern, mass society, is profoundly different from that of ancient Israel or medieval Europe. The sociologist Robert Blauner (1966) would contend that a contemporary society need not, nor does not, organize its social life around the ever-present reality of death, as was the case in the past. He has argued that such social changes as increased life expectancy, medical bureaucratization, and the isolation of the dying person from family and community, as well as other factors, serve to hide death as well as mute the experience of personal grief. Blauner asserted that the changes in the social organization surrounding death found in a large, complex society, have not only relocated the setting of death but also changed its social meaning and psychological valence.

The distinguished sociologist Talcott Parsons (1963) also shared Blauner's views regarding the circumspect and oftentimes muffled response to death found in contemporary society, and the changed perspective in our outlook, but he ascribed a greater role to the individual in accounting for the modern reaction to death. Parsons cited the widespread and dominating belief in science—and concomitantly, the diminished belief in the soul and immortality—together with the growth of personal privacy and apathy, to explain the limited reactions to personal loss that characterize the contemporary encounter with death.

However, the issue that I want to address in this essay transcends the question of how contemporary society deals pragmatically with death, or how an individual reacts to personal loss. Death compels us to ask many other questions in addition to the quintessential or instrumental ones, for instance: Why and for what purpose do we human beings exist? To whom or to what do we owe our lives? Why do we die? What lies beyond death?

Traditionally, the answers to these theological or ontological questions have been found in a society's religious beliefs and sacred texts. In modern secular societies such as the United States, however, where the existence of an anthropomorphic God is challenged and the biblical account of creation is perceived by many as mythical rather than factual, questions concerning the purpose and meaning of life, when they are raised, are often framed within a temporal context. On the other hand, when the discussion turns to society's encounter with death, the focus of the discussion, as can be seen with Blauner (1966) and Parsons (1963), is functional, institutional, and secularly based.

This change in focus has also been observed by another sociologist, Peter Berger (1970). He stated that in the modern world, "the divine, at least in its classical forms, has receded into the background of human concern and consciousness" (p. 5). This shift from a belief system that regards the transcendental as the *primum mobile* of reality, to a secular worldview that maintains a scientific perspective, is not, however, without paradox. Berger noted that even though there is an increase in church participation in the United States, as well as in religious politics, the motivation for such participation has radically changed. Whereas formerly people aspired to achieve religious salvation in order to avoid separation from God or suffer hellfire, Americans today participate in church life "out of a desire to provide moral instruction for their children and direction for their family life, or as part of [their] life-style" (p. 2). The concept of a spiritual world, that is, of another reality that transcends the experience of day-to-day existence, and which is of ultimate significance for humankind, "is allegedly defunct or in the process of becoming defunct in the modern world" (p. 5).

The Transcendental in Contemporary Life

It is true in the United States that formal religious acts or rituals that proclaim the reality and significance of the transcendental are frequently dismissed by secularists as anachronistic, serving no higher purpose other than to provide ethical guidelines and fellowship for the participants. As Berger (1970), Blauner (1966), Parsons (1963), and others have observed, while science and secularism have helped diminish the overall role of the religious experience in modern society and undermine its fundamental message, it has been neither abolished nor silenced. I would contend that one reason for this resiliency is the intrinsic tenacity with which individuals continue to express a belief in immortality, and the fact that the Judeo-Christian paradigm permeates social life to a far greater degree and more deeply than is generally recognized. While formal or public religious rites and observances constitute the most visible expressions of the transcendental or sacred in human life, other manifestations abound in gender relations, everyday speech, inheritance laws and succession practices, sexual attitudes and prohibitions, social display and adornment, and taxes, to name but a few.

Permit me to offer several illustrations. The patriarchal tradition of the Judeo-Christian paradigm that declares "your desire shall be for your husband, and he shall rule over you" (Genesis 3:16), continues to persist in modern, secular society despite dramatic changes in gender equality since the Second World War. It is, for example, still common practice for a woman to take her husband's name upon marriage and for children to carry the surname of their father.

Primogeniture is another case in point. Primogeniture refers to the historic custom whereby the oldest son inherits either all, or a disproportionate share of, his father's wealth. The intent of primogeniture was to provide the son with the wherewithal to say prayers and make sacrifices on behalf of his father's soul; he was, as it were, his father's "funeral priest" (Lewis 1989). The concept of primogeniture is based on the belief that praise and sacrifice to God, endlessly repeated throughout the male generations, secured, for the dutiful, immortality. Even today, primogeniture is observed among many families in contemporary America, and continues to be the basis of inheritance and succession among the royal and aristocratic families of Europe. Primogeniture, expressing as it does the patrilineal legacy of the Judeo-Christian paradigm, is also expressed in those laws that allow men to divorce their wives if they fail to give birth to a male child.

The concept of primogeniture calls forth other observances and practices that find their basis in the Judeo-Christian paradigm. For instance, our laws and taboos concerning adultery find a rationale in the Judeo-Christian context that seeks to assure that the firstborn son be legitimate, that is, identifiable as the father's son beyond question. The efficacy of the firstborn son's role as "funeral priest," it was believed, was contingent upon the spiritual purity of the father–son relationship in keeping with the sacerdotal power inherent in the patrilineal relationship.

The mirror image of these ideas and observances can be found in the Judeo-Christian taboos and prohibitions against homosexuality and prostitution, as well as in the proscription against masturbation. These traditionally proscribed or illegal behaviors are seen to contravene the Divine directive to be "fruitful and multiply," and are thus perceived as abominations. Such acts are judged as putting in jeopardy humankind's obligation to praise God, throughout the generations, as well as imperiling the soul of the offender. By failing to father a legitimate son, in the case of prostitution or by the wasting of seed, as in the case of homosexuality or masturbation, God is blasphemed.

"Gesundheit," or the English equivalent "God bless you," are expressions of good wishes offered to someone who has sneezed, and recalls the belief that the soul resides in the head. The expression is intended to serve as a protective supplication until the soul has safely returned to the body. No such invocation is expected for any other expulsion, or discharge, from the body. On the contrary, all other bodily secretions and expulsions (with the exception of tears) are generally regarded with varying degrees of revulsion. What must, in fact, be acknowledged, is the degree to which the body has historically been viewed as evil and corruptible ("the wages of sin is death"). Rejection and disavowal of the body is found not only in those social practices that demand some form of bodily punishment or mortification, it is also found in the ubiquitous and commonplace use of words and phrases that allude to the body with disgust. In our private speech or in our public discourse whenever we utter a profanity such as "shit," "fuck," "asshole," and "prick" we are, in reality, offering testimony to our disavowal of the flesh. One is hard put to find a profane expression that does not implicitly express repugnance toward, or the desire to distance oneself from, the body. The spirit-flesh dichotomy is expressed, therefore, as frequently in daily speech as it is in religious discourse, finding its basis in the Judeo-Christian perception that the human body is an albatross around the neck of the human soul.

A further illustration of the role of the sacred in the contemporary, secular world is found in our tax laws that provide for charitable or philanthropic exemptions. Such provisions in the law are ultimately based upon the explicit directives from God for humans to act compassionately and charitably toward one another. Given the principle of separation of Church and State that is ostensibly established by law in the United States, these provisions are nothing short of remarkable; they bear testimony to the strength of the spiritual quest for purity and redemption in our secular society regardless of what material gain may be realized by such allowances.

Another example of the manner in which the transcendental manifests itself in the contemporary world can be seen in what Thorsten Veblen (1962), the American economic historian, called "conspicuous consumption," that is, the nonproductive or wasteful expenditure of wealth. The extravagance, for example, of building grand homes and purchasing expensive jewelry, cars, and clothing, can be viewed from one perspective as the way in which the rich identify themselves while enjoying their good fortune. From another perspective, however, such behavior can be understood as a response to the New Testament directive to live like the "lilies of the field" (Matthew 6:28), that is, to trust in God. By consuming in a lavish manner and with seemingly little concern for the future, the wealthy demonstrate their faith in God and the belief that all will continue to be provided for. The possession of wealth, moreover, suggests that for the wealthy, God's punishment, "In the sweat of your face you shall eat bread" (Genesis 1:3), has been somewhat repealed and that the possession of wealth is a sign that God looks favorably upon them. Our contempt for the miser, or those who jealously guard their wealth, needs to be understood in this light. By consuming wealth by acts of charity or philanthropy, the wealthy, moreover, avoid the imputation of pride or arrogance. To the contrary, such generosity earns them social esteem and enhanced repute.

The continued presence of the transcendental in modern secular life is seen most vividly in funeral rites and practices where the distinction between the spirit and the flesh is dramatized, and the belief in immortality signified. The funeral, however, is not like other rituals or ceremonies such as Christmas or Thanksgiving, which are festive, or New Year's Eve or a birthday, which mark transitional events. Rather the funeral is a piacular rite, a ceremony of atonement. Piacular rites address the issue of stigma or defilement. They are ceremonies that are intended to remove an onerous blemish that has been cast on an individual or group by a wrongful act of commission or omission. Death, within the Judeo-Christian tradition, is such a punishment. By definition, a human corpse is evidence of sin, and thus, spiritually unclean. Today, the belief in immortality and the piacular obligations, that is, the sacrifices and oblations that survivors assume on behalf of the dead, are contrary to the ideological beliefs and secular lifestyle of a large segment of the American public. Ironically, however, even those who do not believe in immortality or that it is necessary or proper to waste resources on the dead, can still be seen to respond to a death in a sacrificial or piacular manner. This is observed when one recommends to a survivor that, rather than spend money on flowers or other embellishments for the dead, gifts should be given to medical research or the like, on behalf of the living. What needs to be recognized here is that regardless of the use to which the gift is made, the need to offer sacrifice upon the death of a fellow human being is still keenly felt.

Permit me one last example, albeit somewhat more detailed, that incorporates many of the piacular and other behaviors just described, and that embodies the transcendental vision of the Judeo-Christian world view within the contemporary, secular world. I refer to the celebration of Mardi Gras, which is enacted annually in New Orleans. An examination of this annual festival can provide us with insight into the broad thanatological issues that I am addressing as well as allow us to see the manner in which the Judeo-Christian construction of reality continues to be enacted in the modern public arena. Mardi Gras testifies to the resiliency of the Judeo-Christian paradigm and to the fact that its interpretation of reality, as I have argued, continues to influence everyday life far and beyond general awareness. Mardi Gras captures the ineffable and inextricable relationship between the flesh and the incorporeal. By enveloping the participants in a multiplicity of ritual actions, Mardi Gras both acts out and symbolizes humankind's struggle to preserve its collective existence and its quest for immortality.

At first blush Mardi Gras strikes an observer in much the same way as our contemporary celebrations of Christmas or Halloween, that is, as a ritual reenactment of an historic or spiritual event whose significance has been diminished by time, commercialism, or license. Mardi Gras, however, is more than meets the eye.

Mardi Gras, or Fat Tuesday, which is held annually in New Orleans prior to the beginning of Lent, is generally seen as a time of unabashed fun and public merriment. Revelers, disguised in masks and costumes, put aside the normal rules of propriety and social intercourse in exchange for several days and nights of drunkenness, nudity, sexuality, and, oftentimes, violence. In a word, it would appear to be the devil's workshop, in which law and order are absent, and passion and self-indulgence prevail (Kinser 1990). But there is another side to Mardi Gras, namely the recognition and celebration of the life of society.

To begin, Mardi Gras is sponsored by semi-secret social clubs, called Krewes, that are established along religious, social, racial, and class lines.

While Krewes are often organized by neighborhoods, membership in the most prestigious Krewes is, for the most part, a function of social position. The prestige of a Krewe is reflected in the order of precedence it enjoys in the parades that are held. The most prestigious is the King Rex Krewe, whose parade is held on the evening of Shrove Tuesday, the day prior to Ash Wednesday, the first day of Lent.

Preparation for Mardi Gras by Krewe families begins months and even years before the particular parade and pageant that will include or feature the sons or daughters of Krewe members. Mothers and daughters make forays to shopping meccas—New York, London, Rome, and Paris—in search of the wardrobes necessary for the many different occasions and functions to which the young scions and debutantes of New Orleans society will be invited and presented (Shane 1962).

In the meantime, Krewe organizers arrange for the purchase from Italy, France, and elsewhere, of thousands of dollars worth of trinkets and favors. These token gifts are to be thrown from the Krewes' floats at the time that the parade winds through Old New Orleans, Vieux Carre, to the civic auditorium. In addition, large truck trailers must be rented to haul the floats, a pageant must be planned and rehearsed, a queen and her court must be selected, social engagements must be arranged, and invitations delivered. These are but a few of the innumerable details to be attended to for this yearly social event. These arrangements are both demanding and time-consuming, but of paramount importance to a participating family is the ability to pay. It has been reported, for instance, that parents will bid thousands of dollars to assure their daughter a place on the queen's court (Shane 1962).

A Krewe parade, like the Mardi Gras festival itself, has its own order of precedence. First to appear in the narrow, gas-lit streets of Vieux Carre, are the lumieres. These are African-American men, employed for the occasion to illuminate the procession by carrying lanterns affixed to large wooden crosses. The lumieres proceed in a swaying, snakelike manner down the cobblestone streets of New Orleans, while spectators throw coins at their feet. Without breaking step, the lumieres reach down and pick up what coins they can while holding their large, heavy burdens upright.

Hard on the heels of the lumieres are the mummers, the white, adult male members of the Krewe, who, outfitted in hooded, flowing robes, ride imperiously on their imported Arabian stallions.

The mummers are followed by the elaborately decorated floats. The richly costumed queen and her court wave and receive the applause of the curbside spectators as they pass. Other floats in the parade carry the wives, children, relatives, and friends of the Krewe members, who toss the favors and trinkets that have been previously purchased abroad, thus showering their largesse. Slowly the procession makes its way from Vieux Carre to the steps of the civic auditorium, where a dramatically different, but related social drama, unfolds.

Upon arrival at the auditorium the celebrants change into formal dress for the evening's pageant and ball. After the queen and her court and their escorts have been presented to the assemblage, they stage a theatrical presentation, following which the traditional ball begins. It is the obligation of a young man, honored with a dance, to present the young woman with a small gift, usually of silver.

Following the ball, the celebrations are continued at private parties and receptions. For many young men and women who will receive invitations to one or more of these events, this series of activities will be repeated every evening until the finale, which reaches its dramatic climax with the symbolic killing of the Prince of Misrule (Satan), precisely at midnight on Shrove Tuesday.

Mardi Gras is followed by the 40-day fast of Lent, a Christian observance prior to Easter, the annual festival commemorating the resurrection of Jesus. Traditionally, celebrants are expected to abstain from foods such as meat and dairy products; from activities such as the theater; from sexual intercourse; and from holding marriage ceremonies. They intensify their religious observances: perform penances; wear hair shirts; flagellate themselves; walk without shoes or on their knees; make pilgrimages to shrines; climb holy stairs and increase their attendance at religious ceremonies (masses, prayers, vespers, matins); give alms to the poor; and otherwise atone for their sins.

Mardi Gras, in its full, dramatic richness, embraces two related but significantly different themes. First, the orgiastic festivities express, in the most vivid and dramatic way possible, what the world would be like if it were ruled by Satan. Superficially, it is a world of pleasure, gaiety, and excess, but beneath the pomp and glitter of the festivities it is a world awash in the seven mortal sins of pride, envy, anger, jealousy, sloth, gluttony, and lust. Ultimately, it is a world of darkness and chaos that, perforce, has to be rejected if the individual—or indeed society itself—is to perdure. The Prince of Misrule (Satan), therefore, must be killed. In the burning of his effigy the community expresses its desire to turn away from Satan and his world, and entreat a resurrected Christ's mercy.

The second theme, less apparent, portrays the dual issues of the structure and continuity of society. The shape of New Orleans social structure can be seen in the lavish gift giving by the different Krewe members riding on the floats and the complementary gift giving by the spectators who, in turn, throw coins at the feet of the lumieres. This indirect exchange of gifts, at the same time that it recognizes the superior and inferior roles that are being played out on the part of the Krewe

members and the curbside spectators, confirms the subordinate role of
the lumieres. The lumieres, since they have no place in the system of
gift giving, have their status at the bottom of the social order both proclaimed and confirmed. Thus the different Krewe parades and other
social activities, both public and private, spell out in dramatic fashion
not only traditional religious beliefs, but also the hierarchical character
of social life in New Orleans and the place of class and caste in its community affairs.

The issue of social continuity, on the other hand, can be observed
in the courtship rituals that take place during Mardi Gras. At the invita-
tion-only civic auditorium dances, and in the private parties and family
receptions that follow, the scions of New Orlean's most distinguished
families are presented and introduced to one another, with the expectation that they will marry and that from their loins will arise the next generation of social leaders and responsible citizens.

To understand the spectacle of Mardi Gras, that turns suddenly from
an Bacchanalian orgy into a set of sacred oblations, we must step back
from its colorful pageantry and view it from the perspective of the Judeo-
Christian worldview from which it emanates. To do so permits us not
only to see the connection between what is substantially street theater
and the formal august drama of Easter ritual, it reminds us of the sustaining power of the belief in the transcendental and humankind's quest
for immortality.

Mardi Gras is a public spectacle that theatrically enacts humankind's
condition as a consequence of the Fall from Grace. By engaging in profane and blasphemous behaviors, the participants demonstrate what the
world would be like without God. By burning Satan's effigy and by undertaking the religious tasks and duties of the Lenten period, however, the
participants express their remorse for the sin of their original progenitors. By such oblations they express their desire to survive mortal death
and be reconciled with God. Mardi Gras, inextricably linked as it is with
the Easter rites that announce Christ's resurrection, dramatizes humankind's predicament, mortal death, at the same time that it expresses its
desire to recover its birthright, immortality.

Intimations of Immortality

There are other aspects to the concept of immortality that need to
be discussed in addition to the Judeo-Christian chronicle that intimates
that human beings have the prospect for continued existence after death.
It is to this discussion and its implications for secular society that I shall
now turn.

As it has been observed both archaeologically and anthropologically, the concept of immortality is both ancient and widespread. We can only speculate as to the origin of the idea of immortality, but humankind has always existed amid signs and indications that suggest the cyclical and never-ending nature of things. The regular phases of the moon, for instance, and the constant progression of the seasons, testify to this observation. To look at a tree in the depth of winter when it is totally bereft of leaves, and to know that it will bloom again in the spring—and to witness that blooming—is to open oneself to the prospect that all of life is a cycle—an eternal return.

But many other reasons also account for the fact that humankind, since time immemorial, has embraced the idea that human beings do not die, they merely go somewhere else. Even when the body is destroyed, the conviction is that the soul or spirit lives on. Metamorphosis is one such reason. That a caterpillar weaves a cocoon from which it will later emerge as a butterfly not only challenges the idea of the finality of death, but also, metaphorically, introduces the analogous prospect of transcendent transformation. The snake's annual shedding of its skin and the deer's yearly loss and regrowth of its antlers are two other comparable examples.

Still, there are even more compelling reasons for the belief that mortal death is not the end of human existence. A primary reason, I would argue, is the fact that we humans have the capacity to dream.

One extraordinary aspect of the dream is the fact that following a death, the deceased person can appear in a survivor's dream alive and, importantly, whole. The dreamer may have even witnessed the physical obliteration of the deceased, yet, in a subsequent dream, the deceased appears alive and intact. This mental product is analogous to the phantom-limb phenomenon, that is, a somatic experience in which a person who has lost a finger or limb continues to feel the physical sensations of the missing member. For the dreamer to do for another human being in the dream state something that it does unconsciously on behalf of its own body, that is, project the image of the whole, is a remarkable psychological phenomenon. In this context, however, it is one of the reasons why, since time immemorial, the dream, as a vehicle through which the dreamer can experience an intimation of immortality, has held such great importance for humankind.

The dream is the exhaustless source of inspiration for our hopes of an afterlife because it seemingly restores the dead to life and makes the mutilated or obliterated body appear whole once more. To dream is also a universal experience of human beings. These two facts help account for the widely held belief in immortality as well as its similarity of form.

The importance of dreaming that the dead are alive and whole, for the concept of immortality, cannot be overstated; it serves not only to contradict perceived reality but it also provides a forceful argument for the existence of an unperceived reality. Belief in the living dead—a dead with whom one can communicate, or a dead that seeks contact with the living—becomes psychologically possible.

Delusions and hallucinations are other psychological phenomena that have contributed to the rejection of the idea of death's finality. In the first case, the delusional person believes, despite all evidence to the contrary, that a dead person is alive, while in the second, the dead are reported to be seen or heard or their presence felt. Widows and parents of dead children, particularly, report such hallucinatory experiences.

Personal accounts of an afterworld, such as the contemporary accounts of near-death experiences and the transcendental experiences of psychics and mystics, have also contributed to the idea of an upper and nether world and, by implication, to the belief in a continued existence.

Further, mind-altering drugs such as opium, hashish, peyote, and alcohol have, since recorded time, been integral to the religious ceremonies of peoples worldwide, with the belief that under their influence contact with the spiritual world could be achieved and that its incorporeal nature would be revealed.

Communication with the dead, or with the spirit world without the employment of drugs or other mind-altering practices, has also been widely claimed. History is replete with accounts of persons who have reported having contact with the human dead or with spirits, both benign and malevolent. What should be noted, however, is that the different psychological phenomena that have been reported are not in any direct way connected to traditional religious or spiritual beliefs, per se. For instance, the Christian belief in a Supreme Being who governs the universe and who possesses the power to resurrect the dead represents a tradition of thought that is both separate from, and subsequent to, the personal psychological experiences reported. I would propose that the belief that there is ultimately no death—that in some way, somewhere, human existence continues—originated primarily as a result of the way the human mind fundamentally functions. In this respect, I believe that Feifel and Branscomb (1973) were correct in their observation that there is a "coexisting avoidance-acceptance of personal death" operating simultaneously at the conscious and unconscious levels.

Theologians have argued along similar lines, suggesting that the idea of a Supreme Being (and by implication the prospect of immortality) is intuitive to the soul of humankind. For example, the renowned Catholic philosopher Teilhard de Chardin (1971) asserted that human physical, mental, and moral growth unfolds in an evolutionary way. He viewed this growth as teleological, whereby we are drawn increasingly to recognition, reconciliation, and, ultimately, to reunion with the Creator.

Whatever the ultimate truth may be with respect to the genesis of the belief in immortality, it is important to recognize that humankind has defied the finality of mortal death since time immemorial. It could be said that the historical appearance of Moses, Buddha, Jesus, Muhammad, and the many others who have contributed to the religious beliefs and moral foundations of the world, have but built on the fact of the finite nature of the human body and the infinite vision of the human mind. What this means is that no matter what the degree of decline in the Judeo-Christian belief system may be, or the subsequent changes that have and will take place in the different arenas of contemporary social life, the continued belief in immortality will remain.

The intimation of immortality, I would argue, is so deeply rooted in our psyche as an emanation of mental activity that it is found both in consciousness and in the dream state. The concept of immortality, therefore, is both a primordial and compelling idea in human life, apart from any Judeo-Christian association it might have. As a consequence, I believe that it will continue to vitalize and sustain many nonreligious behaviors that flourish in our contemporary secular world.

Acknowledgments

I would like to thank my research assistant, Mary Drew, for her editorial as well as secretarial assistance in the preparation of this chapter; her contribution went far beyond what one should ask of a mortal friend. I also wish to extend by deep thanks to Stephen Strack, who conceived the idea of a *Festschrift* for Herman, and who, by his dedication and editorial skills, brought this celebratory book to fruition. And, of course, I join my voice with all the others in thanking Herman for his profound contribution to our greater understanding of the human condition.

References

Anthony, S. (1940). *The Child's Discovery of Death*. New York: Harcourt, Brace and World.
Berger, P. (1970). *A Rumor of Angels: Modern Society and the Rediscovery of the Supernatural*. Garden City, NY: Anchor.
Blauner, R. (1966). Death and social structure. *Psychiatry* 29:378–394.
Bromberg, W., and Schilder, P. (1936). The attitudes of psychoneurotics toward death. *Psychoanalytic Review* 23:1–25.
Deutsch, F. (1936). Euthanasia: a clinical study. *Psychiatric Quarterly* 5:347–368.
Feifel, H. (1963). Death. In *Taboo Topics*, ed. N. Farberow, pp. 8–21. New York: Atherton.
——— (1982). Perceptions of death by Western man. In *Death, Dying and Bereavement*, ed. L. Feigenberg, pp. 9–19. Stockholm: Swedish Cancer Society.
———, ed. (1959). *The Meaning of Death*. New York: McGraw-Hill.

Feifel, H., and Branscomb, A. (1973). Who's afraid of death? *Journal of Abnormal Psychol-ogy* 81(3):282–288.

Hall, G. S. (1915). Thanatophobia and immortality. *American Journal of Psychology* 26: 550–613.

——— (1922). *Senescence*. New York: Appleton.

Holy Bible. Revised Standard Edition. New York: Thomas Nelson, 1952.

Kinser, S. (1990). *Carnival, American Style*. Chicago and London: University of Chicago Press.

Lewis, T. J. (1989). *Cults of the Death in Ancient Israel and Ugarit*. Harvard Semitic Mono-graphs #39. Atlanta: Scholars Press.

May, R. (1950). *The Meaning of Anxiety*. New York: Ronald.

Means, M. H. (1936). Fears of one thousand college women. *Journal of Abnormal and Social Psychology* 31:291–311.

Middleton, W. C. (1936). Some reactions toward death among college students. *Journal of Abnormal and Social Psychology* 31:165–173.

Nagy, M. (1948). The child's theories concerning death. *Journal of Genetic Psychology* 73:3–27.

Parsons, T. (1963). Death in American society: a brief working paper. *American Behav-ioral Scientist* 6:61–65.

Shane, P. (1962). Personal communication.

Stouffer, S. A., et al. (1949). *The American Soldier*. Princeton, NJ: University of Princeton Press.

Teilhard de Chardin, P. (1971). *Christianity and Evolution*, trans. Rene Hague. London: Collins.

Veblen, T. (1962). *The Theory of the Leisure Class*. New York: Mentor.

16

The Knowledge of Death as a Stimulus to Creativity

JOHN D. MORGAN

Although we glibly use such phrases as "life and death decisions," fundamentally we know that there are none. Death always wins, always has the last word. The choices with which we are faced deal with death sooner or death later, but never life versus death. The realization of this fact reminds us of the limited control we have over life, and is the root of some answers to the problem of euthanasia.

There are many possible responses to the knowledge that death will end our lives and all our relationships. These responses can be, in general, divided into those that see death as a totally negative, meaningless intrusion into life, or as an opportunity to create meaning in our lives. If one can look at death, and continue to say that life is good, then death has not won. Life has won.

In this chapter I explore the relationship between creativity and the knowledge that our lives and our relationships will end in death. I believe that many people, perhaps in one way or another, most people, find meaning in their lives in spite of death. A few persons even take the opportunity to create something beautiful with their grief (Edwards 1993).

The Human Condition

Since at least the fifth century before the common era, philosophers have sought to understand what it is to be a human person, and having arrived at some tentative answers to that question, have asked what it is to be a good human person.

The terms *individual* and *person* are often interchanged in ordinary discourse, but if we are to gain some understanding of what it is to be a human person, it is essential to make an accurate distinction. *Individual* is a term from logic, the science of efficient reasoning. An individual refers to "one out of the many," that is, the individual is thought of as having no other important characteristics than those common to the whole (Reese 1980). The distinguishing specifics the individual *qua* individual might have are not considered. The computer on which I am working, an IBM Thinkpad type 2620-8yf, is no different from any other Thinkpad of that type. The individual characteristics that it might have, the amount of wear on the keys, the smudges on the cover, or more importantly, the data contained in RAM and ROM, do not change the fundamental makeup of the computer.

If we were content to define human persons as individuals, as philosophers did until fairly recently, and some continue to do, we would conclude that the human person is properly understood as a living, sensate, reasoning, valuing creature. A concomitant conclusion would be that life history and other personalizing characteristics, such as values and goals, disappointments and joys, beliefs and doubts are incidental, and do not fundamentally change the nature of what it is to be this human being, this person. We would think that the characteristics of persons are limited to the characteristics of the class, rather than resulting from personal life experiences.

The computer mentioned above is judged a "good" computer to the extent that it does what one expects of all computers, it stores and processes information effectively. The characteristics uniquely specific to it do not enter into the evaluation. In analogy to the computer, if a human person is fundamentally only "one of the many," then as long as one is living, sensing, reasoning, and evaluating, one has adequately achieved what life has to offer. The unique specifics are irrelevant.

It is precisely because we doubt that the human being is merely an individual that the term *person* is so important. A person, according to Boethius, a fourth century philosopher, is a unique substance of a rational nature (De Wulf 1953), that is, a unique source of knowing and valuing. Each person is a once-in-the-lifetime-of-the-universe event. It is precisely the specific knowledge one has gained, and the specific values asserted—life history—that constitute each of us as a person. In a word, we are our biographies, the sum total of the decisions we have made (Sartre 1957). This view of the person is reflected in such clinically successful treatment modalities as music or art therapy, and telling the story of one's life. One may be healed by putting together the pieces of one's life into a consistent whole.

Persons differ from other creatures in that they determine for themselves what evidence they take seriously, the goals toward which they strive, and the values to which they commit. We are told in the Hebrew Bible that God made persons in His image. In a sense this is a truism. Since whatever exists manifests some aspect that the Divine deemed to exist, everything is made in the image and likeness of God. When we say that persons are made in the image of God, however, we hold that persons not only share in God's act of existence, not only share in His living and sensing characteristics, but also share in His ability to understand and to set goals. Persons self-create values, deciding for themselves what the goals of life shall be (Aquinas 1265). They decide for themselves what kind of person they want to be and evaluate themselves in terms of the goals they set.

This self-creation of goals reflects human spirituality, that is, it comes from the ability to transcend the limits of a particular space and time. Spirituality is shown in many ways, but primarily in rational thinking, secondly in ethical activity, thirdly in religious consciousness, and fourthly in creativity. In rational thinking, the intellect moves from the concrete to the abstract. In ethical thinking, the person moves from the needs of the particular moment to more universal needs. In religion the person considers the "ground of all being" and considers the possibility of trying to establish a relationship with that ground. In creativity, perhaps the highest form of spirituality, the person transcends what is, to establish an imagined might be—to expand the universe. All of the above characteristics point to a quest for meaning, "the journey of the soul—not to religion itself but to the drive in humankind that gives rise to religion in the first place" (Fortunato 1987, p. 8). We are meaning-seeking beings.

Each moment of our lives demands a conscious awareness of who we are and who we want to be. We cannot not choose. Sartre (1957) reminds us that, "We are condemned to be free" (p. 23). Being a self-creating person is not easy for at least two reasons that interest us in this chapter: the first difficulty persons face is insecurity of choice, the second is the knowledge of death.

Choice

The first great challenge of life is the confrontation with freedom. "Once you pose the problem of what it means to be a person, even dumbly, weakly, or with a veneer of pride about your imagined difference from others, you may be in trouble" (Becker 1973, p. 24). The fact that persons are self-creating is a double-edged sword: the agony and ecstasy of being human. On the one hand, persons are not directed only by an in-built nature or genetic code; they have free will. This is the ecstasy. On the other hand, persons must take full responsibility for their own decisions and thus their own lives. They have no one to blame but themselves for their lives. This is the agony.

As Becker (1973) stated with his usual eloquence, "The fall into self-consciousness, the emergence from comfortable ignorance in nature, had one great penalty for man; it gave him *dread*, or anxiety" (p. 69). It is precisely because self-creation demands so much attention and is a risk, that much of the human race chooses a form of slavery—to political or religious ideologies or to consumerism. While the approach of "slavery" is safe, what it misses is the daring to make a contribution with one's ephemerality, either through those great deeds recorded in history, or simply through a commitment to one's family, community, or profession.

If persons are fundamentally self-creative, we must ask why it is so difficult to achieve what Maslow spoke of as actualizing one's full human-ity. If there is a natural urge to do so, why is it so difficult? Maslow believes that "We fear our highest possibility (as well as our lowest ones). We are generally afraid to become that which we can glimpse in our most perfect moments" (Becker 1973, p. 48). Becker takes this a step further and holds that we fear our highest possibilities because of our terror of death.

Death

In spite of the achievements since the 1950s, ours are still death-denying cultures accentuated by four centuries of scientific thought and the materialism of the twentieth century. Wandering through the Vatican Museum, the Hermitage, the Louvre, or the Metropolitan Museum of Art, one is struck by how few paintings depict this central fact of life, that all life ends in death—"the collapse of personal time and space" (Flynn 1987, p. 200)—and all human relationships are limited. Deaths are often de-picted in the visual arts, in opera, or in popular music, but prior to our own times they were usually the deaths of political or religious person-ages. Perhaps the saddest part of our culture is the lack of heroes we deem important enough to memorialize. Rarely, outside of Pieta-type expositions, is grief depicted at all. Philosophy and theology have tradi-tionally examined questions of death, but rarely grief, and the impact that philosophy and theology have on the culture at large is minimal. The social sciences are no more helpful. In a recent article, Robert Kasten-baum (1993) stated that, "Basically, one could have subtracted dying, death, and grief from human experience and it would have made little difference to the studies, texts, and courses promulgated by the social and behavioral sciences until the last few years" (p. 79). He indicates that the dominant attitude of our culture is that "Death is for losers" (p. 78). We continue to find ourselves in a situation in which "we manage to avoid thinking about a highly emotionally charged event that has a 100 per-cent chance of occurring" (Goodman 1981, p. 7).

Herman Feifel (1990), in his usual brilliant synthesis, has pointed out the historical and cultural antecedents of our condition:

We witnessed a shift from spiritual mastery over self to physical conquest of nature. A major consequence was that we became impoverished in possessing religious or philosophic conceptual creeds, except nominally, with which to transcend death. Death became a "wall" rather than a "doorway." A taboo of considerable measure was placed on death and bereaved persons. Death and its concomitants were sundered off, isolated, and permitted into society only after being properly decontaminated. In this context, further circumstances making the area uncomfortable to deal with were (a) an expanding industrial, impersonal technology that steadily increased fragmentation of the family and dismantled rooted neighborhoods and kinship groups with more or less homogeneous values . . . thus depriving us of emotional and social supports with which to cushion the impact of death when it intruded into our lives; (b) a spreading deritualization of grief, related to criticism of funerary practices as being overly expansive, baroque, and exploitive of the mourner's emotions; (c) a gradual expulsion of death from everyday common experience; death has developed into a mystery for many people, increasingly representing a fear of the unknown, and has become the province of the "professional," whose mastery, unfortunately, is more technical than human these days; and (d) in a modern society that has emphasized achievement, productivity, and the future, the prospect of no future at all, and loss of identity, has become an abomination. Hence, death and mourning have invited our hostility and repudiation. [p. 537]

Death teaches us the absolute limits of life as we know it. Sickness is an "uncovering of the limitations and fragility of our earthly condition" (Lepargneur 1974, p. 91). Personal disasters such as the death of a child or a spouse end the feelings of security with which we may have grown. Fundamental assumptions in life are overthrown. Beliefs about the justice and orderliness of the universe are challenged and what remains is the feeling of helplessness (Kleber and Blom 1988). A Trappist monk in Utah, while showing me the monastery cemetery as part of the tour of the monastery, said, "One does not have their feet on the ground, until they have put someone into it." This confrontation with death forces us to accept the basic limits of life and love.

What is perhaps most important, however, is that from death we learn to distrust that physical forces constitute the essential part of what it is to be a human being. "The biological forces indeed make a fine animal, but there is something else in man, something that cannot be mistaken for natural forces" (Lepargneur 1974, p. 95). We are spiritual, meaning-creating beings. Joseph Campbell (1972) believes that the realization of personal death is *the* differentiating characteristic of humans.

> If a *differentiating* feature is to be named, separating human from ani-
> mal psychology, it is surely this subordination in the human sphere
> of even economics to mythology. And if one should ask why or how
> any such unsubstantial impulsion ever should have become dominant
> in the ordering of physical life, the answer is that in this wonderful
> human brain of ours there has dawned a realization unknown to the
> other primates. It is that of the individual, conscious of himself, and
> aware that he, and all that he cares for, will one day die. [p. 22]

Personal death has had several major depictions over the centuries.
For some of our ancestors, it was the dropping-in of an expected neighbor; for others, the last act of a personal drama; for others yet, the end
of a relationship. For those who live in an achievement-oriented culture,
as we presently do, it is consummate failure (Ariès 1981). Whatever else
it may be, for us all it is absolute loneliness. "All the masks must fall, all
roles too must come to an end; all the parts that man plays before the
world and before himself" (Boros 1973, p. 165).

> I have now become finally alone. Alone as never before in my life. The
> loved ones around me have to look on, inactive and powerless, while
> I am being driven into an inescapable whirlpool of solitude. Snatched
> away from unrelieved loneliness, departed to the further outposts of
> the world. This is what dying means. I can no longer even cry for help.
> I am powerless, bewildered, helpless as a child confined in a dark
> place. I have been hurled into the great grey mist of infinite distance,
> into unmoving, muted, silent helplessness. [Boros 1973, p. 175]

Coping with the Human Condition

Ernest Becker believes that there are three fundamental responses
to the finality of death. The first, the most typical of our culture, is to
deny the reality of death, to act as though it won't happen or that it is
not important. The great medieval Italian poet Dante might refer to those
who live this way, because they never threw themselves into life, as ones
who were never alive (Trilling 1967a,b). The second response is that of
mental illness, to become so engaged with death that one refuses to "play
the games of society." According to Berdyaev (1964), Dostoevsky teaches
us that, "For the deeps of human nature are sounded not in sanity but in
insanity, not in law-abidingness but in criminality, in obscure unconscious
tendencies and not in daily life and in the parts of the soul that have been
enlightened by the daylight of consciousness" (pp. 21–22).

The third response is heroism, to realize that since no one can do
more than nature already has done—cut life short—then there is nothing to lose by being a hero, by living as fully as possible. We learn from

Don Quixote that death is, "the great reality, the triumphant enemy of all illusion" (Priestly 1960, p. 49). No longer having illusions about the temporal nature of life, the hero realizes the possibilities of creating a greater level of human achievement, who leaves behind "something that heightens life and testifies to the worthwhileness of existence" (Keen 1974, p. 299). The hero is the one who realizes that an awareness of death enhances life.

Creativity

> [Art] must confront and reflect not only reality at its most painful, but at its most beautiful and meaningful as well. It must, in other words, present evidence of a transcendence over chaos and despair.
> [Theodore Wolff, in Mitchell 1990, p. 59]

Creativity: What Is It

Aristotle pointed out twenty-five centuries ago that art does not deal with theory but with action. The human mind functions in two radically different ways. The "speculative intellect" knows simply for the sake of knowing. "All men by nature desire to know" (Aristotle 335 B.C., p. 689). In addition to this speculative function, the human mind knows for the sake of production. This productive function is known as "practical intellect" (Maritain 1953, p. 45). Practical intellect concerns itself with two basic areas, the production of human actions to be done (moral activity or the virtue of prudence), and the production of works to be made (art). Prudence deals with the development of a good person, art deals with the development of a good product.

There are different types of art, the "right way of doing something" (Aristotle 320 B.C., p. 1026). The arts have been traditionally divided into the servile arts, the liberal arts, and the fine arts. In the servile arts, the only purpose is the production of something useful (boiled water, a clean floor, a clean desk). In the liberal arts, the purpose is the production of a disciplined or liberated (from prejudice) mind. The fine arts differ from servile arts or even the liberal arts, in that they create products, but not "mere products," the products that the arts produce embody a vision.

Creativity is a power of engendering, of producing, not simply reproducing what was already there, but in bringing into existence what has yet to be. Creativity can be defined as a "unique mental process leading to the expansion of experienced reality beyond the already established categorization and classification of it" (Havelka 1986, p. 156). It is a uniquely human gift; not part of the material world, but "a privilege of spiritual organisms" (Maritain 1953, p. 56). Essentially, creativity is an urge to expand in every dimension of being meaningfully alive. Every person desires to be creative, to fulfill the need to form, shape, and express deep feeling (Mitchell 1990). As is seen in the clinical setting of a hospice, the mastering of new skills or the readaptation of old ones has a positive effect: "It is tangible proof that one is still alive and learning" (Melendez 1990, p. 41).

Creativity expands reality by taking the imagined awareness of the human mind and producing it externally. Reality is expanded by the external expression of the internal vision (Havelka 1986). This vision is what Maritain (1953) refers to as "poetic intuition, a musical stir, an unformulated song, with no words, no sounds, absolutely inaudible to the ear, audible only to the heart" (p. 301). This is the "truth" that the creative person wishes to produce. "The fine arts are constituted by the intellect's need to produce externally what is grasped within itself in creative intuition, and to manifest it in beauty, is simply the essential thing in the fine arts" (p. 56). By this process the human person is liberated from the strictures of reality and has the ability to transform reality and control it.

Creativity: Why Is It?

Most of the time, we use length of years as the criterion of the appropriateness of a death, thinking that one should die in advanced age. Correspondingly, we determine that a death is "natural" when it occurs because physical functions fail, regardless of the individual's state of fulfillment at the time (Goodman 1981). For Jung, however, the ultimate aim of life is development and integration of each system and function of personality. A "natural" death, an "appropriate death" would occur when one has reached wholeness, completeness, and self-realization, when all potentialities are actualized and integrated. A premature death would not be determined by length of years but by the incomplete actualization of a person's life. This is confirmed by life-review studies of old or terminally ill patients that show that if a person looks on the past in despair, feeling that life has been wasted, s/he finds it difficult to come to terms with death.

If physical survival were to be the same as actualization of potential, our orientation toward life and attitudes toward death would be fundamentally different. An ideal outcome of life should be the coincidence of the meaning of the words—"His work is done"—for the dying patient and the community. The patient should be "ready to go," when at the same time the community, the physician, has done his best to facilitate a dignified and meaningful death (Parsons et al. 1973). If Jung is correct, the deaths of most men and women today are *"almost always* premature" (Goodman 1981, p. 14). As Sam Keen (1991) said, "Content-ment is probably the rarest of all human virtues. No matter how much we have, few of us are satisfied. We always want more" (p. 122).

Creative persons seem to be satisfied with their lives and its de-mands. The pianist Beveridge Webster states "It never felt like making sacrifices" (in Goodman 1981, p. 48); the actress Eva Le Gallienne adds, "My profession has been the passion of my life" (in Goodman 1981, p. 58). Keen (1991) tells us, "The enlightened person, according to Zen Buddhism, has learned the true miracle of human consciousness—to be satisfied with what is given. The master of everyday life eats when he eats and sleeps when he sleeps and is content" (p. 124). The Irish play-wright George Bernard Shaw says:

> This is the true joy in life, the being used for a purpose recognized by yourself as a mighty one; the being thoroughly worn out before you are thrown on the scrap heap; the being a force of Nature instead of a feverish selfish little clod of ailments and grievances complaining that the world will not devote itself to making you happy. [in Larson 1993, p. 2]

Is it death of which we are afraid or the incompleteness of life? "Once one has succeeded in reaching self-fulfillment by giving form to all the latent possibilities within, death no longer presents a threat: one has won the race with death (Goodman 1981, p. xi). In a series of interviews con-ducted with twenty-three highly creative persons, eleven from the arts and twelve from the sciences, Goodman heard more concern about dying prematurely than about dying. Dying prematurely was defined as dying before one's psychological needs were satisfied. Rather, the cre-ative person is future oriented, rather than present oriented or past ori-ented. "One lives on one's hopes! I am always contemplating, always planning long in advance" (pp. 88–89). What seems to be important for creativity is a different orientation to one's time span. Creativity demands more than a mere long life.

A creative person's orientation to time differs from that of less cre-ative persons. George Bernard Shaw tells us, "Life is no brief candle to me. It is a sort of splendid torch which I have got hold of for the moment, and I want to make it burn as brightly as possible before handing it on to future generations" (in Larson 1993, p. 2). The creative person seems to have little concern with the past and seems to be almost exclusively present or future oriented. The violinist Nathan Milstein says, "Present and future [are important]. Living is important" (in Goodman 1981, p. 39); actor Alan Arkin adds, "Since I have done 'my thing' I am no longer afraid of death" (p. 56). The violinist Isaac Stern says basically the same thing:

"Happily, in the interpretive search there is never an end" (p. 45). Sam Keen (1990), who combines philosophical analysis with his own creative writing, says, "The creative personality is one who is totally here—now, one who lives without future or past" (p. 25). This future concern of creative people does not seem to extend to some far distant future of fifty or one hundred years. The artists and scientists that Goodman interviewed were concerned about accomplishing what they needed to accomplish but were not interested in seeing the effects of it in some remote future.

Some creative persons are explicit about the effect of the awareness of death on their lives. The tenor Luciano Pavarotti (1981) believes that witnessing the execution of members of the Resistance in the Second World War had a great effect on his life. The effect was so great that it is mentioned in the first few pages of his autobiography.

> This was the most important effect the war had on me. Twice during my life I have come very close to death myself. These two experiences—one, an illness when I was twelve, the other, a plane accident just a few years ago—reinforced my reverence for life, my feeling of how precious it is. [p. 13]

Rainer-Maria Rilke warns us not to believe that an author leads an untroubled life, rather, "His life has much difficulty and sorrow and remains far beyond yours. Were it not otherwise, he would never have been able to find those words" (in Larson 1993, p. 138).

We rely on commentaries for the death awareness of other creative persons. Trilling (1967a) believes that these lines from Chekhov's *The Three Sisters* reflect the writer's own concern with death, 'Where has it all gone? Where is it? . . . life's slipping by, and it will never, never return'" (p. 254). "And when Chekhov wrote that 'it will be winter soon, and everything will be covered with snow,' he may well have wished to suggest that in the cycle of seasons the spring will follow and that, sad as we may be over what befalls ourselves and others, life itself is to be celebrated" (p. 255). Trilling (1967a) also believes that Tolstoy's *The Death of Ivan Ilyich* was written for Tolstoy's religious purposes, "for religion often tries to put us in mind of the actuality of death, not in its terrors, to be sure, but in its inevitability, seeking thus to press upon us the understanding that the life of this world is not the sum of existence and not even its most valuable part" (p. 525). The musicologist George Martin (1979) believes that Verdi's operas were almost all responses to death. "Life, [Verdi] suggests, is hard, happiness fleeting, and death the only certainty. He never pretends in his call for generous, noble action that these do not often end in suffering, but offers them as the best response to death" (p. 41).

The symbolic nature of art allows the person to do several things that are more difficult to do from the standpoint of ordinary thinking and acting. First of all, the languages we speak are already structured before we learn them. We inherit other persons' categories (Goodman 1981). The arts, but perhaps especially music, allows us to bypass the limits of language (Ross and Pollio 1991, Salmon 1993). Logical thought processes are, by their very nature, objective, that is, they separate out the personal issues of the thinker from the data being considered. The arts demand no such separation and allow people to "live their questions" (Rilke, in Bailey 1990b, p. 85). The arts also allow the person to express insights that would be too conflicted or too emotionally demanding to be expressed logically (Wald 1990). Norman Cousins (1979) writes that we read in *Dr. Zhivago*, "Your health is bound to be affected if, day after day, you say the opposite of what you feel, if you grovel before what you dislike and rejoice at what brings you nothing but misfortune" (pp. 65–66). "A culture that reveres life maintains its myths and symbols; without them, we dehumanize the life we live" (Hammerschlag 1993, p. 21).

Art is therapy in that it facilitates healing by putting us in touch with the basic issues of life. This is obviously true in such treatment modalities as art and music therapy. "The arts help us to keep our imaginations alive and our connection to the earth and created order of the universe" (Bailey 1990a, p. 17). Wald (1990) tells us, "Engaging in an arts experience can serve to create a sense of integration and community that bridges cultural, religious and racial divisions" (p. 18). Porchet-Munro (1993) believes that the effectiveness of art therapy results from the fundamental healing nature of music. Salmon (1993) adds that the music that a dying or grieving person chooses reflects the particular concerns of the person at the time. In other words, the music is chosen precisely for the purpose of healing.

Music as therapy might be considered a placebo, but placebos work, as Cousins tells us, because of the fundamental will to live. Cousins quotes the physician-organist-author-missionary Albert Schweitzer: "'The witch doctor succeeds for the same reason all the rest of us succeed. Each patient carries his own doctor inside him. They come to us not knowing that truth. We are at our best when we give the doctor who resides within each patient a chance to go to work'" (p. 69). On the basis of his living for a time with the cellist Pablo Casals and with Schweitzer, Cousins says, "What I learned from these two men had a profound effect on my life— especially during the period of my illness. I learned that a highly developed purpose and the will to live are among the prime raw materials of human existence" (pp. 71–72).

More fundamentally the arts heal because they give a reason for living (Porchet-Munro 1993). Creation frees the person from the arbitrary limits culture imposes (Becker 1973, Campbell 1972, Havelka 1986).

> On those rare occasions when I allow myself to think about death, The Terror rises from the pit of my stomach to my throat. How can the universe be designed so that I am to be eradicated? The thought fills me with anger, rage, defiance. And then I get back to work polishing a project that will create a sea wall against the tide of death. I secretly feel a mixture of grief and relief when someone I know dies, because I am still alive. Thus far I have escaped; therefore, I must be special, perhaps even immune to mortality. I know that it's not rational. [Keen 1991, p. 102]

Do we back into death afraid to face it, or do we face it and live in spite of it? We tend to value what we cannot have or whatever is in short supply. If there would always be a tomorrow, if we didn't take seriously that every good-bye could be forever, our only goal would be the satisfaction of immediate needs, as we witness on the animal level. Death, understood to be loss, or fear of loss, naturally causes distress. We create to counteract that distress. On the most basic level the person works actively against its own fragility by seeking to expand and perpetuate itself; instead of shrinking, the person moves toward more life (Becker 1973). Culture is what human beings of all times do to challenge death (Havelka 1986). Perhaps the noblest human characteristic is our desire to challenge destiny, and fight against extinction. The very source of all our endeavors has always been to conquer death, "though it is a goal that probably cannot and should not ever be reached" (Goodman 1981, p. 6).

Energy can be produced only when systems are in imbalance. Artistic creations are examples of sublimated energy. The creative process is a blend of two elements; the overwhelming awareness of death, and the confrontation of our own possibilities, what Havelka (1986) calls "the Holy" (p. 160). Facing death creatively releases energy. A set of keys resting on a table or a battery in complete balance produce no energy. In the words of the Spanish philosopher Ortega y Gasset (1956), each of us is a "radical solitude" (p. 153). At the root of each of us is an incommunicability—a solitude—that no one else can penetrate. This solitude causes us anxieties about who we are and what we should be doing with our lives. It is precisely our anxieties, our confusions, our weakness that are the causes of creativity. The lack of balance of our lives gives us the energy to do something creative with our lives. The violinist Nathan Milstein says, "Satisfied with what I have done so far, yes. But 'fulfilled' is not the correct word. . . . I don't feel I have reached the peak" (in

Goodman 1981, p. 39). Pianist Vladimir Ashkenazy adds, "I am satisfied with the kind of life I am leading, that is, with my whole life-style—I am doing what I want to do professionally—and with my personal life, my children, my wife. But feeling fulfilled? No—that would be the end; I would be finished" (p. 52).

A creative life is a quest for "salvation." Meaningfulness is created intentionally, "Such intentionality, as Rollo May correctly notices, is life's organized patterning which gives meaning to our experience. We intend *to be* to such an extent that the fear of non-being weakens" (Havelka 1986, p. 155). Keen (1990) states, "There are so many lives I want to live, so many styles I want to inhabit" (p. 119). The philosopher Nicholas Berdyaev (1964) believes that all Russian writers, but especially Dostoevsky, writes for "salvation" (p. 30). Campbell (1972) says that the need to transcend human mortality is the first great impetus to mythology. Trilling (1967b) reminds us, however, that even the great writers treat death in a manner that limits its fearsomeness. The scientist Albert Einstein states his view of human fate:

> How extraordinary is the situation of us mortals! Each of us is here for a brief sojourn; for what purpose he knows not, though he sometimes thinks he senses it. But without going deeper than our daily life, it is plain that we exist for our fellow men—in the first place for those upon whose smiles and welfare all our happiness depends, and next for all those unknown to us personally but to whose destinies we are bound by the tie of sympathy. [In Larson 1993, p. 228]

Creative people do fear death, but deal with it in a different manner (Goodman 1981). As meaning seeking, self-creative beings, each human life is a compromise between what is and what might have been, "an intermediate state between the fullness of ideal life and death" (Lepargneur 1974, p. 91). Becker (1973) reinterprets Freud's Oedipus complex to "the Oedipal *project*, a project that sums up the basic problems of the child's life: whether he will be a passive object of fate, an appendage of others, a plaything of the world or whether he will be an active center within himself—whether he will control his own destiny with his own powers or not" (pp. 35–36). The question that each person must ask is the same: Are we playthings of the gods, or do we take our fate in our hands? The response of creativity is to create so as to perpetuate oneself.

What seems to be necessary for a meaningful life is neither refusal to accept death nor acceptance pure and simple, but a "synthesis of revolt and acceptance" (Lepargneur 1974, p. 97). The more positively one evaluates life, the more positively one tends to evaluate death; the less positively one views life, the more negatively one views death (Goodman 1981). An acknowledgment of our finiteness intensifies our awareness of life and acts as a force, propelling us toward the realization of talents or desires. We become free to open ourselves widely and boldly to experience and are exempted from oppressive anxieties about death (Havelka 1986). By transforming death into a product of our own creation, we gain some control over it. It is a way of doing actively what otherwise we would suffer passively. We intend *to be* to such an extent that the fear of non-being weakens. Freedom to act as one desires is possible only with control over one's resources and the ability to channel one's energy in the direction one chooses. The experience of creation can help to restore meaning to the lives of persons who, through illness, have felt a lack of self-worth (Bailey 1990b). The fear of death can be conquered by reaching self-fulfillment and, as a consequence, experiencing life completely. Those who are the least apprehensive of death seem to be free to explore vaster, unfamiliar time regions and can therefore project their needs, wishes, thoughts, and when applicable, their own person into the far distant future as well as extend themselves backward in the distant past (Goodman 1981).

Conclusion

Aristotle (320 B.C.) reminds us that we ought not seek for more precision than is possible in a given investigation. Not all areas of human concern are open to the same precision. When dealing with fundamental realities, we must do the best we can while continually striving for exactitude.

The most important reality human beings must deal with is mortality and death. Whether this topic is approached from the perspective of medicine, psychology, religion, philosophy, music, or poetry, death is often described in terms of figurative images or phrases. Unlike language, the arts have the potential to express diverse themes simultaneously. Through the arts, one can confront life and death on many levels at once. By engaging in an experience in the arts, people can be assisted as they mourn, grieve, celebrate life; they can overcome fragmentation, and find a sense of meaning in their lives. Because the arts are regenerators of the body, mind, emotions, and spirit, persons can be enabled to live more fully while they are dying and grieving.

Becker (1973) believes that culture is a hope that the things that individuals create will outlive death, "that the person and his products count" (p. 5). In the same vein, the ethician Daniel Callahan (1993) says that death becomes acceptable when it comes at the point when there is a good fit between the biological inevitability of death in general and the particular timing and circumstances of that death in the life of the individual. The achievement of such a peaceful death should be the goal of life, and therefore of medicine. "The process of dying is deformed when it is extended unduly by medical interventions or when there is an extended period of loss of consciousness well before one is actually dead" (p. 189). We are, in the words of the philosopher-writer Sam Keen (1990), part of an evolving cosmic adventure. "Nature-God-Life intends something through you" (p. 45). The universe has not come ready-made from the hands of God. Each person completes his/her destiny by creating, by embodying the vision that they have produced. This is both the cause and the effect of creativity.

References

Aquinas, T. (1265). *Summa Theologica*. Part I, Question LXXXIII, Article 1. In *Basic Writings of Saint Thomas Aquinas*, ed. A. Pegis, pp. 786–792. New York: Random House, 1944.

Ariès, P. (1981). *The Hour of Our Death*. New York: Knopf.

Aristotle (335 B.C.). Metaphysics. In *The Basic Works of Aristotle*, ed. R. J. McKeon, pp. 689–926. New York: Random House, 1941.

——— (320 B.C.). Nicomachean ethics. In *The Basic Works of Aristotle*, ed. R. J. McKeon, pp. 935–1112. New York: Random House, 1941.

Bailey, S. S. (1990a). Introduction. In *Creativity and the Close of Life*, ed. S. S. Bailey, M. M. Bridgeman, D. Falkner, et al., pp. 17–30. Brantford, CT: Connecticut Hospice.

——— (1990b). Music. In *Creativity and the Close of Life*, ed. S. S. Bailey, M. M. Bridgeman, D. Falkner, et al., pp. 75–89. Brantford, CT: Connecticut Hospice.

Becker, E. (1973). *The Denial of Death*. New York: Free Press.

Berdyaev, N. (1964). *Dostoevsky*. Cleveland: Meridian.

Boros, L. (1973). Death: a theological reflection. In *The Mystery of Suffering and Death*, ed. M. J. Taylor, pp. 161–178. Staten Island, NY: Alba House.

Callahan, D. (1993). *The Troubled Dream of Life*. New York: Simon & Schuster.

Campbell, J. (1972). *Myths to Live By*. New York: Viking.

Cousins, N. (1979). *Anatomy of an Illness*. New York: Norton.

De Wulf, M. (1953). *Philosophy and Civilization in the Middle Ages*. New York: Dover.

Edwards, D. (1993). Grieving: The pain and the promise. In. *Personal Care in an Impersonal World*, ed. J. D. Morgan, pp. 39–72. Amityville, NY: Baywood.

Feifel, H. (1990). Psychology and death: meaningful rediscovery. *American Psychologist* 45(4):537–543.

Flynn, T. (1987). Dying as doing: philosophical thoughts on death and authenticity. In *Thanatology: A Liberal Arts Approach*, ed. M. A. Morgan and J. D. Morgan, pp. 199–206. London, Ontario: King's.

Fortunato, J. (1987). *AIDS: The Spiritual Dilemma*. San Francisco: Harper & Row.

Goodman, L. (1981). *Death and the Creative Life*. New York: Springer.

Hammerschlag, C. A. (1993). *The Theft of the Spirit*. New York: Simon & Schuster.

Havelka, J. (1986). Creativity and death. In *Thanatology: A Liberal Arts Approach*, ed. M. A. Morgan and J. D. Morgan, pp. 155–162. London, Ontario: King's.

Kastenbaum, R. (1993). Reconstructing death in postmodern society. *Omega* 27(1):75–89.

Keen, S. (1974). The heroics of everyday life: a theorist confronts his own end. *Psychology Today*, April, pp. 298–305.

——— (1990). *To a Dancing God*. New York: HarperCollins.

——— (1991). *Faces of the Enemy*. New York: HarperCollins.

Kleber, R. J., and Blom, D. (1988). Psychotherapy and pathological grief: 1. The search for meaning. In *Grief and Bereavement in Contemporary Society: Volume Two: Counseling and Therapy*, ed. E. Chiger, pp. 59–70. London: Freund.

Larson, D. (1993). *The Helper's Journey: Working with People Facing Grief, Loss, and Life-Threatening Illness*. Champaign, IL: Research.

Lepargneur, F. H. (1974). Sickness in Christian anthropology. In *The Mystery of Suffering and Death*, ed. M. J. Taylor, pp. 91–100. Garden City, NY: Doubleday.

Maritain, J. (1953). *Creative Intuition in Art and Poetry*. New York: Pantheon.

Martin, G. (1979). Verdi and *Risorgimento*. In *The Verdi Companion*, ed. W. Weaver and M. Chusid, pp. 13–41. New York: Norton.

Melendez, B. S. (1990). Fabric arts. In *Creativity and the Close of Life*, pp. 35–50. Brantford, CT: Connecticut Hospice.

Mitchell, H. (1990). Visual arts. In *Creativity and the Close of Life*, ed. S. Bailey et al., pp. 53–59. Brantford, CT: Connecticut Hospice.

Ortega y Gasset, J. (1956). In search of Goethe from within. In *The Dehumanization of Art and Other Writings on Art and Culture*, ed. J. Ortega y Gasset, pp. 123–160. Garden City, NY: Doubleday.

Parsons, T., Fox, R. C., and Lidz, V. M. (1973). The "gift" of life. In *Death in American Experience*, ed. A. Mack, pp. 1–49. New York: Schocken.

Pavarotti, L. (1981). *Pavarotti: My Own Story*. Garden City, NY: Doubleday.

Porchet-Munro, S. (1993). Music therapy perspectives in palliative care education. *Journal of Palliative Care* 9(4):39–42.

Priestly, J. B. (1960). *Literature and Western Man*. New York: Harper & Brothers.

Reese, W. L. (1980). *Dictionary of Philosophy and Religion*. Atlantic Highlands, NJ: Humanities.

Ross, L. M., and Pollio, H. R. (1991). Metaphors of death: a thematic analysis of personal meanings. *Omega: Journal on Death and Dying* 23(4):291–307.

Salmon, D. (1993). Music and emotion in palliative care. *Journal of Palliative Care* 9(4): 48–52

Sartre, J. P. (1957). *Existentialism and Human Emotions*, trans. B. Frechtman. New York: Philosophical Library.

Trilling, L. (1967a). Commentary on Chekhov's "Three Sisters." In *The Experience of Literature*, ed. L. Trilling, pp. 250–255. Garden City, NY: Doubleday.

——— (1967b). Commentary on Tolstoy's *Death of Ivan Ilyich*. In *The Experience of Literature*, ed. L. Trilling, pp. 525–527. Garden City, NY: Doubleday.

Wald, F. (1990). Foreword. In *Creativity and the Close of Life*, ed. S. Bailey et al. New Haven, CT: Connecticut Hospice.

17

What Is the Future of Death?

ROBERT KASTENBAUM

Go and catch a falling star,
Get with child a mandrake root,
Tell me where all past years are,
Or who cleft the Devil's foot. . . .

John Donne

To John Donne's daunting list of challenges we might add the question before us here. Most of us have difficulty enough in coping with the deaths that have already intersected our personal lives and with those that move along with us like companionate shadows awaiting their moment. It could be an exercise in futility to probe the future of death writ large. The question might far exceed the reach of the human mind. Furthermore, even if we did manage to come up with an answer it might not be to our liking.

And yet, didn't Herman Feifel (1959) also encounter doubt and anxiety when he proposed that we consider *The Meaning of Death*? The resulting dialogue and inquiry has not resolved all the questions, but it has helped us to mature as individuals and as a society. Some people needed only encouragement and guidance to break through the taboo against honest communication about death. Others continue to struggle with the challenge. Still others have taken consequential action; the development of the hospice movement, peer support groups, and death education have benefited from the dialogue opened by Feifel.

Once opened, the dialogue cannot be assigned arbitrary boundaries. It would not be credible to insist that we are entitled to explore better ways to assist those who are dying or grieving, but that we must not attempt to fathom death. Our minds don't work that way. For better or worse, we are members of a species that generates questions, enjoys riddles, and longs to discover what is on the other side of the mountain. We do not always answer these questions, solve these riddles, or relish what we encounter in our adventurings. Nevertheless, the uncertain outcome of an inquiry has seldom stopped us for long—unless we have stopped ourselves in fear.

Let us then consider the future of death without the burden of either undue optimism or pessimism about the outcome of these considerations. Humankind's past and present encounters with death will provide an instructive, if imperfect guide to our explorations of the future.

Perspectives on the Future of Death

The future of death can be viewed within multiple frames of reference or perspectives. We will identify and discuss briefly death as conceived through four of these perspectives: (1) numerical operations, (2) predetermination or programming, (3) cosmic destiny, and (4) symbolic interactionism. Because this survey will take us in several directions the reader may at times feel rather far from home. A little adventuring is necessary, however, if we are eventually to examine our relationships to death in a comprehensive manner.

Death by the Numbers

There is at least one thing we know what to do with deaths. We can count them. In fact, we count deaths with such diligence that we might even persuade ourselves that all these numbers add up to knowledge of death. If we are content with representing death by numbers, then our task will be a good deal easier. Some answers are already available; others can be obtained through familiar statistical methods.

Projecting the future of death is an activity that is carried out routinely by experts in population statistics as well as social and political scientists. These projections are based on existing data patterns. For example, the number and rate of deaths expected from smoking-related disorders a decade from now can be estimated from time-trend information that is already available. It is true that all estimates involve a set of assumptions and that these assumptions might prove to be mistaken or be overwhelmed by unexpected developments. Nevertheless, the methodology is straightforward and the results often considered useful by policy makers in many fields (such as public health).

Allowing for a variable margin of error, then, some of the questions we might raise about the future of death could be answered by using accepted methods of obtaining, classifying, arraying, and interpreting statistical data. Here are a few examples:

- Will the overall mortality rate for the United States (or any other specified population) be lower ten years from now? Fifty years from now?
- Will the present gender gap in life expectancy decrease or increase over the next twenty years?
- Will the proportion of total deaths that can be attributed to lifestyle or behavioral choices continue to increase over the next decade?

These typical questions focus on the relatively near future. It is within a limited temporal framework that most of our mortality-related predictions are made and in which they might be expected to be most accurate. The further into the future we project, the more we are subject to unexpected, possibly unique developments. A major volcanic eruption could affect crops and health on a global basis. A disease even more virulent and transmissible than AIDS could appear on the scene. A nuclear accident—or incident—could cause unprecedented loss of life. The mega-earthquake that has been predicted for California might actually occur and have effects that we can scarcely imagine. Our ability to project mortality trends is limited by the possibility of "unscheduled" events whose timing, scope, and consequences also cannot be predicted with confidence.

These questions also share two other characteristics: no attempt to discover the nature of death, and no attempt to discover the meanings associated with death.

Our questions about the future of death are most likely to receive accurate answers, then, if these questions require only quantitative responses and are limited to the near future (the next few generations). The fact that only a restricted range of questions is answerable by statistical operations does not make this a negligible approach. From the health care perspective it is valuable to identify emerging threats and to evaluate prevention programs. From the public policy standpoint it is valuable in decision making about the distribution of resources. From the industrial-commercial standpoint it is valuable to anticipate demographic changes that are related to trends in mortality rates by age, gender, and race.

Nevertheless, we cannot expect statistical operations to answer all the questions that might be raised about the future of death. What we do with numbers, no matter how skillfully, will not touch the most far-reaching questions, such as: Will there always be death? Will death always be what death has been? Will death become something different if our ideas about life and death change? Will death mean or even become something different if the sociotechnological conditions of life change radically? Will every life form have the same death? All these questions are beset with ambiguities and other semantic complications. They should be analyzed and refined as part of a thoroughgoing inquiry process. Even in rough form, however, this set of questions obviously inhabits a different frame of reference than those that are amenable to answer through statistical operations.

A person who trusts only quantitative methods might be inclined to conclude that all the above questions are invalid. If we cannot answer a question by logico-mathematical operations, then the question itself is meaningless. This type of thinking was fairly prevalent in the heyday of logical positivism and is not without its adherents today. Those who place their faith entirely in logico-mathematical operations might opt at this point to dispense with our larger inquiry into the future of death. Perhaps, though, they will stay with us long enough at least to reconsider the appropriateness and validity of logico-mathematical operations when applied to the study of death.

What Logico-Mathematical Operations Are Valid for Studying Death?

Doing death by the numbers requires assumptions about the kind of logico-mathematical operations that are appropriate for this purpose. Perhaps the most important choice-point here is whether or not death requires special treatment. This statement might strike the reader as peculiar. We are accustomed to thinking of numbers as numbers, regardless of their substantive characteristics. Two and two make four, whether we are dealing with cabbages or kings. Why should an exception be made for death? A brief consideration of this question will help us to see what we are up against in our attempt to project the future of death. For the moment I will exclude the ongoing controversies regarding the status of people in persistent vegetative states and other conditions that seem to be on the borderlines of life and death; otherwise we would be venturing beyond the domain of traditional mathematical and statistical operations.

The basic paradigm for quantified death might be described as the digital *either-or*. A person is either alive *or* dead. A nerve fiber is either responding *or* not responding to a stimulus. A light switch is either on *or* off. At any moment of observation, the person, nerve fiber, and light switch will exhibit one of two possible conditions. The digital processing that is utilized by computer-based operations provides a convenient model for construing death. Each data point in a set, then, will read either 1 or 0. It is our choice whether we want to code "alive" as 1 and "dead" as 0 or vice versa.

Valid statistical operations on alive/dead status therefore must follow the rules that are appropriate for discrete variables. It would be an error to treat death as we do continuous variables such as age, height, and weight. From this standpoint, then, death is not unique, but it does belong to a subset of variables whose statistical description and manipulation are governed by the applicable rules. (Sex would be another variable within this subset.)

In comparing two population samples, we probably would not say, "Group A is older, shorter, thinner, and deader than group B." There is some likelihood of making an error of this kind, however, when the data become more complex, and our alertness has been dulled by the relentless proliferation of numbers. Attempts to project the future of death are likely to involve many variables and yield a large harvest of numbers at multiple levels of analysis. One can then miss the point that death is fundamentally different from many of the variables with which it has been associated.

A second problem arises when we turn our attention to the "ownership" and "size" of death. Is death somehow transferable—in a logico-mathematical sense—from one individual to another? We can say that person A is dead. We can say that person B is also dead. We can say that there are two dead people. These statements are well within the bounds of reason. It is here we must catch ourselves, though. Do we want to say that death has somehow been magnified by the fact that there are two dead people instead of just one? Is death twice as deathly? Twice as large? Or must death be regarded solely as a state (nonstate) of the individual?

Habits of thought and language often give rise to the assumption that death is somehow modifiable by numbers. "Death is greater when more people die" is one form this assumption takes. Another form introduces characteristics attributed to the individual or individuals. For example, death is "bigger," or "greater" for:

- Young people who had "their whole lives in front of them";
- Talented people who "had so much to give the world";
- People who had been vigorous, healthy, and alert, and "suddenly had everything taken away from them."

It is understandable that we might attach different meanings and values to a person's loss of life depending on characteristics of the person and the circumstances. Opinion may have it that one death was "tragic" and another "appropriate, a blessing." It is also possible to take a more extreme position and suggest that deaths might actually differ in the ontological sense as well (Kastenbaum 1993). In other words, some deaths are really different in significant ways from some other deaths, just as some life forms are really different from some other life forms. Whatever the merits of these views on their own terms, however, they are likely to distort logico-mathematical operations on "death" unless provided with persuasive justifications that have yet to be offered.

Think, for example, of person A and person B. Each of these people dies. Is it justifiable to make a quantitative transformation of each death and then modify, compare, or summate these numbers? Suppose person A to have been 20 years of age at the time of death, and person B to have been 80 years of age. Is the death of person A four times the magnitude of the death of person B because the former has lost so much potential unlived life? Or is it just the reverse? With the death of person B there is the loss of four times as much life development and experience. Or is it an invalid procedure to compare the death of one person with the death of another? For that matter, is the death of a mouse smaller than the death of an elephant?

The reader who is familiar with epistemology might recognize at this point that we are dealing with a variant of the "cup of consciousness" problem. You and I both observe the Arizona skies transforming themselves into a desert sunset. We both take pleasure in the view. We may also comment on the constantly shifting colors. But are we really seeing the same thing? Philosophers like to tell us that exchanging "cups of consciousness" would be the only way of testing our accord. I would have to experience your experience of the sunset and vice versa. Such a direct sharing of states of consciousness has not yet been achieved and is often considered impossible. The obvious lesson is that each of us experiences the world in our own way and can only infer the experiences of others. We cannot increase, deplete, dilute, or enrich our experiential knowledge by exchanging or blending cups of consciousness.

Similarly, we are on shaky ground if we use numbers to transfer or modify the death of one person through association with the deaths of others. This problem introduces a further note of caution into any attempt to project the future of death by numbers alone. Although we interpenetrate each other's lives and can be fairly described as social animals, each of us has a personal life and a personal death. Those who would pour deaths into a common quantitative vessel must offer a more persuasive rationale than any I have encountered for overriding the unique individuality of each life and death.

Let us take one further step. It has already been suggested that deaths can be subjected to quantitative operations, but that death itself is a dubious proposition for such treatment. We are ready now for a brief look at the choice of mathematical operations. Again, a somewhat peculiar way of putting the question might be the most effective: How should death behave as a mathematical operation? This is a turnaround from the earlier focus on death as the subject of statistical analyses. We are attempting here to envision death when translated faithfully into mathematical operations. The identification or creation of a mathematical model for the behavior of death would provide a plausible foundation for attempts to predict the future of death.

Our first inclination may be to equate death with zero. This inclination may be reinforced by our earlier use of the digital (either-or) model. It is true that dead could be given the 0 position and alive the positive or 1 position. This, however, would be an arbitrary assignment. More significantly, it would still be only a way of representing death, not the more radical attempt to translate death into a mathematical operation.

The concept of zero is among the most fascinating and, in some sense, mysterious, ever to be discovered or invented by the human mind. It has three primary meanings: (1) as naught or nothing, (2) as the starting point of a numbered scale, and (3) as the lowest in an array of numbered points. In its two latter usages, zero has no useful parallel with death. Death is not—or, at least, not obviously—the starting point for a life, nor is it adequately described as only a position lower than life on the same scale. Furthermore, the procedure of specifying various levels of zero (as in temperature) shows no verisimilitude to death. However we say it, death is not well conceived as a different shade, nuance, magnitude, or intensity of life. Death is different from life, and it is this difference that should be identified in the realm of logico-mathematical operations.

How about death as the zero of no-thing, as the absence of any-thing that could be given a number? This is a more promising proposition. When we multiply a number by zero the product is zero. This is more like the death whose behavior we know from experience! Division, the reciprocal operation, takes us down one of two paths. If we choose the path of mathematical theory we will probably accept the prevailing wisdom that dividing by zero yields either infinity or an indeterminate result. However, the path most traveled by most of us is simply the use of division in practical calculations. Whether we use our own brain power or rely on a computer, we find that dividing a number by zero results in zero as product. The operation of division in its most familiar form, unadorned by theoretical considerations, yields the same result as its opposite, multiplication. Multiplication or division by zero is the kiss of death or a reasonable facsimile thereof. Furthermore, a large number is not protected by its magnitude, nor does a small number elude the deadly zero effect.

Even so, zero does not quite make it as an adequate mathematical equivalent for death. Along with the theoretical gloss on division by zero already noted, we remind ourselves that the special power to "empty" numbers does not extend to addition and subtraction. Death cannot diminish 1,000,000 by even 1.

There are further limitations of traditional mathematical operations in modeling the behavior of death. One of these limitations is the indifference to time and direction. Schoolchildren are taught that it makes no difference whether they start with 3 and add 1, or start with 1 and add 3. Logic and mathematics most often present themselves to us as closed systems that are governed by a set of firm rules—quite unlike the open systems we encounter in daily life where time and timing are so consequential.[1]

It is in the principle of reversibility that traditional mathematical logic shows its most significant failure to encompass those operations in which death most clearly shows its hand. (Of course, it is not fair to judge mathematics as a "failure" in this regard, since incorporating death as an operational force does not seem to have been a priority of mathematicians and statisticians up to this point.) In most instances one can reason either forward or backward toward the answer (and only one answer will be correct). Reasoning first in one direction and then the other is a way of checking on one's logic or calculations. Death cannot "show its stuff" within this frame. The most powerful and distinctive operations of death are excluded by the traditional rules. Death is the stopper. Death is the canceler. Death is the final out. Death is the endgame. Death is that which cannot be played backward, cannot be reversed, cannot be outwaited, cannot be set aside to begin anew.

To put it another way, death is not adequately represented by any computer program that generates and displays an outcome. Death does not strike (perform its operations) by adding "death" to any existing array of data or conclusions. Death is the screen going dark and staying dark. Death does not operate as a particular set of computations that appear on the blackboard. Death is the eraser whose touch destroys the blackboard. Coming back to everyday life: death is not simply one more attribute of a person: tall, brown-eyed, married, prosperous, dead. By their very nature, logico-mathematical operations provide still another strategy for denying or trivializing death. Those who give themselves wholly to the engrossing world of numbers will never in that realm encounter reminders of fleeting time, uncertain circumstances, and certain death.

Conclusion? Let us proceed on the working assumption that logico-mathematical operations (of the traditional type, at least) are incapable of modeling the distinctive operations of death. This limitation does not impair the ability of statisticians to estimate deaths by the number at various future projections. It does, however, suggest that we would not

---

[1]"Fuzzy" logic and chaos theory now challenge classical logic and mathematics and might therefore provide the basis for a more "life-like" incorporation of death operations, but this is discussion we must forgo here.

be wise to depend on the assumptions, rules, and procedures of statistical analysis in the effort to understand the future of death in human life.

Death Must Be: Apoptosis

We consider now a more substantive approach to projecting the future of death. In its essence, this approach asserts that death must be. The future may hold many wonders, but every life will end in death. There is an important corollary point: death is not only the outcome, but it is also the fulfillment of a plan, an intention. Some force in the universe wants us dead.

Today this approach is perhaps most challengingly articulated by geneticists. *Apoptosis*—programmed death—is the fate universal for all life forms. There was no escape. There is no escape. There can be no escape.

We will continue to assign particular causes of death for particular individuals. Many deaths will continue to seem remote from the concept of apoptosis. It would be a long stretch of the imagination to blame apoptosis for a drive-by shooting, a suicide, a motor vehicle accident. On the basis of present knowledge it would also be a long stretch to attribute our propensity for warfare and mass violence to genetic codes. The connection becomes more plausible when we consider age-related changes. There is a seeming paradox here. Not only do more people now survive into the later adult years, but more also enjoy robust health and competent functioning. This trend appears to suggest a triumph over built-in deterioration. There is an alternative explanation, however. People in the past often died relatively young or carried debilitating conditions into their later adult years because of pathologies, disorders, and traumas that were not treated successfully. They also were worn down by excessive labor, inadequate nutrition, and other stressors. Improved longevity and health can be seen as the product of a rise in the standard of living (although, unfortunately, not for all people). The boon should be attributed to the avoidance and/or successful management of conditions hazardous to health and survival. Aging, however, still goes on, day by day, year by year. Although it can be difficult to separate normal aging changes from acquired disorders, gerontologists recognize the reality and significance of this difference. We may live longer and healthier lives, but programmed death—operating under the name of "aging"—will remain steadfast at its task.

Apoptosis might be regarded as death's trump card. Individuals in a species will live for variable periods of time, but always within the established limits. With a fortunate genetic inheritance, a positive approach to life, and a bit of luck, some members of our own species live to celebrate their 100th birthday and perhaps a few more. If demographic trends continue, there will be more people who reach the century mark over the next several generations. Nevertheless, mortality and longevity figures have become relatively stabilized in recent years despite continuing medical advances (Gavrilov and Gavrilova 1991). This suggests that industrialized nations may already be approaching the limits of longevity.

Those who take a strong position on programmed death believe that the rate of aging cannot be modified to any large extent. Fundamental biological processes will see to it that deterioration occurs. Research on programmed death has now reached the point where the concept cannot be ignored. Studies conducted by many research teams around the world have implicated programmed death mechanisms in such realms of vital functioning as DNA, the immune system, and neural pathways (Levin and Watters 1993).

Apoptosis, then, serves as the fail-safe assurance that we will die—and that those as yet unborn will also die. Programmed death involves systematic changes in the functioning of cells. All body systems become increasingly vulnerable as the cellular changes become more advanced and widely spread. Any organ system might be the first to crumple, therefore the official cause of death can take many forms. The ultimate cause, however, is the biogenetic plan that builds in both development and deterioration.

It is not politically correct to speak of "nature's plan," and has not been so for many years. Too often scientific progress was obstructed by the insistence that everything happens according to the intention of divinity, nature, or some kind of spiritual force. Furthermore, the insistence on attributing intentionality to whatever happens to happen was often related to political or ideological agendas. "Intention," "purpose," and kindred concepts were booted out of scientific disciplines and were restricted to a sort of underground life. In recent years, though, these concepts occasionally have been rehabilitated and repackaged (e. g., in the 1960s, "thinking" was pretty much taboo in psychology, but the "cognitive sciences" now flourish—and thereby provide a sanctuary and breeding ground for concepts of intention and purpose).

Is it justifiable to speak of programmed death as purposeful? And, if so, what is the purpose? Life scientists have not answered this question in a single voice. Many hesitate to return to teleological explanations (purpose, intention, plan) in general. Others are reluctant to speculate about purpose until the database has been further enlarged. There is, however, one viewpoint that has been around since the early days of developmental biology: aging/programmed death does away with individuals so that the species can flourish and survive. After individuals have passed the reproductive phase of their lives they have no vital function to serve and "should" therefore exit the scene to be replaced by the next generation of progenitors. The emphasis here is on the species rather than the individual, although it is the individual who is marked for deterioration.

A. T. Welford (1958), a major contributor to the study of aging, offered an early theory of programmed deterioration that included both biological and psychological processes, a theory that still remains worthy of investigation. He suggests that aging has an ever-increasing effect on the ability of the central nervous system to process information. Our "channel capacity" becomes restricted and there is an increase in the ratio of "noise" to "signal" within the brain itself as well as in our dealings with the external world. We therefore become less efficient in recognizing, interpreting, and responding to information. These changes occur both on a neural level (e.g., through the death of brain cells) and on a cognitive level. The upshot of all these changes is that the aging person becomes increasingly vulnerable to the loss of the higher cognitive processes. Most critically, it becomes more difficult to plan, execute, and control. Random processes and error interfere with the pursuit of goals and intentions—inflicting damage comparable to that of a virus invading a computer. Programmed death, then, might be seen as operating within the individual as the erosion of control over one's own purposes.

Perhaps the boldest of more recent theories has been offered by Richard Dawkins (1989, 1992). Unafraid to speak directly of purpose, Dawkins suggests that individuals exist to serve as hosts for their genomes (the set of genetic materials we inherit and then pass on to our children). This view is expressed clearly in the titles of one of his books, *The Selfish Gene* (1989). Dawkins presents a lively and informed argument in favor of the proposition that nature is more concerned with the survival of genes than with the fate of the hosts who serve as the conduit for moving genes forward through time. After we have done our bit for our genomes, we have little or no utility value in the larger scheme of things, so it is time for programmed death to get us out of the way.

We are not obliged to accept any particular theory of programmed death at this time, but the emerging facts deserve respect. At the very least, there is a serious case to be made for the proposition that we are designed *as if* decline and death were as intrinsic to our being as growth and development. Therefore, death will continue to continue despite any efforts we might make to the contrary. Death is not a side effect, an accident, or a failure; the forces that shaped the coin of life also stamped the death head on the other side.

There is also another side to this story, however, and it warrants at least brief mention. Programmed death research has emphasized the route from micro- to macro-transformations. One key factor here is the "Hayflick limit," named for the biogerontologist who made the discovery. Cells can divide and replicate themselves only so many times before this process shows signs of deterioration and eventually ceases. The limit for cell doublings—the creation of the successor generation—seems to be in the range of fifty episodes (Hayflick 1987). This finding, which has now been confirmed by other investigators, unseats the influential belief that cells are potentially immortal. The research of Alexis Carrel with cells cultured from the heart of a chick had seemed to support this contention. Eventually, it became clear that other investigators could not repeat Carrel's findings but that Hayflick could demonstrate the finite nature of cell division. We went, then, from a belief in the potential immortality of the cell to the concept of programmed aging and death. Furthermore, other deteriorative changes seem to be built into the non-dividing cells (neurons) that compose the nervous system. It looks very much as though the decline and death of the organism starts in the cell.

As popular as this view seems to have become—especially among cell biologists—it has not been firmly established by the facts. Relatively less attention has been given to the role of the central nervous system (CNS) in the transition from development to decline. There is reason to expect that the CNS has a lot to do with programmed aging and death. It is through the CNS that we exercise purpose and intention, that we develop concepts, acquire information, and develop values. The complex relationship between the CNS and its component units will require much more research on their integrative functioning.

Here is an alternative view. Some years ago I suggested that personal and cultural factors have a powerful influence over the functioning of the nervous system in the middle and later adult years (Kastenbaum 1965). Later adult outcomes will depend much on the loss, maintenance, or renewal of purpose. Let us accept the proposition that there is a built-in psychobiological program that guides early development and also continues into the peak years for procreation. This program supports the command to "Go forth and reproduce after your kind." The individual's developmental trajectory is influenced strongly by this programmed impetus.

Individuals also develop additional purposes and motives as they come of age in their particular societies, responding to the available concepts, symbols, relationships, and cultural ideals. The "grow up and reproduce" program remains a dominant force, although the outcome for each individual will depend on many situational factors as well as that individual's own distinctive personality.

In the later adult years, the programming that guided early development loses its thrust: one has either propagated those genes or passed by the prime opportunity to do so. It is only when no significant alternative program exists that the CNS will lose its purpose, its guidance function. Essentially, the CNS will act as though it has nothing important to do. What is called the programmed death mechanism, then, might actually be the response of the CNS to the loss of its early priorities. Decline may then occur swiftly because it is unopposed by the CNS.

The CNS might continue to function in a robust manner, however, should the individual have other guiding purposes. The individual would then be demanding optimal performance from his or her CNS, therefore keeping it functioning in a robust manner. This is a crucial point for projecting the future of death. If a society expects and demands much of its older adults, if there are powerful models and ideals to which one might aspire, if there are opportunities to remain involved in consequential processes, then the early biological programming may be replaced by effective acquired programming. This outcome would be favored by a preexisting lifestyle in which individuals were accustomed to continued learning, seeking new experiences, and exploring the outer limits of their abilities.

Coming back to the biological side, we might then expect that a vigorous, intact, and active CNS would continue to exercise control over lower centers. The individual would still be vulnerable to all the dangers to which flesh is heir, but might not be absolutely doomed to a programmed death. Furthermore, a note of optimism has been sounded even by those researchers who have contributed to the discovery of programmed death on the cellular level. Hayflick himself is among those who believe that as we learn more about the mechanisms of programmed death we will be in a better position to intervene. Will it prove possible to overcome programmed death at the cellular level through genetic engineering or other techniques? It is too soon to know; therefore, it is also too soon to conclude that this project is doomed to failure.

Is it possible for sociocultural and individual factors to halt or reverse programmed death—or can behavioral choices only shunt the process over to a slower track? This is also a question that we are a long way from answering, but it is at least a viable hypothesis that the future of death could be affected by the way we live, especially in the postreproductive years (which are themselves perhaps more modifiable than previously supposed).

Before leaving the "death must be" arena, perhaps we should remind ourselves that the concept of doom was with us long before the life sciences took hold. The belief that death is punishment for sin is at the root of much Christian thought and practice. Salvation would have little significance without the conviction that our deaths are the result of divine intention. If we simply withered and passed away like the grass there would be no spin of guilt on our mortal move. It is the idea that God wants us dead that makes the end of life something more than just the natural conclusion to a natural existence. For those who align themselves with this facet of Christianity, death is programmed by God. (And if God happens to use genetic codes to achieve this purpose, this is only the technical side of the matter.)

More complex versions are also available. For example, death can be viewed as a partner or associate of God ("Good cop, bad cop") in running the universe. Death is an intrinsic part of the show, and perhaps only another face of God. Either way, death is not the result of accident or failure, but is programmed into the fundamental purposes and forces of the universe.

There is another widespread tradition that views death as a necessary component of life. This tradition includes the practice of sacrificing humans, animals, or symbolic substances to the gods to ensure a good harvest. It may even be considered necessary to sacrifice a god (or proxy) to make sure that the life-to-death-to-life loop operates effectively. Some ancient civilizations were well aware of the process through which decaying organic matter provides the nourishment for life-giving sustenance. The respect given to the dung beetle in dynastic Egypt is one revealing example. From a people's agricultural practices to its theology we at times can see that death is regarded as a crucial element in life's ongoing program. The quest for personal immortality arose as an attempt to transcend the cycle of growth and decay, life and death. Even as one dared hope for a life beyond death, one understood clearly that in *this* life, death must be. In myth, imagination, ritual, and psychosis we have attempted to reconcile in some way the recognition that each life has its death and the wish that it might be otherwise.

Cosmic Destiny and Death

A term such as *cosmic destiny* invites immediate rejection. It sounds too much like the title of a tract left at our doorstep by a religious cult or an overblown quasi-philosophical essay covered by a century of dust. Perhaps, however, we should not be too abrupt in closing the door. Let us first ask ourselves these questions:

Do we live and die in the universe? Or only in Toledo or Spokane?
Does death have some relationship to life?
Does life have some relationship to the status of the universe?
Has the universe changed in significant ways since its time-point of origin?
Is the universe continuing to change in significant ways?

What we call "life" is a phenomenon that has arisen during the course of cosmic events, and what we call "death" has little or no meaning apart from its association with life. In thinking about the future of death, then, we might well consider the changing relationships between life/death and the cosmos. If the universe is going some place, then we are going there, too.

My limited purpose here is to identify aspects of the frame of reference within which it might prove stimulating to examine death and cosmic destiny. The following basic propositions are offered for your consideration.

1. The universe—all that "exists"—did not begin with the configuration that is familiar to us today.
2. What we call "time," "space," and "matter" are emergent characteristics.
3. "Life" and "mind" are phenomena that developed only when the universe became capable of hosting these emergents.
4. Death did not enter the cosmic frame until life forms appeared.
5. Just as $death_g$ (general case) had no meaning until $life_g$ appeared, so $death_p$ (particular case) had no meaning without reference to $life_p$.
6. We tend to obscure the situation when we use the word *death* to refer to the "off" state of widely diverse life forms (e.g., primal scum and politicians).
7. The nature of the life forms that are subject to $death_p$ is conditioned by the current status of the universe and by its direction of change. As we examine any space-time slice of cosmic history, then, we will discover life/death configurations that are unique to this sample.
8. A thorough description of a particular life form ($life_p$) would include its environmental context. A fish, for example, would be difficult to understand if we knew nothing of water. The identity of *who it is* that lives and dies always assumes context—and context always assumes the state of the cosmos as well as local conditions.
9. $Death_g$ may differ between and within types of life form. The mosaic tobacco virus, the liver fluke, and the butterfly, for example, each undergo transformations so radical during their lives that one can raise such questions as "Which phase is the real organism" and "Who dies when life is extinguished at one phase or another?" We do not know the full past extent nor can we know the potential future extent of diversity in life forms and, therefore, do not and cannot know all the forms taken by $death_p$.
10. Individuation, complexity, and experience (acquired attributes) are among the factors that make a particular life what it is. The

cessation of highly individuated and unique lives is sufficiently different from the cessation of essentially interchangeable or redundant lives that much valuable information is lost when all instances of death$_p$ are subsumed under the rubric of death$_g$. (A unicell organism that has divided into two successor cells has itself vanished/died—or has it? Is it adequate to equate the death of one of the two successor cells with the death of a unique person?)

These propositions only begin the task of establishing the case for considering death to be a concept relative to its circumstances as distinct from a reification floating free of particulars and contexts. It would be understandable if many readers were reluctant to open themselves to the prospect of relativistic death and all that might follow from this unorthodox idea. We need time to accustom ourselves just to the possibility that it might be worth exploring. Perhaps this somewhat unsettling enterprise will seem a little less bizarre if we consider briefly its epistemological/methodological underpinnings.

Common sense tells us that there is a "real" world that is external to our personal thoughts and feelings. In this assumed real world we assume there is real death. It is not just that we use words and symbols that refer to death. Beyond our language, beyond our concepts, there is an implacable reality. These are familiar and reasonable assumptions. Nevertheless, they must remain as assumptions because we cannot get out of our own skins; we cannot climb out of our habits of thought and language. The cognitive-lingual skills that enable humans to employ an impressive range and versatility of thought also limit what we can know for sure. There may be an absolute and absolutely real death "out there." We, however, cannot be absolutely sure because even this formulation is a function of our cognitive-lingual systems. (What is "real"? What is "absolute"? What is "relative"? What is "out there"?)

Most philosophers of science agree that our perceptions and cognitions of the world are not pure and faithful representations of an objective reality. Rather, our acts of observation and measurement bring something of ourselves to the endeavor. From physics to psychology, it is now well recognized that we must consider both the observer and the situation in considering the "findings." Furthermore, observations must also be communicated to others, a process in which both the sender and the receiver influence the message.

There is not much new in what has just been stated. It is useful, though, as background to our challenge to the assumption that death is the exception to the rule. We know about things, processes, people, and events only through particular operations of knowing and communication. Tradition has it, however, that we know death as an absolute, that we know the Real Death that is beyond the representation of death in our thought and language. This is not a tenable assumption. At the very least, it is an assumption that must be defended vigorously, not simply asserted. The opposing proposition is that all that we know about death is what we have learned from particular deaths within particular contexts. We are best qualified, then, to consider contextualized death, death as part of a given situation.

By implication, each individual's death must be construed within its own unique context (Kastenbaum 1993). The future of death will therefore depend much on how people live and die. It will also depend on the changing ecology of planet Earth and on larger processes throughout the cosmos. (Will our traditional conceptions of death even be relevant to emerging cosmic conditions and life or "postlife" forms?) This vista may seem quite out of scale with our everyday way of looking at life and death. We may prefer to continue thinking of death as an immutable reality, but death may nevertheless have other ideas on the subject.

Symbolic Interactionism and Death

Several general frames of reference have been identified as possible approaches to thinking about the future of death: logico-mathematics; life sciences (especially microbiology and genetics); and theoretical physics/philosophy of science. What do these realms have in common? All were engendered by the human mind. All are symbolic constructions. It is not really a new topic, then, when we turn now to symbolic interactionism. Creating meaning and constructing our own versions of reality are activities that must be included in any definition of what it is to be a person. It is time now to explore briefly some of the ways in which symbolic interactionism pertains directly to the future of death. Again, we will limit ourselves to a few propositions that may be useful in preparing for more extensive inquiry.

1. Concepts of futurity and death are intimately related. If I do not have a firm sense of futurity (and therefore also a firm sense of past and present), then I will not comprehend death or, at the least, my construction of death will be much different from the consensual adult view. Whatever influences our symbolic construction of time is also likely to influence our construction of death. A searching comparison of time and death concepts in agrarian, industrial, and postindustrial society would reveal much about the ways in which the "future of death" has already been altered and in what directions it might continue to develop. (For

example, "the failed machine" and "disposable relationships" are death-relevant concepts that would have been difficult to anticipate for those living in hunting-gathering societies.)

2. Changing ideas about whether the world will end "with a bang or a whimper" will influence the way we think about the future of death. And, in turn, the way we construct the future of death will influence the way we live in the prospect of death. Will the children of our children's children believe that there is a spiritual destination beyond their years on earth? Or will they suppose themselves to be living a meaningless existence on a small, dying spheroid within a universe hurtling toward self-destruction? How we project (or fail to project) purpose and fulfillment into the future will be a major influence on how we construct both life and death.

3. Changes in political ideologies and their acceptance by the people will influence the future of death. War, genocide, and other human violence have been major contributors to death throughout much of history. Although the causes of group violence are still being debated, it is clear that dividing people into "Us" and "Them" facilitates lethal aggression. How much of future death will take the form of the natural ending of a coherent life in a coherent society and how much the form of killing and exploitation? This will depend much on the extent to which individuals are willing to see themselves as members of a group and, therefore, having a communal rather than a personal life to surrender.

4. The future of death will be influenced by the alternative and competing definitions that are offered of both life and death. These variant constructions are already coming from multiple sources. For example, have scientists already succeeded in creating life forms? The answer to this question will depend much on how we choose to define life. The answer probably will be subjected to continued revision as research continues. The questions of *who* is alive and *when* life ends have become the subject of an ongoing series of disputes in law and ethics. Is the person who has slipped into a "persistent vegetative state" still a person? Still the same person? Who or what is still living during "brain death" or "clinical death"? Has death occurred at the moment a physician makes the pronouncement, even if efforts are already under way to prepare the body for cryonic storage with the goal of subsequent resuscitation? The transplantation of brain tissue for therapeutic purposes is a technique already in use as an experimental treatment in Parkinson's disease. In the future will we believe that a "deceased" brain donor still lives in the new host, and will we

consider the recipient to have a dual identity? The main point here is that all the key terms are symbolic constructions. All are subject to critical analysis. All are subject to being accepted or rejected by health care professionals, legal experts, philosophers, and the public. "Brain death," for example, is not the solid entity that popular discourse would suggest. It is a construct that was motivated by the need of physicians to respond to changing technologies (McCullagh 1993). Medical observations were only part of the process. Constructs such as brain death have already been modified as they go along, and there is no reason to assume that we have heard the last of new definitions of life and death. The future of death, then, will to some extent be determined by the definitions of life and death that win favor at a particular time, and the consequences of accepting these definitions.

5. "Virtual reality" will influence the future of death. Reference here is not only to the recently introduced technological wonder that goes by this name, but to the entire spectrum of computer and electronically generated images. It is probable that throughout human history we have been constructing memories, expectations, and outright fantasies. Today— and tomorrow—the world with which we interact is furnished with technological versions of memory, expectation, and fantasy. Our ancestors might have had the opportunity to communicate with an occasional discarnate spirit. Remote control or computer mouse in hand, we can interact with discarnate images at our convenience, day or night. Our sphere of symbolic interaction is populated by television reruns featuring deceased performers. Aging performers at times must compete against their younger and more celebrated selves. Many of us are compiling personal archives on camcorder videotapes, the "home movies" that will bring the past forward into the future. "Morphing" one form into another and postproduction wizardry in general make it possible to transform images that at first were accurate representations. In these and other ways we are leading more than one life: our daily trudge through "real time" and our interpenetrations with computerized electronic images. The commonsense notion of one life and one death is being challenged—perhaps *seduced* is the better word. We see this in the proliferation of parasocial relationships and their sometimes lethal consequences, as when a person imagines that a celebrity is actually part of his life and becomes a stalker. Constructions of life and death that have endured for centuries may or may not prove capable of withstanding the influence of cybergenetic reality. The future of death is still under construction and its out-

come will be significantly affected by the choices we are already starting to make (Kastenbaum 1995).

A Final Word

It is reasonable to persist in our familiar belief that "death is death" and therefore must be the same through all time. In our more adventuresome moments, however, it might be stimulating, even useful, to consider alternative possibilities. For example, I have asked people what life would be like for them if death were no longer inevitable. Almost all respondents to this "world without death" exercise focus on the negatives (e.g., overcrowding, boredom, lack of motivation to get things done, possible loss of heaven and eternity). Many are surprised at their own responses. "I always thought it would be great if I didn't have to think of death, not that I think about it much anyway. But I guess we really need death, or at least I do, for everything to make sense." Thinking about the possible futures of death, then, may help us to monitor our hopes, fears, needs, and expectations in the here and now.

We might also be less passive and uncritical when exposed to competing concepts of life and death. For example, "brain death" would arouse our curiosity, but not lure us into a premature evaluation. And we might, at least now and then, raise our eyes to the heavens and contemplate our place in the mysterious, swirling, ever-changing universe. The meaning of life may be written in the cosmos or it may be only the uncertain product of our fertile but fallible minds. For myself, I do not expect to catch a falling star, get with child a mandrake's root, discover where past years are, or who cleft the devil's foot—yet I grant myself the pleasure of wondering about the future of life and death and hope that others are doing the same.

References

Dawkins, R. (1989). *The Selfish Gene*, 3rd ed. Oxford, New York: Oxford University Press.
——— (1992). *The Extended Phenotype*. Oxford, New York: Oxford University Press.
Feifel, H., ed. (1959). *The Meaning of Death*. New York: McGraw-Hill.
Gavrilov, L. A., and Gavrilova, N. S. (1991). T*he Biology of Life Span*. London: Harwood.
Hayflick, L. (1987). Cell aging in vivo. In *The Encyclopedia of Aging*, ed. G. L. Maddox, pp. 101–102. New York: Springer.
Kastenbaum, R. (1965). Theories of human aging: the search for a conceptual framework. *Journal of Social Issues* 21(4):13–36.
——— (1993). Last words. *The Monist, A Journal of General Philosophy* 76:270–290.
——— (1995). *Dorian, Graying: Is Youth the Only Thing Worth Having?* New York: Baywood.
Levin, M., and Watters, D., eds. (1993). *Programmed Cell Death*. New York: Gordon & Breach.
McCullagh, P. (1993). *Brain Dead, Brain Absent, Brain Donors*. New York: Wiley.
Welford, A. T. (1958). *Aging and Human Skill*. London: Oxford University Press.

Herman Feifel—Then and Now

World War II, an officer in the Adjutant General's office, 1944.

At the side of the Enola Gay, two days after its historic mission of bombing Hiroshima, August 8, 1945.

Savoring the good life, Los Angeles, 1989.

Appendix: Highlights of Herman Feifel's Career

1915 Born in Brooklyn, New York, on November 4, 1915, to Jacob and Rebecca (Katz) Feifel.

1935 Receives B.A. degree from the City College of New York with a major in psychology and minors in philosophy and English literature.

1939 Obtains his M.A. in psychology from Columbia University. Is influenced by Robert S. Woodworth and Otto Klineberg. Meets George S. Klein, with whom he inaugurates a lifelong comradeship.

1941 Develops a mentor-friend relationship with Irving D. Lorge, who stimulates a sustaining interest in the area of adult development and aging.

1942–44 Enlists in the U.S. Army Air Corps. Joins Psychological Research Unit #1, Nashville, Tennessee, and functions as an Aviation Psychologist dealing with the selection and classification of flying crew members.

1944–46 Directly commissioned as an officer in the U.S. Army Adjutant General's Office as a clinical psychologist. Is assigned to the island of Tinian in the Marianas in anticipation of the forthcoming invasion of Japan. While there he works with combat and operational fatigue cases resulting from the Iwo Jima and Okinawa campaigns. He is also witness to the takeoff of the Enola Gay to bomb Hiroshima, which ushers in the Atomic Age in warfare.

1946–49 Joins the Personnel Research Section of the Adjutant General's office as a civilian research psychologist and works on such issues as leadership, career guidance, and training while stationed at the Pentagon.

1948 Awarded his Ph.D. in psychology from Columbia University. His dissertation, *Qualitative Differences in the Vocabulary Responses of Normals and Abnormals*, is published as a *Genetic Psychology Monograph* in 1949.

1950–54 Joins the Winter Veterans Administration Hospital staff in Topeka, Kansas, as a supervisory clinical psychologist, and serves as a lecturer at the

Menninger School of Psychiatry. While there he interacts with a bevy of outstanding colleagues and psychologists, among whom are Robert R. Holt, George S. Klein, Martin Mayman, Gardner Murphy, Helen D. Sargent, Martin Scheerer, and Bernard Steinzor.

1952 Awarded the Diplomate in Clinical Psychology by the American Board of Examiners in Professional Psychology.

1954–59 Accepts a position at the Los Angeles Veterans Administration Mental Hygiene Clinic as a supervisory clinical and research psychologist. Again, he is fortunate in the caliber of his colleagues, among whom are Norman L. Farberow, Bertram Forer, Bruno Klopfer, Mortimer M. Meyer, Vita Sommers, and Ruth S. Tolman.

1955 His first paper dealing with death, "Attitudes of Mentally Ill Patients Toward Death," is published in the *Journal of Nervous and Mental Disease.*

1956 Organizes and chairs the first scientific symposium on the topic of "Death and Behavior" at the annual convention of the American Psychological Association in Chicago. Participants in this historic program are Irving E. Alexander, Arnold A. Hutschnecker, Gardner Murphy, and Jacob Taubes.

1958–63 Appointed Assistant Clinical Professor of Psychiatry (Psychology) at the University of Southern California School of Medicine (1958–61), and later Associate Clinical Professor (1961–63).

1959–62 Awarded a three-year research grant by the United States Public Health Service, National Institute of Mental Health (NIMH), to study "Attitudes Toward Death and Their Relation to Behavior." This is the first time in history that NIMH supports research on the topic of death.

1959 *The Meaning of Death* is published by McGraw-Hill. A paperback edition is published in 1965. The book is also translated into Dutch and Japanese.

Serves as panelist on the symposium "Existential Psychology" presented at the annual convention of the American Psychological Association in Cincinnati, Ohio. Other participants are Gordon W. Allport, Abraham H. Maslow, Rollo May, and Carl R. Rogers. Symposium papers are later published as a book titled *Existential Psychology* by Random House in 1961. The book is translated into Spanish.

1959–60 Awarded a Special Research Fellow grant by the United States Public Health Service. On leave from his Veterans Administration post, he spends the year as a Visiting Senior Research Scientist at New York University's Research Center for Mental Health. There he renews his contacts with co-directors Robert R. Holt and George S. Klein.

1960 Accepts appointment as Chief Psychologist at the Los Angeles Veterans Administration Outpatient Clinic.

1963 Organizes and chairs symposium on "The Nature of Man" at the annual convention of the American Psychological Association in Chicago. Distinguished participants are George A. Kelly, James Miller, Henry A. Murray, and Edward J. Stainbrook.

1964–65 Serves as President of the Los Angeles County Psychological Association.

1965 Receives a Special Commendation from the Chief Medical Director of the Veterans Administration, Washington, D.C. His citation reads, "Your work has helped enhance the image of the V.A. even beyond the borders of the United States and has contributed to the entire field of human behavior."

1965–present Appointed Clinical Professor of Psychiatry and the Behavioral Sciences at the University of Southern California School of Medicine (1965–90), and later Emeritus Clinical Professor (1990–present).

1966–67 On leave from his Veterans Administration post, he serves as Visiting Professor of Psychology at the University of Southern California.

1967–70 Serves on the American Psychological Association's Council of Representatives for the Division of Philosophical Psychology.

1970 Receives a Certificate of Appreciation from the Director of the National Institute of Mental Health for his "contributions to the work of the Suicide Prevention Review Committee."

1974 Receives the Distinguished Scientific Achievement Award from the California State Psychological Association.

As a founding father, participates in the first meeting of the International Work Group on Death, Dying, and Bereavement at Columbia, Maryland.

1974–75 Serves as President of the American Psychological Association's Division of Maturity and Old Age.

1974–77 Serves on the American Psychological Association's Board of Professional Affairs.

1975 Appointed Consultant to the Vaad Lishikum, Department of Defense, and to the Ministry of Health, State of Israel.

1975–77 Selected as National Lecturer for Sigma Xi, The Scientific Research Society of North America.

1977 *New Meanings of Death* is published by McGraw-Hill. A paperback edition is published in 1978, and it is translated into Dutch and Japanese. It is selected as Book of the Year by the American Journal of Nursing.

Receives a second Special Commendation from the Chief Medical Director of the Veterans Administration, Washington, D.C. This is in recognition of "outstanding leadership as Chief of the Psychology Service, VA Outpatient Clinic, Los Angeles, California; initiative in organizing the service to become a major catalyst in promoting an interdisciplinary approach to the health care of patients; and in bringing prestige to the Agency's research program."

1978 Honored with the Harold M. Hildreth Distinguished Award by the American Psychological Association's Division of Public Service.

Is invited to deliver the Annual Ontario Ministry of Health Lecture, Ottawa, Canada.

1978–86 Elected to the Board of Directors, International Work Group on Death, Dying, and Bereavement. Serves two consecutive terms, 1978–82 and 1983–86.

1979 Receives the Distinguished Human Services Award from Yeshiva University.

1982 Delivers keynote address, "Perceptions of Death by Western Man," to the Swedish Ministry of Health in Stockholm.

Inducted as a Distinguished Practitioner and Member of Psychology, National Academies of Practice, Washington, D.C.

1984 Awarded the Doctor of Humane Letters, honoris causa, by the University of Judaism, Los Angeles.

First recipient of the Plaque and Award in Thanatology, given by the National Center for Death Education.

1985 Delivers the keynote address, "Death in Contemporary Society," at the First International Conference on Grief and Bereavement in Jerusalem, Israel.

1986 Delivers the keynote lecture on "Care of the Terminally Ill," at the Sixth World Congress in Montreal, Canada.

1987 Awarded its Distinguished Service Medallion by the Los Angeles County/ University of Southern California Medical Center.

1988–91 Serves on the Dean's Committee, University of Southern California School of Medicine/Veterans Administration Outpatient Clinic, Los Angeles.

1988 Receives the American Psychological Association's Distinguished Professional Contributions to Knowledge award.

Reaches the quarterfinals in the Diamond Doubles at the National Tournament of the American Handball Association.

1989 Is honored with the Federal Executive Board's Outstanding Professional Employee Award.

Receives the Outstanding Contributions to the Advancement of Psychology award from the City University of New York.

1990 Accepts the Distinguished Scientific Contributions to Clinical Psychology award from the American Psychological Association's Division of Clinical Psychology, and a Distinguished Death Educator award from the Association for Death Education and Counseling.

Receives a Letter of Recognition from the Secretary of Veterans Affairs, the Honorable Edward J. Derwinski, for "the honor you have brought to VA through your work. Your leadership and pioneering research efforts in the study of death and dying have been of great moment to researchers and clinicians . . . and to society as a whole."

Delivers the keynote address, "The Thanatological Movement: Respice, Adspice, Prospice," at the First National Congress of Thanatology, Columbia-Presbyterian Medical Center, New York City. Also delivers the keynote address, "Death and the Helping Professions," at the University Clinic of Trondheim, Norway.

1991 Awarded a Fellow Rosette by the American Association for the Advancement of Science.

   Becomes a Charter Fellow of the American Psychological Society.

1992–present Retires as Chief Psychologist of the Los Angeles Veterans Affairs Outpatient Clinic. Asked to serve as Consultant to the Psychology Service.

1993 Installation and dedication of bronze sculpture at the Los Angeles Veterans Affairs Outpatient Clinic.

Print Bibliography of Herman Feifel

1949   Qualitative differences in the vocabulary responses of normals and abnormals. *Genetic Psychology Monographs* 39:151–204.

1950   Qualitative differences in the vocabulary responses of children. *Journal of Educational Psychology* 41:1–18 (with I. Lorge).

1951   Ego structure and mental deterioration. *Journal of Personality* 20:188–198.

1952   An analysis of the word definition errors of children. *Journal of Psychology* 33:65–77.

1953   Group psychotherapy with acutely disturbed psychotics. *Journal of Consulting Psychology* 17:113–121 (with A. D. Schwartz).

1954   Let's add life to years. *Menninger Quarterly* 8:27–29.
        Psychiatric patients look at old age: level of adjustment and attitudes toward aging. *American Journal of Psychiatry* 111:459–465.

1955   Attitudes of mentally ill patients toward death. *Journal of Nervous and Mental Disease* 122:375–380.
        Note on hypothetical situations in personality appraisal. *Journal of Clinical Psychology* 11:415–416.
        Personality factors in post-encephalitic parkinsonism. In *Clinical Studies of Personality*, ed. A. Burton and R. E. Harris, pp. 365–386. New York: Harper & Brothers.

1956   Older persons look at death. *Geriatrics* 11:127–130.

1957   Judgment of time in younger and older persons. *Journal of Gerontology* 12:71–75.

Research with projective techniques. *Journal of Projective Techniques* 21:341.

Some aspects of the meaning of death. In *Clues to Suicide*, ed. E. Shneidman and N. Farberow, pp. 50–57. New York: McGraw-Hill.

1958 Relationships between religion and mental health. *American Psychologist* 13:565–566.

1959 Attitudes toward death in some normal and mentally ill populations. In *The Meaning of Death*, ed. H. Feifel, pp. 114–130. New York: McGraw-Hill.

The dying patient. *Bulletin of the Los Angeles County Medical Association* 89:25 (with A. M. Kasper).

The Meaning of Death (editor). New York: McGraw-Hill. (A paperback edition was published in 1965. Editions have also been published in Dutch and Japanese.)

Psychological test report: a communication between psychologist and psychiatrist. *Journal of Nervous and Mental Disease* 129:77–81.

1961 Attitudes toward death in older persons. *Journal of Gerontology* 16:61–63.

Book review. *Proceedings of the Academy of Religion and Mental Health: Religion, Culture and Mental Health.* New York: New York University Press, 1961. In *Journal of Religion and Health* 1:84–86.

Book review. Sulzberger, C. *My Brother Death.* New York: Harper, 1961. In *New Leader* 44:16–17.

Clinical perception of the therapeutic transaction. *Journal of Consulting Psychology* 25:93–101 (with B. R. Forer, N. L. Farberow, M. M. Meyer, V. S. Sommers, and R. S. Tolman).

Death—relevant variable in psychology. In *Existential Psychology,* ed. R. May, pp. 61–74. New York: Random House. (Translated into Spanish.)

1962 Normalcy, illness, and death. *Proceedings of the Third World Congress of Psychiatry* 2:1252–1256 (with J. Heller).

Scientific research in taboo areas—death. *American Behavioral Scientist* 5:28–30.

1963 Death. In *The Encyclopedia of Mental Health: Vol. 2,* ed. A. Deutsch, pp. 427–450. New York: Franklin Watts, Grolier.

Death. In *Taboo Topics,* ed. N. Farberow, pp. 8–21. New York: Atherton.

Patients and therapists assess the same psychotherapy. *Journal of Consulting Psychology* 27:310–318 (with J. Eells).

The taboo on death. *American Behavioral Scientist* 6:66–67.

1964 Book review. Meerloo, J. A. *Suicide and Mass Suicide.* New York: Grune & Stratton, 1963. In *Teachers College Record* 65:460–461.

Philosophy reconsidered. *Psychological Reports* 15:415–420. Reprinted in *The Science of Philosophy: Critical Reflections,* ed. D. P. Schultz, pp. 30–35. New York: Appleton-Century-Crofts.

1965 Attitudes of mentally ill patients toward death. In *Death and Identity,* ed. R. Fulton, pp. 131–142. New York: Wiley.

The function of attitudes toward death. In *Death and Dying: Attitudes of Patient and Doctor; vol. 5,* ed. Group for the Advancement of Psychiatry, pp. 632–641, 654–655. New York: Author.

The problem of death. *Catholic Psychological Record* 3:18–22. Reprinted as a Classic in *Illness, Crisis, and Loss* 3:29–33 (1993).

1967 Book review. Keniston, K. *The Uncommitted: Alienated Youth in American Society.* New York: Harcourt, Brace & World, 1966. In *Contemporary Psychology* 12:275–277.

Book review. Munnich, J. M. A. *Old Age and Finitude: A Contribution to Psychogerontology.* Basel, Switzerland: Karger, 1966. In *Journal of Gerontology* 22:378–379.

Physicians consider death. *Proceedings of the 75th Annual Convention of the American Psychological Association* 2:201–202 (with S. Hanson, R. Jones, and L. Edwards).

1968 Book review. Shneidman, E. S. *Essays in Self-Destruction.* New York: Science House, 1967. In *Science* 161:1336.

Perception of death as related to nearness of death. *Proceedings of the 76th Annual Convention of the American Psychological Association* 3:545–546 (with R. Jones).

1969 Attitudes toward death: a psychological perspective. *Journal of Consulting and Clinical Psychology* 33:292–295.

Book review. Weisman, A. D., and Kastenbaum, R. *The Psychological Autopsy: A Study of the Terminal Phase of Life.* Community Mental Health Journal Monograph No. 4. New York: Behavioral Publications, 1968. In *Journal of Gerontology* 24:218–219.

Perception of death. *Annals of the New York Academy of Sciences* 164:669–677.

1970 Book review. Kübler-Ross, E. *On Death and Dying.* New York: Macmillan, 1969. In *Bulletin of Suicidology* 7:51–52.

The paradox of death and the "omnipotent" family doctor. *Patient Care* 4:14–75.

The psychological autopsy in judicial opinions under section 2035. *Loyola University Law Review* 3:17–18, 36–40.

Commentary. In *Death, Property, and Lawyers,* ed. T. L. Shaffer, pp. 166–167, 183–187). New York: Dunellen.

1971   Book review. Brim, O., et al., eds. *The Dying Patient.* New York: Russell Sage, 1970. In *Social Case Work* 52:239–240.

Book review. Pearson, L., ed.. *Death and Dying.* Cleveland, OH: Case Western Reserve University Press, 1969. In *Contemporary Psychology* 16:305–307.

Book review. Toynbee, A., et al. *Man's Concern with Death.* New York: McGraw-Hill, 1969. In *Life-Threatening Behavior* 1:67–73.

The meaning of death in American society: Implications for education. In *Death Education: Preparation for Living,* ed. D. P. Irish and B. R. Green, pp. 3–12. Cambridge, MA: Schenkman.

1972   Foreword. In *On Dying and Denying,* by A. Weisman. New York: Behavioral.

1973   Book review. Lester, G., and Lester, D. *Suicide.* In *Contemporary Psychology* 18:284–285.

Book review. Susman, J., and Davidson, D. L., eds. *Organizing the Community to Prevent Suicide.* In *Contemporary Psychology* 18:284–285.

Death fear in dying heart and cancer patients. *Journal of Psychosomatic Research* 17:161–166 (with J. Freilich and L. J. Hermann).

Fear of death in the mentally ill. *Psychological Reports* 33:931–938 (with L. J. Hermann).

The meaning of dying in American society. In *Dealing with Death,* ed. R. H. Davis, pp. 1–8. Los Angeles: Gerontology Center, University of Southern California.

Who's afraid of death? *Journal of Abnormal Psychology* 81:82–88. (with A. B. Branscomb).

1974   Book review. Kastenbaum, R., and Aisenberg, R. *The Psychology of Death.* New York: Springer, 1972. In *OMEGA* 5:277–278.

Death—center stage. *The Jewish Funeral Director* 42:12–24.

Psychology and the death-awareness movement. *Journal of Clinical Child Psychology* 3:6–7.

Relation of religious conviction to fear of death in healthy and terminally ill populations. *Journal for the Scientific Study of Religion* 13:353–360.

1975   Book review. Grollman, E. A., ed. *Concerning Death: A Practical Guide for Living.* New York: Beacon, 1974. In *Contemporary Psychology* 20:28–29.

Book review. Weisman, A. D. *The Realization of Death.* New York: Jason Aronson, 1975. In *Psychiatry* 38:393–394.

Death and dying in contemporary America: teaching seminar. *Highlights of the 20th Annual Conference, VA Studies in Mental Health and Behavioral Sciences* 59–62.

The meaning of dying in American society. *Journal of Pastoral Counseling* 9:53–59.

1976   Book review. Ariès, P. *Western Attitudes Toward Death: From the Middle Ages to the Present.* Baltimore, MD: Johns Hopkins University Press, 1974. In *Societas—A Review of Social History* 6:141–143.

1977   *New Meanings of Death* (editor). New York: McGraw-Hill. (A paperback edition was published in 1978. Editions have also been published in Dutch and Japanese.) Selected Book of the Year by the *American Journal of Nursing.*

Death in contemporary America. In *New Meanings of Death,* ed. H. Feifel, pp. 4–12. New York: McGraw-Hill.

Death and dying in modern America. *Death Education: An International Journal* 1:5–14.

Epilogue. In *New Meanings of Death*, ed. H. Feifel, pp. 352–355. New York: McGraw-Hill.

1978   Cui bono? *American Psychological Association Division 18 Newletter* 6–7.

1979   Crisis and opportunity. *Direction* 10:1–4.

1980   Death and dying in modern society. In *Issues in Adult Development,* ed. D. Rogers, pp. 280–285. Monterey, CA: Brooks/Cole.

The death movement. In *New Directions in Death Education and Counseling,* ed. R. A. Pacholski and C. A. Corr, pp. xi–xvi. Arlington, VA: Forum for Death Education and Counseling.

Death orientation and life-threatening behavior. *Journal of Abnormal Psychology* 89:38–45 (with V. T. Nagy).

Life-threatening illness, death, and bereavement. *The Jewish Funeral Director* 48:6–12.

Meanings of death and the hospice. *Journal of Pastoral Counseling* 15:23–27.

1981   Another look at fear of death. *Journal of Consulting and Clinical Psychology* 49:278–286 (with V. T. Nagy).

Book review. Farrel, J. J. *Inventing the American Way of Death, 1830–1920.* In *Journal for the Scientific Study of Religion* 20:392–393.

Death outlook and social issues. *OMEGA* 11:201–215 (with D. Schag).

1982   Book review. Ostow, M. *Judaism and Psychoanalysis.* New York: KTAV, 1982. In *Contemporary Psychology* 27:970–971.

Book review. Rowe, D. *The Construction of Life and Death.* Chichester, England: Wiley, 1982. *In Death Education* 6:285–286.

Guest editor and discussant. Symposium. Death in contemporary America: reformulations and copings. *Death Education* 6:III-174.

Perceptions of death by Western man. In *Death, Dying and Bereavement,* ed. L. Feigenberg, pp. 9–19. Stockholm: Swedish Cancer Society.

1984   Thanatology. In *The Encyclopedia of Psychology: Vol. 3,* ed. R. Corsini, pp. 415–417. New York: Wiley.

1986   Book review. Shoham, S. G. *Rebellion, Creativity and Revelation.* New Brunswick, NJ: Transaction Books, 1985. *In Contemporary Psychology* 31:813–814.

Foreword. In *In Quest of the Spiritual Component of Care for the Terminally Ill,* ed. F. S. Wald, pp. 15–18. New Haven, CT: Yale University School of Nursing.

Humanity has to be the model. *Death Studies* 10:1–9 (with J. D. Morgan).

1987   Coping strategies and correlative features of medically ill patients. *Psychosomatic Medicine* 49:616–625 (with S. Strack and V. T. Nagy).

Degree of life-threat and differential use of coping modes. *Journal of Psychosomatic Research* 31:91–99 (with S. Strack and V. T. Nagy).

The human reality of death and bereavement. In *Bereavement: Helping the Survivors,* ed. M. A. Morgan, pp. 13–18. London, Ontario: King's College.

Old is old is old? *Psychology and Aging* 2:409–412 (with S. Strack).

Thanatology. In *Concise Encyclopedia of Psychology,* ed. R. Corsini, pp. 1116–1117. New York: Wiley.

1988   Grief and bereavement: overview and perspective. *Bereavement Care* 7:2–4.

1989   Coping with conflict situations: middle-aged and elderly men. *Psychology and Aging* 4:26–33 (with S. Strack).

1990   Psychology and death: meaningful rediscovery. *American Psychologist* 45:537–543. Reprinted in *The Path Ahead: Readings in Death and Dying,* ed. L. A. DeSpelder and A. L. Strickland, pp. 9–19. Mountain View, CA: Mayfield, 1995.

1991   Foreword. In *Facing Death: Images, Insights, and Interventions,* by S. L. Bertman. New York: Hemisphere.

1992   The thanatological movement: respice, adspice, prospice. In *The Thana-
       tology Community and the Needs of the Movement*, ed. E. J. Clark and
       A. H. Kutscher, pp. 5–16. New York: Haworth Press. (Printed simulta-
       neously in *Loss, Grief and Care* 6:5–16.)

1993   Commentaries. In *A Time to Mourn, A Time to Comfort*, ed. R. Wolfson.
       New York: The Federation of Jewish Men's Clubs and The University of
       Judaism.

1994   Attitudes toward death: a personal perspective. In *Dying, Death, and Be-
       reavement: Theoretical Perspectives and Other Ways of Knowing*, ed. I. B.
       Corless, B. B. Germino, and M. Pittman, pp. 49–60. Boston: Jones and
       Bartlett.

1996   Age differences, coping, and the adult life span. In *Handbook of Coping*,
       ed. M. Zeidner and N. S. Endler, pp. 485–501. New York: Wiley (with
       S. Strack).

Credits

Index

Pollak, J. M., 12, 15, 16, 20, 23
Pollio, H. R., 355
Pope, A., xxi
Pope, R., 167
Porchet-Munro, S., 355, 356
Postmodernism, death attitudes, 125–128
Potter, S., xxvii
Powell, F. C., 15, 23
Power, horrendous death concept, 311
Pratt, C. C., 23
Pratt, M., 74
Prayer, medical care and, 63–64
Price, R., 169
Priestly, J. B., 351
Psychopathology, death anxiety
    correlates, 19–21
Public violence, 48–50

Quadrel, M. J., 202
Quality of global health, horrendous
    death concept, 307–308
Quality of life, 137–152
    complexity in, 137–140
    defined, 140–141
    future improvement, 147–149
    measurement deficiencies, 142–146
    measurement rationale, 141–142
Quinlan, K. A., 160
Quint, J., 59
Quint-Benoliel, J., 143

Ragon, M., 116
Rando, T. A., 244, 263, 264, 265, 268, 271,
    272
Rank, O., 291
Raphael, B., 199, 259, 264, 267
Rapport, R., 36
Rathbone, G. V., 141
Read, G. D., 60
Redlich, F., 62
Reed, P. G., 143
Reese, W. L., 346
Reilly, T. P., 200
Reisenberg, L. A., 210
Reisner, A. I., 87, 88, 90
Reiss, A. J., Jr., 307, 315, 320
Religiosity. See also Spirituality
    cosmology, death and, 374–377
    death anxiety correlates, 22–24
    Judeo-Christian worldview, 331–332
    medical care and, 63–64
    transcendentalism, death, 334–340

Rembrandt, 176, 177, 184
Renner, M. G., 319
Rhudick, P. J., 5, 21
Rigdon, M. A., 8, 23
Rilke, R. M., 354, 355
Rivera, C., 47
Robbat, B. G., 33
Robinson, P. J., 15, 16
Roediger, H. L., 9
Rogers, D. E., 43
Ron, A., 43
Rosenberg, C. E., 43, 44
Rosenblatt, P., 197
Rosenfeld, S. S., 318, 319, 324
Rosenstock, I., 308
Rosenthal, T., 140
Rosett, A., 81
Rosner, F., 97, 99, 102
Ross, L. M., 355
Roth, J. A., 307, 315, 320
Roy, D. J., 141
Rummel, R. J., 305, 307

Saigh, P. A., 197
St. Thomas Aquinas, 347
Salmon, D., 355
Sandelowski, M., 31, 38, 39
Sandoval, J., 200
Sankar, A., 42
Santa Maria, L., 322
Sartre, J. P., 346, 347
Saul, J. R., 312
Saunders, C., 59, 66, 67, 68, 139, 165
Schag, C. C., 142, 143, 145
Schag, D., 6, 7
Schilder, P., 201, 218, 329
Schipper, H., 142, 143, 144
Schools, death education, children, 209–211
Schuetz, A., 305
Schultz, R., 19, 242
Schweitzer, A., 355
Scofield, G. R., 51
Scott, J. P., 208
Segal, R., 306
Selby, P. J., 142, 145
Selzer, R., 170, 177
Seneca, 153
Sexton, A., 169
Shane, P., 338
Sharkey, F., 170
Shaw, G. B., 353
Shiu, W. C., 17